SOUTHEAST ASIAN TRIBES, MINORITIES, AND NATIONS

PUBLISHED FOR THE PRINCETON CENTER OF

INTERNATIONAL STUDIES

A LIST OF OTHER CENTER PUBLICATIONS

APPEARS AT THE BACK OF VOLUME II

VOLUME II

SOUTHEAST ASIAN TRIBES, MINORITIES, AND NATIONS

EDITED BY

PETER KUNSTADTER

PRINCETON NEW JERSEY

PRINCETON UNIVERSITY PRESS

1967

CONTENTS VOLUME II

PART VII: THAILAND (*continued*)

PART VIII: VIETNAM

PART IX: THE ROLE OF PRIVATE FOUNDATIONS

SOUTHEAST ASIAN

TRIBES, MINORITIES,

AND NATIONS

PART VII, CONTINUED

CHAPTER 13

The Rural "Haw" (Yunnanese Chinese)
of Northern Thailand

F. W. MOTE[1]

INTRODUCTION

The people described in this paper, the rural "Haw" or, more properly, recent migrant Yunnanese Chinese of Northern Thailand (with a total population of about 6,700) are numerically unimportant as a minority group in Thailand. Nonetheless they are illustrative of a number of significant points. First, they are representatives in the hill areas of a "High Culture," and in spite of numerous physical disadvantages are managing to retain and transmit that attachment to their younger generation. Second, in spite of (or, more accurately, because of environmental advantages of) their transitional ecological location, they have become relatively prosperous in a short time, in comparison to their hill tribe and rural Thai neighbors, without a primary dependence on opium cultivation. Third, as a migrant population from a nation involved in international struggles and the rem-

[1] Professor Mote, with his wife, spent approximately eight days in the two Haw villages described herein. Because of their ability to speak the dialect of Chinese in use in these villages and their previous acquaintance with the general pattern of life in Yunnanese villages, the Motes were able to establish rapport very rapidly and to gather far more information in a short time than would the average visitor. The importance of these materials is increased by the fact that there are only brief, scattered journalistic accounts of the Haw in print.

The occasion of Professor Mote's visit to the Haw was a request from the Hill Tribes Division of the Thai Department of Public Welfare. The Hill Tribes Division was familiar with some of the general features of the agricultural techniques of these people and their relationships with other ethnic groups in the same area, and with the fact that "Haw" traders traveled to many of the hill tribe villages. The specific purposes of Professor Mote's trip were to determine, if possible, the origins of this population; to describe briefly their way of life; to suggest ways in which further research might be useful to the Thai government; and to gather information on ways in which the "Haw" might contribute to the modernization of other hill peoples. (Ed.)

nants of a civil war, their situation indicates the sorts of international pressures to which such minority groups may be exposed. Fourth, their relationships with rural Thai and tribal peoples exemplify the sort of acculturative influence that can exist in rural areas from settled communities, in spite of the fact that they are not deliberately established as "model communities." In all of these variables the contrasts of the two communities which were studied show the difficulties of making valid generalizations.

WHO ARE THE HAW?—SOME DEFINITIONS

The Amphur Fang Haw District. This is an internally cohesive zone, but it is not administratively defined as a "district" (*amphur, tambon,* or *muban*) by the Thai government. It is the area comprising the mountain border area plus the foothill villages of Ban-yang, Ban-mai, and Mae-nom, plus the planned village (at present only an empty site) of Kuang-wu (Chinese name only) and the sub-village of Hui-tsung-p'o (Chinese name). All of these lie within twenty-five kilometers of the southwest, west, and north of Fang. The residents recognize two such separate and internally cohesive districts, this one on the Burmese border and the other near Chiengrai on the Laotian border.

Refugees. This term is used here in the sense in which it is used by the village "Haw" themselves, although officially their status is that of irregular immigrants like many of the hill tribes of the region and not that of "refugees." They are Chinese (Yunnanese, with some admixture of minorities races) who fled from Yunnan Province into Burma, mostly in 1951–1952, and after two or three years there started migrating in a diffuse movement infiltrating portions of the border zone in Thailand in 1954. The vast majority are natives of Yunnan Province; exceptions are a few from other southwestern Chinese provinces, wives married in Burma or Thailand, and children born in the last fourteen years. Three-fourths of the Yunnanese come from those few prefectures lying closest to the Burmese border. A much smaller proportion come from the established Yunnanese community in northern Burma, and some, both directly from Yunnan and from established residences in Burma, have entered Thailand only within the past year. These recent arrivals, however, represent

TABLE 21
POPULATION OF RECENT YUNNANESE REFUGEES
IN NORTHERN THAILAND, 1965

Location and Village Names[a]	Total Population
Changwad Chiengmai—Amphur Fang	
Wan-yang (Ban Yang),[b] Lower Level	1,830
P'an-lung (Mae-Nom), Mid-level	152
Huo-fei (Ban Mai),[b] Lower Level	680
Hui-tsung-p'o, Mid-level	? 100+
Changwad Chiengrai—Amphur Chieng-saen	
Man-t'ang	2,257
Amphur Chiengrai	
Lao-chia-t'ang	1,151
Amphur Thoeng (?)	
Ch'ang-k'ung	547
Total	6,617+

a Thai names are in parentheses, following the Chinese names.
b Only Ban-yang and Ban-mai were visited by the writer.

a very small fraction of the total. There is little or no movement at present, and conditions making possible such movement of "refugees" do not seem likely to exist again in the foreseeable future.

The Haw (Also Written "Hor," "Hô," or "Chin-haw") in Thailand. Yunnanese have been coming into Burma, Laos, and Northern Thailand for a hundred years or more, though in Thailand their numbers have been small. Here they came mostly as single peddlers, driving a pack-horse or two, coming in the winter and dry seasons (October to May) and returning before the rainy season.[2] The majority were Chinese Moslems from the

[2] For an earlier reference to the "Haw" see Hallett (1890:210), who quotes the 1887 journal of Mr. Archer, the British Consul at Chiengmai, describing caravans from Yunnan to Utaradit, the head of barge navigation on the Menam:

The route followed by this caravan was from Yunnan (Fu) to Puerh, Ssumao, Kiang Hung, Muang Long, Muang Lim, Kian Hsen, Kiang Hai, Peh, and Utaradit or Tha-It. These caravans come down to Tha-It, but the greater part go eastward toward Chiengmai (Zimmé), and some as far as British Burmah. ["Eastward" in this sentence must be a misprint for westward.] These traders are pure Yunnanese, and are called Ho by the Siamese.

There are interesting early references to the Haw (spelled "Ho") and much valuable information on present circumstances in the article by Halpern (1961:22, 24, 26–7, 32, tables).

[489]

heavily Moslem southwestern part of Yunnan. They traded mostly in the villages, both upland and lowland. The word "Haw" is something of a mystery; it is neither a Yunnanese nor a Thai word. Thais, including officials, have questioned the meaning of the word, and hill tribes "experts" think that it is the word by which the people of this "hill tribe" call themselves; they do not realize that the so-called Haw are simply ordinary Chinese of Yunnan. Thais have observed that the majority of overseas Chinese in Thailand cannot communicate with the "Haw," and make the mistake of thinking that their Teochiu language is the standard for China, hence the "Haw" must be something other than Chinese, that is, another minority people like the Yao, the Meo, etc. Most of the "Haw" who have come within the last ten years and do not know Thai are not even aware that such a name exists. Those who do know the word, as well as other Chinese and Sino-Thais in the region, accept the word "Haw" simply as a curious and somewhat insulting Thai term for Yunnanese Chinese, a term having both official and popular currency. From this point onward this report will adopt the word "Yunnanese." Questioned about the meaning of the word, the people in Northern Thailand give a variety of answers (five different explanations have been collected), none of which makes much sense.[3]

---

[3] Among the explanations for the word "Haw" the following are cited as typical attempts to rationalize the explanation, rather than as approved or acceptable explanations:

(a) "Haw" is the Thai equivalent of the southwestern Chinese sound of the word *ho* of the expression *ho jen*, meaning "what people?" It is said that when asked who they were, the Chinese would reply somewhat rhetorically: "*Ho jen?!*" ("What people, indeed?!") This explanation came from a Yunnanese gentleman in Chiengmai. It sounds most improbable.

(b) "Haw" is the Thai equivalent of the southwestern Chinese sound of the word *ho*, meaning "peaceful, friendly." The early Yunnanese were so designated because they were peaceful, friendly traders, and their designation of themselves as such was accepted as the ethnic name for them. This came from a Yunnanese leader of the Moslem community in Northern Thailand and is also improbable.

(c) "Haw" is the Thai equivalent of the southwestern Chinese sound of the word *huo*, which is the name of the semi-historical tribal chieftain Meng Huo (in Thai usually called Beng Haw), a character in the Chinese novel *The Romance of the Three Kingdoms*, well known among Thais in the translation made over a hundred years ago called *Sam-kok*. Meng-Huo was supposed to have been a fierce local chieftain who was seven times captured and seven times released by the Chinese general Chu-ko Liang (K'ung Beng) in the effort to pacify him and bring the southwest of Yunnan under Chinese control. The

The early Yunnanese occasionally became permanent immigrants; they settled in small numbers, always in towns, never forming mountain villages of their own, and never practicing agriculture in Thailand. Chiengmai, Lamphun, and Chiengrai have been their major centers. It is said by the Chinese school principal in Chiengmai that there are now seven hundred to eight hundred Chinese or Sino-Thai households in that city, of which about one-third are Yunnanese, though in the smaller communities of the North the proportion runs higher. Linguistically distinct, they tend to remain a community apart from the Teochiu-speaking overseas Chinese; we might also call the Yunnanese the "overland" Chinese.

Of the two mosques in Chiengmai, the smaller and newer one (fifteen years) is exclusively Chinese; its leader reports that about two hundred to three hundred men and sixty to eighty women attend the major service each week. The other mosque has a larger congregation and a considerably longer history, but is no longer exclusively Chinese, having Thai and Indian members as well. It was founded fifty years ago by an immigrant from Yunnan surnamed Cheng, who became a leading Chiengmai citizen. He donated the land for the city's airport, for which he was knighted. He died last year in Mecca at the age of ninety-three. Another leading Yunnanese Moslem was Mr. Lu

---

modern "Haw" are regarded as this general's descendants, hence they are called by his name. This explanation seems improbable since, if the analogy has any meaning, "Haw" should then be the name by which Yunnanese call the Thais.

(d) "Haw" is the Chiengmai (Northern Thai) word for walnuts (man haw means "nut oil"). The Yunnanese traders used to arrive in Chiengmai each fall with walnuts to sell, and they were identified by their association with this product above all else. The Chinese word for walnut is ho t'ao, the first syllable of which, in southwestern Chinese, sounds something like "haw." This explanation, minus the Chinese word for walnut, came from an elderly Thai agricultural expert who grew up in Chiengmai fifty years ago and who remembers the annual arrival of "haw" traders in the city after the end of the rains in November.

(e) "Haw" is a variant pronunciation of the Chinese word hao, meaning "good," and shows either bilingual tribal peoples' appreciation of the Yunnanese traders or Chinese self-esteem in having labeled themselves this way. This story is current among the Chinese in Northern Thailand.

(f) It is assumed by some amateur anthropologists that "Haw" may be some tribal name for the Chinese, unrelated to any Chinese or Thai word. But no such tribal word has been found that corresponds phonologically to this.

The origin of the term "Haw" as applied to the Yunnanese in Thailand remains an unsolved mystery.

THAILAND: F. W. MOTE

of Lamphun, knighted for his contributions to the building of the rail line between Lamphun and Chiengmai.

Such Yunnanese have settled in the area and have become familiar as "Haw" peddlers or even as leading citizens without the Thais having come generally to realize that they are not analogous to the other minority groups classed as hill tribes. Were it not for the attention now being focused on the "refugee" Yunnanese who have arrived since World War II, the old "Haw" of Thailand's northern towns would probably go unnoticed today except as one further constituent of the ubiquitous Chinese shop-keeping population.

The new arrivals, in Thailand at least and in their present circumstances, are properly classed as "border region minority people." Although an analogy to the hill tribes is misleading in terms of understanding their culture, it is realistic in terms of the Thai government's administrative tasks in the border regions. For the Yunnanese are not immigrants to Thailand in the usual sense, and their activities play a central role in the lives of the hill tribes.

Since similar "overseas" Chinese groups, especially those from Yunnan and neighboring provinces where hill tribe minorities are most numerous, appear to have an analogous position in the present-day life of Burma, Laos, and even in Vietnam, some aspects of the more readily studied situation in Northern Thailand may have significant implications for these areas as well. The pattern of Han relations with non-Han peoples is itself a major domestic Chinese problem of the whole Chinese border zone, as Mr. Diao's paper in this volume attests.

Some Misleading Political Identifications. Several groups that should be carefully distinguished from each other are by customary usage rather indiscriminately labeled in ways that identify them with the Chinese Nationalist government. Such usage is not analogous to the usage current among the Yunnanese themselves, and indeed is not even comprehensible to them. But the historical reasons for the confusion are easy enough to understand.

In the large-scale movement of refugees from Yunnan into Burma in 1951–1952, the most important group politically (though not the largest) was that consisting of military units loyal to the Republic of China. Such military units were called Kuomintang (Chinese Nationalist) forces, and were given some protection as political refugees in Burma. Later these units became guerrilla irregulars; their activities created an international crisis, and under outside pressures they were withdrawn to Taiwan (although it is an open secret that some small numbers of them remained). Those remaining elements are often confused with the Yunnanese villagers. They occupy, in part, adjacent areas; moreover, some of the villagers were formerly military personnel of one kind or another. But the villagers today are living as civilians. Moreover, they have no direct organizational links with the government in Taiwan and in fact feel themselves very lucky to be in Thailand and not in Taiwan. They are not happy to find themselves politically identified in any way. It is proper to distinguish them from the "old Haws," i.e., Yunnanese who have been in Thailand since before World War II, some of whom also still work as petty traders in the hills, although no political label seems to make this distinction.

The Chinese Nationalist label is equally misleading when applied to two other groups in the hills. One is made up of the bandits who were also forced out of China by the Communist take-over. The Yunnanese villagers say that all the scum of southwest China fled ahead of the Communist armies and formed bandit bands that preyed especially on the Chinese refugees themselves as they tried to flee with a few possessions into Burma. They recall also that such bandit gangs when confronted by Burmese military forces would pose as fleeing Chinese army regulars, thereby receiving protection. Finding it at times useful to continue to claim that label for themselves, these bandits have continued to be the scourge of the Yunnanese villagers as well as of the hill tribes and other people they encounter in Burma, Thailand, and Laos. At one time several years ago the Yunnanese villagers, with the support of the original guerrilla forces, created an extermination force to track down and annihilate one bandit group operating in their area, and though their area is now clear, they know that other such bandit elements are still operating in some places.

Another group popularly labeled as belonging to the former Chinese regular armies, whose behavior also threatens the reputation of the "Haw" in general, is that relatively small group (three hundred to four hundred) of overaged and useless ex-soldiers who refused to be evacuated to Taiwan because they were in an advanced stage of opium addiction and knew that they could not get opium in Taiwan. They are discussed below (pp. 506, 514).

To summarize, it is inappropriate to apply any political labels to the villages under discussion, and it is especially inaccurate to refer to all of the disparate groups mentioned above by any general and inclusive label and to imply that they constitute one coherent group.

THE VILLAGE OF BAN-YANG (Chinese name "Wan-yang," alternate Chinese name "Yang-tzu-chai")

Wan-yang is simply the Chinese transliteration of the Thai name; "ban" means "village" and "yang" means "Karen." The alternate Chinese name means "Karen people's stockade." Both Thais and Chinese state that a small Karen village occupied the location at the time the Yunnanese moved in, after which the Karen all left.

History. Yunnanese first moved in to the site from the higher hills above and from the Burmese side of the border exactly ten years ago (the winter of 1954–1955). They came as civilian refugees fleeing Yunnan, and most had spent two or three years in Burma on the way. After the first major evacuation of Chinese Nationalist troops in Burma (by air to Taiwan) in 1954, these peasant families had to move down out of the hills and establish settlements where they could live by farming. All of the so-called Haw villages came into being at that time, some as early as late 1953, and some a year or two later.

At the time the Yunnanese arrived, the Karen village of a few houses stood in an isolated small clearing in the midst of a forest, just at the lowest edge of the foothills and above the paddy fields cultivated by Thais in the valley bottom.

The Yunnanese cleared the jungle, laid out streets following the curve of the hill, and cleared extensive fields now totaling (with the village area) about 1500 *rai*, extending principally to the south of the settlement and up a draw to the west. Two streams run out of the hills at this point; they are reliable year-round sources of water and power, and the residents have devised an elaborate system of open ditches and split-bamboo elevated culverts to divert running water to most homes and household gardens. In this way they have also provided a stream of water to power the machinery of a home-built rice-polishing plant; they have also considered using it to produce electricity, but haven't the capital to purchase equipment needed for installation. Formerly they also supplied water and power for a bamboo-paper factory, no longer in production.

Some scattered trees have been left for shade; their great size gives evidence of the magnitude of the task of clearing the site.

Appearance of the Village. The village has much of the appearance of a typical peasant village of the interior of China, except that the houses are mostly built of bamboo and other flimsy materials, whereas in Yunnan they would be built of brick and tile, with some stone in lintels and doorways. Each residence consists of three or four separate one-story buildings built on the ground, having raised (to a height of one foot or more) tamped-earth floors and consisting of a central room through which the main door enters and two side rooms entered by interior doors. These three or four buildings form the sides of a courtyard comprising usually half or less of the household area, the rest being vegetable garden. One or two of the buildings will be living or sleeping rooms, one a detached kitchen and storage room, another a bath house or further storage area. Only two houses, one the village headman's (the chairman's), are built on pilings raising them well above the ground in the Thai manner. Each residence has an outside privy, a deep pit boarded over and enclosed in a small hut for privacy, containing also a water urn for washing. Beyond or adjoining the courtyard there usually are found a stall for horses and oxen, a pen for pigs (pigs are not allowed to roam free at any time), chicken roosts, duck pens, etc., and a place for tools, grain, storage, etc. Each yard is enclosed in a fence of bamboo or a living hedge, and many are planted with fruit trees or decorative flowers. The large vegetable gardens are intensively worked and neatly maintained, with a constant rotation of crops providing a steady supply. There is no electricity in the village. Roads are deep in dust that must become mire in the rainy season. A wide bridge crosses

the stream at the entrance to the village, and many narrow ones
cross it at other points as it winds through the place. The main
street has a number of shops occupying the fronts of houses,
the courtyards of which then lie behind. Doorways are decorated
with last year's New Year couplets, faded and tattered. Immediately on entering the village, one realizes that it is a Chinese
village from the layout, style of houses, and evidence of characteristic Chinese activities, yet it does not seem like a village
in China because it is so flimsy and new. The streets are unim-
proved, there are no decorative stone gateways, pavilions, stone
inscriptions, imposing doorways of more substantial homes—none
of the things reflecting long establishment, gentry pride, and
wealth.

Population. The official registered population of Ban-yang is
1,830, of whom 88 are very recent arrivals from Burma. Ten
years ago, at the time of founding, the population is said to
have numbered about a thousand. There are something over 200
"households," of which 120 include a man and his wife (the
large number of incomplete households reflecting the refugee
character of the population). Of the 120 couples, 90 of the wives
are Chinese from Yunnan and 30 are non-Chinese wives married
in Burma or Thailand, among whom the largest number are
Pai-yi (Thai-Lue). In the ten years since the village was
founded, 550 babies have been born (not counting stillbirths
and infant mortalities within the first month). There are local Thai
husbands in three or four households at the edge of the village,
whose Pai-Yi wives are connected in some way to the Yunnanese
villagers. There are no Teochiu-speaking or other overseas types
of Chinese in the village, but there are a few who, though they
had been resident in Yunnan, claim a "native place" (usually
ancestral, not personal) in some other province in the southwestern part of China.

Religions. About one-third of the population are Chinese Moslems (Hui). They maintain a mosque (one of the largest and
best buildings in the village) with attached school and residence
for their *A-Hung* or religious teacher. About forty very young
boys study Arabic in this school late each afternoon; their two
or three years of such study is adequate only to teach them
how to recite the Koran without really understanding Arabic

syntax or vocabulary. An itinerant Pakistani Imam also had been invited to spend the month of Ramadan and help with the extra services. Both of the town's two noodle-shops (the only restaurants in the town) are Moslem. As the non-Moslems said on several occasions, "We can easily observe their food practices, but they cannot observe ours, so theirs tend to prevail." It appears that the Moslems observe their religious practices meticulously.

Two-thirds of the population are non-Moslems, identifying themselves as *Han-chiao* (a term not generally used in China, but current where the distinction from Islam, or *Hui-chiao*, becomes important; *Han-chiao* literally means "Chinese teachings"). These households raise pigs, make liquors, hang their sausages and hams up to cure in the public gaze, and otherwise go about their infidel ways with no sign of friction or communal ill will of any kind. All persons questioned about this denied any friction or sense of communal opposition or separation of any kind. Moslems often marry non-Moslem wives; Moslems will be invited to eat in non-Moslem homes, but normally will decline; non-Moslems do not decline Moslem invitations. Each ward (*tsu*) of the village contains both Moslem and non-Moslem households, and about half of the ward captains are Moslems. These conditions and proportions prevail in both of the villages visited: one (Ban-yang) has a Moslem chairman, and one has a non-Moslem. A first impression that should be studied however is that the Moslems tend to include relatively fewer of the poorest families and exercise a strong leadership role.

The non-Moslem people have built a small and pitifully poor-looking temple to the spirits of the locality. This is not specifically sectarian in any sense, but displays the character of popular or vulgar Taoism. It has no priest or attendant. It consists of three mud-plastered buildings, earth-floored and leaf-thatched, on a commanding hilltop. The central hall contains an altar-table with three spirit tablets, the central one dedicated to "the efficacious spirit of this place imperially-enfieffed to receive and respond to offerings," and the side ones to the spirits of crops and fields and domestic animals. Candles and incense are burned before these, especially on the first and fifteenth days of the lunar month, by individuals singly and not in any formal ceremony. Banners attesting to petitions made or answered, crudely lettered in black on cheap red cotton cloth, hang before the altar and form the only decoration in the place. The side buildings contain one room each, and are used for cooking and serving congregational meals a few times a year at celebrations that mark the limited community life of the believers.

There is no Buddhist temple nor shrine in the village, and no villagers are identified as active Buddhists, though that does not mean that some do not practice private Buddhist devotions in their homes. The village or some persons in it have made donations to the Thai Buddhist *wat* five kilometers down the road in the larger Thai village near the highway. However, it is not known whether these were acts of piety or diplomacy.

There are seven or eight Christians in the village, all those noted being younger single men. A Canadian missionary and his American wife from Chiengrai (Pastor Carlson of the China Inland Mission) occasionally visit the village. Pastor Carlson has spent some years in Yunnan in the past, speaks the language well, and is respected for his learning and his ability to hike the hills alone carrying a heavy pack.

The Moslem mosque is decorated with Chinese sayings and couplets, one of which reads: "Trace Islam, Christianity, Confucianism and Buddhism to the one root with its many branches." This notably ignores "superstitious" Taoism, but suggests an atmosphere of mutual respect and goodwill that in truth seems to prevail, as far as religion is concerned, in these villages.

Occupations. Many of the adults are illiterate or barely-literate peasants who practiced farming in Yunnan and who live principally by farming now. (The character of their agriculture is discussed below.) Many of these at one time served as conscripted soldiers or were attached to households of better-off refugee families, some of whom have since left the villages.

A number practice subsidiary occupations such as carpentry, smithing and horse-shoeing, carting, cooking and food-processing, sewing and tailoring, etc. There are two barber shops, two noodle-shop restaurants, two rice-milling plants (one water-powered; one with gasoline-powered machinery), two or three full-time tailors, and several full-time shopkeepers. There are seven teachers, and there is one "doctor," perhaps the only regular college graduate resident in the village; he studied electrical engineering at Southwest Union University in Kunming and received some kind of medical training in the army after that, but cannot be considered a real doctor. However, he gives shots and dispenses medicines on daily rounds and still is addressed by his former title, "Medical-Officer Wu." The teachers have had mostly the old-style Chinese private education, except the younger ones who attended modern-type country high schools in Yunnan. Commerce as an occupation is discussed elsewhere.

Government. Each of the Yunnanese villages, being in the border zone beyond normal Thai habitation, is required by Thai regulations governing the hill tribes to have a village chief or headman, in Thai the *puyaiban.* On analogy to this, the "Haws" too are required to conform to the tribal convention. The Yunnanese have met this incongruity by organizing "self-governing committees" (*Tzu-chih-hui*) whose chairman (*hui-chang*) functions as the *puyaiban* vis-à-vis the Thai government and as head of government internally. The relationship to the Thai government is very important; he receives instructions from the local officials, is required to keep a registry of all the village inhabitants, and is responsible for them. And he can deal directly with Thai officials at the *amphur* (district) level. (No inquiry was made about taxation.)

But primarily the chairman is important as the actual governor and leader of his village. The Ban-yang chairman has held office since the founding of the village. He is not regarded as a highly effective village head as far as the village's internal affairs are concerned, but he is respected as a competent and vigorous man, especially successful in dealings with the Thais. He speaks Northern Thai readily; his wife is a Pai-yi (Thai-Lue) from a village near Fang, with whom he communicates in Thai. He spends much of his time attending to personal business out of the village, and because responsibilities are not effectively delegated, nothing can be decided in his absence, and government tends to lag. Thus the spirit and quality of government in Ban-yang is quite different from that in Ban-mai (see below), a fact remarked by residents of both villages. Nonetheless, the essential tasks of community government are accomplished.

[499]

The self-governing committee is made up of the eleven or twelve ward chiefs (*tsu-chang*). The wards are areas of the village, divided off so as to provide convenient groups of eighteen or twenty contiguous households without respect to religion, occupation, or status of the householders. Within each ward one household head is "advanced" by the others to be their ward chief, to serve indefinitely until he gets tired of the office and wants to get out of it. The committee "elects" its chairman and vice-chairman by procedures known to it, not stated in any constitution, and for indefinite periods. They hold meetings from time to time, but accomplish most of their business in *ad hoc* meetings singly or in small groups with the chairman as need arises. The village business keeps him quite busy whenever he is at home or walking about in the village.

There is little or no crime in the village. The streets are safe, and homes are left unlocked. There have been two murders of villagers by other Yunnanese in ten years, but both are declared to have been the work of Communist provocateurs. A constant vigilance is maintained to ferret out any Communist activity, but there is a general feeling of security about this and confidence that everything which goes on in the village is known to the proper authorities. In fact, though the only policemen are the two BPP teachers, there is an effective informal system of surveillance of the kind that naturally develops in a small rural village where everyone knows everyone else. Some opium-smoking and petty gaming go on, but probably less than in a rural village in Yunnan before 1949. No prostitution is allowed within the village limits, and prostitutes who ply their profession beyond the limits are from Thai villages farther away. There seem to be no secret societies, protection rackets, extortion, or other such practices; at least, no one could be found to complain of such, and the village is probably too poor to support many parasites.

The Village Primary School. The Yunnanese had organized schools for their children from the beginning of their refugee existence in Burma, and as the present villages were being built, sites were set aside on which the schools were to be erected. The support of elementary education has the automatic acceptance of the citizenry and is a virtue professed by all leaders.

The differences among the schools in the various communities derive from the varying degrees of effectiveness with which the village leaders have been able to organize and utilize the resources available to them.

But it must be pointed out that these are poor villages, and the best schools, reflecting the best organization and the greatest sacrifices, still are skin-and-bones operations. Aid to education is one of the greatest needs of the villages. The only aid to the schools from the Thai government is represented by the services of two BPP teachers in each village and, at Ban-yang, a small contribution toward the roofing of one of the school buildings now under construction. The schools need support for children who cannot pay the tiny tuition fee, textbooks, equipment, better pay for teachers, and many other kinds of aid in order better to accomplish their educational goals. Yet their very existence indicates the importance which these people attach to education, and they stand as monuments to a significant achievement in community action.

The school at Ban-yang consists of two shed-like buildings and a third under construction (though work is not at the moment in progress because of a lack of funds); these buildings stand on three sides of a spacious courtyard and playground. The main building has an office and two large classrooms. The second building has three classrooms. The third building will be one very large room that can be used as classroom space or as a meeting hall. These buildings are in bad repair. Their only furnishings are battered desks and chairs of rough make, many falling apart. There are few decorations, pictures, maps, or teaching aids. The walls are papered with newspapers, tattered and dirty. Everything looks dusty and in bad repair. Recreation facilities consist of a few swings and a slide; the students themselves collected contributions to buy one basketball and a pair of badminton rackets.

Adjoining the schoolyard is a compound in which the two Thai teachers (one with wife and child) live, and where one bachelor Yunnanese teacher also lives. This housing is provided by the village for the Thai teachers, who also receive a regular gift of vegetables, wine, and foods,—e.g. there is a convention that every time anyone in the village slaughters an ox or a pig,

THAILAND: F. W. MOTE

each Thai teacher receives one kilo of the fresh meat. The Chinese teachers nominally receive five hundred baht per month and no regularized gifts, and sometimes go without salary.

Thai is taught during the regular school hours from 9:30 to 3:00 to children who (by regulation) have not passed the age of fourteen, but attendance is not compulsory, and only a little over half of the students in the Ban-yang school attend the Thai classes. One of the two Thai teachers is a lively, friendly man much liked by the villagers and students; observation of his classes has shown that he is an excellent teacher. The other is notably less effective. Parents are glad to have their children learn some Thai, for convenience, but many of them have not yet learned to value it as education. It is doubtful that any student, under present conditions, would learn enough Thai to go on to regular Thai middle-school. The Thai education, however, is taken much more seriously by community leaders at Ban-mai and appears to accomplish more there. The contrast between the Ban-yang school and that at Ban-mai points up the impossibility of generalizing about the quality of education in the villages. At Ban-yang the school has had a history of starts and failures, of inadequate organization, weak leaders, and repeated financial crises. At present only one-half or slightly more of the children of school age are enrolled (total enrollment is 122), while at Ban-mai all of the children of school age are in school. Fortunately, two or three of the Ban-yang teachers are now quite concerned about the condition of their school and are striving to bring about a reorganization of it. The visit of the writer was opportune from their point of view as it helped focus attention on the school's need.

Chinese education is conducted in off hours, before and after the regular school hours devoted to Thai. It is fair to say that the community (understandably) regards the Chinese education as something very important, has sacrificed to create the schools for that purpose, and will strive to maintain and improve them for the same reason. But a fairly effective teaching program in Thai is also launched, and it will inevitably grow in importance as the community becomes more adjusted to its new life in Thailand. In any event, the schools are the sensitive spot in the community at which influence can be brought to bear, where the community can be made to work together now, and where the character of the community in the future is now being molded.

Agriculture. Despite some small-scale commerce within and emanating from them, the Yunnanese villages are essentially agricultural. The villagers, though they arrived a short ten years ago destitute and empty-handed after having fled repeatedly, are rather proud that with their bare hands they have succeeded in creating viable communities. Moreover, they feel that their trial period was passed two or three years ago and that now their economic foundations are established and their future security assured. With their growing awareness that they will be here awhile and that they can remain in their present locations, they are beginning to take a longer-range view of their agricultural planning. Already their impact on the wet-rice-growing Thai and Thai-Lue villages below them and on the hill tribes above them is evident, and it is sure to become stronger.

When they first arrived, the villagers had to clear fields where neither habitation (beyond the temporary Karen village of a few houses) nor permanent cultivation had existed before. They located their village at the bottom edge of the slopes, above existing paddy fields, and constructed some new paddy fields to grow wet rice in the manner to which they were accustomed from their Yunnanese experience, but their wet-rice fields were confiscated by neighboring Thai farmers, apparently with local government approval. So the villagers took to making new fields just above them, in which they could grow dry rice as a staple crop in the main growing season and a second crop of vegetables or other produce during the winter growing season. The boundary between paddy-rice lands has remained the boundary between Yunnanese and Thai (and Pai-yi) at Ban-yang, although at Ban-mai they have found ways of leasing some paddy fields for three- to five-year periods in order to grow some wet rice also. At Ban-yang they hesitate to convert dry fields to wet ones even where it could be done, for fear of losing them, and though they talk about eventually being able to lease some paddy lands, they still have not done so except for a single winter season at a time, to grow dry or irrigated crops during the season that the Thais normally let the fields lie fallow.

Almost all the regular residents of the village work in these fields lying near the village, both the 1,500 *rai* of fields that they consider to be their own and the fields rented in the winter from their Thai neighbors. Even the school principal, a man from a scholarly family who had never used his hands before, tells with self-deprecation mixed with humor how he had to learn to dig the soil and do peasant labor. Most of the leading people in the village were classed as "rich peasants" or "landlords" by the Chinese Communists, were made the object of class war, and hence were forced to flee. This means that agricultural management skills and experience tend to be high among them, and the agriculture of the village is consequently quite progressive. This has helped them to raise their status since their arrival. They note that when they arrived they had to hire themselves out to the Thai farmers as day laborers at the rate of three baht per day (collected in unhusked rice). Now they have become employers of large numbers of Thais to help them work their fields, at wages of seven or eight baht per day, paid in each case day by day. This change from hired laborers to employers of labor is symbolic of the rapid advance that their superior agriculture plus their hard-working habits have made possible.

Farmers with a little capital are beginning to develop fruit orchards. Tangerines do well, but one must wait three years after planting small grafted trees before a crop can be harvested. Some poorer villagers spoke with envy of those who could afford this kind of development. The best orchard in the village has been producing tangerines for two seasons, and the owner is now transforming it gradually to lamyai, which bear for a longer life after the trees get started (tangerines bear for a total of only about seven years), and which earn bigger profits per man-year-per-acre. This orchardist is also experimenting with other fruits, grows commercial vegetable crops, raises large numbers of chickens and ducks, and has experimented with raising fish. He uses chemical fertilizers applied according to soil tests, insecticides, scientific procedures. His further development is not limited by lack of water or land, but by lack of labor.

Most farmers grow their wet-season crop of dry hill-land rice, then plant a winter cash crop of garlic, onions, ginger, soy beans, etc. Market conditions have fluctuated, and some have suffered losses. Three years ago there was overproduction of potatoes, and last year overproduction of garlic, the latter because so many neighboring Thais began to grow garlic in imitation of the Yunnanese. But gradually they are learning how to plan for the market and how to enlarge their marketing area. In addition to the field crops, each household maintains fine vegetable gardens for table use, raises pigs and poultry, and produces its own eggs. Moslems, being unable either to raise or to eat pork, tend to raise more poultry.

The villages at the lower level (just at the edge of the paddy-rice zone) have counterpart villages at mid-level between themselves and the highest mountain elevations. At the mid-levels there are some fine plateaus of extensive area, easily worked, where some crops grow particularly well. The exact relationship between the lower-level villages and the mid-level is not entirely clear to the present writer (who has not observed the mid-level agriculture), but in part it is a matter of crop diversification, made possible by the varying climate of the two levels. For example, good potatoes cannot be grown at the lower level, hence the Thais cannot seriously compete in the potato market. The crop coming in from high Burmese growing areas formerly controlled the market in Northern Thailand, but in the last two seasons Burmese potatoes have not been able to enter, so local prices have risen, making potato-growing in Thailand a very profitable activity. Seed potatoes are grown at the lower elevation in the winter season, then the small and unmarketable seed potatoes are taken to the higher fields and planted during the main growing season. This crop needs little attention after being planted, so the farmer can return to the lower fields (four or five hours' walk) after a few days of labor in the potato fields and devote most of his time to the lowland dry-rice crop. The upland fields can also produce certain other crops of vegetables and grains (especially maize) better than the lower fields, so there seems to be reason enough to have some small part of the farming population permanently stationed there. The population figures show something of the relationship: Ban-yang with 1,830 people and Ban-mai with 680 are related to the mid-level villages of Maenom (Chinese name P'an-lung) and Hui-tsung-p'o, of which the former has 152 people and the latter a similarly small population (exact figures not ascertained).

Another factor in the relationship between the levels is the production of opium. It seems apparent from the reports of villagers (corroborated by Manndorff's observations) that there are a number of derelicts, overaged soldiers in advanced stages of addiction, who cannot be productive farmers but who can produce enough opium for their own needs and who therefore must stay at the higher elevations at which opium grows. Their number is small and is decreasing, for the profits from opium are not enough to attract the normal hard-working Yunnanese farmer. But a small amount of such opium production probably will continue until the hard core of otherwise useless derelicts liquidates itself. (See below under "Aspects of the Opium Problem.")

The villagers speak of themselves diffidently as backward people from a remote border area of Yunnan, not worthy representatives of China's more advanced regions. To some extent their agriculture reflects the partial truth of this, though their own awareness of the fact shows their susceptibility to innovation and improvement. An agricultural expert currently working among them states them to be "fifty years behind the most advanced agriculture in Japan or Taiwan, but to a similar degree in advance of the agriculture at present practiced all about them," and he notes their keenness to learn new methods. This same expert states that the methods of the Yunnanese as now practiced in the villages, particularly in winter cropping, in the use of fertilizers, in the introduction of new crops, in the improvement of varieties through selective breeding, and in their approach to agriculture as a commercialized activity, are already being widely copied and are bringing about a transformation of the agriculture of the region. This is said with particular reference to the lowland farmers—Thais and Pai-yi especially—but it could also be applied to the hill tribes. Although the impact among the hill tribes is less evident, the Yunnanese villagers have started giving vegetable seeds to tribesmen in neighboring villages, have taught them how to plant vegetable crops, and have provided them with a market for their production. Lahu women were noted selling Chinese-type vegetables in Ban-yang, and the Yao villagers were reported to do the same.

A responsible official in Ban-yang said that in a good year

like the current one and the previous year, the total sale of agricultural produce out of the villages of Ban-yang and Ban-mai
reaches a gross in excess of one million baht, and that it is steadily increasing. Potatoes are the best single cash crop, but fruit
may displace them in first place in a few years.

Because of the importance that the Thai government attaches
to experiments with wheat production in Northern Thailand,
some questions about it were put to a number of farmers and
village leaders. They are experienced wheat growers, wheat having been a staple crop in Yunnan and during their years in
Burma. They are also familiar with buckwheat, barley, and other
grain crops that grow at high elevations. They insist that wheat
will not produce the yield or the quality, in these lowlands of
Northern Thailand or in the adjoining hill locations like those
of Ban-yang and Ban-mai, to justify the Thai government's
present efforts to introduce it there. They also report that seed
wheat brought in from Burma and planted some years ago by
themselves even at the middle and high elevations above the
present villages produced excellent yield of high quality in the
first season, but so exhausted the soil that they could not get
a second crop despite attempts to rotate and fertilize. The technical problems of growing wheat in these soils at present remain
unsolved. But these farmers should be useful participants in any
joint experiments with Thai agricultural experts, especially if
their present level of knowledge and experience is not overlooked
by such experts who, it was suggested, occasionally tend to be
somewhat bureaucratic and arbitrary in dealing with their "poor
ignorant cousins" of the hills.

Animal Husbandry. Cattle for slaughtering are purchased from
the Thais. One main reason for this is that at Ban-yang animals
cannot be herded and protected from thievery by residents of
neighboring villages (Ban-mai reports much less difficulty of this
kind). Draft animals, mainly humped-oxen and mules (there are
no water buffalo in either village) are important for carting and
for packing produce, and many households have such animals.
Since wet rice is not grown, and also partly because of the pov-
erty of many of the villagers, fields are tilled by hoe and not
plowed by animal labor; this remains true even as conditions improve, despite the fact that these people are accustomed to the

use of the plow in Yunnan and have experimented with deep cultivation at high elevations in Burma and even in Thailand.[4] The failure to use plows at present probably is to be explained as a temporary adjustment to changed environmental conditions and economic circumstances. Some of the villagers talk about using light power-cultivators in the future, when they can afford to buy them, and some first experiments with such equipment are reported to have commenced in the summer of 1965, after this writer's visit to the villages.

Horses are a status symbol, and they are necessary for travel in and out of the hills in the wet season. The better-off families often have one or two horses of the small Yunnan breed (mistakenly called by many outsiders the "Mongolian pony"); these are strictly used as saddle and pack horses, and customarily are not gelded. Donkeys are used chiefly for breeding mules which carry the bulky agricultural produce down the mountain trails to the levels where they can be shifted to ox-carts. Horses can pack fifty kilos, mules eighty.

Non-Moslem households usually keep a pig or two, always tightly penned and under a shed roof, and never allowed to roam freely; pigpens usually adjoin the household garden patches, but are kept as far from living quarters as possible.

No count of animals was made, but there appear to be fewer than would be normal for a village in Yunnan.

Commerce. The six or eight commercial establishments in the village are all of very small size, and most villagers make periodic visits to Fang to purchase supplies. But cloth, foods, soap, notions, candies, trinkets, simple medicines, cosmetics, batteries for transistor radios, kerosene for lamps, etc., can be bought in the village.

A number of peddlers who travel among the hill tribes are based in the village; they usually farm in the wet season and peddle their goods in the winter and dry seasons. The local shops supply most of their stock, probably on a partnership basis. This trade appears to be very small, involving little capital investment

---

[4] Cf. Gordon Young's brief report of a village in Amphur Fang called Pha Luang, where, at an elevation of 6,000 feet, Yunnanese were using oxen to plow fields for the staple crop of buckwheat (Young 1962:83). The exact location of this village, its population size, and its Chinese name are unknown to this author, and the villagers may have moved since Young's description was written in 1961.

and small profits. Although a little opium gets into this trade, these mountain peddlers are not primarily opium traders, and all persons questioned said that to break into the opium trade in a way to make it worthwhile required large capital and involved great risks.

There is also some peddling of simple wares to Thai and other lowland villages, but it is less extensive than the trade among the hill tribes and is not expected to increase.

The marketing of agricultural produce is the major business activity of the village. The village production is in part marketed in Fang, though increasingly it reaches markets as far away as Chiengmai (150 km.). The same buyers who specialize in buying up village production for sale in large lots elsewhere also buy up produce from Thai and Thai-Lue villages nearby, arrange transport, and deal with the big buyers. In this, connections with merchants in the towns are important, and these are not exclusively with fellow Yunnanese.

The commercial life of the villages was only casually observed; it was not possible to study it carefully.

Contacts with the Outside World. In terms of the movement of persons, contacts with the outside world (farther than Fang or Chiengmai) are extremely limited. Though some leaders travel several times a year to Chiengmai, and even occasionally to Bangkok, most of the population have not gone farther than Fang (23 km.) in the direction of Thailand. Persons coming into the village are noted and recorded. Tribesmen come to sell things and to buy, to borrow, and to seek advice. Thais and other lowlanders come occasionally; young monks of the Thai temple five kilometers away are frequently to be seen in the village. Thai officials, mostly Border Patrol Policemen, come regularly, and local civil officials come occasionally. Non-Yunnanese Chinese merchants from the outside are said not to come into the villages and not to be welcome there, although the villagers buy from them in the Thai towns nearby. There is no regular transportation in and out of Ban-yang; goods must be moved by ox-cart at twenty baht per cart-load per trip (7 kilometers), and persons usually go on foot in the dry weather, and by horseback when the road becomes nearly impassable to all vehicles and to pedestrians in the wet season.

USIS and British Information film trucks have come into the

village on two or three occasions; their visits were highly appreciated. During the past five years malaria-control workers have come once a year to spray insecticides, but no other public health or other services have ever come. (A TB survey is badly needed.) The missionary Pastor Carlson from Chiengrai walks over two or three times a year and once came with his wife. A traveling Pathan Imam was in the village to help with the special activities of the month of Ramadan, 1965. The Chinese Embassy in Bangkok, after several years of little or no direct contact, in 1964 sent some officials in for a brief visit. Four technical advisers from Taiwan, in the fields of medicine, food processing, agriculture, and animal husbandry were in the villages in 1965 for a period of six to twelve months. The Princess Mother of Thailand visited the village briefly by helicopter in 1964, on her way to visit a new school she had sponsored in the Yao village above Ban-yang. Her visit made a deep impression, and photographs of her taken in the village hang in several places. The Governor of Chiengmai with an entourage of more than a hundred persons made an inspection of the village in the fall of 1964.

An American anthropologist spent a few months in the village some two or three years ago, using it as a base from which to study the Yao people nearby. Other than this limited movement of persons, the villagers see no outside faces.

But the isolation has been greatly ameliorated in the past two or three years by the widespread use of inexpensive transistor radios. Almost every household has one, and some are well-installed with good aerials. However, radio reception leaves something to be desired. The Communist Chinese station in Kunming, a 700-KW transmitter, comes in loud and clear at all times and carries special broadcasts to the region, but the hatred for things Communist Chinese is so great that, without any outside effort being made to prevent people from listening, these broadcasts receive very little and always scornful attention. The only Mandarin broadcasts that are reliably loud and clear are those from Radio Australia, twice a day; these are the chief source of news for the villagers, and they are avidly followed. The Thai radio stations are listened to for music, but knowledge of Thai is not widespread enough to make the Thai news and commentary broadcasts effective. Thai-language broadcasts of educational or instructional nature could be effective with the school children. Voice of America can be located on the radios but cannot be received clearly enough so that anyone tries to listen to them. Radio Taiwan cannot be received. The villagers are intent radio listeners and try doggedly to find broadcasts to listen to.

A few copies of some Bangkok Chinese dailies reach the villages, many days late. They are not widely circulated and seem to be little read. There is an interest in magazines, pictures, audiovisual education materials, books, and the like that far exceeds the meager supply; when questioned about the need for a bookstore, however, everyone replied that there was not enough money in the village for books to have any sale. A free lending or reading library in each village, directed toward recreational and self-study needs of children, youth, and village leaders undoubtedly would be very popular.

Relations with the Thai. When asked how they feel about Thailand, all villagers, from headmen to common villagers in the privacy of their own homes, express gratitude to the country for the opportunity it has given them to start life over again. This seems to be a general and a sincere sentiment. Moreover, they love the land they now live on and remark on its beauty and fertility. Their attitude toward the Thai king and royal family is one of respect, and toward the central government of Thailand one of confidence.

But their attitude toward local petty officials is one of distrust, partly a carry-over from the usual Chinese peasant distrust of government at the lower levels, and partly a consequence of the insecurity of their refugee status. They have learned that small officials expect to be bribed; this neither surprises them nor arouses resentment as long as the amounts remain reasonable. But they try to avoid all contact with officials, feeling they will be found vulnerable to larger-scale extortion, and all having some distant examples to point to. It is unlikely that they would ever willingly go to the Thai courts to seek justice or to Thai law-enforcement officers to seek protection.

Most important in their lives is the character of the local Thai farmers, their neighbors in the villages just below them on the wet-rice land. They call Central Thais "T'ai-tzu," and call the local Northern Thais "Kuo-lo," distinguishing them as two different races. "Kuo-lo" is not a Yunnanese word; it appears to be one they learned from one of the hill tribes. The relations between Ban-yang and the near-by Kuo-lo villages in the past have been marked by violence; more than twenty of the villagers have been murdered by the Kuo-lo in ten years, mostly in connection with armed robbery. Ban-mai, by contrast, reports very good relations with its neighboring villages (although the nearest ones are Thai-Lue, not Kuo-lo); although the villagers in Ban-mai share the unflattering clichés about Kuo-lo character, they report a lack of violence and much better relations. And even at Ban-yang the relations between the two kinds of villages are more constructive than destructive. The problem of order and safety on the road leading into the village has greatly improved, and although considerable loss is regularly sustained (particularly theft of poultry and animals, uprooting of fruit trees in newly planted orchards, theft of tools, plundering of crops, and the like), the Yunnanese on the one hand constantly devise better means of guarding against this and on the other tend to shrug it off as part of the price they must pay for being allowed to live here. And, in any event, it is a controllable and diminishing problem which does not seriously affect the future of the villages.

As the young Yunnanese children learn Thai in school, and as marriage and other relationships with the Thais increase, understanding between the two communities will improve. At present it can be noted that the Kuo-lo are anxious to work for the Yunnanese as winter-season laborers in their farms, depend on the Yunnanese to buy their agricultural products, and imitate the Yunnanese in patterns of livelihood, especially in agricultural technology and in diet. The nearer villages have notably increased in prosperity in recent years—evidenced in the building of many new and better houses—and the departure of the Yunnanese would have a serious adverse affect on the region.

Relations with the Border Patrol Policemen-teachers are rather good. The Yunnanese regard them as policemen primarily and feel that some of them are not highly qualified to teach, but nonetheless grant them the respect that teachers should be accorded. No doubt these teachers are making an impact on the minds of the children in their classes. The children gather in the school yard every morning at 9:30 to recite the oath of allegiance, salute the flag, and sing the national anthem (all in Bangkok Thai), and proudly claim that they sing the anthem better than the children in the nearby Kuo-lo village. If there were some bilingual teaching of the Thai, the language instruction could be made more effective; many of the children say that they can pronounce to the teacher's satisfaction, but cannot explain. No doubt the Yunnanese villagers are both better able to profit from the presence of the BPP in their villages and to defend themselves against abuse than are the hill tribes, among whom complaints against BPP encroachments are sometimes much more serious. Realistic cooperation between the Yunnanese and the BPP in any enlightened program could be expected.

On the level of contact between village leaders and mid-to-high-level Thai officials, the Yunnanese say that quite satisfactory understandings have been achieved in recent years. The village leaders themselves profess to feel that no serious problems between themselves and the Thai government exist or are in danger of erupting.

Relations with the Chinese Government in Taiwan. The scope of personal contacts with Taiwan and with the Chinese Embassy in Bangkok (as noted above, p. 510) has been very limited. The present writer has no basis for discussing the real nature of any organizational contacts, but the attitude of the villagers toward Taiwan can be known with some certainty. The calendar system of the Republic of China, outlawed by the Chinese Communists, is retained by the villagers, and this is sometimes taken to imply allegiance to the government on Taiwan. A negative and perhaps more accurate explanation is that there is no other modern calendar, excluding the one the Communists have promulgated, for Chinese to adopt. Nominally the village authorities profess allegiance to the Republic, and Chiang Kai-shek's picture is hung alongside that of the Thai king in their official rooms, but here again a negative or passive explanation probably comes closer to the truth. For the one definite political attitude that all of these people share in unshakable conviction is that Chinese Communism is evil. Beyond that, they are politically passive. They are well informed on the true nature of Chinese Communism, having lived under it and having been forced to flee in order to preserve their lives. The Moslems among them add to that a deep-seated resentment of the Chinese Communist treatment of their religion. But it would be incorrect to say that the Yunnanese villagers feel a positive loyalty to the government in Taiwan. Moreover, they have no interest in Taiwan as a place; they feel lucky not to have been evacuated to Taiwan and say that they would refuse to go there in the future. They explain this by saying that Taiwan is so poor and overcrowded that unskilled and destitute peasants like themselves would have no way of supporting themselves there. This lack of enthusiasm toward Taiwan is similar to the attitudes noted among the more recent refugees in Hong Kong and elsewhere, and is perhaps not surprising.

Aspects of the Opium Problem. Opium affects the daily lives of a number of the inhabitants of the villages, as it does the daily lives of most of the people in Northern Thailand. Although outlawed in Thailand in 1958, it was still smoked openly in Fang City as late as 1961 or 1962 (according to village gossip) and can still be procured there without too much trouble. However, the general trend toward suppression pushed vigorously by the Thai government has had the effect of inducing the use of heroin, which the Yunnanese villagers greatly fear and which they claim is not used by any of themselves.

The traditional attitude toward opium, as contrasted to heroin and the other more powerful derivatives, is that opium is not a bad or dangerous thing if used in moderation, and that it can be used in moderation indefinitely without addiction. Mild use of opium was particularly prevalent in peripheral areas of China like Yunnan. Thus it is not surprising that a number of older villagers have been mild users of opium at one time or another, and that most people think first of a pipe when they feel any illness or discomfort. Serious discussion of the problem with some younger schoolteachers and other more modern-minded persons in the villages leads to the conclusion that the number of steady users is small and that there is a strong feeling against even the mild use of opium among the young. Strengthening the schools and the youth clubs and providing recreational and educational material to sustain the modern-minded resistance to it should be adequate means for controlling the opium-smoking problem. Although it is important that the schools and other progressive forces in the villages be aided in their work of keeping up the community morale, the opium consumption problem at present must be regarded as a minor issue, not greatly different from the problem as it has existed in Yunnan for a century, and in no danger of getting out of hand under present and foreseeable conditions.

Another aspect of the opium problem concerns its production and the economics of production vis-à-vis other kinds of agricultural production. The 1961 report of the Hill Tribes Division on tribal peoples and the opium problem presents a rough formula: one man's labor for one growing season, working one *rai* of land, produces one kilogram of raw opium, worth about 1,000 baht at the prices paid to the producer in the hills. Discussion with the Yunnanese villagers, without suggesting knowledge of this formula, tended to corroborate its validity. But they also added the opinion that opium production required intensive labor and that the production can be cut in half by a sudden change in the weather during the few days of collecting the sap. Thus they claim that since they now have other good agricultural opportunities, among the Yunnanese of all kinds only a derelict unfit for productive labor, i.e., an addict willing to live a minimal existence for the sake of smoking opium, would waste his time growing opium. According to the villagers, potatoes which grow best at the same elevation as opium can in one growing season gross one man 4,000–5,000 baht; moreover, the labor is far less intensive (enough so that the farmer can live at the lower elevation, simultaneously growing another winter crop of some other cash product there), and the yield is certain. In addition, other winter crops grown at lower elevations, such as garlic, ginger, etc., can gross a man 3,000 baht in one season. Although market variability can (and has at times) upset these figures, in general the hard-working Yunnanese farmer always has a choice of several other crops in the winter (opium) growing season that can guarantee him greater income with less labor and risk. These figures were checked out with many persons in all kinds of conversational situations, and there seems to be no reason to doubt their basic validity.

Attitudes toward the Various Hill Tribes. Yunnan is ethnically the most complex region of China. The Yunnanese villagers in Thailand have lived all their lives with minority groups of the same ethnic identifications as most of those now present in Northern Thailand and classed by the Thai government as hill tribes; they know them well, and have generally good relations with them, especially those they know best from Yunnan.

Chinese-influenced Hill Tribes. They class three tribal groups as being most influenced by Chinese culture and most susceptible to their leadership and influence now. These are the Lisu, the Yao, and the Meo, in that order. They state that usually 70–85 percent of the Lisu and Yao people of both sexes and all ages are able to speak fluent Chinese of the Yunnanese dialect, honor Chinese writing, and occasionally are even literate in Chinese. The Meo are less reverential toward things Chinese, but among most groups known to the Yunnanese at least 50 percent of the total, including almost all of the adult males, are able to speak Chinese. They particularly like the harmonious character of the Lisu and Yao, though they object to their loose sexual morals. They state that all three groups come to them for guidance in religious matters, for seeds and growing instructions, for loans and other aid, and to conduct business.

The relationship described by the villagers between themselves and these hill tribes was particularly evident in the Yao village near Ban-yang, visited one day in the company of some of the villagers. The Yao village headman's wife, when asked how it happened that she spoke such perfect Yunnanese (and her village has been more or less in its present area of Thailand for forty years), replied: "Why not? We come from the 'Great Dynasty' [*ta-ch'ao*] and we speak the language of the 'Great Court.'" The Yunnanese find the Yaos' conservative attachment to things Chinese somewhat touching and slightly amusing. They say the Yaos all want a pair of mock copies of oldfashioned cloth shoes to be buried in, so that their spirits can present themselves at the court of the Chinese emperors. And, it is said, the Yaos will pay higher prices for oldfashioned staple commodities from China than for new superior goods from elsewhere. Their shamans recite incantations from Chinese texts, and this makes some knowledge of Chinese essential to them. In the village visited everyone encountered, from very young children to old grandmothers, spoke quite passable Yunnanese and was proud to do so. The forms of courtesy extended to the visitors were all consistent with Chinese models.

The Thai-Lue (Pai-yi). The Yunnanese know the Thai-Lue (Pai-yi) from Yunnan, from Burma, and as residents in Northern Thailand. They like them and find them very tractable and pleasant people. Thai-Lue outnumber all other non-Han wives among them. At Ban-mai there are two neighboring villages of Thai-Lue who came out from Burma with the Yunnanese. At Ban-yang the headman (*puyaiban*), though a Moslem, has married a Thai-Lue girl from a village near Fang.

Asked what "Pai-yi" means in their usage of the word, the best informed of the Yunnanese agreed in explaining that it means any of the peoples known to them who speak the Tai-related languages, excluding Central and Northern Thai and Lao. These languages are said to vary only slightly from China to Burma to Thailand, and from "dry Pai-yi" to "water Pai-yi," so that all the Pai-yi are one great community. When asked specifically what the Shans of Burma are in relation to the Pai-yi, the answer given is that "Shan" is simply a local Burmese name for Pai-yi. The difference between "dry" and "water" Pai-yi, as these people understand it, is not that between dry-rice farming as opposed to wet-rice farming. Rather it has to do with other economic and cultural distinctions. The "dry" Pai-yi are described as more backward and poorer, living in low hill regions where there are no large streams. The "wet" Pai-yi are valley-bottom people living in conjunction with major streams, and water has ritual significance for them. For example, they defecate only when standing in water, and consider the signs of human defecation in their fields to defile them. (Ban-mai, incidentally, is located *up*stream from their villages.) Even the "dry" Pai-yi are merely foothills people, and none of the Pai-yi should be classified as true "hill tribes" since they never occupy the higher elevations.[5]

Other Tribes. Many of the Yunnanese can speak at least a

---

[5] This "folk ethnology" is not completely accurate, but does reflect the attitudes of these Yunnanese toward the Thai-Lue. "Pai-yi" is a name for some Tai speakers in China, notably those in Yunnnan, but is not used for the Tai speakers in, for example, Kwangsi, such as the Chuang and Chung-chia, who call Yunnanese Tai speakers "Pai-yi," but would not refer to themselves in this way.

smattering of many of the hill tribe languages, especially Lahu and Karen, which they had to learn while in Burma. Local Lahu women come frequently to Ban-yang to sell vegetables; as they walk through the village (their costume, exposing their bare breasts, is bizarre to the Yunnanese eye), young men idling in doorsteps make joking banter with them, to everyone's amusement. But few Karens or Lahus know much Yunnanese, and relations with these other tribes clearly are not like the relations with the Lisu, the Yao, and the Meo. And, although they do not let it affect their relations with the local Lahu, the Yunnanese much resent the fact that the Burmese in recent years have hired some Lahu groups to fight them as infiltrators, snipers hidden along jungle paths, and as guerrillas.

Among all of the hill tribes of the region, the Yunnanese exercise considerable authority; their prestige and their obviously superior way of life give them much leadership potential. The Yunnanese know this and under proper conditions would be willing to cooperate with Thai authorities in using their influence to bring about the guided transformation of the hill tribes, particularly in matters of agricultural technology. And among those tribes which use the Yunnanese language and honor the Chinese script as the language of their religious texts, the prestige of the Yunnanese villagers' example in sending their children to schools to learn Thai might be particularly helpful in persuading tribesmen to take the study of Thai more seriously. In matters of medicine and public health (in which they are accustomed to look to Chinese for advice) the leadership of the Yunnanese villagers might also be important. In short, the Yunnanese villagers represent an asset that might be exploited in many ways to improve the conditions of the hill tribes.

THE VILLAGE OF BAN-MAI: COMPARISONS AND CONTRASTS

The village has two Thai names, "Ban-mai" meaning "new village," and "Vieng-wai," the meaning of which is unknown to this writer. The Yunnanese villagers call it by a third name, "Huo-fei," which has no meaning in Chinese, but is simply the Yunnanese transliteration of another Thai name for the place, meaning "the chief dam"; the Thai equivalent does not seem to be current any more.

Ban-mai is located three kilometers south and five kilometers west of Fang City, off the road leading to the hot springs and the provincial agricultural experimentation station. Like Ban-yang, Ban-mai is located just above the border of the paddy fields, in the lowest foothills, on a fine river, and on a main trail leading up into the hills. Ban-mai is closely linked to the mid-level village of Mae-nom (Chinese name, "P'an-lung"), from which many of its residents have come; it is also closely linked to a mid-level sub-village known to the writer only by the Yunnanese name of "Hui-tsung-p'o," located north of Ban-mai and Fang at the mid-elevation.

Ban-mai was founded one year earlier than Ban-yang, but in the same movement of people and under the same conditions. Its present population is 680, among whom 75 are recent arrivals from Burma, and 108 are babies born in the village in the last eleven years. A new street is now under construction to accommodate new arrivals from Mae-nom. The proportion of Yunnanese to non-Han wives is about the same as at Ban-yang.

On first glance, Ban-mai seems to be just a smaller and more compact copy of Ban-yang, but on a second glance it reveals some interesting differences. Its streets are neater and better kept; its gardens are smaller, permitting less space for vegetables, but they are much neater and more attractively planted. There is no open water running through the village to each house; instead, many houses have good wells (average 40 feet deep, reaching gravel-rock stratum, costing 1,000 baht to dig and improve), cemented and enclosed in protective walls. Many houses have cement floors and terrace areas in front. The village manages to look more prosperous simply by being more orderly. Each of these villages insists that the other has the more well-off inhabitants, but the truth is that both have very few who are not quite poor.

The religious situation is comparable to that at Ban-yang. A new modest-sized mosque is being built. A temple to the local spirits is said to exist, but was not seen by the writer. There are said to be no Christians in the village, and no active Buddhists, but the village headman welcomes to his village Pastor Carlson of Chiengrai on his infrequent rounds.

The village has one noodle-shop (Moslem, as at Ban-yang)

[519]

and another shop that sells pastries, and a number of small general stores. However, it is closer to Fang and on a better road (served by two daily round trips of the local bus), so it is more dependent on shopping facilities in Fang.

The pattern of governmental organization is identical with that at Ban-yang, but the conduct of government is strikingly different, and most of the contrasts between the two villages seem to derive from this fact. The chairman is an extremely vigorous man in his forties who spends all his time in the village, working his own farm and tending to the affairs of his people. He says that the Thai officials have learned that to find him they must go to his fields and not to his house, as he works on the land every day. He has three children of school age and another who soon will be, and he works intimately with the school authorities to keep the school well financed (relatively speaking), well organized, and running properly. One gains the impression that this village chief walks the streets of his village every day, talking with the people in a friendly and egalitarian manner, imparting a morale and a cohesiveness to the social group that keeps everyone performing at a high level. And the village chief has able aids. Ban-mai appears to be run by a triumvirate of the chairman or village head, the school principal, and an elderly man called the guidance officer (*chih-tao-yuan*, a position nominally higher than that of the chairman, but more or less honorary). They are an effective trio.

The school at Ban-mai has less than one hundred students. Its buildings and school grounds are roughly comparable to those at Ban-yang, except that they are in excellent repair, clean, and better equipped. It has the reputation of being the best school in the several Yunnanese villages, and parents who can afford to do so are beginning to send their children to live with friends at Ban-mai so that they can attend this school. It is reported that there are no children of school age in this village who are not enrolled in the school. The teachers receive only three hundred baht per month. Tuition, as at Ban-yang, varies from ten to forty baht per semester. Like the school at Ban-yang, the Ban-mai school lacks books and teaching aids as well as recreation equipment.

[520]

The school at Ban-mai is served by a board of trustees and by an active "youth club," occupying school premises. The youth club, run by village teen-agers with the direction of two or three young teachers, gives many recreation programs for school and village. A performance for the visitors' benefit was quite remarkable. In a series of vaudeville acts young children in improvised costumes sang, danced, and acted out pantomimes with great cleverness, while the officials and citizens of the town watched. The show was pure entertainment, free of any political meaning or propaganda.

The school needs more buildings and needs books and other materials, but it is functioning admirably and could well serve as a model for the reorganization of the school at Ban-yang; its leaders discussed the Ban-yang situation with concern and intelligence and indicated that they would be willing to help. The Ban-mai school has a more positive attitude toward learning Thai. The two BPP teachers are much appreciated, and in order to keep them in the village and on the job more fully, the village, at its expense, has built them homes and given them some cash for moving expenses so that they will bring their wives and families to live in the village. In this as in many other things the leadership of Ban-mai displays positive and constructive attitudes toward the Thais, and the village follows that leadership. As the village school becomes an enlarged boarding school, it might be used to aid the cultural assimilation of Lisu, Yao, Meo, and other tribal peoples for whom the Chinese model has great prestige.

The agricultural situation at Ban-mai shows some minor deviations from that at Ban-yang, but they might become important. Relations with the Thai (Kuo-lo) neighbors is much better, and losses due to theft and plundering are said to be insignificant. In addition, the residents of this village are pressed for space (they claim about 570 *rai* of fields as "theirs") and have little area for easy expansion into the steep hills behind them, so they have to keep their residence area as small as possible, meaning that home gardens are smaller, and more vegetables are grown in the fields, in the winter season only, and a larger proportion of vegetables is purchased. But most important, at Ban-mai they

[521]

have found ways of leasing or renting nearby paddy fields on three-to-five-year contracts; thus they can raise some wet rice in the rainy season and enlarge their production of cash crops and vegetable crops in the winter season. And, under the stimulus of the guidance officer (formerly a large landlord with great interest in agricultural management in Yunnan), they are experimenting actively with crop improvement. Six improved strains of Taiwan and Japanese wet rice were being grown experimentally alongside the best two strains in the village as a demonstration to the village. These efforts to improve agricultural technology are being followed with interest in the village and are reported to be having an impact on the Thai-Lue and Thai villages nearby as well.

Potatoes and other upland crops are important cash crops grown at higher elevations by Ban-mai farmers, as at Ban-yang.

The shorter time spent at Ban-mai made it impossible to talk to as many of the villagers and to verify all of the first impressions. In retrospect, the main point of contrast seems to be atmosphere or morale, rather than any material difference.

CONCLUSION

The presence of the Yunnanese rural minority poses some difficult problems for the Thai administration. From the standpoint of the Thai government, there are several disadvantages in these people: one is the fact that their general *cultural* orientation is, without question, Chinese. The other item which must be of great concern is the military organization and involvement in large-scale opium trade of Yunnanese Chinese in the more remote and higher terrain of the border regions, reports of which have reached the public press.[6] I was unable to observe directly

---

[6] Dennis Bloodworth, for example, states, "In North Thailand the (opium) commerce is run by remnants of the 93rd Nationalist Chinese Infantry Division, which was forced out of Yunnan when the Communists overran China 15 years ago" (1965).

On May 18, 1965, the *New York Times* carried the following story, under the byline of Seymour Topping, datelined Bangkok:

A Chinese Nationalist military force based in Northeast Burma is reported to be carrying out raids in Yunnan Province of Communist China. Troops commanded by Gen. Ma Chuan-kuo operate from the mountainous areas of Hsi Meng, 170 miles northwest of the junction of the borders of Burma,

the relationships between those Chinese and the peaceful-appearing, non-opium-growing villagers in the Fang area.

This no doubt brings into question the many advantages which the existence of the Yunnanese brings, or could bring. But there are some very real advantages. Their political loyalties are strongly anti-Communist, and as refugees from the Communist Chinese regime, they have a more realistic view of Chinese Communism, its methods and its dangers, than any other minority population. Their influence on the hill tribes is widespread in Thailand, Burma, and Laos, because of trade connections which have been established over hundreds of years. These trade connections also make the Yunnanese potentially great sources of information on activities in the hill areas which Thais do not frequent. Their permanent settlement in areas the Thais have considered to be only marginal or unproductive means that these areas are blocked off to other immigrants, and this effectively controls migration of hill tribes in areas which Thais have otherwise been unable to consolidate. Their potential influence as innovators and introducers of new agricultural, economic, educational, and social organizational techniques is particularly great because of the traditionally high esteem with which Chinese culture is viewed among such peoples as the Meo, Yao, and Lisu (see Kandre's paper in this volume for further examples of this among the Yao). But this latter condition is precisely the heart of the problem which faces the Thais in building a culturally Thai (rather than Chinese) nation within the boundaries of Thailand. The question remains whether a sufficiently flexible and imaginative administrative device can be developed to assure the integration of these Yunnanese into the Thai nation and make possible their use as a link between the Thai administration, Thai culture, and the hill tribes.

Thailand and Laos. The raiders are said to be able to cross easily into Yunnan and sometimes escort out dissident elements and refugees.

The article also reported that there were 10,000 Chinese former Nationalists in eight settlements in the North Thailand frontier areas, which were independent of Peking and Taiwan. It is not known what sources of information may have been available to the *New York Times* writer, but his report clearly contains some inaccuracies of detail.

Young (1962:83) asserts that the Haw "owe a degree of loyalty to the Kuomintang guerrillas."

THAILAND: F. W. MOTE

BIBLIOGRAPHY

BLOODWORTH, DENNIS
  1965   Chasing the dragon. The Observer, January 24, 1965. London.
HALLETT, HOLT S.
  1890   A thousand miles on an elephant in the Shan States. Edinburgh
         and London, William Blackwood and Sons.
HALPERN, JOEL
  1961   The role of the Chinese in Lao society. Journal of the Siam
         Society 49(1):21–46.
TOPPING, SEYMOUR
  1965   New Chiang raids in China reported. The New York Times,
         May 18, 1965.
YOUNG, GORDON
  1962   The hill tribes of Northern Thailand. Bangkok, the Siam So-
         ciety, 2d edn.

CHAPTER 14

The Hill Tribe Program of The Public Welfare Department, Ministry of Interior, Thailand: Research and Socio-economic Development

HANS MANNDORFF

PREFACE

This paper is intended to present a concise review of the Hill Tribe Project in Northern Thailand, as conducted by the Ministry of Interior, Public Welfare Department, Hill Tribe Division. It gives a brief description of the history and present state of the Hill Tribe Project, including research, planning, and development activities. Reference is made to a number of reports, articles, and government papers on this subject, from which more detailed information may be obtained.

HILL TRIBES AND CENTRAL GOVERNMENT BEFORE 1959

There has been a continuous historical process in Southeast Asia by which peoples and tribes, such as speakers of the Tibeto-Burman and Thai-Shan-Lao languages, have gradually moved toward the south. Repeated southward migrations of populations and spread of cultural traits can be detected since the Bronze Age, and even neolithic times. This is reflected not only in the linguistic and racial affiliations, but can also be inferred from archeological evidence and historical record (Manndorff 1965B).

At the same time as the extension of populations and civilizations from the north was taking place, there was also a continuous seaborne cultural impact into Southeast Asia from India and Indonesia, starting with the beginning of the Christian era. This southern impact is reflected, for example, in the early Indochina civilizations of Funan, Angkor, and Srivijaya, and later influences repeatedly extended inland from the coasts, spreading upstream along the great rivers of the subcontinent. In recent centuries overseas influence has been represented increasingly by European and American civilizations.

In the hills of the entire region, stretching from Burma and Thailand to Laos and Vietnam, the southward movement of various tribal groups continues. In Northern Thailand, a number of hill tribes lead a semi-nomadic or migratory way of life, at elevations ranging from 800 to 2,000 meters (2,500 to 6,100 feet), often crossing the borders to and from Burma and Laos. The general direction of this movement is from north to south. Estimates of the number of tribesmen involved range from 50,000 to 400,000. One report estimates that as of November 1960 the total Thailand hill tribe population was 217,000 (Young 1962:85). However, all these figures are only estimates and should be used with considerable caution. Unlike the tribes of such nearby countries as India, Burma, French Indochina, and Malaya, the Thailand hill tribes have never been included in any census reports or district gazetteers compiled by the government. Until recently, many of the remote hill tracts of the fourteen northern provinces were virtually non-administered areas, and, until the Border Patrol Police was set up in 1955, the mountainous frontier regions were never effectively controlled.

Besides the hill tribes, an as yet undetermined number of Chinese and Shan people have moved into the hills of Northern Thailand in recent times. These dwell primarily in the frontier regions near the three-country corner of Burma, Thailand, and Laos. Many of them are the remnants of retreating military units, such as the former Kuomintang (KMT, Nationalist Chinese) and Free Shan Armies from Burma. Others are stragglers or refugees from political and military disturbances in the neighboring countries. Thus the majority of them are male. Only a fraction of these recent immigrants have brought their families with them. Those of Chinese origin are generally labeled "Haw" in Northern Thailand.[1] It is quite interesting that no one is able to give

[1] These are only the most recent movements of Shan and Chinese into Northern Thailand. Most Chinese in urban areas have moved by sea to central Thailand and thence have moved to other parts of Thailand. Many of the Shans in the North remain from invasions as recent as the turn of the century. There are records of "Haw" (Yunnanese Chinese) in the mid-nineteenth century (see e.g. Hallett 1890). See also Mote's paper in this volume for a more complete description of the "Haw." (Ed.)

a satisfactory explanation of the derivation of this name. However, it should be clearly stated that the so-called Haw, who have recently settled in the mountains of Chiengmai and Chiengrai provinces, can not be regarded as a "hill tribe" in the same sense as the other groups treated in this paper. Many of these Haw have spread into hill tribe villages, without, however, losing their identity as Chinese. We will have to deal with these people repeatedly in this report because they live in a remarkable symbiosis with the hill tribes. As traders in the hills and key men in the opium traffic, they not only exert control over financial transactions, but also manage to have considerable influence upon the headmen and other members of tribal communities.

Anthropologists who are concerned with the ethnography of Southeast Asia have traditionally distinguished between lowland and upland groups. The differences between the culturally diversified tribal groups, dwelling in the mountain ranges, and the developed civilizations of the river valleys have been referred to frequently in the anthropological literature. Thus the term "hill tribes" has been created. We shall not argue about the validity of this term, but since it has been created, we shall use it when needed.

Nonetheless, it should be mentioned that these hill tribes have never lived in a state of complete isolation, and that cultural traits of the surrounding great civilizations have been adopted by them and assimilated to various degrees. For example, an analysis of the religious beliefs and rituals of many hill tribes leads to the impression that they have preserved (and possibly reinterpreted) some of the concepts and teachings prevailing in ancient China and Tibet. This is especially true for the Meo and Yao, and also a lesser degree for such tribes as the Lisu and Lahu. On the other hand, if some popular magico-religious practices of remote lowland Thai villages are observed, it becomes evident that a number of them bear striking resemblance to those of certain hill tribes, a phenomenon which might be traced to former historical relationships, or even to a common cultural stratum from which these seemingly distinct populations derived.

Many of the hill tribes that can be found in the fourteen northern provinces seem to be rather recent immigrants. Specifically those of the Tibeto-Burman stock (like Lisu, Lahu, and Akha), as well as those Chinese-affiliated tribes (like Meo and Yao), probably did not enter the country more than 100 to 150 years ago. Others, such as the Lawa and other Mon-Khmer-related tribes of Austroasiatic linguistic stock, as well as some early groups of Karen, have had their homesteads in the area between the Salween and Mekong rivers for a very long time. Some have even been there since before the emergence of the early Thai city-states in the northern provinces in the tenth to twelfth centuries. However this may be, there has evidently been a tremendous influx of hill tribesmen in the last eighty or one hundred years.

In some provinces the hills are close to being overpopulated, a situation that threatens to become worse due to two factors. First is the constant flow of newcomers in recent years, and the second is the absence of any inclination on the part of most hill men to move down to the lowlands. Even if they should move, the demographic expansion of the rural Thai people living in the lowlands will probably lead to a saturation of these lands within the near future. Some sections of the lowland population are already pressing into the upper parts of the valleys and up the hill slopes.

Traditionally, the relationship between the lowland population and the hill people in Thailand has been one of mutual tolerance and non-interference. There has been little open antipathy, but rather there has been apathy between them. Up to now, the average *khon muang* ("Northern Thai," literally "man of the principality") considers the *khon doi* ("mountain man") to be a rather strange-looking but no less respected countryman. In some neighboring countries, various disdainful denotations are given to hill tribesmen (e.g. *kha*, "slave," in Laos; *moi*, "savage," in Vietnam). The name "Kha" is also applied by the Thai to some tribes living near the Laotian border, e.g. the Khamu (or Kha Khmu?) and Khatin. These, however, are exceptions, and concern only small groups which have migrated into Thailand from Laos, where this derogatory name was already attached to those tribes. The Thai term *khon pa* ("forest man") or *khon doi* ("mountain man") is without pejorative meaning.

It is true, however, that tribesmen are sometimes discriminated against in business dealings. This is especially true of the non-opium-growers, e.g. the Karen and Luaꞏ, who do not have the benefit of possessing cash crops, and whose economic relations with the lowlanders are on a less advantageous basis.

Among the opium-growing tribes, trade relations between lowlands and uplands are largely determined by the opium production of the hill people and by their demands for certain commodities which can be obtained only from the lowlands. These trade relations are carried on either by Thai petty traders or by Chinese (Haw) merchants. These intermediaries bring news from the outside world and stimulate new demands and desires by exhibiting merchandise previously unknown or unobtainable by the hill people. The opium, as a marketable cash product of high value, encourages the traders to penetrate even into the most remote parts of the hills and guarantees a relative economic security and even wealth to the hill tribesmen. By means of this cash product they can buy luxury or fancy goods and can even occasionally hire lowland people as laborers.

Until about ten years ago the Thai government did not care much about the tribesmen in the hills. Establishment of contacts with them was largely left to the discretion of the province (*changwad*) and district (*amphur*) authorities. Usually the local officers maintained that they had enough problems with their own people (in the lowlands) and did not feel compelled to bother about the people in the inaccessible hills.

With few exceptions there was no taxation, no conscription, no education, and no legal registration of hill tribesmen. The population census did not include them. Their legal position as residents or citizens of the country was never clearly defined, and virtually no governmental administration was extended into the remote mountain areas.

Even during our hill tribe survey in 1961–1962 we felt that many local authorities appeared to lack a clear understanding of, and concern for, the hill tribes and were uncertain about the Thai government's policy toward them. Some responsible persons thought that it was government policy to bring the hill tribes down to the lowlands. Others admitted that they had little or no contact with the hill populations and had little information concerning their number and whereabouts. As an example, we were told several times that since there was now a law prohibiting opium production, there was no more poppy cultivation by hill people. Some explained that their current activities gave them little or no time to learn much about the hill people. The prevailing ambiguities of government policy resulted in a lack of coordination in the approach of responsible authorities toward the hill tribes.

On the other hand, the recently arrived hill tribesmen seem to have been quite content with this state of affairs. As traditionally self-reliant and independent mountain peoples, they have always been able to take care of themselves. There is reason to believe that their prevailing attitude is to hail any government that leaves them alone. We may not be mistaken in assuming that many migrations of hill tribe communities are caused by government actions which the tribesmen feel to be oppressive. These tribal communities are, in general, not aggressive or warlike. They tend instead to disappear, to retreat deeper into the jungle if they fear any undue interference in their internal affairs. For them it does not make any difference if the hill tract in which they dwell is in Burma, Laos, or Thailand, as long as they are allowed to practice their customary social, economic, and ritual life in peace. It may well be that the expectation of being left alone has guided many tribal communities into Thailand in the past, and in recent years.

Of course, it is no longer possible for the government to leave these ethnic minorities entirely alone today. It is the inevitable logic of events in our times that administration and modernization are extended even into those remote parts of the country which were traditionally self-sufficient.

The deliberate process of government involvement with the northern hill tribes was started in 1955, with the program of the Border Patrol Police, and was intensified in 1959, when the Ministry of Interior assigned the Public Welfare Department to carry out certain research and development activities in the remote mountain regions.

INTENSIFICATION OF RELATIONSHIP SINCE 1959

In the last ten years the government of Thailand has increasingly become aware of its responsibility for including the hill people of the North in its public policy and for providing administrative services. These steps were taken to show, in a practical way, that the welfare and problems of the hill tribes in Northern Thailand are a concern of the government. It was implied that if the government would not care for them, someone else might attempt to do so.

When the late Prime Minister, Marshall Sarit, banned the production of opium in December 1958 (2501 Buddhist Era), the Ministry of Interior was given the responsibility of abolishing opium cultivation. This added urgency to the problem of dealing with the hill tribes, since several of these mountain people were opium producers. Thus the opium problem became the reason for intensifying relations of the central government with hill tribe societies.

The major problems which the government faced at this time were as follows: (1) to replace opium cultivation without striking a deathblow to the economy of the hill people; (2) to prevent further forest destruction by assisting the hill people to develop a more conservative system of shifting cultivation or, if possible, to promote stabilized farming in the hills; (3) to render health, educational, and other welfare services to the mountain population; and (4) to extend administration and control to remote hill and frontier regions.

Since 1955 the Border Patrol Police had been operating with regard to the fourth point, as they were assigned to provide for "control and public safety in the remote hills and frontier regions." Besides, or for this purpose, they also established schools and distributed some medical and agricultural equipment to hill tribesmen. However, it was felt in several quarters that education, vocational training, agricultural assistance, etc. should be in the hands of a civil agency with an adequately qualified staff.

In a decision of June 3, 1959, the Council of Ministers approved a Ministry of Interior plan for the establishment of Land Settlement Projects for hill tribes in various North Thailand provinces. The Public Welfare Department was entrusted with the implementation of this project. The primary purpose was to settle hill tribes in locations suited for them, by means of establishing "settlement areas" (nikhom) on the ridges and high plateaus which are the most favored sites of the hill peoples,

[531]

and by encouraging the tribes to migrate to these settlement areas.

Four land settlement pilot projects were established for hill peoples in 1960–1963: in Tak Province (Doi Musser); in Chiengmai Province (Doi Chiengdao); in Chiengrai Province (Maechan); and in Loei Province (Bhu Lom Low). The hill projects were administered by a superintendent and were usually staffed with agricultural workers, health workers, tractor- and truck-drivers, etc. They were also equipped with some modern agricultural machinery and road-construction and transport equipment.

The first few years were occupied with the mere establishment of these projects. The Thai officers were feeling their way, since they were faced with an entirely new situation, socially and culturally, as well as economically. The Thai were not at all experienced in hill agriculture. In the nine hundred years of their history in Thailand they had never taken great interest in the mountains. It took some time to realize that the concepts and experience derived from lowland settlements could not easily be transplanted into the hills. So it was not at all surprising that these hill projects suffered some setbacks during their initial period of operation.

On the other hand, the hill tribes were rather reserved and restrained, though never hostile or rejecting in their response to the projects. They took a "wait and see" attitude, occasionally passing by or stopping at the office bungalow, accepting invitations for social gatherings or for tribal dance performances, without making a final commitment to resettle. We should note at this point that tribal leaders are usually quite shrewd and able politicians, and even diplomats. In the end, they did not voluntarily migrate into the settlement areas, and it would have been unrealistic to think that they could easily be ordered to leave their villages and join the projects.

The administrative and planning officials of the Hill Tribe Project were probably quite right in following a policy of moderation, since premature activities could possibly have aggravated the already delicate situation in the hills. They did not take any drastic measures to transplant tribal populations or to resettle them in the project areas, and they refrained from

[532]

enforcing the laws prohibiting slash-and-burn agriculture and opium cultivation.

Confronted with so many pressing problems, the Public Welfare Department, led by its Director General, Khun Pakorn Angsusingha, reacted in three ways. Carefully selected officers were sent to neighboring countries to study comparable problems in other ethnic minority programs, international technical assistance agencies were invited to render aid, and a socio-economic survey of the Northern Thailand hill tribes was inaugurated. The Hill Tribe Project proceeded slowly as the main effort was directed toward gathering more experience.

THE SOCIO-ECONOMIC SURVEY OF SELECTED HILL TRIBES IN NORTHERN THAILAND 1961–1962

Soon after establishing the Doi Musser (Tak Province) and Doi Chiengdao (Chiengmai Province) settlement projects, the government felt the need for reliable information about hill tribes, to be used as a basis for effective planning of the hill tribe welfare and development projects. For this purpose, the Department of Public Welfare initiated a socio-economic survey of selected hill tribes.

This research project was the first government-sponsored survey of the mountain peoples of Northern Thailand. It was conducted by the Ministry of Interior, with assistance and cooperation from several organizations. The Asia Foundation gave financial assistance for training the government officials and for the field survey and final survey report; the United Nations provided a social anthropologist (the author of this paper) as a technical assistance expert; ECAFE Division of Social Affairs drafted an observation schedule and interview guide which was pre-tested and refined after field experience; the Ministry of Agriculture and the Border Patrol Police participated in the project by seconding their officials to join in the field work; the Ministry of Public Health provided medical supplies; the Siam Society furnished information by making available its rich library resources; and advisory services were also received from Chulalongkorn University during the training period, as well as during the later stages of the study.

The field survey, which covered the Meo, Yao, Lisu, Lahu,

and Akha, all of whom are opium growers, was carried out between October 1961 and May 1962. The tribes covered were selected in accordance with the wishes of the government and were those with which the land settlement projects were primarily concerned. The Karen, another populous hill tribe in Northern Thailand, were only included in the Hill Tribe Project at a later date. Special emphasis was given in the survey to the role of hill traders, i.e., Thai peddlers and the "Haw."

The field-survey personnel was grouped into five teams, each consisting of one official from the Department of Public Welfare, one official from the Ministry of Agriculture, and an associate from the Border Patrol Police, who gave medical assistance and was dressed in civilian clothes. The survey teams were stationed in sample villages, usually for a period of from one to three months, and were constantly advised and guided by the social anthropologist. Great pains were taken in the beginning to establish a friendly relationship with the tribesmen and to gather information in a casual way through "participant observation." More systematic interviews were started only after a good amount of mutual confidence and amicability had been developed. In several cases it was three weeks or more until this could be accomplished. Eighteen sample villages of the above-mentioned tribes were studied rather intensively, and some twenty to thirty more villages were visited more briefly.

Following the field survey of the five research teams, a smaller group made month-long visits to check the data which had been obtained and to supplement it, particularly through studies of attitudes and opinions.

The *Final Report of the Socio-Economic Survey of Hill Tribes in Northern Thailand* was prepared in Bangkok during June 1962, and was presented to the Ministry of Interior and to UNESCO. With their approval it was published in a preliminary mimeographed form in August 1962 (Thailand 1962).[2] This report has become an authoritative source of information, and its recommendations are used as a basis of the present Hill Tribes Development and Welfare Program of the Ministry of Interior.

It is not possible to go into all the details of the survey report. But it may be mentioned that it attempted to give a comprehen-

[2] A revised and illustrated edition is now in print.

sive account of the ethnic and socio-economic situation in the hills, stressing the contemporary patterns of acculturation and basic facts of economic activities and social structures of the tribes concerned. It discussed the major problems, including: (1) promoting a more stabilized economy; (2) replacing opium-growing by developing new cash crops; (3) administration and control in the remote hills and frontier regions.

The authors of the report did not assume that this survey would give the final answer to the many questions which were covered. Instead, it was stressed that this survey pointed to problems which deserved intensive study by qualified experts. These were problems related to such things as soil conservation, land use, hill agricultural techniques, preventive veterinary methods, development of effective transport and marketing mechanisms, livestock-raising and pasture improvement, etc. There were, in addition, problems in which human factors played an important role, for which more intensive anthropological and sociological research would be required.

Recommendations for further research, experimentation, and continuous evaluation were made throughout the survey report.

RECOMMENDATIONS OF THE 1961–1962 SURVEY

On the basis of the survey a number of recommendations were submitted to the Thai government. These included policy measures, administrative measures, and development activities. An action program was suggested, with three major projects: (1) intensification and broadening of settlement project activities; (2) mobile development workers to approach the hill peoples outside the settlement project areas; (3) establishment of a Tribal Research Centre to serve as a permanent advisory institution (see Geddes' paper in this volume).

Development Activities. The implementation of these major projects will be dealt with below. Here we can discuss only some of the main principles which were recommended on the basis of the survey findings.

1. In regard to the Land Settlement Projects, it was suggested that, for the time being, they should not be regarded as resettlement areas into which the tribal groups should be relocated, but that they should become hill bases in which intensive agricul-

tural (and other) experiments should be carried out, and from which, at a later stage, useful innovations should be spread into the surrounding hill tribe villages. Thus these hill stations should be looked on as pilot development blocks incorporating such activities as:

(a) cultivation of experimental cash crops, which might ultimately replace opium-poppy cultivation and development of improved and modernized methods of hill farming;

(b) training and demonstration centers for hill farmers who may be encouraged to come in from the nearby villages outside the project sites;

(c) marketing and trans-shipment centers for the promotion of trade envisaged in the program;

(d) health, education, and welfare centers for the hill people living in or near the project sites.

Through the intensified experimental development process it is hoped that the settlement project areas can gradually become regions of more stabilized agriculture in which the opium poppy will be completely replaced by economically valuable crops which are in short supply in the country, from which the hill people can derive an adequate income. The development of live-stock-raising, and possibly some handicraft activities could play an important role in this context, at least in some areas.

Within the settlement project areas, proper roads should be built to link the tribal villages together, and to connect them with the national highway system in order to facilitate the transport of hill farmers' products into lowland markets. Other facilities, such as schools, dispensaries, public meeting places, etc., should also be set up in the hill stations.

2. Secondly, the hill stations should be considered as:

(a) training centers for development workers who will work among the hill people in several fields of economic and social activities;

(b) hill bases from which mobile development work should be launched, in order to introduce useful innovations to the hill tribesmen in the remote areas.

The settlement projects at Tak and Chiengdao have only two and three tribal villages respectively within their prescribed project areas. Suitable provisions should be made for the large number of villages outside the project areas. Since it would be unrealistic to expect that those tribesmen scattered over the hills would migrate into the sphere of the settlements (or even visit and study their demonstration plots), the hill tribes should be approached in their own villages. They should be met in their own world, in their own physical and social environment. Everything possible should be done to prevent the settlement centers from becoming "ivory towers" with the officials living inside, while the hill tribes remain outside.

Of course, such a mobile extension scheme can be successful only if it is conducted by adequately trained personnel, who are experienced and dedicated, who in fact have something valuable to extend to the tribesmen. The training of such personnel is, therefore, a prerequisite for a successful mobile development scheme. Two proposals were made to render this kind of thorough training. The first channel for training should be the hill stations, or settlement projects, through which valuable practical experience in work with hill people could be obtained. The second channel should be the Tribal Research Centre, which, at the same time, should serve as a permanent advisory and training institution.

It is quite clear that this action program is a long-term project, the implementation of which will need much time. It may take several years before the experiments in the hill stations yield the first useful results. And only after these have been achieved can proper training be given to the mobile development workers. Several years may be required before the Tribal Research Centre will be in a position to render substantial advice and training.

3. The establishment of a Tribal Research Centre for Northern Thailand was another major project recommended on the basis of the survey findings.[3] The objectives of this project are covered in Professor Geddes' paper in this volume.

[3] The text of the recommendations with regard to the Tribal Research Centre was as follows:

In order to facilitate effective work in connection with the tribal minorities in this country, anthropological research and a variety of socio-economic studies should serve the practical purpose of preparing a basis for formulating realistic plans directed toward the improvement of social and economic conditions. Apart from this they should contribute to our

These were the three major projects of the action program recommended in 1962. It is most gratifying to report that their implementation was prepared and started in 1963 and 1964.

Administrative Measures. Another section of recommendations dealt with administrative measures. These are listed under their major headings in order to give an idea of the issues which were dealt with.

It was recommended that:

1. Action regarding the hill tribes should be given priority consideration, and an appropriate administrative machinery should be established to this end.

2. Consideration should be given to means which would increase the effectiveness of communications between the Central Tribal Welfare Committee and the administrative authorities of the provincial and district levels.

Action on these two issues has not been completely satisfactory. The administrative machinery has been created by establishing a Hill Tribe Division in the Public Welfare Department. But this Division ranks too low in the bureaucratic hierarchy, and the higher echelons of the Public Welfare Department are too occupied with other responsibilities to produce effective results. Operational communication between those persons in the field and those in positions of higher authority in the government is lacking. The Central Tribal Welfare Committee has set up

---

knowledge of the tribes and peoples concerned, their culture, their ways of life, and their history. The one cannot easily be separated from the other.

We recommend that a Tribal Research Centre be set up in Northern Thailand, preferably in the town of Chieng Mai on account of its central location. It could, perhaps, be associated with the University of Chieng Mai, which is about to be inaugurated, but should cooperate also with other national universities as well as with the Siam Society in Bangkok.

The Tribal Research Centre should serve as:

(a) a center for studies in applied anthropology;
(b) a documentation center for anthropological (and other socio-economic) studies carried out in the region,
(c) a briefing and training center for tribal officers, extension workers, administrators, educators, specialists in agriculture, live-stock, transport and marketing, being concerned with development activities among hill tribes;
(d) a bureau providing advisory services to the government of the problems of the hill tribes.

It is plausible to conceive that this Centre might well be utilized for coordinating regional efforts in regard to the hill tribes. (Thailand 1962)

six subordinate subcommittees, but it is felt that this committee organization is not too effective. The feeling is growing that the status of the Hill Tribe Division should be raised to that of a separate Department of Hill Tribe Affairs.

3. Consideration should be given to methods of bringing hill people into participation in the Thai local and central government.

So far, this very important issue of organizing effective local government in hill tribe areas has been entirely neglected.

4. Establishment of "tribal officers" attached to district officers of provincial governors.

It was recommended that a special administrative post of "tribal officer" should be established in areas with large tribal minority populations. This position should be held by a fully authorized government official, who at first might be a Thai, but in future might be recruited from the tribal minority concerned. He might be attached to the district officer (*nai amphur*) and act as a liaison at the administrative level. Nothing has been done in this regard.

5. Creation of a cadre of workers in a wide variety of technical fields including community development, who will be dedicated to the hill people and will live and work with them.

6. Training programs for these workers.

7. Provision of incentives for young Thai officials to work among hill tribes.

The Thai authorities gave great attention to these recommendations, since they have a direct bearing on the implementation of two of the major projects mentioned above, the settlement projects and the mobile development project. However, the quality of the training programs and the provision of incentives are still unsatisfactory.

Policy Measures. A final section of the recommendations dealt with policy measures. The Thai government has assumed responsibility for the administration, welfare, and development of the hill people. Consequently, it seemed appropriate to clarify certain basic issues in order to fulfill these aims, and it appeared important that rapid action be taken in view of the growing uncertainties in the hill region.

[539]

The section on policy included considerations such as the following:

1. The government's relations to the hill tribes should be clarified.

It was mentioned that the competent government authorities should decide the legal position of persons in tribal communities, including questions of citizenship, registration, taxation, conscription, compulsory school education, the right to hold official positions, etc. It was suggested that the competent government authorities should give due consideration to the need for special laws which allow for the special cultural and linguistic characteristics of these ethnic minorities. For example, the question of bilingual school education, school curricula, marriage and inheritance laws, village administration systems, etc. should be considered. Finally, it was mentioned that the government should consider ways and means of creating loyalty to the Thai nation, so as to facilitate the integration of these ethnic minorities into the social, economic, and political life of the country.

2. The question of legal land ownership in the hills should be examined.

The existing Land Code of Thailand does not allow private ownership of the highlands. If this code is taken literally, the hill people may be declared outlaws at any moment. In view of the serious problems which could result from such a measure, ways and means should be developed to provide legal security for the people in the hills. The question of land ownership for hill farmers will become imminent when the semi-nomadic shifting cultivators adopt stabilized farming. Any discrimination against the hill dwellers in favor of the lowland dwellers should be avoided. Therefore, the competent government authorities should either decide upon a modification of existing land codes, or should seek an alternative solution favorable to the hill populations. The authorities should study the possibilities in this regard, keeping in mind the following factors: (a) the production unit of all the hill tribes concerned is the family, either in its nuclear or extended form; (b) tribal people have a concept of private property and real property, and there is a preemptive privilege of the family unit, recognized by all others, to return to its old clearings as long as the village remains in the same vicinity;

and (c) tribal people do not like forced relocation to areas where there is a risk that they will become merely hired labor, without land of their own to live on and cultivate.[4] In its relations with the hill peoples, the government should accept their existing social structure, without attempting to bring about immediate changes which would unnecessarily disturb their social equilibrium. If it should appear that the formation of new types of associations or corporations would be desirable, their implementation should be discussed with the formal and informal leaders of the tribes, and their advice should be given serious consideration.

3. The question of using some of the hill forest areas for agriculture should be examined.

The present forest reservation policies declare that the practice of slash-and-burn agriculture in the hills is unlawful. Two considerations were brought to the attention of the government in this context: (a) The settlement of semi-nomadic populations can only be achieved gradually. A long-term project requires a continuous, patient approach. In the initial stages, severe penalties for cutting trees in protected areas may not yield the desired result, because the hill men do not yet fully understand the nature of their offenses. We have already observed grave reactions in cases where tribesmen were arrested. In the long run it would be more profitable if a more lenient approach were used during the first phase of law enforcement. The relevant authorities should stress the positive aspects of teaching the hill people how to stabilize their agriculture, rather than using a punitive approach. (b) The stabilization of hill tribes will have to be done in various parts of the hill areas. It is impossible to group them all together in two or three or even five settlement project areas. Though some regrouping may be considered, most of the hill people may remain in the area and the villages they now occupy. This means that several parts of the highlands now reserved for forest might have to be legally allotted for cultivation. The alleged negative results of deforestation caused by hill agriculture seem to have been greatly exaggerated. The com-

---

[4] See papers by Kandre and Kunstadter in this volume for an indication of some of the variability among some of these tribes in concepts of property, land allocation, and production units. (Ed.)

petent government departments should cooperate in reaching the decisions on this subject.

4. The policy toward opium-poppy cultivation should take into consideration the conditions prevailing in the hill and frontier regions.

In addition to their presently illegal use of reserved forest lands, the hill peoples may be declared outlaws at any time because of their age-old economic tradition of poppy cultivation and sale of raw opium to traders. The tribesmen themselves cannot be blamed for this state of affairs. The policies of various governments toward opium production and consumption have frequently changed during the last century. Sudden enforcement of the prohibition on the main cash crop, opium, is liable to lead to more dangerous situations than exist at present. Therefore, the following suggestions were made: (a) At present there should be a sympathetic policy toward the hill people who produce opium. (b) Strong measures should be taken in the lowlands against the trade in opium and opiates. (c) Government authorities should put primary stress on the positive objectives of enabling hill people to develop a new cash economy, by rendering technical assistance through experienced hill agriculturalists. Only in this context should they be gradually encouraged to give up opium cultivation.

5. The final policy suggestion was that consideration be given to the use of hill tribesmen as members or associates of security forces or Border Patrol.

The hill tribesmen are the only ones who really know the hills and jungles. They know how to find their way and also to move and survive in this environment. They are far superior to anyone else in this environment. They also know what is going on in the hills. In fact, they have amazing communications among the various groups. It would therefore seem of great benefit to ensure their cooperation in matters concerning control and intelligence. Selected members of hill tribes may be used as local informants, local guides, and as associates attached to the Border Patrol Police. They should be specially briefed for these tasks. A program of this kind is already being carried out by the Border Patrol, and there is no reason why it should not be accelerated. But however it is done, it should be based on voluntary, not compulsory, conscription of hill tribesmen into the Thai military services in the near future. They do not seem prepared for this type of function for some time yet. Abrupt confrontation with a world different in society, technology, and climate would probably lead to a disruption of their social systems, values, and ethics, without allowing them to establish roots in their new environment. On their return to the tribal villages after the service, they would not have any prospects of becoming leaders, since the traditional social systems would not recognize their new knowledge as qualifying them for tribal leadership.[5]

This is the outline of recommendations submitted to the Thai government in 1962 on the basis of the survey findings. In the following year a number of these recommendations were implemented, primarily through the newly established Hill Tribe Division of the Public Welfare Department, Ministry of Interior.

THE IMPLEMENTATION OF ACTION PROGRAMS, 1963–1965, AND SOME REMARKS ON THEIR EVALUATION

There are three major projects in the action program, dealing with the expansion of the functions of the hill settlement stations, the development of mobile extension services, and the establishment of a Tribal Research Centre, respectively. Expenses for the implementation of these programs were met by the Thai government. Technical assistance was rendered by the Asia Foundation and by the Australian government. The Asia Foundation provided an anthropologist (the author of this paper) to serve as adviser to the Hill Tribe Division for two years (1963–1965) and granted financial aid for training government officials and conducting an experimental mobile extension scheme. The Australian government, through SEATO, provided an anthropologist (Professor Geddes) to serve as a special adviser to the Tribal Research Centre for one year (1964–1965) and presented fourteen jeeps to the hill tribes project of the Public Welfare Department. The following paragraphs discuss the progress made from 1963 to 1965.

[5] See papers by Huff and Moerman in this volume for suggested use of returning veterans in minority Thai villages, and papers by Kandre and Kunstadter for the functions in tribal villages of individuals who have had experience in the outside world. (Ed.)

1. Intensification and expansion of the activities of the settlement projects in the hills has included development of (a) agricultural experiment stations, (b) demonstration centers for hill farmers, (c) marketing and trading centers for cash crops, (d) training centers for development workers, and (e) hill bases for mobile demonstration and development work. No spectacular progress has been achieved in these regards in existing stations. Some modest experiments have been conducted at Tak (Doi Musser) and Chiengrai (Maechan) in the course of the last year. They have not served as demonstration centers because the experiments were limited in scope and success. The idea of establishing trading stores has been discussed at various levels, but none are operating so far. Due to the fact that the hill stations have not yet made the desired progress in these fields, they cannot yet serve as training centers for development workers. The station at Tak was used as a base for an experimental mobile scheme in 1963 and 1964. Its impact and success were rather limited due to lack of knowledge and trained personnel.

A formal request has been made to foreign aid agencies to obtain the services of three qualified men with experience in tropical hill agriculture, livestock-raising and pasture improvement, and plant ecology. These experts are supposed to assist and advise the research and experimentation on modernized hill agriculture. This would include the promotion of more rationalized systems of shifting cultivation, with short cropping periods and adequate fallow times, cover crops, and growth of shade trees in abandoned clearings, experimentation with suitable annual and perennial cash crops, continuation of work on the experimental cattle farm at Tak, and research on the reaction of natural vegetation to various kinds of agricultural activities.

In 1963 a soil specialist (provided by the Food and Agriculture Organization) and a plant ecologist (provided by the Colombo Plan) were brought up to the Tak hill tracts to study soil types and plant associations and to determine prospects for agricultural development. The preliminary report on their activities (Keen 1964; Moorman *et al.* 1964) is very valuable. In 1964 a New Zealand cattle specialist worked at the Tak hill station for five months. He established an experimental cattle farm in cooperation with the project officials. Pasture land was cleared, a wide variety of new grass species was introduced experimentally for improving grazing, and eleven cattle were brought to this livestock farm. The project seems quite promising, and hill tribesmen of surrounding villages take an interest in it. However, it is absolutely necessary to have continuous expert advice for it to become a success.

It is hoped that the experts mentioned above will give a new stimulus to the activities of the settlement projects, but one will have to wait for at least two to four years for the first valuable results to appear.

Besides the activities mentioned above, the hill stations are engaged in (f) establishing educational institutions such as primary schools, (g) rendering medical services, and (h) promoting good relations between government and the hill people. The Hill Tribe Division cooperates with the Ministry of Education to establish schools in relatively accessible tribal villages. The process is slow, due to lack of funds and to the difficulty of finding dedicated teachers willing to devote themselves to work in these remote areas. Moreover, curricula and teaching methods properly adjusted to the aspirations and expectations of the hill people are still lacking. As in other matters, basic research into these aspects of tribal life is required. It may be mentioned here that schools run by the Border Patrol Police have not been too successful either. This is probably not due to low intelligence of tribal children, for their alertness and intellectual ability have been noted by several previous observers who have studied them closely (Finlay 1962), but it may be attributed to a variety of other reasons. In many hill tribe villages growing interest in learning and writing is clearly evident. It appears that many tribesmen would prefer to have teachers from their own tribe, but there have been very few tribesmen in Thailand who would be qualified for a job as primary school teacher. Much attention is being given to these questions, but no satisfactory answer has been found so far.

Medical services are usually accepted gratefully by hill tribesmen, but, as in education and agriculture, their extension is hampered by the lack of trained, experienced, and dedicated personnel, as well as by the physical factors of inaccessibility of the widely dispersed villages.

As far as the relationship between the field officers of the Hill Tribe Division and the tribesmen is concerned, a sympathetic and friendly approach prevails in the entire project area. There has never been any forced labor, for example, in road construction or field-clearing. If the hill people work in groups near the hill stations, it is commonly done on a voluntary basis of mutual aid—they will receive another benefit in return for their assistance, either in cash or in kind.

2. The second major project is the mobile extension scheme. An experimental mobile development project was launched from Tak (Doi Musser) hill base in 1963 and 1964. Four teams, each composed of an agricultural extension worker, a health worker, and a social worker, were sent to remote villages of Meo and Karen tribesmen. Some of these villages were relatively well known from previous contact and study. Others had never before been visited by local government officials or even Border Patrols. Their relations with lowlanders had been confined to the bartering of opium during occasional contacts with traders, "Haw" merchants, and Thai peddlers.

The mobile extension work started with a reconnaissance survey of twenty-six Meo villages in the Tak and Mae Sod hill tracts and fourteen Karen villages in Amphur Mae Sod. On the basis of these surveys, strategically located villages were selected in which the four mobile teams settled down. Temporary huts were built with the assistance of the villagers. A more intensive survey was carried out in the key villages, and operations were sometimes extended to neighboring villages.

One of the valuable lessons learned was that much more preparation and training of field workers is required if the scheme is to become successful. More emphasis is now given to training in the relevant skills. It was also learned that it would be of great value to introduce some kind of government administration into these villages. For example, official recognition could be given to a headman who might be chosen by the tribesmen in accordance with their own traditions. Then communications could be established between the officially recognized village government and the authorities of the nearest Thai lowland administration. Throughout their history, up until today, these tribal communities have been largely self-governing and have received few, if any, services from the central government, so it is not surprising if they have no understanding of the purpose and intentions of the mobile extension workers who visit or settle down in their villages.

Of course, the introduction of an appropriate system of government administration, adequately adjusted for tribal culture and conditions would need active cooperation between the Hill Tribe Division and the Department of Administration, as well as the district and province authorities. Thus the political integration could be promoted through a moderate regional autonomy, by which tribal chieftains, village headmen, formal and informal leaders are recognized as officials of the villages and even of the *tambon* ("commune" or group of villages). This has already been done in a few areas, as in the case of the Yao of Phu Langa (Nan Province) and in some of the Karen districts of Maehongson Province.[6]

The idea of having mobile extension workers who go to the hill tribesmen, meeting them in their own setting and extending their useful skills in agriculture, health, education, marketing, etc., seems excellent to the tribesmen. However, several dangers are involved. If it is done with a lack of basic understanding and knowledge on the side of the mobile workers, it may result in a loss of confidence by the hill people.

First of all, these mobile workers need to have a proper attitude toward the tribesmen and appreciation for their mode of life. Second, they must be dedicated to their work, since their job is not easy. And last but not least, they have to be trained in such fields as community development among tribal minorities, and hill agriculture, as well as such subjects as anthropology and sociology, in order to develop an adequate understanding of how tribal societies operate.

As mentioned above, the hill stations and Tribal Research Centre could serve as training channels and permanent advisory institutions. However, it may require two to four years until they can really do so. In the meantime, training and advice is rendered, as the need occurs, by the staff of the Hill Tribe Division and by the two anthropologists attached to the hill tribe projects.

[6] This pattern is already well established in other areas as well. See, for example, Kandre's and Kunstadter's papers in this volume. (Ed.)

Some preliminary training courses have been held, and three manuals for field workers have been produced on initial development activities, reconnaissance survey, and village community survey (Thailand 1964 A, B, C). Finally, and equally important, the field staff is continuously learning by doing, following the trial and error approach.

In the official policy of the hill tribe project, more and more importance is attached to the use of mobile work, i.e., approaching the hill people in their own villages. The resettlement idea, on the other hand, is slowly fading, or at least has been postponed, because it was learned that the hill tribesmen were not inclined to be relocated and resettled in the prescribed project areas. These areas were not properly selected in all cases. We do not think it a wise policy to impose any force on the hill people, since this could well result in annoyance and even hostile feelings among the hill tribesmen and might finally lead to obstinate fights in the jungles.

Another basic problem is to provide incentives or inducements to the field staff, both mobile workers and hill station staff. It has been realized that not all of them are fully dedicated to the work to which they are assigned. They complain about the hard living conditions, low salary, isolation in remote areas, and small opportunity for promotion in a physical and cultural environment which is quite strange to them. Such complaints are quite understandable. Yet as a consequence, in many cases the workers do only just enough work as is absolutely necessary to avoid trouble with their superiors. Without personal motivation no progress can be achieved, as this is the kind of work which requires as much individual initiative and sincere dedication as skill and experience.

A remedy for this problem might be to recruit hill people into the hill tribe project field staff as soon as possible. However, in the beginning, a small cadre of Thai officers is needed. Moreover, there are administrative and bureaucratic difficulties in recruiting tribal people, since, according to present govenment regulations, certain qualifications and examinations are required in order to become a Thai official. At present discussions are being held on these problems.

Two further experimental mobile projects were carried out in 1965. In the first, eight student volunteers from Chulalongkorn

University were sent to some hill villages to make friends with tribesmen and to exchange opinions. These students were properly selected and thoroughly briefed. They stayed for one month and reported to the Hill Tribe Division on their return. This project seems to have succeeded because of the excellent qualifications of the persons concerned. In the second case, a selected group of Buddhist monks volunteered to contact tribal people in their mountain villages, perhaps for the first time in history. This experiment, which is now going on, is being closely observed. Both projects were sponsored with financial aid from the Asia Foundation.

3. The Tribal Research Centre is the third major project in the action program. The Centre was established during the fiscal year 1964–1965 through the Public Welfare Department and in association with the University of Chiengmai. Professor Geddes, the anthropological adviser attached to the Centre, has submitted several substantial recommendations for its future administrative setup, staffing, organization, and field research, and his paper on these subjects is included in this volume. Therefore, only the most essential facts will be discussed here in order to summarize the present state of the project.

Staff is being recruited and trained in the course of this year (1965). The current budget allows for one senior research officer, two junior research officers, one librarian, and maintenance personnel. A grant has been received from the British Embassy to purchase books for the library. This is in addition to the grant of the Australian government, previously referred to, which consisted of fourteen jeeps presented to the hill tribe project through SEATO. The Centre was inaugurated in June 1965 with a training course for government officials.

A number of research projects are envisaged for the coming years, including (a) comprehensive studies of selected tribes, giving primary importance to Meo, Yao, Lahu, Lisu, Akha, and Karen; (b) community studies; (c) studies on trade systems in the hills and market conditions in selected areas, specifically near the existing hill stations in Tak, Chiengdao, Maechan, Lom Sak, and Maesariang; (d) linguistic studies, particularly on Meo, Lahu, and Karen; (e) agricultural and animal husbandry studies, with attention to the social factors involved; (f) population studies, with emphasis on an accurate hill tribe census; (g) edu-

[549]

cational research, with an examination of such questions as adjustment of curricula to hill tribe societies, language instruction, use of audiovisual aids, etc.; (h) health studies; (i) study of the role of the Chinese "Haw" in relation to the hill tribes; (j) studies of administrative systems which would be acceptable to the tribal people and would facilitate their integration into the life of the Thai nation.

In addition to these activities, the Tribal Research Centre is being developed to serve as a documentation center, including a library, museum, and archives. It is also used as a briefing and training center for officers and workers among hill tribes, as well as for members of the hill tribe societies. Finally, it is to become a coordination center for foreign and domestic researchers who work on various aspects of hill tribe life.

The foundations are being laid so that the Tribal Research Centre will carry out as well as stimulate and coordinate research work in the hills of Northern Thailand, with a view to assisting the hill tribe projects.

It should be stressed here that applied research cannot be easily separated from pure scientific research. Something must be known before it can be applied. This means that thorough research on several aspects of tribal life is a prerequisite to successful action. Any attempt to launch large development projects without the necessary knowledge would be worse than useless. It is easy to cite numerous instances from various parts of the world in which well-intentioned measures were nullified by the lack of knowledge. It was not known in advance that these actions were incompatible with social institutions or deeply rooted sentiments of the people concerned. Such lack of knowledge has often led to real catastrophes, social or economic disintegration, and even loss of life. There have been examples in which ill-considered agricultural innovations, undertaken precipitately, have led to remarkable damage to soil and vegetation. As a result of such action, the population lost confidence, and further administrative action became more difficult.

It is to the credit of the authorities of the hill tribe project in Thailand that they have always been prepared to facilitate research in connection with the planning and implementation of the program, and they have contacted various foreign and domestic agencies to assist in the conduct of specific research programs. The establishment of the Tribal Research Centre in Chiengmai is an outstanding achievement in this regard.

Since this project is of worldwide interest, there is good hope of continuing support from international organizations and foundations concerned with the promotion of human welfare. It can be hoped that its organization will advance independent and concentrated scientific work and that it will facilitate cooperation among the relevant national and international research institutions.

BIBLIOGRAPHY

The following is a list of scientific articles, survey reports, and government papers which have a direct bearing on problems dealt with in this paper.

BENNINGTON-CORNELL ANTHROPOLOGICAL SURVEY
1964   A report of tribal peoples in Chiengrai Province north of the Mae Kok river. Bangkok, Siam Society, Data Paper 1.

BERNATZIK, HUGO ADOLF
1947   Akha und Meau: probleme der angewandten Völkerkunde in Hinterindien. Innsbruck, Wagnerische Universitäts Buchdruckerei. Two vols. Although this book is an account of field research done in 1936–1937, it is still the only anthropological monograph on hill tribes of Thailand. Several sections of the book deal with problems relevant to topics under discussion in the present volume.

CAMPBELL, P. D. J.
1963   Report on survey of tea-growing areas of Thailand. Colombo Plan.

FINLAY, DOUGLAS
1962   Report on visit to Chieng Dao to study child and family needs of hill tribes community. Bangkok.

HEINE-GELDERN, ROBERT
1962   A proposal for the establishment of a tribal research center in Thailand. Bulletin of the International Committee on Urgent Anthropological and Ethnological Research 5:21–22.

KEEN, F. G. B.
1964   Prospects for land development and settlement of hill tribes in the uplands of Tak Province. Bangkok, Ministry of Interior, Department of Public Welfare.

KUNSTADTER, PETER
1964   Research on the Luaʔ and Sʔkaw Karen hill people of Northern Thailand, with some practical implications. Bangkok, mimeographed.

MANNDORFF, HANS
1965A Socio-economic research in support of socio-economic development in the hill tribe project. Journal of the Public Welfare Department 5:30–36. Bangkok, Ministry of Interior.
1965B Some observations on the southward migration of hill tribes in Thailand. Mitteilungen der Anthropologischen Gesellschaft in Wien. (Published in German, with an English summary.)
MOERMAN, MICHAEL
1964 A diary of activities in Thailand. Bangkok. Contains a review of tribal programming under Para. IV.
MOORMAN, F. R., K. R. M. ANTHONY, and SAMARN PANICHAPONG
1964 Note on the soils and land use in the hills of Tak Province. Bangkok, Ministry of National Development, Land Development Department.
PATYA SAIHOO
1962A The hill tribes of Northern Thailand and the opium problem. United Nations Bulletin on Narcotics 15(2):35–45.
1962B Report on the hill tribes of Northern Thailand. Bangkok, mimeographed. Contains a bibliography and review of anthropological studies of hill tribes of Northern Thailand, including a number of recommendations on possible areas of research pertaining to the socio-economic development of hill peoples in the North.
THAILAND, DEPARTMENT OF PUBLIC WELFARE
1959 Land settlement project for hill tribe people in Thailand as of 1960 (B.E. 2503). Bangkok, Ministry of Interior, Department of Public Welfare.
1962 Report on the socio-economic survey of the hill tribes in Northern Thailand. Bangkok, Ministry of Interior, Department of Public Welfare.
1964A A manual for field workers among hill tribes: initial development activities. Bangkok, Ministry of Interior, Department of Public Welfare.
1964B A manual for field workers among hill tribes: reconnaissance survey. Bangkok, Ministry of Interior, Department of Public Welfare.
1964C A manual for field workers among hill tribes: village community survey. Bangkok, Ministry of Interior, Department of Public Welfare.
UNITED NATIONS ECONOMIC COMMISSION FOR ASIA AND THE FAR EAST (ECAFE), DIVISION OF SOCIAL AFFAIRS
1961 Report of a field trip undertaken in connection with the project on a socio-economic survey of the hill tribes of Northern Thailand.
YOUNG, GORDON
1962 The hill tribes of Northern Thailand: a socio-ethnological report. Bangkok, Siam Society, 2d edn.

CHAPTER 15

The Tribal Research Centre, Thailand: An Account of Plans and Activities

WILLIAM R. GEDDES

INTRODUCTION

This paper deals with the subject of the Tribal Research Centre which the Thailand government established in 1964. The creation of the Centre was recommended in the report, prepared by Dr. Hans Manndorff, of the socio-economic survey of the hill tribes in Northern Thailand carried out by the officers of the Department of Public Welfare in 1961–1962 (Thailand 1962). On April 21, 1964, the Cabinet of the Government of Thailand decided that the Department of Public Welfare, working in co-operation with the University of Chiengmai, should establish a "Tribal Research Centre" with the following activities (Thailand 1964):

(1) To conduct research projects in the fields of education, health, economics, sociology and anthropology of the hill tribes in northern Thailand. The outcome of such projects will be used as as basis to reformulate a better plan for hill tribe work.

(2) To procure books, films, journals, etc. in the fields of social science and other studies relating to the hill tribes. These books will be for library which will be part of the Centre.

(3) To procure artifacts of the tribes and films of them to be kept in the museum which is also to be part of the Centre.

(4) To evaluate continuously the hill tribe projects conducted by both the Government and private organizations.

(5) To participate in the training of officials who will be working with the hill tribes.

(6) To give advisory services and cooperation to institutions, both domestic and foreign, interested in conducting studies among the hill tribes.

Prior to this final Cabinet decision the government had approached the Southeast Asia Treaty Organization (SEATO) with a request for assistance in planning and equipping the Centre. The Australian government undertook to supply transport and the services of an anthropological adviser in the initial year, a position which I assumed in July 1964. Later the British government undertook to provide books for the library up to a value of £600 sterling, and in July 1965, the U.S. government announced a gift through SEATO of $12,000 worth of photographic and recording equipment.

In translating the Cabinet decision into action, a number of problems have been encountered. These are the normal birthpangs of a new institution. Some of the problems are financial and organizational, such as the small size of the present budget and the comparatively low status of the Centre in the institutional structure of the Thailand civil service. These problems I shall discuss toward the end of this paper. An immediate problem was to formulate a research program. Although by no means unconscious of the academic value of research on the hill tribes, the government was most interested in its practical use in the service of policy.

Therefore, in formulating the plan, one had first to understand the policy towards the hill tribes. In fact, in the opinion situation of 1964 one could do something more than merely seek to understand. Serious thought on the nature of an active policy towards the hill tribes was fairly new, and although there was general agreement on the basic lines of policy among the persons most intimately connected with the hill tribe program, many other persons were uncertain as to what the policy was or what it should be. Thus here was opportunity for one to use one's judgment of the already known facts and comparative knowledge of similar situations elsewhere in the world in support of the agreed policy, and so help to promote a greater, and hence more effective, consensus.

It is agreed that the tribes can no longer be left isolated from the Thai people. There has to be a greater relationship. Should this take the form of complete absorption of the tribes into the general Thai community—that is to say "assimilation"—or should it take the form now generally known in English as "integration," in which the tribes would remain more or less separate social entities with cultural distinctiveness, but participate in the overall economic and political structure of Thailand? Decision on this question will affect the nature of the development program.

If the policy were to be assimilationist, then effort would be directed toward educating the people in Thai language and culture and encouraging the interchange of persons between Thai and tribal areas. There would be less need for the study of tribal languages and cultures. If, on the other hand, the policy were to be the milder one of integration, then the aims would be to promote economic, social, and political development through existing tribal institutions.

It is unrealistic to view the two policies of assimilation and integration as extreme alternatives. Complete assimilation of the tribes within the foreseeable future is not a possibility. Especially in some of the tribes the sense of tribal integrity is very strong.

The Meo, for instance, almost never intermarry even with other tribes whose territories intersect their own. Attachments to languages, customs, religions, and family and group systems cannot be broken on a mass scale within the space of one or two generations, except perhaps by the use of force, which is interdicted in a free country.

Attempts to hasten assimilation usually produce social disruption and eventually hostile reaction. The resources of personnel and wealth which would be required for economic assimilation of the tribes are beyond the means of the Thai government.

Finally, there is the specifically national reason for keeping the tribes in the hills. If they move away from the hills other groups will manage to come in, thus creating a never ending task of assimilation and pressure on the lowlands which will be needed for the constantly increasing Thai population. As long as the tribes do remain in the hills, however, their relatively isolated existence will tend to uphold their distinctive social structures and cultures.

But just as complete assimilation is not a practical possibility in the foreseeable future, neither is a form of integration which would not result in some loss of tribal culture or some loss of the identity of tribal people with their original groups.

A degree of assimilation is an inevitable consequence of an integration policy. The people will learn economic techniques

[555]

common to the Thai but foreign to their traditional ways. They will go more to the market place, and some of them will probably stay there.

Although the integration policy would foster respect for tribal languages, political and economic integration and educational development will demand increased knowledge of Thai language, and some persons, having acquired the necessary language ability, will find greater opportunities of advancement by identifying themselves more or less completely with the Thai. Pressure on the land may in time expel some tribesmen from the hills.

The most realistic policy, therefore, appears to be one of open-ended integration. It would not be anti-assimilationist. It could recognize the right of tribesmen to assimilate the Thai culture and blend with Thai society if they wished and would also recognize the pressures which would induce many of them to do so.

It would facilitate the process for them, but the policy's primary aim would not be assimilation. It would be to promote the welfare of the tribal peoples and the development of their economics within their present hill environments.

It would not seek to break up their social institutions but would instead seek to make them more effective. It would respect tribal religions, so long as the people wished to hold them, and utilize tribal languages.

It would allow the tribal people maximum control over their local government, although it would require loyalty to the crown and subservience to the central political institutions of the country. This is the policy upon which a consensus appears to have been reached. It, or a policy very like it, guides the programs of hill tribe development which are currently being pursued. It also guides the practical research program of the Tribal Research Centre.

Let me now speak of the program in some detail. It is not yet approved by the Thailand government. But I have submitted it to the government and it is currently under consideration.

SOCIO-ECONOMIC STUDIES

Basic studies are required of the six main tribal groups—Meo, Yao, Karen, Lahu, Akha, and Lisu. The studies should be of two types: socio-economic community studies and studies of languages. The first requirement, then, is for six social anthropologists and six linguists to make the studies. If funds or available personnel are limited, I should give priority to the socio-economic studies. We need them for basic knowledge of tribal cultures and for the interpretation of later research findings. Therefore, I shall speak of these studies first.

Ideally, the persons to carry out the studies should be Thai. This is because there is a need to build up a corps of Thai experts on the tribes who will remain in the country, constantly increasing the information on the tribes and keeping it up to date, and who will act as advisers on development projects.

But there are very few Thai at present qualified in social anthropology, and none who seem likely to be able to serve the Centre permanently. Therefore, I have suggested the appointment of six junior research officers who would, until such time as graduates in anthropology became available, be recent university graduates in any subject. Each one of them should be assigned to specialize on a particular tribe. Each should learn to speak the language of the tribe on which he is specializing and should be responsible for keeping an up-to-date record of all available facts on the tribe. In selecting the junior research officers, an attempt should be made to get a group with diverse initial training—some in economics, some in politics, some in agriculture, for example—and they should be encouraged to develop their special interests along with their general anthropological interests in the tribes of their choice in order to increase their value in joint discussions on problems affecting any or all of the hill tribes. As early as possible in their careers the junior research officers should be given a chance to study for a period in a university anthropology department in Thailand or overseas.

The junior research officers will not be capable of carrying out the basic socio-economic studies on their own. Therefore, it will be necessary to have outside experts conduct the studies. The junior research officers should then be assigned to the experts as assistants in order that they be trained to carry out later research projects on their own.

For the outside experts to be engaged, financial grants will be necessary. Funds are being sought for this purpose, and I hope a sufficient amount to finance the socio-economic studies will become available in the near future.

The socio-economic studies should be planned to occupy two years. A period of at least six months will be required to allow the anthropologist to gain a general familiarity with the tribal area and the people and to acquire a working knowledge of the language. Thereafter there should be detailed observation and collection of quantitative data on a whole year's cycle of social and economic activities. If there is any time left after the observational year is completed, it can be occupied by checking data, by brief comparative studies in neighboring communities, or by a preliminary write-up of field results.

To some persons the period of two years may seem too long. But the whole *raison d'être* of the Research Centre is to supply information in depth as distinct from the more superficial type of information which is all that can be hoped for from quick surveys. The tribal cultures are unfamiliar. It is a difficult task to gain true rapport with the people and a greater task still to appreciate all their cultural differences.

The research work of the Centre has a practical intent. There is, of course, great scope in the hill tribe areas for research work of a more purely academic kind. I hope that the Thailand government, in the interests of international scholarship, will always remain friendly to such work and the Centre will give it every facility in its power. Indirectly, it will profit by the improvements to anthropological theory which the work should provide. But the projects which the Centre itself adopts as parts of its own program must be so governed as to yield the type of knowledge it wants and to ensure that the results of the studies become known within a reasonable length of time. Therefore, it is proposed that the following conditions be attached to grants made to foreign experts for the purposes of the socio-economic studies:

(1) The project must be subject to the general supervision of the Director of the Tribal Research Centre.

(2) The anthropologist should have one of the junior research workers of the Centre attached to him—that is, the research worker who is to become the permanent specialist on that tribe. The anthropologist should allow this research worker to participate in the research activities, acquaint him with the facts dis-

covered in the research work, and give him training in research techniques.

(3) The research plan should embrace a complete socio-economic study of a single community, analyzing its demography, ecology, kinship system, general social structure, politics, religion, and subsistence and trading economy.

(4) Within six months of the completed field research a full report should be given to the Centre with the right to publish it (although special circumstances—such as university requirements for advanced degree theses—may be taken into consideration in deciding the date of publication). The final payment under the contract should be deferred until the report is received.

Direct financial aid, as distinct from help with transport, accommodation, and other facilities which the Centre may be able to render, should be confined, in the initial stage of the Centre's activities, to research workers who are willing to accept the conditions given above.

I do not myself feel that these conditions would infringe the independence of the anthropologist or impede his work. But in the United States some of the anthropologists with whom I have discussed the proposal—although by no means all of them—expressed concern at the conditions. Therefore, it is desirable to explain them in more detail and to state the reasons for them.

Let it be understood, first of all, that the conditions apply only to projects which are part of the Centre's research scheme. The Centre does not wish to monopolize all scientific work in the hills, and scholars whose projects are not part of the Centre's scheme will be free to make any arrangements they can, or their consciences will allow, with their own sponsoring agencies and with other sections of the Thailand government.

In the case of its own sponsored projects the Centre commits its resources to them. It also obtains the cooperation of other government agencies, particularly the provincial and district administrations and the police, to protect the research workers and facilitate their work. In return for this government effort it is fair that the research workers should supply the information resulting from their studies and assist the development of further research work. At least it seems to me so. The second requirement—the assistance with further development—may be debatable, and I shall discuss it in a moment. But there can scarcely be any debate about the fairness of supplying a full report on the research work. There is no restriction on freedom of speech in this. The anthropologist is being invited to widen his audience. He is not being asked to give the information confidentially. He can also publish it wherever else he likes.

Although this development may be regrettable, the tribal region of Thailand has become of great strategic importance. An anthropologist can, in fact, no longer work there without government support. The supplying of a report is the minimum condition under which free anthropological research is likely to be permitted to continue in the area. Severer conditions imposed by the National Research Council of Thailand already exist on paper governing all foreign research in the country, but I hope that the Tribal Research Centre will be permitted to operate on the lines outlined above.

Undoubtedly a main reason for the decision of the Thai authorities to request reports from foreign scholars was that certain foreign government agencies were sending into the field persons who reported directly to them and whose reports could, at the wish of the agencies, be kept confidential. It does not seem to me to be excessively nationalistic of the Thai government to wish to have the same information as was sent abroad. It does not ask that the scholars give their results to it alone. It does not wish to dictate the way in which the studies are carried out, although it provides facilities for them. It is a curious fact that some of the scholars who have criticized the conditions set out above have themselves accepted far more restrictive conditions imposed by their own fund-supplying agencies. In such cases it is the foreign scholars and not the Thai who are being the more nationalistic.

The above discussion has been concerned primarily with the fourth, general condition—the supplying of a terminal report on the research. I should like now to speak briefly of the other conditions. The first and third conditions are necessary parts of the Centre's specific scheme for a systematic coordinated study of tribal socio-economic structures. Scholars who do not wish to take part in this scheme can pursue their own independent lines. But those who do elect to participate in it can justifiably be asked to adopt a study plan which will allow their work to fit into the total scheme. The Director's "supervision" would in fact be of a very general nature. He would not attempt to impose particular research procedures, but he should be consulted as to field locations and be able to suggest modes of coordination between the various research workers.

The second condition—that of accepting a junior research worker of the Centre as an associate—requires more explanation. As mentioned earlier, the Centre, for the continuance of its work after the initial studies are completed, needs the services of Thai workers who will remain in its service. Help with the training of these officers is a return which the foreign scholars could give for the help which they themselves receive. Advantage to the anthropologist and not disadvantage should be the result of the arrangement. The junior workers will probably prove highly valuable assistants. They will all be university graduates selected for their intelligence and keenness to work in the tribal areas. Naturally they will be fluent in Thai. They will wish to perform well because it is upon the quality of their performance that their future opportunities will depend. These opportunities will include, it is hoped, a period at a university in Thailand or overseas to enable them to gain higher qualifications in anthropology. Difficulties of cooperation with the junior research workers, therefore, need not be expected. But should they arise, there are several ways in which they could be overcome. The junior research worker, who would be under the field direction of the anthropologist, could be given supplementary tasks which would not involve a close daily association between him and the anthropologist. In extreme cases when cooperation became impossible, the Director of the Centre could be asked to withdraw the junior research worker.

Finally, it might be said that neither the Director of the Centre nor the foreign anthropologists are expected to be imbeciles. The imagined problems discussed above will probably have little reality. The scheme and its associated conditions are similar in many ways to the Colonial Development and Welfare Fund scheme under which a good deal of the best recent British social anthropology has been carried out. It was on the British scheme that the proposal was modeled, although with some necessary adaptation to the Thai political reality. It may be even more productive because it offers a unique opportunity for a number of anthropologists in neighboring field areas to work coincidentally and in a coordinated manner.

LANGUAGE STUDIES

There are a number of linguists from overseas already at work on hill tribe languages. Others have displayed an interest in coming and may get support from sources other than the Centre. It may, therefore, be possible to get the basic language studies done without the need to make maintenance grants to the field workers. The Centre should, however, provide subsidies for the publication of dictionaries and grammars. If enough finance can be found, the Centre should also offer grants along the same lines as those proposed for the socio-economic studies in order to get a complete coverage of tribal languages as soon as possible.

Ideally, the Centre should have on its staff a trained linguist to supervise language research and publication. He or she should, if possible, be Thai. If no suitably trained person can be found in Thailand, encouragement should be given to an interested graduate to get his or her linguistic training in an overseas university with a view to an appointment as a linguistics research officer of the Centre.

OTHER RESEARCH PROJECTS

The socio-economic studies are basic because they will provide fundamental information useful to practically all other studies in the tribal field. But there are a number of other urgent studies required to supplement them, or to provide information on specific issues. The most important of these studies seem to me to be as follows:

1. An Agricultural Study of Shifting Cultivation.
   a. A detailed study of the effects of shifting cultivation on soil
      fertility is required. The complete study should cover:
   (1) A full description of the present methods of shifting cultivation practiced by the six main tribes in respect to paddy, corn, opium, and any other crops of significance.
   (2) A study of a selected area of land within which shifting cultivation is being practiced, this study to comprise accurate

land-use maps, the determination of vegetation and soil characteristics at the outset of the study, and a recording of the changes
in these characteristics as the cultivation proceeds.

(3) Experimentation in an area (perhaps adjoining that in
"2" above) with different methods of land use under shifting
cultivation, such as, for example, fallow periods of different
length, leaving forest strips between fields, or deliberate planting
of trees, such as casuarinas, during fallow periods.

Let me speak briefly of the importance of this study in general
and of each of its parts in particular. All the groups living in
the hill areas of North Thailand practice shifting cultivation, even
those who, like the Karen and Lua?, also have some terraced,
irrigated fields or, like the Yunnanese near Fang, who have large
permanent foothill vegetable gardens. Shifting cultivation is the
only method for most tribes. It is also practiced by millions of people elsewhere in the world and is the predominant method over all
of upland Southeast Asia. It is unlikely, therefore, that the
method will be abandoned in the foreseeable future, although
some modifications may be introduced. Sections of the present
population of shifting cultivators in Thailand may be resettled
in the lowlands, or the area of permanent cultivation may be
extended into the hills by further terracing or by the spread
of tree crops. But under present conditions it is likely that if
sections of the present hill population do leave the hills, their
place will be taken by new immigrants from Burma and Laos.
The land formation and drainage pattern will make an extensive
spread of terracing difficult. The introduction of tree crops will
depend upon the development of a market for them and a marketing organization, and upon the training of the hill tribesmen
in methods of tree-crop cultivation. Probably also the extent to
which such crops can be introduced will be limited by the demographic situation, that is to say, by the amount of labor which
can be absorbed by them. Some tree crops require a larger area
of land than is available to certain groups. Others, such as tea,
have only a limited market. As pointed out by Dr. Campbell
in his report, tea production according to the present rates of
consumption in Thailand could at the most absorb the labor of
six thousand hill tribesmen (Campbell 1963).

It seems quite clear, therefore, that shifting cultivation is going

[563]

to remain the major method of agriculture in Thailand's hills for a very long time to come. Acceptance of this fact by the planners of hill tribe development schemes and by agriculturists concerned with the hill tribes is highly important. Far too often is the view taken that shifting cultivation is bad, that it must be abandoned, and that therefore it is not a fit subject for agricultural study. There is error on all these points. Properly practiced, shifting cultivation is not bad and, in fact, is probably the only method by which many of the hills can be farmed at all. The only alternative to it is to abandon the hills to forest or allow their exploitation only for lumbering, which, as practiced sometimes, does as much permanent damage to the forest cover as does shifting cultivation. Nor, for the reasons already stated, will shifting cultivation be abandoned. Finally, it is a fit subject for study because it is the most important part of the hill tribe economic reality.

The opprobrium with which agricultural scientists have so often viewed shifting cultivation has been a serious handicap to economic improvement in all the hills of Southeast Asia. Professor Harold Conklin, in a work published first in *Current Anthropology* and later as a monograph issued by the Organization of American States (Conklin 1963), has reviewed all the literature to date in the world on shifting cultivation. The number of adequate studies is very small, and nearly all of the studies are purely descriptive. There are none involving controlled experimentation. Thailand, through the Tribal Research Centre and the Hill Tribe Division, has a chance to redress this situation, thereby making an important contribution to knowledge valuable to all Southeast Asia.

Let me consider now the three parts of the proposed study in more detail. The first part is to be a description of the existing methods of shifting cultivation practiced by the various hill tribes. Such a description is a normal part of an anthropological socio-economic survey, and therefore the data would be supplied by the anthropologists working on the community studies proposed earlier. But they should be especially requested to collect the information in detail, briefed as to what to look for, and asked to report their findings in all the relevant social context.

The hill tribes apparently practice different methods of shifting cultivation. The Karen in the Maesariang District, for instance, appear to rotate their fields according to a system which places a field in fallow after only one year's cropping for paddy. Probably because of this system, their residence pattern is stable, some villages having been on their present sites at least during the lifetime of the oldest inhabitants. For a system of this kind to work, there is an upper limit to the population size relative to the land area available. In other words, the populations remain sufficiently small to allow the fallowing fields to stay out of use long enough for new forest growth to regenerate them completely. It is important to determine what the upper limit of population is. It will vary, of course, according to the soil characteristics of an area. Therefore, the anthropologist who makes the study of the Karen should report not only on the modes of land use, but also on the sizes of populations using defined areas. He should pay attention to divisions of land ownership within the community because population pressure on the land may vary throughout the community territory and a study of the variations and their effects may help to indicate what the upper limit of desirable population is.

The Meo, on the other hand, do not practice a rotation system of the kind described above. They normally divide the land into paddy land and corn-poppy land. To some degree they seek different types of soil for the two purposes, because the soil type which favors paddy is not the most favorable for poppies. The extent to which they can find the two types of soil in the same general locality is limited, especially as each household wants its paddy and its poppy cultivations to be fairly close together in order to save the labor of building two farmhouses. Therefore, in practice, a community has to choose to some extent which crop to favor in its selection of land, the favoritism at present generally being given to poppies. Sometimes a community has no scope for choice. It must take the land which happens to be available.

Even so, there are limiting factors affecting the sites of Meo cultivation, the strongest influence being the predilection for growing poppies. It is extremely rare to find Meo communities living at a height of less than 3,000 feet. In the Thailand environ-

ment the greater the height the better the poppies grow, and
this is at least the rationalization the Meo give for living so
high. There may be other factors, of course, accounting for the
height. It is the tradition of the Meo to live high. They are
adapted to the climate at this level. Also the factor favoring
the growth of poppies may not be simply the height but the
drainage pattern of the soil and its chemical characteristics due
to this or other causes. The Meo do not appear merely to seek
height. They seek the sources of streams and then settle near
these sources. All the factors which possibly determine settlement
require study to determine their role.

The Meo farming patterns on land chosen for paddy and on
that chosen for poppies are different, but in neither case do they
resemble the Karen pattern of regular fallow after a short period
of use. Paddy land is never used for poppies (although the reverse is occasionally true) because poppies will not grow well
after paddy. A paddy field is normally used for two years in
succession. It would be used in subsequent years, too, if it would
yield enough crop, but it cannot do so, and therefore the paddy
fields are abandoned after two years. Poppy fields have in each
year a succession of two crops—corn and poppies. In the case
of new fields the corn is planted after the fields are cleared by
burning in late April or early May. In July, before the corn is
harvested, the poppies are planted between the corn so that the
corn leaves will shelter the young plants from the heavy rain.
(This is the common practice. Sometimes the poppies are planted
in fields which do not have corn, but this is considered a risky
procedure.) When the corn is harvested, attention is devoted
to the poppies until the harvesting of the opium in January.
Thereafter corn and poppies are grown on the field for up to
five years in succession, until the productivity of the field has
become so low that further cultivation is not worthwhile.

A village area farmed under this pattern soon becomes
exhausted. Although the Meo often claim that poppy land
farmed for several years will regrow scrub and trees and thus
be refertilized, the condition of areas they have once used and
their own frequent migrations suggest that this is not so, or at
least that the period required for jungle regeneration is extremely
long. The paddy land, being farmed for only two years, may

be refertilized faster, but this is the smaller proportion of the land being brought under cultivation, so that even if it does regenerate, the area so made fit for farming again is often too small to support the population any longer.

Therefore, a frequent pattern appears to be as follows. The Meo move into a new area. They break in land for paddy and poppies, feeding their animals on the corn raised in the poppy fields. They extend the areas used for paddy in the following years and farm their initial poppy fields for five years. After five years there is usually enough land left for another set of poppy fields to be made. Therefore, they can remain in the area for a further five years, making ten years in all. (Five years appears to be the maximum period to use for a poppy field under optimum conditions. If soil conditions are not perfect, the period may be four years or less. Thus the total period of residence possible in an area shows variation.) Frequently, after ten years there is no more suitable land left, and the group must migrate. In many parts of Thailand ten years is the average period of settlement of Meo communities, although the common range is from six to fifteen years.

When the Meo do move, they often move in leaps. This means that they do not go to an area adjacent to the old one, but move to an area perhaps twenty or even over a hundred kilometers away, sometimes even much further. Great significance lies in the last two facts which have been given—that the migrations come every ten years or so and that the move is often to a completely new area. These facts suggest that the Meo pattern of farming is dictated not simply by tradition, lack of knowledge of the exhausting effects on the soil of repeated cropping, and by the ease of not having to clear jungle every year, but also by necessity. The land available to them in any one place may not be sufficient for them to farm according to the rotation system practiced by the Karen even if they knew it and wished to follow it. If the land were enough, their period of residence under their present system would not have to be as short as ten years. If there were sufficient land nearby, they would not have to migrate by leaps but could move to areas adjoining their old farms.

An important fact appears to be that the Meo are latecomers

to Thailand. In some areas, at least, they were probably the last of all the tribes to come, some of their major migrations being as recent as sixty to eighty years ago. They often have had to fit themselves into areas already occupied by other tribes. Thus they frequently populate small enclaves of uncut forest between the territories of, for example, Lahu or Karen groups; or they may not be able to find any areas of virgin jungle but be forced to make do with an area previously used by another tribe but abandoned for many years. Areas which have been abandoned in this way are usually the marginal regions of other tribes' territories of use. The conditions which make them marginal are that the land is at high altitudes and often steeply sloped. Therefore, the necessity to locate themselves on areas of land unused by other tribes or on the marginal areas of other tribes' land reinforces the Meo custom of living high up.

It may be that in other provinces the Meo do have larger areas of virgin land available to them and that the situation suggested here, which is derived from study in Chiengmai Province, does not apply (Anthony and Moorman 1964). But this does not mean that the description of the situation is without importance. If it is atypical now, it is likely to become typical in future years because the Meo must soon begin to run out of hills in Thailand. Their southern migration from Yunnan has now extended well into Tak Province. The remaining hill areas to the south are quite densely occupied by Karen. So where can the Meo go next?

It shoud be noted in passing that the fact that the Meo must often take second place in the competition for land does not mean that they are inferior to other tribes in wealth, status, or self-estimation. Due to their superior skill in poppy cultivation, they are often richer than neighboring tribes; they employ Lahu and Karen in a system which could perhaps be termed "opium slavery"; they are jealous of their independence (although cooperative with government officials) and are proud of their culture, this pride being indicated not only by their words but by the fact that, unlike most of the other tribes, they rarely, if ever, intermarry with other tribes.

The above considerations make it clear that an understanding of the Meo system of shifting cultivation requires full study, not only of their types of crops and conditions under which they grow best, but also of the extent of land areas available to them and the population sizes of their groups.

As with the anthropologist studying the Karen, so too the person studying the Meo must watch for all the relevant facts. One task of the Research Centre will be to prepare a survey guide for him and to ensure that it is revised and refined through periodic joint meetings, arranged by the Centre, of all anthropologists working on the community studies. At these meetings, the anthropologists will give one another the benefit of their experiences, their insights, and their criticisms of one another's procedures.

A feature of the shifting cultivation practiced by many of the tribes in Thailand is the clearing by numbers of households of very large blocks of land without leaving any strips of jungle between the household clearings. This probably has an adverse effect on forest regeneration because it leaves no seed reservoirs, and it may also increase erosion. How extensive is this block-clearing? What are the inducements to it? The inducements may be social, in that the people prefer to work together or exchange labor; they may be religious, in that the people fear spirits in isolated areas; they may be political, in that village leaders select the main planting areas each year and the rest of the people abide by their decisions; or they may be purely economic, in that land is in too short supply to allow the leaving of uncultivated strips, or that better tracks can be made to a combined planting area and thus the total amount of labor need for crop production is reduced. Or is it that none of the above factors are compulsive, but simply that the block clearance system, admittedly more sociable and generally more convenient, is practiced because the people are ignorant of its deleterious effects on soil fertility? If the last explanation is true, then great improvement might be effected by simple education in strip farming and in the advantages of it. The answer to the situation cannot be found, however, until full investigations are carried out in each tribal area. The situation may vary in different tribes.

As the discussion has been long, let me summarize its main theme. We are discussing the proposal for a detailed study of the effects of shifting cultivation on soil fertility, the aim being twofold: firstly, to determine how urgent is the need for alternatives to the system and secondly, to discover how the system itself may be improved. We said that the first part of such a study should be a full description of the existing methods of shifting cultivation as practiced by the six main tribes in respect to all their main crops. To fulfill this part of the study, the anthropologists making the tribal community studies should be fully briefed on what to look for, should collect information on all agricultural practices in detail, and should present this information in all its relevant social context. There is one other way in which the anthropologists might help. They might put markers in the fields they study (mapping their locations accurately) to note in code form the date, the size of the field, and the crop grown there. The Research Centre is to be a permanent organization. It should be possible for its officers to check up in subsequent years on the use or non-use of at least a selection of these fields and thus get quantitative data on shifting cultivation practices which will have a higher degree of scientific validity than has been recorded on this topic.

The second part of the proposed study was said to be a detailed investigation of a particular area in which shifting cultivation is being practiced to determine the vegetation and soil characteristics of particular parts of it both before and after use. This part of the study is to be of a different order from the first. The first part will be descriptive of existing methods and can be carried out by the anthropologists. The second part is intended to be a purely agricultural study and will require the services of a trained agricultural scientist. A convenient area to investigate would be that embraced by the Chieng Dao *Nikhom*.[1] Shifting cultivation is spreading in this area to parts which are still under primary jungle. The study would aid *nikhom* planning as well as provide the scientific information needed for general use. Cultivation is proceeding in the area of all the recognized hill tribe crops as well as of tea and coffee. The study would give added value to the *nikhom* because of all the *nikhoms* this one has the lowest population, which probably numbers not more

---

[1] A *nikhom* is a government land settlement area. In the case of the hill tribe areas, the *nikhoms* now operate as government welfare stations for the tribes.

than 450 people, and therefore it is less suited to the development of the social welfare program which the *nikhoms* were intended to promote. At the same time, the population relative to the land area is dense enough to provide the right conditions for the study now proposed.

The first task would be to prepare a detailed land-use map of the area. This would require aerial photography from a low level. Thereafter the agriculturalist would study the characteristics of the parts of the area under use, in fallow, or not yet used, and progressively record the changes and their effects on the map. The information so derived would permit the interpretation in agricultural terms of the information on various tribal practices supplied by the anthropologists.

The third part of the proposed study is controlled experimentation with different methods of shifting cultivation. This experimentation could also be carried out in the area of the Chieng Dao *Nikhom*, utilizing the areas of primary jungle which will otherwise soon succumb to the present largely uncontrolled shifting cultivation.

On the basis of the information derived from the whole study, a truly scientifically based agricultural education program could be prepared for the hill tribes.

Ideally, a fully trained agricultural scientist should be appointed to the research staff of the Tribal Research Centre. The project is a long-term one. To yield significant results, the experimentation would have to be carried on for at least five or six years and preferably much longer. The project, therefore, requires a person who is prepared to devote his whole attention to hill agriculture, which differs greatly in nature from the agriculture of the lowlands. Although the first and main task of such an agricultural research officer would be to carry out the research project proposed above, he would advise the anthropologists and assist them in their descriptive studies in such ways as classifying vegetation and soils for them. He might also supervise experimentation in the *nikhoms* and villages.

To carry out the project, the Centre will need additional finance. It may also be difficult to find in Thailand a person with sufficient qualifications who is able to free himself from prior commitments. It may be necessary, therefore, to seek a foreign expert to initiate the project. It is doubtful if a foreign agriculturalist would be able to stay in Thailand long enough to do more than just initiate it. For this reason, if such a person is brought in, then a junior research officer with a degree in agriculture should be appointed to be trained by him to continue the study on a long-term basis. Every effort, however, must be made to find a qualified Thai senior agriculturalist willing to devote himself to problems of hill agriculture.

2. *A Study of Pastoral Possibilities.* The Hill Tribes Division of the Department of Public Welfare is hoping to engage the services of overseas experts to study the possibilities of using the upland grasslands for cattle-raising. Although these experts would probably not be working directly from the Centre, they would receive every possible assistance from the Centre. The Centre should also be able to help in the interpretation of their results in terms of practical development schemes by investigating such socio-economic factors as the density of the population which could be supported by cattle-raising (and relating it to the existing population densities in the areas), the land tenure system which would be most practical in the cattle-raising areas, and the marketing system which would be most suitable. There are other considerations too, which might affect the success of a cattle-raising scheme. For instance, if the cattle-raising is intended to provide only a part of the people's income, leaving them dependent on agriculture for the rest, there will be the problem of keeping the cattle from the cultivated areas. All such matters will require investigation.

We are arguing that the purely pastoral study must be but a part of a wider investigation. We certainly do not intend to imply that it is not highly important, but it is true that pastoralism, like tea cultivation, can probably at best provide employment for only a small proportion of the total hill tribe population. But this will be the situation with many forms of hill tribe development. There can be no panacea for all the problems. The answers must be piecemeal.

3. *Population Studies.* At present no one is certain of the number of tribes-people in Thailand. Generally the number is assessed at around 200,000, but estimates have ranged as high

as half a million. There is no certainty as to the population sizes of any of the tribes (Bennington-Cornell 1964)

The National Statistical Office is now planning a census, and the Centre has been cooperating in drawing up plans for it. It is hoped to collect information not only on the numbers of people in the various tribes, but also on family size and type, clan membership (where there is a clan system), land holdings, types of crop and annual yields of each type, holdings of animal stock, and, if possible, cash incomes. It will be possible to collect some of this data only according to a sample system.

When the census is completed, it will be necessary to keep the information up to date, especially that relating to village locations and the movements of tribal groups both within the country and into the country from Burma and Laos. It is hoped that a statistical officer for this purpose can be permanently located at the Tribal Research Centre.

4. *Education Studies.* A number of schools have already been established in tribal areas, some by the Border Patrol Police and a few in the *nikhoms* by the Department of Education. The demand for schools, although still slight, is bound to increase, and the rate of economic and social development can be speeded by a well-adapted educational system.

In order for the scheme to be well adapted, investigation is needed of the relative places to be assigned to tribal languages and to Thai as media of instruction; of the curriculums of schools; of the timetables of schools; and of possible forms of adult education.

When resources permit, it is hoped that an educational research officer can be appointed to the staff of the Tribal Research Centre to devote his whole attention to these and other related problems. Using the information on tribal cultures supplied by the anthropological research officers, he would supervise or advise experimental schools as they were established and assess the results of their programs.

5. *Other Research Projects.* There are many other matters into which the Tribal Research Centre could carry out investigations, such as the relationships between the several different categories of Chinese immigrants and the tribes-people, the problems in-

volved in giving the tribes-people citizenship and land rights, and the development of information services for the tribes. But adequate consideration of these matters seems to me to require the information from the socio-economic and statistical studies outlined above. It is hoped, therefore, that these studies can be carried out first. The list is long enough to occupy the probable resources of the Centre for at least the first two years. If other matters should become so urgent as to demand action, the persons working at the Centre would, of course, try to give such information on them as they could accumulate from the investigations already carried out.

THE ACTIVITIES OF THE TRIBAL RESEARCH CENTRE TO THE PRESENT DATE

The discussion so far has been futuristic. This is because the Tribal Research Centre is a new thing born a bare year ago on paper only. But its material existence has now begun, and I shall briefly review its infant progress to date. Then I shall discuss the obstacles it must overcome.

The construction of a building to house the Centre has almost been completed on the campus of the University of Chiengmai. The building incorporates a lecture hall, a library, a central office, five offices for research staff, a room (to be air-conditioned) for the storage of tapes and films, and a photographic darkroom. Possibly by 1967 an extension to the building will be constructed comprising an auditorium and more office space, whereupon the present lecture room would become part of a museum for which collections are already being made.

It is hoped to provide the library with as complete a collection as possible of books and articles on hill tribes in all areas of Southeast Asia. An excellent beginning has been made through the generous donation from the British government, and it is expected that funds will be provided by the Thailand government for further acquisitions each year. The library also includes a number of general works on social anthropology, linguistics, and tropical agriculture.

The government has already approved in principle a plan for a museum. According to this plan the museum will have two sections. In the main Centre building there will be an exhibition of perishable and valuable objects, such as tribal costumes and jewelry. In addition, on an area of land which it is hoped the University of Chiengmai can make available, there will be erected actual houses of the six main hill tribes. These houses will either be bought in the hills and reassembled on the museum site, or they will be erected from new new materials by tribal craftsmen. Each house will be furnished in typical tribal fashion and will contain exhibits of agricultural implements and other items of tribal material culture. Together these houses will form a small composite tribal village in natural surroundings. The houses may also be used on occasion to accommodate tribespeople visiting the Centre.

At present (May 1965) the research staff of the Centre comprises only two persons. Khun Wanat Bhruksasri is acting as Senior Research Officer. Because of his outstanding talent, it is hoped that he will remain with the Centre in a senior capacity. The other member of the research staff is a junior research worker who at present is on secondment from another section of the Department of Public Welfare. He is a most able and enthusiastic worker, who we hope will occupy a permanent position on the staff. Provision exists for the appointment of another junior research officer, and the establishment is to be increased in the next financial year, which begins in October. But the Centre faces a problem in recruitment which will be discussed later.

Arrangements have been completed for the holding at the Centre of a training course for officers from all agencies concerned with hill tribe development work. The course will comprise instruction in elementary anthropology, language study, policy towards the hill tribes, and development programs. The aim of the course is to stimulate a scientific attitude in the officers and to promote coordination between the agencies. It is also intended to familiarize the officers with the objectives of the Centre and to encourage them to cooperate with it.

Because the establishment of the Centre has required a good deal of office work and consultations with government officials, and because of shortage of staff and the recentness of the appointments of the two persons who do constitute it, we have been able to make only a small beginning with our research work. It seemed wisest to apply our very limited resources and time to the study of a single community. There were two main reasons for this.

1. Serious research on the hill tribes has so far taken the form, in most cases, of wide-ranging comparative surveys utilizing a questionnaire prepared in advance.[2] Useful as these studies are for providing a general conspectus of the situation in the hills, full understanding of the structures and economies of the hill tribe societies demands more intensive investigations. This is especially so in the case of those hill tribes whose main source of income is an illegal crop. Because it is a government agency, the Tribal Research Centre is bound to be called upon often to conduct quick surveys to gain information which is said to be urgently required for this or that purpose. The more dependent the Centre is on government funds, the lower its status in the government institutional hierarchy, the greater the pressure for this kind of research will be. Sometimes, no doubt, the Centre must concede to the demands. But the chief value which it has as a permanent research organization, as distinct from *ad hoc* research terms, is that it is in a position to carry out longer-term investigations which will yield more substantial, more accurate, and ultimately more valuable information. Therefore, I wished to make our earliest research venture a demonstration of the type of study which I felt the Centre should have as its main interest.

2. The second reason for concentrating on a single community was to provide training methods of field work for the two members of the staff, neither of whom is a trained anthropologist.

We selected the Meo village of Meto, which is at a height of 3,700 feet in the Amphur Hod District of Chiengmai Province. For several months we visited the village for about a week at a time, whenever opportunity permitted. We have now had a house built in the village, and we hope that one member of the staff will be able to carry on the study more continuously. For myself, the study is a continuation of one I began in 1958,

[2] I am referring here to the six main hill tribes. I am therefore not taking into account the excellent study of the Lawa by Dr. Kunstadter, which would serve as an example for studies of the hill tribes proper. A field study of the hill Karens has also just been completed by Shigeru Iijima of Kyoto University, but only preliminary results have been published so far.

the main group in the community at Meto being the same group I lived with then at Pasamliem in Amphur Chieng Dao. In the intervening six years the group moved more than 120 miles, having resided en route for two years in Amphur Mae Cham.

We are carrying out a socio-economic analysis of the community. It is certainly not a model study, because of the constant interference of other duties. But we have already gained a great deal of useful information. We have learned much about the Meo systems of kinship and clanship and about Meo religion. We have discovered many interesting facts about the economy, of which I may quote just a few as examples. Having witnessed the opium harvest, we know that the average productivity of a household is about five to six kilograms of raw opium, which yields a cash income of five to seven thousand baht (approximately $250–$350).[3] A few of the larger households may have an income of ten thousand baht. The people live in a symbiotic relationship with Yunnanese Haw traders (immigrants from Yunnan now resident in Thailand) of whom, at the height of the opium season, there are seventeen families in a village of sixty-two households. The Meo employ neighboring Karen to work in their fields, paying them a very low wage but rewarding them also with opium for smoking. On the average, about half the opium income of the Meo is used to buy necessary foodstuffs. There is an interrelationship of crops, especially paddy-maize-opium-stockraising, which is basic to the present Meo economy. Many Meo would be willing to forego opium production if suitable crop alternatives could be found. Meo communities have wide-ranging connections through marriage with other Meo groups, which influence their migration patterns. The study of the Meto community is so fascinating that it is difficult to resist the temptation to spend all our time up there. In the heat of the Chiengmai Plain our noses twitch for the mountain air, and we know why the Meo want to stay where they are, or at least in some like place where the air is cool and the flowers bloom. Perforce, however, the Centre is our main concern. Its heart must always be in the mountains if it is to have any life at all, but for it to function properly as a research institution certain

[3] One U.S. dollar equals approximately 21 baht.

problems must be overcome, and these form the subject of the concluding part of the paper.

THE STATUS OF THE TRIBAL RESEARCH CENTRE

The Tribal Research Centre was established on a recommendation emanating from the Department of Public Welfare. The Department gave it birth and has mothered it solicitously. If it is to remain a section of any single government department, it could have no better home than in the Department of Public Welfare, because the Director General and his deputies and the senior officers of the Hill Tribes Division are all keenly interested in its welfare and do their best to promote its interests.

But the Department of Public Welfare is only one of several government agencies engaging in work with the hill tribes. A most important agency is the Border Patrol Police, which has extensive programs to improve conditions in the hill tribe areas. If the Tribal Research Centre is to have maximum utility, it should supply information to all agencies and also receive aid from them in the gathering of information. While it remains under the administrative control of a single department, working cooperation, although not impossible, is rendered more difficult. The government is aware of the need for closer coordination of hill tribe programs, and measures to effect this coordination are under consideration. The position and role of the Tribal Research Centre should form an important part of this consideration.

Another problem arises from the location of the Centre within the Department of Public Welfare. Every department has an order of subdivision, and the status of officers depends on their relative positions within this order. At present the Tribal Research Centre is a section of the Hill Tribes Division, which itself is subsidiary to the Bureau of Land Settlement. Although the Centre does receive special consideration from the Department, it must operate through the existing ranking order, and its staff has to be graded according to it. The position of the Director is still undetermined, but in the cases of all other positions the present situation means that they are all of relatively low grade. Thus they cannot attract persons of sufficient qualifications to carry out independently the skilled work of anthropological research. In the case of junior persons with the talent to be trained as efficient research workers, the present situation does not offer them opportunities for career advancement which would encourage most of them to regard work with the Centre as a permanent occupation.

The problem may be overcome in time by a departmental reorganization which would give the Centre a higher status. Or a solution may emerge from the consideration now being given to the coordination of the hill tribe programs of different departments.

A solution along the second lines would have one advantage. The fourth function of the Centre as set out in a Cabinet decision quoted earlier (p. 553) was "to evaluate continuously the hill tribe projects conducted by both the Government and private organizations." It would not be easy for the Centre to carry out this function while it remains a section of the Department of Public Welfare. It would be difficult enough for it to evaluate the projects of its own department. It would require considerable temerity to offer evaluations of projects of other departments.

Both the above solutions would leave the Tribal Research Centre as a part of the ordinary civil service organization. A different way of overcoming the problem would be to give the Centre independence in some form. There are two possibilities here. One is to attach the Centre to a university, probably the University of Chiengmai.

There is, it seems to me, considerable merit in the suggestion of a university attachment, provided the position accorded the Centre in the university structure is sufficiently high for it not to have to face the same problems of control and status which it now has in the Department of Public Welfare. This affiliation would allow the Centre to carry out its evaluative function. And it would relieve the Centre of some of the pressure for quick results which tends to inhibit the intensive work which I feel should be its main task.

But a university attachment would have its own problems, chief of which would be the recruitment of staff. In Thailand at the present time the universities do not have the same degree of prestige as is often accorded to them in the Western countries. University leaders do, of course, often exercise considerable influence on government activities, but frequently they do so through holding dual positions, one in their university capacity and one in the government. The junior person cannot see himself, at least for very many years, the holder of dual positions. Therefore, if he is ambitious, as the ablest young Thais concerned to aid their country's development naturally are, he usually elects for government service because that seems to offer him the greater opportunity for influence and authority.

This is a more serious problem than it may seem to those outside the Thai scene. In the case of the Tribal Research Centre it may be overcome by two means operating conjointly. First, in drawing up conditions for a university attachment, provision could be made for a definite relationship of the Centre to government agencies working with the hill tribes. The Centre should have an advisory and an evaluative role, and it should be able to call on the resources of the agencies in collecting information. Second, it should have sources of funds which would allow it to offer special inducements to staff and carry out extensive field-research programs, produce publications, and employ foreign experts, when needed, for special projects.

For this to occur, a source, or sources, of funds must be found outside regular government funds. One such source is the Southeast Asia Treaty Organization, which has already been generous to the Centre and may be inclined to further generosity. However, the Centre will need funds which are assigned on more than a yearly basis, and it remains to be seen whether this can be so in the case of the Treaty Organization.

An alternative would be support from one or more of the large overseas foundations. Here one's thoughts naturally turn toward American magnanimity. The support given would have to be large, because a condition which the Centre would probably have to accept in order to secure it would be a relinquishing of SEATO assistance.

The case for foundation assistance is very strong. In the Tribal Research Centre the Thailand government has created an institution which could be of major importance to Southeast Asia. There is no similar institution, as far as I know, in any of the other countries of the region. At the time of the Centre's creation it was envisaged that ultimately it might become a Regional Centre. This is a bright vision which could be made a reality.

BIBLIOGRAPHY

ANTHONY, K. R. M. and MOORMAN, F. R.
  1964 Agricultural problems and potentialities of a hill tribe area in Thailand. Bangkok. This paper surveys conditions in Tak Province.
BENNINGTON-CORNELL ANTHROPOLOGICAL SURVEY
  1964 A report on tribal peoples in Chiengrai Province north of the Mae Kok river. Bangkok, Siam Society, Data Paper 1.
CAMPBELL, P. D. J.
  1963 Report on the survey of tea-growing areas of Thailand. Bangkok, Colombo Plan.
CONKLIN, HAROLD C.
  1963 The study of shifting cultivation, Washington, Pan-American Union. Studies and Monographs VI.
THAILAND, DEPARTMENT OF PUBLIC WELFARE
  1962 Report of the socio-economic survey of the hill tribes in Northern Thailand. Bangkok, Ministry of the Interior, Department of Public Welfare.
  1964 A brief on the hill tribe development and welfare program in Northern Thailand. Bangkok, Ministry of the Interior, Department of Public Welfare.

CHAPTER 16

Autonomy and Integration of Social Systems: The Iu Mien ("Yao" or "Man") Mountain Population and Their Neighbors

PETER KANDRE

INTRODUCTION

This paper does not deal directly with an action program, nor does it propose any definite course of action; however, some of the topics discussed may be relevant for the planning of action programs. On the basis of my research experience with one minority group, the Iu Mien (or "Yao" or "Man") in Thailand and Laos, I discuss some internal and external adaptations of a population, by which a characteristic organizational framework and concomitant values are maintained under the impact of changing political and economic conditions. Some understanding of the adaptive mechanisms of this society may be useful, at least for those administrators in contact with this people.

The Research Project. The research on which this paper is based has been carried out among the Iu Mien of Chiengrai Province, Thailand, and in Houei Sai Province, Laos. The main part of the data was collected among the Iu Mien now living in Maechan District, Chiengrai Province. The greatest part of this population has immigrated to Thailand from the Houei Sai region since 1945. The most detailed information comes from Ban Lao Tsii Khuen (Thai name Ban Phalae) in the area of the Maechan Hill Tribe Welfare Center (*nikhom*) of the Public Welfare Department, Thailand Ministry of Interior. I currently reside in this village. Information concerning the Iu Mien of Yunnan, China, and Mung Sing and Nam Tha areas in Laos has been collected in the Nam Khyng settlement, Houei Sai Province, Laos. The villages that constitute the settlement come from

Mung Sing and Nam Tha. One of these villages moved from Yunnan to Laos after 1950.*

Two kinds of data have been collected: information of a general nature, gained through interviews with well-informed persons over a period of about one year; and information obtained through systematic investigation of selected households and villages with regard to factors which I have judged, on the basis of more general information, to be of strategic importance in shaping social processes. The questionnaires have been revised continuously as a result of progress made in the analysis.[1]

The Categories of Iu Mien, and Yao or Man. Populations commonly called Yao or Man are found in portions of southern China (parts of Kwangtung, Kwangsi, and Yunnan provinces), North Vietnam (Tonkin), northern Laos, Northern Thailand, and northeastern Burma. The total number of Yao speakers has been estimated to lie somewhere between half a million and one million, with the main part of them living in China, from where they have gradually moved to the other regions (LeBar *et al.* 1964:64).[2]

The present paper is not concerned with the Yao as defined by linguistic classification, but only with populations having a certain socio-economic-ritual system and which, on the basis of

* Geographical names have been spelled phonetically, except where usage is well established on maps or in published literature. Some confusion is inevitable because of the different standards of transcription employed in different places. For example, the Tai word *huaj* ("small mountain valley") has ordinarily been transcribed by the French as *houei;* the Tai word *myang* ("city" or "principality") is ordinarily transcribed *muong* by the French, but sometimes appears in Indochina, Thailand, and Burma as *mung,* and sometimes is rendered *muang* in Thailand.

[1] My current research has been financed by UNESCO (a Fellowship under the Major Project for Mutual Appreciation of Eastern and Western Cultural Values, 1964) and grants from the following Swedish research institutions: the University of Göteborg; the Swedish State Council for Social Science Research; the Swedish State Council for Research in the Field of Humanities. Valuable administrative support has been given me by the National Research Council of Thailand and the Public Welfare Department of the Ministry of Interior of Thailand. To all these and other agencies, and to all the private persons who have assisted me in various situations, I offer my sincere gratitude. I am particularly indebted to Professor K. G. Izikowitz of Göteborg University for help and encouragement, and to Mr. Lej Tsan Kuej, of Ban Phalae, Maechan, Thailand, who has been a true friend and a patient tutor. Parts of the sections of this paper on political structure are modified from Kandre (1964).

[2] Unfortunately, it is not possible to draw from this condensed compilation of data from various published sources any usable information concerning Iu Mien social organization.

this association, distinguish themselves from other populations and refer to themselves as *Iu Mien*. Although Iu Mien are speakers of various dialects of the Yao language, they do not use the Yao language as a basic criterion for self-identification, but instead refer to various traditions which are discussed at length below.[3]

In Thailand there are about 10,000 Iu Mien, settled in approximately seventy villages or hamlets, mostly in the mountain regions near the northern borders with Laos and Burma. There are two main concentrations, one in the *amphur* (districts) of Chiengkham and Mung Pong and another in Amphur Maechan, Chiengrai Province. Most of those living in the Maechan area have migrated from Laos since 1945. The settlement in the Chiengkham-Mung Pong area is older. Apparently there have been Iu Mien living in this region, and also in adjacent Nan Province, for the last hundred years. Recently a number of them have moved into Thailand from Chiengtung (Kengtung) Province, Burma.

The Iu Mien population in Laos seems to be much more numerous than in Thailand, but I do not have reliable information about their total numbers. Information on their population in Burma is also lacking, but my informants believe them to be less numerous in Burma than in Thailand.

Ecology of the Iu Mien. The Iu Mien socio-economic-ritual system operates, with few exceptions, in a mountainous natural environment, where the people practice swidden (slash-and-burn) agriculture. The main subsistence crop is dry, glutinous rice. For at least the past fifty years opium cultivation has been the main source of cash. At present in Thailand, as a result of the gradual suppression of poppy cultivation and the opium trade and as a result of improved communications, the raising of pigs and peppers for sale is becoming increasingly important. More

[3] I should make it clear that I am speaking of a socio-economic-ritual *system* whose participants call themselves Iu Mien. The members are recruited primarily by sexual reproduction, but approximately 10 percent of the population called Iu Mien have been incorporated by purchase or marriage and ritual adoption through introduction to the proper spirits. Strictly speaking, Iu Mien who become Christians are no longer Iu Mien—they have "thrown away the ancestor spirits" and no longer participate in the Iu Mien ritual system. They may, however, continue to participate in the Iu Mien social system (through exchange of wives) and economic system (through economic alliances). (See below for further discussion of methods of incorporation of new population elements.)

than most other mountain populations in this area, the Iu Mien have excelled in trade.

None of my informants remembers ancestors who have lived on the plains. Among the terms they use for self-identification there are some which refer to the ecological setting of the Iu Mien, for instance "men of the high mountains," and "sons of the mountain rice."[4] Nonetheless, a few villages have moved, or are planning to move, down to the plains in order to practice wet-rice cultivation. For these communities soya beans and peanuts, in addition to pigs, are the main sources of income.[5] Some villagers located in the mountains also plan to start wet-rice cultivation. In one such village, Phalae, where I live, some paddy fields have already been prepared. The Department of Public Welfare is carrying out systematic experiments at the Maechan *nikhom* for the introduction of new crops and agricultural techniques.

THE SYSTEM MAINTAINED AS AN INTEGRATED WHOLE THROUGH CONSCIOUS APPLICATION OF DIFFERENT TECHNIQUES OF ADAPTATION TO ACTIVE FORCES OF THE TOTAL ENVIRONMENT

At an early stage of my research among the Iu Mien, I found that my informants used two different terms when referring to formal rules governing their social and ritual practices: *lej njej* and *lej fing*. Lej can be translated as "custom" or "tradition." No direct translation is possible for the words *njej* and *fing*.[6] When I followed this lead, I found that they are clearly aware of, and also say that they act on, the premise that their welfare depends on successful adaptation to the demands of two distinct power structures which belong to two different, though not strictly separated, spheres of existence: (1) the power structure of the spirit world, which has special relevance to long-term action-orientation; and (2) the political systems affecting short-term action-orientation. The power structures belonging to the latter category are usually referred to as "governments," and

---

[4] The existence of these two terms was pointed out to me by Dr. Gordon Downer, School of Oriental and African Studies, University of London.

[5] For a brief but accurate description of Iu Mien economy and contacts with other groups in Thailand see Young 1962:47–48.

[6] The word *fing* in this context is not the same as its homonym, which means "clan."

particular importance is attached by the Iu Mien to relationships with central governments, *hung gjaa* ("the king's government").

It is considered essential to know and apply a distinct set of rules of conduct for each of these categories of power. My informants also stress the importance of flexible adaptation to other individuals—the "polite approach" in day-to-day interactions—in order to avoid open conflicts. This conscious and systematic approach to problems of adaptation between individuals is important in determining the general character of social life among the Iu Mien and in the relationships between them and other populations. Because this is a form of institutionalized behavior which is not defined by the Iu Mien as tradition (*lej*), I call it *institutionalized politeness*.

Another class of behavior frequently referred to is *phou tung* ("ordinary"). This term refers to fields of action in which individual choice or judgment is considered to be the proper criterion for determining action.

Lej Njej. This term refers to a body of knowledge about the nature of the universe and the place of the Iu Mien in it. *Lej njej* also refers to rules of conduct which define the long-term action-orientation that will result in the best possible adaptation of a particular individual to conditions affecting his ultimate welfare. Because these rules are believed to correspond to the permanent order of the universe, the idea that they could change is considered to be absurd.

Thus *lej njej* is both a world view and a theory of action (it is not, however, the complete theory of action of the Iu Mien). It prescribes stable forms of cooperation between individuals and groups in the populations defined as descendants of Iu Mien. It gives to this population what social scientists call "social structure." It also prescribes the use of an instrument to facilitate cooperative action and, finally, it serves as a boundary-maintaining mechanism with regard to interactions between different social systems. Because *lej njej* refers only to the inevitable conditions affecting persons with a particular association with the past, it counteracts linkage of that population with other social systems.

A World View and a Theory of Action. To the Iu Mien the universe is the habitat of a multiplicity of actors, the two main categories of which are referred to as *men* and *spirits*. The *spirits* (*mien*)[7] have the capacity for enjoyment and suffering. Like men, the spirits need food (ritually transformed into "spirit food"), and they value security and social recognition of their intrinsic worth. They want to be respected. Spirits have a social organization in which the observance of contractual obligations is supervised and enforced by the coercion of "the great group of spirits" (*tum toong mien*). This group of eighteen specialized functionaries, with a host of assistants, forms a veritable central government. Protected by this government, each spirit enjoys existence in absolute security according to his intrinsic value or merit. This value or merit is gained by investments in the world of men, either made by the individual himself (before he dies and becomes a spirit) or, he has already passed to the spirit level of existence, made for him by living men.

These investments must be made in the world of men in the form of merit-making ceremonies, in which the individual's spirit receives a status in the spirit world from the spirit central government. Merit-making (*fiu too*) is carried out under strictly controlled conditions and requires expenditures of various amounts of wealth,[8] particularly *silver*. The spirit government has strong likes and dislikes in two respects: It likes silver and dislikes sexual intercourse.

While accumulating wealth, particularly money, during his existence in the world of men, a person's physical welfare depends largely on correctly fulfilling duties toward ancestor spirits (*ung thai mien*). A living person's safety also depends on protection received from temporal political powers. However, his ultimate security depends on his relations with the central government of the spirit world.

The spirits' goverment does not regularly interfere with relations between men, but they have the power to do so if desired. Ancestor spirits cause illness if the obligation to feed them has not been fulfilled. In addition, man is exposed to aggression from a multiplicity of evil spirits (*tsung mien*), one for each ailment

[7] The word *mien* in the middle tone means "man," and in the high tone means "spirit." The correct tone indication for Yao words is given in the glossary.

[8] There are three main grades of merit-making, each associated with its own ceremony: *kwaa tang, tou saj*, and the highest, *gjaa tse*. All ceremonies are carried out according to the same basic principles, but they require different amounts of wealth.

[588]

or category of accident, all properly catalogued by the ritual experts. Man is also protected by certain local spirits toward whom he has contractual obligations.

Men may propose cooperation on a contractual basis to spirits, asking them for help to become rich in the world of men. Such propositions are often made by the Iu Mien, but, because it is not certain that the spirits will cooperate in the world of men, they are never paid in advance for their assistance. When it is a question of obtaining status in the spirit world, the procedure is the other way around. A man ritually contacts the great spirits and, after feasting them and paying them respect, he expects to receive, after his death, a particular position in the spirit world.

In the world of the Iu Mien there is a defined network of relationships between living men, which motivates various stable forms of cooperation with regard to common obligations toward ancestor spirits and various other spirits (but not with regard to the government of the spirit world, which is a matter for individual action). The competitive efforts of individuals are based on processes of wealth accumulation and on notions of the universe as an organized whole where the advancement of the individual is inconceivable without flexible adaptation to certain power relationships. It is only possible to make this adaptation by accepting the responsibilities of a loyal member of Iu Mien society.

The Notion of the Unified Iu Mien Community and of Stable Social Relationships. The spirits of the descendants of the Iu Mien are subjects of the spirit government—the eighteen dignitaries who administer the community of spirits. Ultimate security and social recognition are enjoyed as a member of this hierarchy under the protection of the spirit government. A person may qualify himself for future positions in the hierarchy of spirits by carrying out a series of merit-making ceremonies during his lifetime or by having them carried out on his behalf after his death. But a person's ability to advance is dependent in part also on cooperation. There are rules which bind the individual, in a network of ritual obligations, to various categories of progenitors, and these obligations link the individual to others with similar obligations.

The notion of a unified Iu Mien community and the character

of stable relationships implied by such an idea are founded on
the belief that the descendants[9] of Iu Mien have all contracted
ritual obligations to ancestors and creator-gods. The living population is divided by patrilineal descent into subdivisions, each
of which is charged with ritual responsibilities for a corresponding group of ancestor spirits. These are ritual cooperative units,
and common ritual obligations sometimes impose economic cooperation in the pooling of resources for individual merit-making
ceremonies. For example, when the parents help sons to make
merit before the sons have accumulated sufficient capital, the
sons have the obligation to compensate the parents, after their
death, by carrying out expensive death ceremonies.

The house (*peo*) is *lej njej* because it is the place where the
ancestor spirits are fed and the spirit government is honored.
The house is always associated with a descent group, which is
obligated to a corresponding group of ancestor spirits, that of
the "owner of the house" (*peo tsiu*) and his descendants.[10]

There may be persons living in the house who do not belong
to the descent group of the houseowner, but the in-married
women are integrated into this group. Therefore, the household[11]
is distinct from the ritual group, and its operation is regulated
primarily by a concern for productive efficiency. The ritual
leader, who is the houseowner, is not necessarily the actual leader
of the household production team. However, these two roles tend
to coincide in one person. Because of the usual orientation to-

[9] "Descendants" include all those from other ethnic groups who have been
ritually integrated into the Iu Mien community, as well as the biological descendants of the Iu Mien. Iu Mien rules of descent do not refer to biological descent,
as understood by modern science, but to ritually established connections with
the ancestor spirits. The child is believed to be the product of cooperation
between a male and a female ancestor spirit (both of the father's group),
who give the young life spirit to the human parents, who then give it a body,
feed it, and make it grow.

An individual is not really a member of the Iu Mien until he has undergone
initiation, that is, an introduction to the ancestor spirits after he has reached
twelve years of age. Because the Iu Mien believe in a cycle of rebirth, there
is no formal objection to the initiation of a child from another ethnic group.
After all, the child of one's own flesh and blood may be the reincarnation
of a person who formerly belonged to another ethnic group. (For further information on this topic see Kandre and Lej Tsan Kuej 1965).

[10] This ritual group is called *chuang ung thaaj* ("those who cooperate with
regard to ancestor spirits").

[11] The household is called *jet peo mien hoo khii haj* ("one house people
that cooperate without quarreling").

ward individual wealth accumulation, men found their own houses as soon as they are able to recruit and manage successfully an efficient production team.

The clan (*fing*) is the largest of the ritual descent groups. Clan membership is inherited patrilineally, for life, unless the person is transferred to the clan of his adoptive father before the ritual initiation. Members of each *fing* are supposed to have descended from a common ancestor, who was a member of the group that "came over the sea" (see below). Clans and their larger subdivisions do not keep genealogies and have no internal organization. Individuals keep the name of their father's clan and add it to their official name (*tum mien bua*), which is used in contacts with persons outside of the circle of close relatives and friends, and also add it to their spirit name (*fa bua*), which is used in ritual contexts.

Fing cut through different villages (*laang*) and households which are associated with particular places and particular men. They cut through households because women do not change their clan membership at marriage.

When defining the Iu Mien as distinct from other populations, the clan system as a whole is referred to in the context of an origin myth known as "crossing the sea" (*phiu jiu gja koe*). This myth, which is part of a longer cycle of stories, tells how the ancestors of the Iu Mien set off to cross the sea in boats because of a severe drought in their own country, "Nanking." Some of the boats were lost, and the crews of the other boats were saved by one of the creator-gods. Pien Hung thereupon pledged always to honor and reward this god. The twelve Iu Mien *fing* (clans) were founded after this voyage, and thenceforth the Iu Mien have called themselves *Pien Hung fun fa* ("the children and granchildren of Pien Hung").

Because all of the Iu Mien respect "ancestors" who cooperated when crossing the sea, they all must honor the obligations those ancestors contracted. They must bring up their children to take care of the ancestors' rights, and they must all cooperate in teaching and reminding each other of the respect they owe to Pien Hung.

The Iu Mien stress that Pien Hung is known to all Iu Mien. They say that Pien Hung is one of the first things their children are told about, together with knowledge of respect due to parents and ancestors.

It is significant that Pien Hung is not explicitly referred to as the biological progenitor of the Iu Mien, but as a benefactor who remains an outsider. The ultimate unity of the Iu Mien population is thus defined in terms of common ritual obligations contracted by the ancestors with regard to an outsider. These obligations refer both to the living and to the dead generations, who continue to honor Pien Hung after they have passed to the spirit level of existence.

Clan membership among the Iu Mien is not associated with positions of power and prestige. Statements referring to a fixed rank ordering of the clans are phrased in terms of the relationship between elder and younger brother. In general, I have found such statements of ranking to be inconsistent with one another, because there is no notion of a common progenitor for the whole population. To an outsider, such statements seem to be like occasional squabbles between people who, in fact, are used to treating each other as equals.

The elder brother-younger brother relationship is often referred to when describing the connections between the Iu Mien and the Lanten. Linguistically these two populations are both Yao, and even with regard to social organization there seem to be many similarities. However, from the point of view of the Iu Mien, the differences are important enough to make them maintain that these two have different *lej njej* traditions.

All Iu Mien who belong to the same clan are supposed to be "almost like relatives" (*tsien tse*—the term refers to patrilineal relatives). When persons meet for the first time, the two first questions are: "Where do you live?" and "What is your *fing?*" After this basic information is given, a more precise patrilineal kinship relationship, based on a common known ancestor, may be established by comparing genealogies. Membership in the same clan establishes patterns of long-term cooperation in neither the realm of economic production nor in the political sphere.

Economically and politically the *fing* provides a basis for informal person-oriented (i.e., non-spirit-world oriented) relationships, which may become the nucleus of economic and political cooperation, but which are not binding in advance to fixed patterns of cooperation. Only in cases where relationship can be defined in terms of exact kinship terminology are there certain restrictions and rights. The restrictions apply only to formation of marriage alliances. The rights give access to a house when certain ritual activities are being carried out, for instance at the birth of a child.

The restrictions governing marriage are never formulated as categorical prohibitions to be enforced by political institutions. Payment of adequate compensation in silver ("washing the face") seems to be the solution to most such problems. It may happen that biological descendants of the same father and mother fall in love and want to marry, and by moving far away they are able to establish their own household. It is admitted that they cannot possibly stay and cooperate with people who know about their kinship relationship, because "they are too ashamed." However, the idea of persecuting such deviation from the approved pattern by following the couple and putting pressure on them is quite contrary to Iu Mien ideas of ultimate individual responsibility. It is not the business of anyone to interfere in the private life of other people.

According to my experience, the common reaction in such and similar cases is, "They do wrong, but what can you do? This is love, and it is better that they run away and marry than that they commit suicide." Several cases of marriage between biological brother and sister have been reported to me, as have many cases of passion dramas ending in suicide or murder.

I believe that this intensity in relationships between the sexes has something to do with the codification of erotic behavior which has resulted from the reading of literature glorifying love, and also may be a result of the very real difficulties men have in getting married. Marriage among the Iu Mien is a business transaction involving the transfer of important amounts of wealth, and it is fundamental to the individual's success in life.

Lej njej is never categorical with respect to obligations. Men cannot force an individual to fulfill his ritual obligations. He can only be taught why it is in his own interest to do so. Ultimately the spirits themselves are supposed to be able to enforce respect for their rights.

Relationships to Other Populations. Other ethnic groups are also sometimes referred to as *fing* (clan), and they are supposed to have obligations, prescribed by their own *lej njej* traditions. Therefore, the idea that, for instance, an Akha would like to become Iu Mien does not make much sense to many of the latter because of the dominant belief that one cannot get away from one's obligations to ancestor spirits without giving them substantial compensation. The person who does not follow his *lej njej* rules risks serious trouble sooner or later.

Despite this, the Iu Mien population in Laos, Thailand, and Burma contains a high proportion from other ethnic groups. At least 10 percent of the present Iu Mien population has been purchased directly from such groups as Meo, Akha, Lahu, Shan, Lamet, Khamu, Lao, and Thai. These people have been ritually incorporated into the Iu Mien community. Almost all were very young children when they were purchased, but, particularly in the past, grown married couples have been bought and ritually incorporated.

One case may be cited of a Meo married couple who were sold to the Iu Mien by the husband's father in about 1860. A daughter of this couple, now aged eighty-seven, is still alive. She married a high-level Iu Mien headman in Laos, and one of her sons, Lej Tsan Kuej, is my tutor. Another of the grandsons is Lej Tsan Fin (Lao Tsii), the headman of the village where I live. Both keep in touch with their Meo relatives, who live in Tak Province, Thailand.

Because of the ritual integration, the 10 percent who have been adopted are considered as Iu Mien in every respect. I have discovered no sign of a feeling of shame or oddity or inferiority attached to being a "bought child," or being born to parents from another ethnic group. These persons readily admit the fact and joke about being Akha, Lahu, or some other tribe. But "bought children" are not always treated with the same affection as the others.

The reason for buying children is almost always the desire to build quickly an efficient working household, which is the main instrument for the enrichment of the "houseowner." If the household has not yet reached the limit for profitable expansion, the head often invests some of his surplus in expanding his future productive capacity. There is no evidence that this is a recent phenomenon, nor is it associated specifically with the cash income from opium cultivation. The cause lies much deeper, in the desire to maximize household production.

The importance of the Iu Mien institution of buying children is illustrated by the following example. About three hundred to four hundred Iu Mien have been converted to Christian ritual in the past ten years. These marginal Iu Mien have not given up the practice of buying children and, indeed, oppose the missionaries in this. They stress that "this is such an old custom that we cannot give it up." Furthermore, these marginal Iu Mien have not given up the idea of marriage as a business transaction between two persons, one of whom is going to lose manpower while the other gains it. Thus they have agreed, only under missionary pressure, to abstain from taking bride-price if the marriage is between Christians. But if the girl is a "bought child," compensation is demanded for the original outlay.

There are also persons belonging to Iu Mien households who have not ritually become Iu Mien. It is not necessary that every member of the household be integrated with the houseowner's group of ancestor spirits. It is sufficient if the spirits are informed about the new household member and asked not to harm the person.

Several women in my village of residence who belong to different ethnic groups have been members of Iu Mien households for shorter or longer periods. One is an Akha woman, divorced by her husband, who had previously sold their daughter to Iu Mien. The mother, who wanted to live with her child, was accepted as a permanent member of the household. Her daughter has become an Iu Mien, but the mother maintains her Akha dress. An Akha male lives in the village under similar conditions.

The attitude of Iu Mien toward other ethnic groups seems to be one of great tolerance as long as it is a question of productive cooperation. Meanwhile, the ritual distinctions are maintained with great care.

Thus *lej njej* rules affect the internal operation of the social system, but do not delimit the demographic expansion of the population.

Money: The Instrument of Action. The rules of *lej njej* are associated with a view of the universe as an organized whole, in which the Iu Mien operate on two levels of existence: the world of men (*jaang keen*) and the world of spirits (*jom keen*). On both levels goals can be reached by individuals using silver as an instrument called the "bridge of spirit silver" (*gjaa jom kiu*, lit. "making the bridge of the spirits"). The spirits bridge can be used for many purposes, including strengthening health and predicting a person's life span.[12]

The premise of the ritual is that a person is able to act and attain various goals by knowing how to use silver (money). He will live as long as he can accumulate silver. *Lej njej* offers a method of action and an instrument for evaluating progress of the individual's life. By making the individual's ultimate success require the financing of a number of expensive merit-making ceremonies, *lej njej* makes accumulation of liquid wealth the main goal for the individual.

In the Iu Mien world view, the individual's life is goal-oriented. His progress can be evaluated in terms of merit-making ceremonies that have been carried out and in terms of his poten-

---

[12] The following is a brief description of these techniques. The basic assumption is that general vigor is a matter of the proximity of the "life spirit" (*uən*) to the body. The ritual expert uses techniques prescribed by *lej njej* for finding the life spirit and inducing it to stay with the body. He orders a number of special spirit assistants (spirits, not men) to visit all quarters of the universe in search of the life spirit, and he instructs them how to do it. Laying out pieces of ritual paper money across the floor of the house toward the ceremonial door, he tells the spirit assistants:

> This is the bridge that leads into the sky;
> This is the bridge that leads to the earth;
> This is the bridge for spirits and for men;
> This is the bridge to the spirit world;
> This is the bridge through the forest;
> This is the bridge across the waters;
> This is the bridge that leads through all countries;
> This is the bridge that leads in all directions.

He shows the spirit assistants how to follow the bridge by jumping from one piece of money to the next. Then, falling into a (simulated) trance, he departs for the spirit world.

When the life spirit has returned (in the form of an insect found in front of the ceremonial door of the house), it is offered food. Uncooked rice is placed in a bamboo tube in the middle of a tray covered with ritual money. Using a sticky string, the ritual expert tries to catch as many pieces of the paper money as possible. The number of pieces caught indicates how many more tens of years the subject will live.

tial to accumulate further liquid wealth for merit-making. *Lej njej* defines silver as the ideal medium of exchange and the fixed standard of value.

The preoccupation with the accumulation of wealth, particularly in the form of silver (which is ritually defined by *lej njej* as the universal "Open Sesame"), has undoubtedly been a main determinant of the action-orientation of the Iu Mien for a long time. The whole system of merit-making ceremonies directed toward the "central government of the spirit world" uses silver as the bridge between the world of men and the world of spirits. Payment of silver, at least a small quantity, is a basic *lej njej* requirement for all important ritual transactions, including marriage.

Because money is the key to success (but by different paths) both in the world of men and in the world of spirits, the individual has to choose between the bridges that can be built with money. If a person decides to invest in his future existence in the spirit world, he spends his money for merit-making ceremonies. Thus he purchases in advance a respected position in the spirit world, and after he is dead this may affect the success of his living descendants. However, I have been told repeatedly that a person is not particularly respected among living men because of his spirit rank. This rank is indicated by his spirit name, which is never used in relationships with men. His relation to the spirits is his own business. Only a person's ability to act in this world counts with his fellowmen. The saying is, "One is respected for three things: money, intelligence, and good heart—and money is the great thing." If a man has all these qualities, it is largely attributed to help from ancestor spirits—if the ancestor spirits are clever, they will not lead a life-soul of bad quality to their descendants.

A man who is simply rich, without being clever or generous, is still respected, but above all he is feared, because it is thought that a rich man is free to do more or less what he wants. There is also the idea that virtue is attached to silver. It is believed that spirits, particularly those of the central government, value silver just as much as they dislike sexual intercourse. The heavens where the top eighteen spirits live are called "the pure land." Only by offering enormous amounts of spirit money can the individual gain the necessary merit and increase his intrinsic value so as to attain his heavenly goal.

Money, in particular silver, has special symbolic connotations. Fifty or sixty years ago, when my oldest informants were young, "silver was so rare that it was cut into tiny pieces. They used to say about a person who had much silver, 'This person has much silver. His life is good. He is very good.'" I have also been told that in the old times only wealth was respected, and it is only recently that the "clever" persons, for instance ritual experts, have gained respect.

I know of poorer men who have withdrawn from competition for the post of village headmen after learning of the ambitions of rich men. The idea that a rich man can do whatever he likes has been pointed out to me frequently, as in the following example. I once commented on the peculiar and ungentlemanly behavior of a man who was an alcoholic. When I suggested that his very unhappy childhood might have something to do with his present behavior, I was firmly corrected. "That has nothing to do with his childhood. He is so rich that he thinks he doesn't need to bother about other people, but can do whatever he likes."

In spite of their general preoccupation with money, the Iu Mien have not become corrupted. They are friendly and reliable people, with very great respect for the rights of their fellowmen. Money, in their society, is associated with positive values: the good life, respect and care for parents and children, and respect for the traditional way of life. It would be misleading and unfair, on the basis of their emphasis on money, to visualize the Iu Mien as a mercenary and cold-blooded lot.

Ritual Techniques. Spirits are thought to be powerful but rather stupid. "They believe everything the ritual expert says. When he gives them pieces of paper saying it is silver, they believe it is real. When he gives them bad alcohol, they enjoy it because he says it is good." Ceremonies are often occasions for hilarious joking at the expense of even the most powerful of spirits. The Iu Mien lack a concept of an omniscient, omnipresent god. Their spirits, big and small, are powers with whom man can cooperate on a contractual basis. Although they can travel fast, they are not always present and do not know what is going on in the world of men unless they are properly told. The spirits,

particularly those of the central government, do not easily understand the Yao language, so these spirits must be addressed in
ritual Chinese. Thus the spectators at the ceremony can make
their comments if they do not interfere in the activities of the
ritual expert.

Lej njej prescribes the techniques of communication with the
spirits, the office of "ritual expert,"[13] and an educational and
examination system for recruitment of specialists, in which the
teacher-pupil relationship is essential. This relationship is thought
to be a continuous process of cooperation which is not ended
by the death of the teacher. Teacher and pupil cooperate across
the borders dividing the world of men from the world of spirits
in the same way as ancestor spirits and their descendants are
supposed to cooperate.

Techniques of communication with spirits are strictly
regulated by *lej njej* prescriptions, largely in written manuals
(*saj zung sǝu* or *tsǝu míen sǝu*). The texts are written in Chinese or use Chinese characters, often copied from Chinese origi-
nals. An archaic form of literary Chinese (sometimes called
"Cantonese," sometimes "Nanking dialect") is prescribed because the spirits have difficulty understanding other languages.
Usually the ritual experts have a very imperfect knowledge of
this form of Chinese, and the spirit of the teacher of the expert
is always called upon to lead his pupil. A priori, the teacher
is supposed to be more competent than the pupil.

Lej njej does not refer to the use of any other language. All
other languages, including Yao, belong to the category of non-
ritual techniques and are classed as *phou tung*, which means
"ordinary" (see below).

Lej Fing. The *lej fing* tradition defines an approach to the
problem of adaptation to political power in the world of men.
These are rules aimed at the protection of life and property of
the Iu Mien population in interactions between members of the
Iu Mien community and in relations with the external political
powers dominating the regions where the Iu Mien live.

While *lej njej* affects long-term planning, *lej fing* is concerned

---

[13] *Tum saj kung* ("the great teacher"), the high-level expert who takes care
of relationships with the spirit government, and *mien sib mien,* the man who
takes care of smaller spirits.

with the short term—with adaptation to a changing total environment. *Lej fing* is a general principle for adaptive behavior and is an essential element in the Iu Mien theory of action, as indicated by their use of the term *lej* ("tradition").

In earlier days the need was for adaptation, primarily to loosely organized (often "inter-tribal") political systems of a feudal type, controlled by high-level headmen exercising a characteristically charismatic form of leadership. Now the *lej fing* refers primarily to the administration carried out by central governments. "When you live in Thailand, you have to follow the *lej fing* of Thailand. If you live in Laos, you follow the *lej fing* of Laos, and in Burma, you follow the *lej fing* of Burma. . . ."

The size of fines and the method of recruiting the village headman and council are *lej fing* matters. As units of production and elements in a political system, the constituent households of the village are not covered by conscious application of *lej njej* rules. But *lej njej* affects household routine more than it does the communal life of the village (*laang*), since the nucleus of the household is always a ritual descent group associated with a particular group of spirits, while the village is merely an aggregate of households.

Actually, *lej fing* and *lej njej* are mutually reinforcing, and when describing the impact of one on the behavior of the Iu Mien, it is impossible to disregard the other. The distinction is a conceptual one and refers strictly to the Iu Mien model of the universe, a world view in which a basic distinction is made between *stable* and *unstable* power relationships. The two sets of rules will be treated simultaneously in the remainder of this paper.

Phou Tung. All practices not affecting the rights of the spirits or not stemming from the need to protect men from men or to conform to demands of political powers are called *phou tung* ("ordinary"). This term refers to fields of action left to be governed by individual judgment. Important examples include agricultural techniques, the decision to live in the hills or on the plains, and even the Yao language and traditional dress used in everyday life (this does not refer to the dress of ritual experts, which is *lej njej*). The spirits are supposed to be interested only in getting their just compensation for cooperation, for instance for "helping the rice grow." For this they are offered ritual "spirit money."

Institutionalized Politeness. This is a technique for facilitating daily personal interactions, particularly in competitive situations. It is applied systematically to avoid getting into open conflicts. "You cannot speak in an unfriendly manner to each other. If you are impolite, then somebody will lose face, and this will cause a quarrel. Then you cannot cooperate any longer. That makes you weaker and you make less money."

Ideally, the polite approach should apply in all situations. "For instance, if two children fight, then you have to separate them. But you should not beat them, only teach them nicely." The Iu Mien try as much as possible to keep social interactions free from overt friction. Undoubtedly this preoccupation is connected with other elements in their theory of action.

Forming Household Units with Strong Internal Discipline. Institutionalized politeness, applied to interaction between members of a household unit, contributes to strong internal discipline. Struggles for leadership are stopped at an early stage, because quarrels are not tolerated. If two grown members cannot get along, the "houseowner" (*peo tsiu*) will ask one of them to leave, or someone will move out on his own initiative.

The household units usually split after the death of the houseowner, when married sons establish their own households. If brothers continue to live under the same roof, with a common household (eating together, making fields together, etc.), both of them may be called *peo tsiu*. Sometimes they may have separate households but care for their ancestor spirits together at a common spirit platform.

I inquired systematically in forty households, not limiting my interviews to household heads, regarding the optimum size of the household. The desired number of grown persons (over fifteen years of age) varied between five and twelve. The reasons given for limitation of household size were invariably that bad talk and quarrels would start if too many lived together, and that this made cooperation difficult. The houseowners always refer to disciplinary problems. A frequent opinion is that if it were not so difficult, they would like to have as many working hands as possible, "to make it big, have large fields, and be strong."

[601]

Some Techniques of Social Control and Boundary Maintenance: Security of Life and Property. Deviant behavior in Iu Mien society is counteracted and corrected by various formal and informal procedures. Non-observance of contractual obligations is checked mainly by exclusion of the offender from benefits of cooperative activities. The fact of a breach of contract is communicated to the community, and the offender is always excommunicated to some extent. He loses face and will find it difficult to secure profitable cooperation until he has "washed his face" by honoring his obligations. Because contracts are so important, the presence of witnesses is stressed both in ritual contexts (cooperation between men and spirits) and in economic cooperation between men.

The lack of formal social control over contractual relationships accounts in part for a marked distrust of long-term contracts and the preference for exchanges of goods and services on a cash basis. On the other hand, extension of credit improves a man's reputation and attracts partners for cooperative enterprises.

There are formal procedures for repair of damage to physical well-being or property caused by direct action. In this situation communal organs get involved and apply corrective measures in accord with *lej fing* tradition. The judicial process aims at establishing a contract ex post facto and at the transformation of a conflict into a relationship of cooperation and exchange. The victim and the offender, under pressure from mediators (for example, the headman and the village council), agree upon reasonable compensation for the damages and the services of the mediators. The decision is made easier by established precedents for amounts to be paid and procedures to be followed. As long as the offender shows readiness to cooperate, he is given the opportunity to negotiate and bargain. The main principle of the Iu Mien judicial system is not revenge, but repair of damage to individuals. It is founded on the idea of the community as a cooperative going concern.

This idea is frequently expressed in the statement that "Iu Mien do not kill Iu Mien." For example, when informants have reported robbery combined with murder, they have stressed that these are really peculiar times—in the past "such a thing was unheard of." When older cases of killing have been reported, they have been presented as accidents, with one exception. In this case (see below) the killer was a person who had been adopted recently from a different ethnic group. After investigating these cases in more detail, the circumstances of the accidents sometimes seem rather strange. But it is quite characteristic of the Iu Mien processes of conflict resolution that their explicit interpretations avoid the admission of aggression, even as a *fait accompli.*

The formal procedures for conflict resolution (for instance, in the case of theft) are carried out in an atmosphere which is made as pleasant as possible for everyone. The plaintiff, the accused, the headman, and the spectators sit together and discuss the matter politely, drinking and eating the food brought by the accused if he has already admitted his guilt, or that brought by the plaintiff.[14]

The purpose of the meeting is clearly understood to be reparation for damage and restoration of the smooth functioning of social interactions once the offense has become known. The motive is not revenge, and the blood feud is not an Iu Mien institution. The victim, the accused, and the community as a whole act as if they were equally interested in removing the conflict. Everyone cooperates in solving the unpleasant matter as smoothly and with as little offense to the involved parties as possible. Of course, the Iu Mien are no more saints than any other people, but even if there is desire for pure revenge, public expressions of it are not ordinarily tolerated.

The idea that anything can be repaired with adequate compensation, which makes aggression against the culprit meaningless (if he cooperates), is founded on the principle that assets of various persons are commensurable. Even in the case mentioned below, when a person was actually executed, it was stressed by my informants that the act for which he was punished could have been neutralized by the payment of a certain amount of money. In the old days, in fact, there was a fixed blood-price.

The logic of this attitude is explained as follows. To kill a man is to deprive him of money-making capacity and to deprive those who have been in contractual relations with him of the money he could help them make. Consequently, everything can

[14] This and the following paragraph are taken from Kandre (1964:30–31).

be put right by paying compensation in silver, and it is in the interests of many people in addition to the accused to see that this is done.

The method for conflict resolution is not permissive or lenient. Money means the capacity to act and survive. The person who has caused the death of another must make up to the dead person's spirit by financing merit-making ceremonies and also by honoring the obligations which the dead person had contracted with other men. This normally means that the killer must forego his own possibilities for advancement.

According to Iu Mien standards, one has to be rich to get away with murder without extremely serious consequences for oneself. This is one reason why rich men are feared.

If the killer is a young unmarried man, it is probable that his parents and other close relatives will pool their resources to pay compensation rather than letting him be executed. But this means that the young man's life chances are spoiled. He will not be able to build an efficient, independent household. Unless his parents are very rich, they probably will not finance his marriage, and it will be difficult for him to find anyone who wants to marry him. He is tied by too many obligations to his creditors.

About twenty years ago in Laos an adoptive son shot his father in circumstances that were considered very extenuating. The fourteen-year-old boy and his twelve-year-old brother had been bought only a few years before from the Red Lahu. They were very badly treated by their adoptive father, who beat them and made their lives miserable in every way. One day the father came to the field where the two boys were working and scolded them for not working fast enough. Before he left, he told them he was going to kill them. The boys panicked, and when they found the rifle the father had forgotten, the older boy shot him. In this case the killer was shot, much to the regret, it seems, of everyone in the village. The younger boy was not touched. The execution was motivated by the fact that the killer had no relatives who could have paid the compensation, and it was assumed that if he were left alive he would run away (the only logical thing for the boy to do if he wished to avoid virtual slavery).

In another case, also in Laos, a man is said to have shot another man by accident with a crossbow during a tiger-hunt. The circumstances were considered very incriminating. The killer hid the body, which was not discovered for quite a while. Compensation was agreed upon, amounting to over U.S. $1,000 (calculated in terms of the present exchange rate between dollars and silver in Thailand).[15] The killer belonged to a wealthy family and thus he survived.

These are illustrations of the traditional methods by which the Iu Mien provide security for life and property. Prosecution of the killer traditionally depended on the action of the victim's relatives. With the expansion of central governmental jurisdiction into hill regions of Laos and Thailand, cases of theft and murder are sometimes brought to government courts. But the prevailing opinion among the Iu Mien seems to be that their own way of handling such problems is more satisfactory, at least from the point of view of the victims. "What is the use of putting a man into prison or executing him if he can be made to work and repair the damage he has done? Later on he may leave prison and start the same thing again."

We can conclude that the idea of the "bridge of silver" provides an efficient method for social control of the individual. Because the individual is able to operate successfully only by using this instrument, the possibility that he may be deprived of its use is indeed a meaningful threat.

Informal Cooperation in Village Communities: Maintenance of Village Solidarity. Both the village council or group of assistant headmen and the headman are involved in the process of conflict resolution inside the village community. The headman and his assistants rely primarily on the agreement. A household head who does not want to conform is always free to leave the village community and go somewhere else where the social climate is more congenial.

Semi-informal control is exercised by the village headman in the following situations. Uncooperative behavior such as refusal to help in defense of another house if it has been attacked does

---

[15] The average lifetime earning capacity of an Iu Mien at that time is estimated by my informants to have been U.S. $100, calculated on the same basis. The standard compensation for a man at that time was $150, for a woman $40.

not cause immediate punishment or reprisal. Instead, gradual pressure is put on the recalcitrant party to repair the split in village solidarity. Repeated failure to shoulder responsibilities for common security will ultimately result in expulsion from the village. But before this point is reached the offender will be "taught the right ways" by the headman and eventually fined if the offense is repeated.

An informant has given a hypothetical example of the round-about way in which communal discipline is imposed. If there is a good field near the village, but it is too small for everyone to get a portion of it, it may be agreed that no one will use the field. If someone then starts to use it in spite of the agreement, he will not be forced off it, but the headman will probably come around and tell him politely, "Go on—it really doesn't matter. But don't come and complain if the pigs from the village come into the field."

It is characteristic of the "loose structure" of Iu Mien villages that a social behavior of the kind described above is not considered to be criminal. It is disapproved, however, and the person or household that goes against the cooperative practices will eventually come into difficulties.

Techniques of Communication: Authority and Ideological Control. It has already been stressed that the cooperation between individuals in processes of production is regulated largely through contracts between individuals, and that some of the most important forms of contract involve obligations to be honored after the death of one of the parties to the agreement. But what is the guarantee, for instance, that the descendants will in fact honor their ritual obligations once their parents are dead and cannot apply economic sanctions? There is no political authority to enforce these obligations. Enforcement depends on *lej njej* tradition.

Knowledge of *lej njej* is communicated in writing, orally, and by participant observation. The Iu Mien are literate (in a Chinese script) and have a variety of books, mostly concerned with ritual and myth. There are also collections of love songs and, finally, circular letters usually coming from persons with such firm reputation and high prestige that they have reason to believe their opinions will have strong impact.

Messages from these opinion leaders is one of the characteristic ways in which knowledge about the system is comunicated. There is great general interest in these letters; young and old sit for hours singing their texts, which always contain some moral lesson. Before the present political situation blocked communications, these circular letters traveled quickly all over the vast area inhabited by Iu Mien. The possibility of written communication has no doubt been important in maintaining the integrity of Iu Mien culture. Persons who have never been in Yunnan take it for granted that the Iu Mien there keep alive the same *lej njej* traditions because "if there had been any change [at least before the present regime in China] we would have heard or read about it."

The two following examples are summaries of letters of a type called "song for making good." The author of both, Fu Oon Uang, is a sixty-six-year-old ritual expert of highest distinction and is a high-level headman of a number of Iu Mien and Meo villages in the Chiengkham District, Chiengrai Province, Thailand. His Thai government title is *Phya* Kham Daeng.

Song No. 1

Everybody must respect his father and mother

When you were still a child, your mother carried you on her back, and you ate her milk. Father is like the sky, and mother is like the earth. Therefore you should respect them.

Marriage

Everbody should cooperate in harmony. One must not fight or make trouble. Husband and wife must love each other, and not do what is wrong.

Relations to spirits and to the governments

You have to do good and not do wrong against the spirits and the goverment. It is more serious to do wrong against the spirits than against the goverment. With government you can usually come to an agreement. If you do wrong against the spirits, you will die.

The actual letter, which is more than a thousand words long, begins by telling the origin myth of the Iu Mien. It was probably written in 1962 and is now said to be widespread among the Iu Mien of Thailand.

Song No. 2

Marriage

It is important to see in the books whether the two people who are going to marry are a good combination [reference is to horoscopes of date of birth, etc.]. If this is not done, the marriage may fail because perhaps the two will not cooperate.

Opium

Opium is not good. Some people become rich by trading with it, but others lose their wealth smoking it. Because of opium one often comes into opposition with the government, and the result is suffering. [The author of this letter neither smokes nor drinks.]

This letter was written around 1947 and is well known and widely circulated both in Thailand and Laos.

The following is a circular letter from the high-level headman I Kien (Lao government title, *Chao La*), one of the two main political leaders of Iu Mien in northern Laos.[16] He now lives in the Nam Khyng settlement in the Houei Sai Province and has a position in the Royal Lao Government administration. The letter, written in Chinese, sets down regulations for the size of the bride-price and is addressed to both Iu Mien and Meo in Laos. Chinese is the lingua franca in this case. In translation, the letter reads as follows:

Talking openly to all Iu Mien and Meo, to all headmen, to all households. From now on there will be four different levels of bride-price. In all cases the "mother's milk money," and the "grandparent's money" will be counted as one, and for the best quality [bride] it is fixed at 66 *lung;* for the second quality, 56 *lung;* for the third quality, 46 *lung;* and for the fourth quality, 36 *lung.* The "gold custom money" is counted into the "mother's milk money-grandparent's money." In addition to what has already been counted you have the *mui mien* money [money for the organizer of the marriage ceremony, who is the leader and go-between].[17] You have to pay that separately. For this, two *lung* is the correct amount. Furthermore, there is the "pork custom" [the food consumed during the marriage ceremony]. For

[16] The other is I Fu, older brother of I Kien. His government title is *Chao Mai.*

[17] It is significant that the *mui mien* money has to be counted separately. The *mui mien* belongs to *lej njej* tradition and is described in the creation myth. The saying is "without clouds no rain will fall, and without *mui mien* there will be no marriages."

this you will use not more than three pigs, and the middle way custom is to have two pigs. *The way it has been up to now, it has been difficult for poor people to do it* [emphasis added]. The duration of the great variety of marriage [ceremony] is one day and two nights. The middle variety is finished in one day, with two pigs. The poor people, who make it small, finish it after a single meal. The custom that guests receive pork to take with them when they leave is to be discontinued. The goodness of the parents must be remembered later on by giving them one pig. It has been decided that this custom must be followed exactly. Everyone must follow it, and they must not take more.

The third month of the year 1965
(Signed) *Chao La* Tsan Ngin

These letters are examples of the kind of social control exercised by leaders whose positions are founded mainly on personal prestige and further cemented through connections with the central governments.

The relationship between these opinion leaders and the other Iu Mien is analogous to that between a ritual expert and his teacher. The latter acts as a go-between and leader in the pupil's relations with the spirit government. Likewise, the ritual expert who conducts the merit-making ceremonies for an individual is called the teacher of this person because he explains the significance of the ceremony. This teacher-pupil relationship clearly reflects the central role of communication of knowledge in Iu Mien society.

But how efficient is this communication, for instance, in the economic sphere of life? I Kien's letter is clearly directed toward regulation of economic activities, because the size of bride-price is not fixed by *lej njej*, but belongs to the *phou tung* ("ordinary") category. My informants believe that the Iu Mien in Laos will follow the directives. Perhaps this will not happen at once, but after a few years everyone will conform "because everybody there has troubles with money now, and also, earlier [thirty to forty years ago], the prices of women in silver weight were just about what I Kien ordered. But of course silver had more value then." Compared with the current (1965) price level, the ordered reduction is more than 70 percent, if all costs of the ceremony are added together.

The Theory of Action and the Potential for Adaptation. Success (*meeng nuung haj*) is believed to result from intelligent adjustments with regard to the power relationships dominating particular situations. The general idea is one of flexible adaptation to the demands of the powers (*liing*), while safeguarding one's own vital interests. The principles for action-orientation are formed in terms of the advancement of the individual on the two levels of existence: the world of men and the world of spirits, from which the soul of the individual comes and where it returns at his death. In theory, everything else is either instrumental or an obstruction to the individual's advance.

This individual-centered approach is clearly expressed in the idea that in the afterlife in the spirit world everyone—man and woman alike—has an individual house and is unaffected by sentimental attachments.

With these notions in mind it may be easier to understand why the Iu Mien are so articulate in their approach to problems of adaptation. The individual is left to care for himself in a competitive, production-oriented social environment. If disruptive conflicts are to be avoided, there must be communication of general but efficient principles of adaptation. This in turn means that the rational, empirical element can be expected to be prominent in representations of the nature of the universe. Thus, as has already been pointed out, the ideal state—the successful achievement of adaptation to fundamental power relationships— is conceived as one where sentimental attachments are lacking.

Like all models of complex systems, the world view of the Iu Mien is a simplification and does not account for all the observable processes taking place in a given social and ecological situation. The principles of action referred to as "institutionalized politeness," *phou tung*, and *lej fing* are thus complementary to the general long-term principles of action, *lej njej*. The *lej njej* tradition is considered invariant, because it is assumed to correspond to the true nature of the situation of man in the universe, seen from long-term perspective. At the same time, *lej fing* tradition is considered to be the intelligent approach to problems of adaptation in a changing political environment. *Lej njej* refers to stable power relationships, and, ultimately, it is an elaboration of empirical knowledge about death, disease, and loss as inevitable elements of human existence.

I believe that in its present formulation the *lej njej* of the Iu Mien may be an elaboration of an earlier experience of drastic changes in political power relationships that occurred in the past as a result of confrontation with the Chinese imperial political system. The Iu Mien socio-economic-ritual system, which operates on the premise that an intelligent adaptation to changing power conditions is possible and necessary, is well armed to deal with more powerful political-social systems.

According to Iu Mien beliefs, spirits do everything backward compared with men. They eat food raw, instead of cooked; they are stupid, while men are clever; they are strong, while men are weak; and finally they are free of sentimental attachments, while men are not. But the appreciation of money is a common denominator between men and spirits. The world view of the Iu Mien is an explanation of the processes of life in terms of complementary oppositions. This is a dialectical method of reasoning, in which the contradictions are resolved in the notion of human action directed toward its own advancement, achieved through the use of a generally approved standard of value. Thus the notions of power, security, and value cannot be applied separately when describing the behavior of the Iu Mien because ultimately they refer to the same thing, survival.

POLITICAL BEHAVIOR

Village and Household in Iu Mien Society. There is no formal rule that every Iu Mien settlement must have a headman. It is a matter of convenience whether a group of households chooses its own headman or prefers to ask a headman from some other village to take care of the *lej fing* side of communal life. The Iu Mien have a tendency to spread out into small hamlets, sometimes comprising only a few households. This is to some extent symptomatic of the concept of individual enterprise which is favored in their society. Individuals are always on the move searching for better opportunities, better soils, or a more convenient social climate. There is nothing special about the Iu Mien in this regard as compared with other ethnic groups living in the same hill regions; the pattern of settlement is in part conditioned by the ecological pattern of swidden agriculture.

In this setting it is common for residents of very small or poor settlements to ask the headman of a bigger, wealthier village to be their headman too. This is especially true if the headmen has a reputation of "good heart."

Because the matter of village political structure is a matter of *lej fing*, practical convenience in such factors as size of village, relative size and wealth of neighboring villages, reputation of headmen of neighboring villages, nature and extent of control exercised by state authorities, and the general social climate (for instance, whether there is a war going on) mean that decision-making in various villages may operate under radically different conditions. A small settlement in the war-ravaged region around Mung Sing in Laos cannot be expected to follow the same practices in selecting a headman as a large wealthy village in the region of Chiengkham, Thailand.

By saying that the village government is *lej fing*, the Iu Mien state explicitly that it does not matter how the collectivity of the households is managed as long as the operations of the households are not impeded. The village government is thought of as instrumental for the protection and preservation of the households, which are the basic production and ritual units.

There are some *lej njej* rules which affect the cohabitation of constituent households of a village. Nonconformance to these rules by a household or section of the village—for example, non-observance of the closing of the village to communications with the outside world as prescribed by the ceremonial calendar—is incompatible with co-residence. Thus in Thailand there have been instances where conversion to Christianity has resulted in the splitting of villages when the ritually opposed halves moved to a safe distance from one another. The *lej njej* rules apply to the village, not as a politically organized unit, but as an aggregate of households in common residence, which implies certain common ritual obligations. Because of common residence on the same mountain slope, all the households are subject to the same geomantic rules with regard to obligations toward a body of local spirits of earth and water, and these obligations must be fulfilled in accordance with the same ceremonial calendar. My informants stress that the constituent households cooperate in these ritual activities, but the political organization has no relevance to this cooperation. The households act as if they were free and independent of one another and only unite in a common desire to fulfill obligations to the spirits that have been contracted independently. These spirits are not connected with the ancestors, so clan membership or kinship relations do not affect these activities. The only exception is that sometimes the spirit leaders of the groups of ancestor spirits associated with particular households are supposed to act as intermediaries and witnesses when transactions are carried out with the local spirits.

In fact, *lej njej* ignores the village as a distinct category. For instance, there is no ritual village gate, nor a common playing ground, nor a communal house. Villagewide public works are not an institution of the Iu Mien. Economic cooperation is carried out by groups of cooperating households; it is not dependent on ritual or political cooperation. There is no clear notion of a common village territory. Distribution of fields is decided on the basis of informal negotiations between leaders of the households each year, and a general direction is agreed upon in which the fields are to be prepared.

With regard to the notion of village territory, the prevailing idea seems to be that if some households of a different ethnic group want to settle near the village, there are no formal obstacles (there are many informal ones) except that they are not allowed to occupy a place above the Iu Mien on the same mountain slope. This rule is strictly enforced and is founded on the same geomantic considerations as the rules regulating the relative location of the households of an Iu Mien settlement: no house is allowed to obstruct a clear line between any other house and the local spirit shrines which are located above the village.

The idea that the house (*peo*) is primary as compared with the village (*laang*) appears clearly in the Iu Mien ideas of the afterlife. The same geomantic principles as those followed for home sites are followed, and much more carefully, for grave sites (the spirit homes of the dead). Often large amounts of money are paid to Chinese geomancers for their services. It is believed that if the grave is favorably located, the ancestor's spirit will be respected by all other spirits, regardless of rank. Thus descendants born after the ancestor's death will be protected against attacks of bad spirits and will be helped by friendly spirits. They will be clever and rich.

The geomancy, in its present form, is clearly Chinese. Several well-informed Yunnanese state that Iu Mien geomancy is identical with that practiced in Yunnan before the present regime. Freedman (1958:77 ff.), on the basis of several literary sources, stresses the great importance attached to geomantic correctness of grave sites in southeastern China, motivated in exactly the same way as described to me by Yunnanese and Iu Mien informants.

In the spirit world, the Iu Mien believe, every individual has his or her own house. Husbands and wives have separate houses, although "at night, when nobody sees, they visit each other."[18] This idea of an individual spirit house reflects the importance attached to the position of "houseowner" (*peo tsiu*). The household is the main institution for the attainment of the dominant goal of individual action: wealth, particularly in the form of money. In this context, the village has no meaningful function except the short-term one of providing security against attack from other men.

Resolution of Conflicts Caused by Political Rivalry. Conflicts of political rivalry are usually solved in the following way. If a man strongly aspires to the office of headman, but fails to be chosen, he may start to break away from the village, alone or with a group of followers. But this process of fission is carefully restrained in order to minimize the risks of "throwing away face" and thus losing the possibility of returning if things do not turn out as hoped.

The split works as follows. The man who plans to found a new village and has selected a suitable place for it will not abruptly declare that he is moving away and invite others to come with him. Instead, he starts cautiously, building a small hut at the chosen place, calling it "a shelter that it has been necessary to erect at the distant field." Gradually he moves most of the things belonging to his household and is seldom seen in the old village. He has not yet made a formal move. If the site proves good, it may attract other households from his old village and perhaps from other villages. Thus, gradually, a new village community has come into existence, "and nobody knows when

---

[18] According to *lej njej*, sexual intercourse is incompatible with life in heaven, "the clean land."

they really moved." If calculations prove wrong, they slowly move their things back to the old village. "This they can do because they have not lost face by telling others that they were going to move away."

Of course, sometimes things do not work so smoothly. Open disputes may occur in a village, and a whole section may leave together, but manifest conflict seems exceptional among the Iu Mien.

The Iu Mien and Inter-Tribal Political Systems. Iu Mien governmental structures have gradually become parts of the administrative systems of Thailand and Laos. I have no information about the continued existence of the traditional systems in Yunnan, but it is probable that under the present regime these semi-feudal political structures built around local charismatic leaders no longer exist there.

The terminology given in this discussion is from Iu Mien sources and refers to principles of political organization that are, or have been, practiced by them. The existence of a common approach to political organization among the larger community of hill populations in this area is indicated by the existence of inter-tribal political structures. However, this paper is concerned primarily with the adaptation of one population, the Iu Mien.

Whatever similarities may exist between the socio-economic-ritual systems of the various "tribes," there is no common ideology or institution for the enforcement of a permanent supra-tribal political organization. Thus the alignments on this level are unstable and conditioned by changing realities of power politics in which the main contestants are individuals of established reputation. These realities are ultimately conditioned by pressures coming from more powerful and expansive power structures of the valley regions.

In this situation individuals may gain power and influence by cooperating with the external powers, who need agents for the control of the mountain regions. This is the secret of the careers of many Iu Mien political leaders who started as wealthy and respected village headmen and gradually secured their reputations by skillful mediation of conflicts in the mountains. In some cases they finally established themselves as semi-feudal princes over huge collections of villages with a wide range of

[615]

distinct socio-economic-ritual systems which were veritable multiple societies.

Before the extension of central governmental administration to mountain regions, governmental functions above the village level were carried out by persons who held office as high-level peacemakers and mediators. It was common for such a political system to be created and maintained by such a peacemaker and to include elements from different ethnic groups.

The *tum tao mien* ("big headman") carried out his functions as mediator and peacemaker (*hoo si mien*) within a group of villages (*tsaang laang haa laang*, "upper villages, lower villages"). Several such groups could be combined into larger units under top-level chiefs (*tsuang tsi*, lit. "owner of the whole").

The constituent village (*laang*) headmen (*fiu tao mien*, "small headmen") were often chosen and appointed by the high-level headman.

The *tum tao mien* was assisted by the "helping man," usually a brother or son who was not a headman in his own right, but who often became his successor. The system was broken up if some of the constituent villages preferred another *tum tao mien* after his death. Thus the combinations of villages were not stable, but varied with the attraction of individuals of greater or smaller reputation and with the power delegated by them by the dominant political powers of the valleys.

The institution of *tum tao mien* was not limited to the Iu Mien population. High-level Iu Mien headmen have been recognized, and in some cases are still recognized, by populations with different socio-economic-ritual systems. The terminology used in such cases is different, but the leadership exercised by the Iu Mien headmen is the same.

Some Iu Mien chiefs have exercised authority over wide areas and received titles indicating their relations to external governmental structures. Uen Tsoe, a *tum tao mien* whose government title was Phya Luang, was a notable case. When he died about twenty years ago, his authority was recognized by more than a hundred villages associated with seven different socio-economic systems (Iu Mien, Lanten, Akha, Khamu, Meo, Lahu, and Kato) located in the Mung Phon-Mung Mang area of Yunnan and the

[616]

Mung Sing-Nam Tha area of Laos. He gained his position on the basis of his personal qualities, the prestige of his ancestors (several of whom had been distinguished high-level headmen), and through his competence as a skillful mediator with the French colonial regime. Two of his sons, Tseu I Fu (government title *Chao Mai*) and Tseu I Kien (government title *Chao La*), are now important high-level headmen in northern Laos, holding positions in the administration of the Royal Lao Government.

Likewise in Thailand Iu Mien men have been *kamnan* (headman) of a *tambon* or "commune" including Iu Mien villages and Meo villages in Amphur Pong, Chiengrai Province. This is an old pattern, as one of the headmen is said to have held the same position, with a government title of *Phya*, for forty years. In turn, his father, Tang Tsan Khuen, is said to have been a *tum tao mien* in the Luang Prabang region of Laos for about fifty years.

The Iu Mien in Laos did not always belong to systems where the high-level headman was Iu Mien. Sometimes Iu Mien villages had Meo or Lahu chiefs. This illustrates the Iu Mien attitude with regard to political power, expressed in *lej fing* tradition. Villages or village segments that move in search of better soils or more congenial social climates conform to the prevailing power structure of the area into which they enter.

I have investigated the questions of qualifications of high-level headmen and the processes by which they attain office, relying on information from I Fu, I Kien, Uen Lin, and others. When a man is in trouble, he will consult a ritual expert if the problem is believed to originate in a conflict in relations with the spirits. But if the difficulties are caused by disturbed relations with men, a man with a reputation for knowledge and ability will be consulted. The person, or persons, in trouble will give a sum of money to the peacemaker (*hoo si mien*) and ask for his services as mediator. If the mediator is successful, more people will request his help, and his reputation will grow. By traveling on business or pleasure trips and talking with many people, by displaying his intelligence and knowledge, his reputation will spread even more. In due time, as a result of his reputation, he will be appointed headman by some high-level chief. Eventually, when his reputation has become very great, a group of "small headmen" will invite him to be their *tum tao mien*. Wherever such a man goes, his reputation will precede him, and he will always have a position of authority.

Competence in solving inter-personal conflicts, which is the starting point for a political career, is demonstrated only in part by actual deeds. Actual accomplishments are essential, but the reputation of a person's ancestors is also important for building the confidence so essential to a headman's career. Descent does not give any particular right to an office, but is is commonly believed that if the ancestors were "good" then their descendants will probably be "good" as well. The basis for this belief is the notion that the soul of the child is led to its parents by the ancestor spirits. If the ancestor spirits are good and intelligent, they will not recruit spirits of bad quality, because if they do, they themselves will suffer as the child grows up to neglect his duties to his ancestors. A man who does not respect his obligations to the spirits is necessarily an unreliable man. The rights of spirits and the rights of man are blended in the sense that the most imperative obligations between living men have ritual motivations. A man whose spirit has been selected by the spirits of persons who proved themselves reliable during their lifetime seems therefore a good choice. The past deeds of the individual reinforce this judgment.

In this context the quality of the ancestors is not judged on the basis of their presumed status in the spirit world (achieved by merit-making) but on the basis of what they accomplished during their life in the world of men. Because the merit-making system is a standard open to all, the true quality of a man cannot be determined on the basis of his ancestors' merit. It is thus not surprising that descent lines whose ancestors included many high-level officeholders sometimes keep special records of the political positions of the ancestors. Such records are distinct from the genealogies used in ritual.

In all maneuvering for positions of power and influence, wealth, particularly money, is essential. The office of a high-level headman is no exception. His position is, to an important extent, the combined result of his own and his ancestors' capacity to spend. There is a definite tendency among the Iu Mien for political offices to be allocated to people of lineages whose members have previously held similar offices. In part this happens because men who are in office often use their sons or brothers as assistants, and thus the latter are in a good position to build the necessary reputation. Also, the brother or son will capitalize heavily on the prestige of his relative. Among the Iu Mien, as among more highly organized states, the incumbent administration is usually in a favorable position at the time of succession. There is also the reinforcing factor of accumulated capital of silver or money, as well as the fear that this inspires. Thus, in spite of the absence of formal rules for the recruitment of high-level headmen, the offices tend to be occupied by persons from certain lineages because of their privileged positions, accumulated capital, and favorable ancestors.

This tendency is further reinforced by the role of high-level chiefs as mediators for the central government. Through allocation of government titles which are sometimes hereditary, and through the additional prestige gained by delegating to relatives the powers of command of the government office, some lines of descent attain positions that are doubly supported. They are reinforced on the one hand through factors which are effective in the value structure of the hill society (or societies) and on the other hand through the policies of the political structures of the valley societies which tend to continue, with sons or brothers, the forms of cooperation that have already proved useful. One reason for this policy is simply the lack of alternatives; there is also the fact that sons and brothers of a "government man" get introduced to the relevant authorities.

The monopolization of the channels of communication with the valley governments is further reinforced by the seemingly common attitude among hill people of fear and frustration dictated by their ignorance of the ways of the valley people. The hill people, who think of themselves as simple and honest, think of valley people as being clever. In such situations a man who can communicate with the government agencies is relied upon heavily.

Phya Luang Uen Tsoe is a good example of this process. His father, and many ancestors, had been important *tum tao mien.* He was intelligent and rich, had a "good heart," and helped the hill people and the French government. At that time the hill people were scared of government officials and were often in difficulties when they had to deal with them. Uen Tsoe spoke for the hill people, and he also helped the French defeat the Akha, who did not obey the government.

Relations with valley government authorities have been continued by his two sons. Their titles, *Chao Mai* and *Chao La*, are said by my informants to be hereditary and to belong to the older and younger son of a *Phya Luang*. There are similar examples in Thailand.

The Compatibility of Various Hill Societies and the Terms "Hill People" and "Valley People" as Meaningful Categories. We shall now consider some of the non-political aspects of relationships among the various hill populations, and between them and the valley peoples. During my research I have heard statements concerning the relative ease with which different kinds of communities are able to co-exist in close proximity. The statements often refer to the relative permissiveness of the various social systems. For instance, it has been commonly agreed that "the Akha forbid much, the Iu Mien less, and the Lahu very little."

This statement was made in Ban Chaguoo, a Red Lahu village in Amphur Maechan, Chiengrai Province, during a discussion among nine Red Lahu men, my Iu Mien interpreter, and myself. The starting point of the discussion was the following event, told to me by the headman, Chaguoo, in the course of his life story.

> In Huej Mukhang I became headman and stayed ten years. I was nominated when there were twenty-four houses in the village. Before that there was no headman. I first lived there alone with my household for one year. Then my relatives arrived, and thereafter, the others. In the end two Akha villages (Ban Adju and Ban Saen Chaj) came and settled down quite near. For two years they lived close together, but it became very difficult in the long run because the Akha forbid all kinds of things. The customs do not fit together. And also there were not enough fields. Therefore the whole village moved to Huej Chaj . . . .

Similar statements have been made by several Iu Mien and Akha informants, and a similar order of cultural incompatibility is suggested by other research workers (e.g. Bennington-Cornell

[620]

Survey 1964; Ministry of Interior 1962). It is an important subject for systematic research to investigate the internal consistency of the various traditions of what might be called "the greater hill society," and to see whether there is a common attitude among the hill populations toward the valley populations.

For example, the general categories "hill people" (*jɔm bung mien*) and "plains people" (*jɔm pɛɛng mien* or *jɔm mung mien*) occur in the Iu Mien creation myth.

> . . . Then the man cut the fruit into small pieces as he had been told. But he got mixed up, and threw the seeds on the plain, and the pieces of the fruit on the mountains. Therefore, there are many people on the plain, and very few in the mountains . . . . But, as the saying goes, "the hill people are better" [referring to them as the meat of the fruit].

One common distinction between mountain and valley is based on literacy. Books, in this context, are symbols of prestige and power. My Akha and Red Lahu informants say that both of these groups used to have books. Books made of rice were given to the Lahu by the creator-god, but the people ate them because they were too heavy to carry around. The Akha say that the dogs ate their books. Among the Akha of the Maechan area it seems that literacy is associated with ideas of economic and political domination, as indicated in the following paragraph.

About ten years ago the well-known Akha chief, Saen Chaj, had a reputation as a "strong man." For various reasons many Akha, Lahu, and Iu Mien villages sought his protection. Much to their surprise, he did not want to be connected with any of the Iu Mien. He is said to have remarked: "I don't want to have the Yao. They have books, and sooner or later, they will give trouble. You cannot control them."

The progressive-minded Iu Mien are well aware, and proud, of the fact that they differ from the other hill people (except their "younger brothers," the Lanten) because they have books. But they still consider themselves inferior to the lowlanders and to some other hill peoples, for example the Meo in Laos. "The Yao have their own books, but few read them. The Meo in Laos have no books of their own, but still they send their children to schools where they learn to read and write and speak an important foreign language."

EFFECTS OF FORCED ADMINISTRATIVE INTEGRATION:
A COMPARISON OF IU MIEN AND LAMET

One of the basic assumptions which the Iu Mien hold about social relationships is the notion of reciprocal rights and obligations, created on a contractual basis. The idea of the Iu Mien community, as a united whole, is phrased in terms of common obligations contracted by common ancestors to one of the creator-gods, Pien Hung. The idea of correct fulfillment of mutual obligations permeates Iu Mien social relations and has its ritual counterpart in the regular feeding of ancestor spirits.

The idea of the spirit government is associated with the idea of an objective merit system for advancement in the spirit level of existence. Positions in the hierarchy are reached through merit-making ceremonies for individuals, carried out under strictly controlled circumstances.

Given the historical background of the Iu Mien, there is little doubt that the idea of a central government of the spirit world, which offers complete security, is the projection of an idealized view of the traditional imperial administration of China (cf., for example, the description of Yang 1961). Even the painted images of the eighteen great spirits depict these dignitaries in traditional Chinese dress.

Because of the lack of relevant documentation, it is not possible to state the history of *lej njej* and *lej fing* traditions. But if we consider the preoccupation of the Iu Mien with the individual accumulation of wealth, and particularly the importance placed by *lej njej* on money, it is obvious that the Iu Mien's ecological position makes the achievement of the necessary surplus a matter of strenuous efforts by a well-disciplined production team. Personal initiative and mobility are of utmost importance in this context. Often this means that individual households, or small aggregates of households, enter into the spheres of various previously established power structures, and they must either adapt themselves to the demands of these power structures or leave.

The stress on individual accumulation of wealth is clearly an obstacle to the formation of larger and more politically potent production units. The frequently expressed desire to "make it big, to be strong" is usually frustrated by the difficulty a leader has in imposing discipline and keeping a large slice of the profits in a situation where everyone wants to have as much as possible for himself. As soon as an individual thinks he can enrich himself faster on his own, he will either try to impose himself as the leader (in order to get control of the purse-strings), or he will quit the household. His ritual obligations to his parents do not necessarily oblige him to stay in their house.

In this kind of a social setting the rational approach, expressed in the *lej fing* tradition, seems to be the one used in most situations affected by power relationships.

The Lamet, described by K. G. Izikowitz (1951:85–142, 294–355), have an ecology and social system similar to those of the Iu Mien in many ways. One striking similarity is found in the role of certain categories of wealth as a dominant goal for individuals—and the association of these forms of wealth with positions of power and influence in the community. With the Iu Mien the goal is silver; with the Lamet it is buffaloes and bronze drums. In both societies the household is instrumental in achieving the necessary surplus, and in both cases individuals must be highly mobile in search of profitable opportunities for the acquisition of wealth. The Iu Mien engage in extensive trade, and the Lamet (as described before World War II) earn salaries by working in distant places like the Siamese teak forests.

In both systems power and influence are in the hands of the rich. However, these people do not constitute a distinct class in the society among the Iu Mien as they do among the Lamet, where they are ritually initiated into a class called *lem*. In both societies the preferred form of wealth has ritual functions.

There are also important differences: the preferred form of wealth of the Lamet has less universal application as a medium of exchange in relationships between men than does the preferred form of wealth among the Iu Mien. It is not quite clear from Izikowitz' description whether the preferred wealth of the Lamet is explicitly thought of as a medium of exchange with the spirits or whether its efficiency lies in the fact that the spirits like them. It is rather evident that some sort of exchange is involved with regard to buffaloes, but there is no clear explanation of the role of the bronze drums. The circumstances in which the drums are used suggests that they are employed as instruments for the propitiation of spirits in the same way as the Iu Mien use music, dancing, and recital. Among the Iu Mien the spirits, particularly the eighteen members of the spirit government, are supposed to like silver.

Izikowitz stresses that the *lem* have no formal prerogatives in daily life—they are just generally respected, and their influence is based on respect. Thus their situation is similar to that of the rich men among the Iu Mien who are feared and also respected because they have silver. The Iu Mien spirits like silver, and therefore silver is associated with the idea of virtue or cleanliness. "Silver makes things clean," they say, and they pay fines with silver "to wash the face of someone." Because silver gives capacity to act, rich men are feared, and this gives them a position of power and importance.

The important thing about the Iu Mien form of preferred wealth is that it gives them possibilities of operating in other social contexts: silver is used and accepted by everyone. The preferred wealth of the Lamet has a more limited field of application.

There is an important difference between Iu Mien and Lamet world views. The most important spirits of the Lamet are their ancestor spirits, while the governors of the Iu Mien spirit world are the non-ancestral dignitaries of the spirit government. The merit-making ceremonies of the Lamet are directed toward their ancestor spirits, while among the Iu Mien they are oriented toward the spirit government. Among the Iu Mien the feeding of the ancestor spirits is a very important ritual, but it is done to fulfill an obligation, while the merit-making ceremonies are held to insure certain rights for the individual in his future life. According to the Iu Mien, the ancestor spirits are not strong enough to provide security in the spirit world, where ultimate power is in the hands of the spirit government.

Perhaps before the Chinese conquest the Iu Mien had a socio-economic-ritual system similar to that of the Lamet. Because of the prestige of Chinese political power and culture, silver was substituted for buffaloes, bronze drums, or similar objects vested with symbolic value. At the same time, the merit-making ceremonies were re-directed from the relatively impotent ancestors to a government of the spirit world which had brought the ancestor spirits under control in the same way as the Chinese imperial government had brought the living generations of Iu Mien under control.

Although this is a purely theoretical reconstruction, it seems plausible enough to form a basis for research in the historical sources. In any case, it would be difficult to explain how the Chinese script and ritual language would have become an element of the *lej njej* tradition without assuming a period of strict Chinese political control and close contact with Chinese culture.

Chinese influence on the Iu Mien socio-economic-ritual system has been of great importance. But this does not mean that the Iu Mien *are* Chinese or that they have any particular attachment to modern Chinese culture.[19] Archaic literary Chinese, mixed with Yao in ritual, and the writing system belong to the *lej njej* tradition and are considered to be central to the Iu Mien social scheme. But this situation is roughly comparable to the use of Church Latin or Pali in the modern world. Spoken Chinese (Yunnanese) is still widely used as a trade language, but is maintained only for commercial reasons. The most significant contributions from Chinese traditional culture seem to be the idea of a central government of the spirit world and the money economy.

DEVELOPMENT PROJECTS AND SOCIAL SCIENCE RESEARCH

The practical use of information furnished by sociological research requires that it refer to reality, and not just to a construction that may be of interest for pure research but useless as a working tool for the formulation of concrete administrative policies. There is also the question of the relevance of the information to the problems that the development agencies are working with at a given moment. Some problems could be overcome if the research workers were informed about current development policies and if the technical language used in research reports were translated into terminology more familiar to non-specialists. The part that gets lost in translation (if the translation

[19] There is little hope of rediscovering ancient Chinese social patterns in the contemporary Iu Mien system. The ecological conditions of Iu Mien life impose definite limitations on the possibility of conforming to "traditional" Chinese practices.

[625]

is done competently) will not be important compared with what is gained in increased efficiency of planning. Nonetheless, various difficulties seem to be almost endemic in the relationships between social science research and programs directed toward the rapid solution of concrete problems.

Relevance of Social-Anthropological Research to Directed Social Change. The motivation for far-reaching intervention in the social, economic, and cultural life of various minorities comes both from a need to promote national security and from a concern for reform and improvement of living conditions. In some cases these interventions have produced disastrous results and have created more problems than they were meant to solve.

Perhaps more efficient approaches could have been found if the policies were based on relevant information about the social, economic, and cultural realities of the situation. But the usual anthropological monographs and doctoral dissertations are not much help in constructing policies. How can these faults be remedied?

It seems reasonable to assume that those who make integration policies are interested in attaining their goals with minimum time, effort, and expense. It also seems reasonable that they would try to use to their own advantage the conditions prevailing in the minority groups. If they are not interested in smashing doors that are already open (although this sometimes happens), then they should be interested in the adaptive mechanisms of the community which they wish to integrate.

Crash programs are rarely successful. They usually seem to result from three factors: urgent need, lack of time, and deficient information, which excludes the possibility of a more differentiated and less destructive approach. Even if the ultimate goal is a socially and culturally homogeneous society rather than a multiple society (though this goal in itself may be unrealistic), the policy-makers cannot be expected to welcome an element of the population consisting of socially badly adapted persons who may become a serious burden.

The notion of balanced growth which is, to some extent, always present in planning for economic development, is certainly relevant in the context of nation-building. It is just here that intimate knowledge of the adaptive mechanisms of the various socio-economic-ritual systems which are to be combined to form an integrated whole is of greatest importance.

Unfortunately, as Fredrik Barth has recently pointed out, the problems of adaptation have been treated rather one-sidedly in the anthropological literature. Too frequently these things have been forgotten: "Firstly, that an adaptation involves people not only in a relationship with the natural environment, but also in relations of competition, cooperation, and symbiosis with each other which may profoundly influence the structure and distribution of groups. Secondly, that in human adaptation cultural factors such as systems of politics and property, and demographic factors, are as vitally involved as are the more commonly considered technological factors" (Barth 1964:15–22).

The problems discussed in the present volume are mainly problems of mutual adaptation of different social, economic, and ritual systems. On the basis of data that are now available concerning the other social systems of the region where I am carrying out research, the Iu Mien seem quite exceptional for their differentiated and explicitly formulated approach to various categories of problems of adaptation. However, I doubt that there is really a basic contrast. It may well be that we are simply short of relevant information, for reasons indicated by Barth.

Among the Iu Mien, I have investigated the range and character of adaptive techniques by systematic questioning. I would have remained relatively ignorant of the existence of these theories of action had I relied only on the techniques of participant observation and the recollections of informants concerning past events. Perhaps it is not surprising that once I had been informed about the adaptive techniques of the Iu Mien, I quickly discovered a similar differentiated approach (though not so systematically verbalized) among the population associated with the Akha socio-economic-ritual system.

The Akha have a body of formal rules, analogous to the *lej njej* of the Iu Mien, pertaining to general ritual activity, called *ne tu thuu* ("feeding the spirits"). These rules are considered invariable, and the social organization owes its stability to their enforcement. While the Iu Mien have a verbally articulated tradition of adaptive techniques to be used in relations with political powers (*lej fing*), such a verbal tradition seems to be absent among the Akha. However, in their village communities they have a political institution, an office charged with external political relations, called *nangεε*. I have been told that this institution can be found in every Akha village. There is in addition another functionary called *djumaꞁ*, who is the founder, or close patrilineal relative of the founder, of the village. He is the leader of the ritually determined village activities involving economic cooperation. Besides these two offices there are the separate functions of ritual expert and smith. All four of these functions may be carried out by the same person, but the method of recruitment is different for each office.

Knowledge of the existence of these offices will undoubtedly help those who need to approach Akha communities in order to secure economic or political cooperation. Cooperation should be sought from *all* key persons, not only from the *nangεε*. He is the official contact man with regard to outsiders, but in this capacity he is not in a position to impose his personal policy on the population of the village except by methods of force. Unfortunately, confused ideas about the leadership patterns in Akha communities have led to the failure of many action programs and have resulted in some unnecessary frustrations and bad feelings.

But the leadership pattern only makes sense if it is seen as the application of a theory of action or adaptation. Therefore it seems to me that the principles of planning for the future, upon which the various groups base their activities, are proper subjects for study and have practical value in social science research for directed social change.

Anthropologists sometimes tend to look at the communities they study as if they were closed systems, and therefore they rely too much on the technique of participant observation. If applied too one-sidedly, this technique is bound to be self-defeating because the processes of rapid change have already started to make an impact on people's knowledge concerning the total environment. These processes of change have altered the previously stable bases on which members of communities used to be able to plan their lives and activities in consistent patterns. Under these changed conditions it would seem more realistic to inquire into ambitions and plans for future activities rather than to rely on a one- or two-year period of just observing what the people do. Because of the rapid development of communications which feed in new information, traditional frameworks also sometimes appear more clearly in the conflicts created in the thinking and planning of the individual than they would appear in externally observable actions.

It seems commonly agreed that one of the main objects of social science is to produce predictive models of social systems. In order to do this, the research worker must pay particular attention to the views that the members of the community under study have of the future. The accuracy of these expectations should be compared with the better-informed guesses of the observer about changes which can be expected in the total environment. This has not been the orthodox approach in social or cultural anthropology, although it is more common in economics and sociology. It can be hoped that the integration of the social sciences will occur faster than the growth of the problems of integration of minority groups.

A Short Iu Mien Social Grammar for Practical Use. As I pointed out in the beginning of this paper, I have not proposed concrete action programs. But I can offer a few general "rules of thumb" that might be useful for those who plan or carry out action programs among the Iu Mien or "Yao."

1. Changes that increase money-making capacity are welcomed.

2. Changes that decrease money-making capacity are strongly resisted because the Iu Mien measure the individual's chances to survive and succeed in terms of his money-making ability. This concept belongs to their religious tradition, *lej njej.*

3. Change in religious practices prescribed by the *lej njej* tradition will affect the social organization and the motivations that have made the Iu Mien in their present environment a disciplined, hardworking people, mainly interested in the peaceful accumulation of wealth, particularly in the form of money.

4. Political government is a matter of practical adaptation of the basic productive and ritual unit, the household, to the demands of external political powers. In the present situation, this means adaptation to central government agencies. The word *lej* means "custom" or "tradition," and the term *fing* is used by

[629]

the Iu Mien to indicate that they consciously and systematically seek good relationships with governments.

5. In all inter-personal and inter-group relations, the Iu Mien consciously and systematically try to avoid involvement in open conflicts. If they do get involved in conflct, it means that the matter is of vital interest to them. They attach extreme importance to the correct fulfillment of mutual rights and obligations.

6. Production techniques are governed only by considerations of efficiency. Thus the Iu Mien can be expected to be interested in all technical innovations that promise to increase their production and thereby their income.

7. The location of settlements in the hills is governed by strict religious rules. No other settlements should be established on the same mountain slope above an Iu Mien settlement without careful consultation with the Iu Mien villagers, especially their religious experts. The rules governing the location of settlements do not prescribe that the Iu Mien must necessarily live in the mountains. When they move down on the plains, the geomantic rules no longer apply because there are no mountains. The rules are not replaced with other ritual regulations concerning the location of settlements on the plains.

8. While Christianity is incompatible with the Iu Mien religious tradition, in the sense that a person cannot subscribe to both these religions at the same time, there is no such opposition, at present, between Iu Mien religious beliefs and the teachings of Gautama Buddha.

Suggestions for Improving the Yield of Field-Work Projects. It may be evident from what I have already said that I do not consider the survey method as a very useful device to advance our knowledge of the adaptive techniques of various populations. Neither do I believe that the time is ripe to organize social-anthropological field work on a team basis, though the idea of large laboratory-like settings for social science is very attractive to me. Unfortunately, at present most research workers seem to guard their own small fields of study jealously, and it is not easy to see how this situation could be changed rapidly.

The basic problem is, of course, that everyone wants to develop his own data and the implications of these data to the fullest extent possible. While nobody is unhappy to get information which helps them along in their own research, few are ready to furnish others with unpublished data or ideas. This means that the exchange of really stimulating ideas is indeed a slow process. Whatever may be the true interests of science, these are the rules of the merit-making system in the world of the anthropologists, and they must be reckoned with when planning reform of the working conditions of the research workers.

Under the circumstances, the most efficient research organization for anthropology still seems to be the individual field worker with his native tutors. However, his efficiency would be improved if he had the opportunity for rapid publication and thus could establish a claim on his findings. As it is now, it may be years before the information is published: the advance of the science is retarded, and the practical usefulness of research is diminished. If a research worker by his own choice waits for years before publishing the results of field work, then the expenses of his activities may not be justified. But I believe if facilities for publication (including adequate research libraries) were available in the countries where much research is done, then the ratio of the input of time and money for field projects to the output of valuable data would be more reasonable.

Because I am working in Thailand and particularly concerned with problems of research there, I would suggest that high priority be given to the establishment of a reasonably complete research library at the Hill Tribe Research Centre in Chiengmai. This library should include first of all the most important periodicals of social science, particularly those oriented toward the integration of various branches of the social sciences, as well as the classics of social anthropology. The information services of various countries, the United Nations agencies like UNESCO and ECAFE, should be interested in extending their activities in this direction.

It now seems commonly agreed that social science research can give valuable assistance to the developing countries. If this is so, the research workers should be given the practical facilities to formulate and disseminate their findings.

APPENDIX ON THE MOBILITY OF INDIVIDUALS AND SETTLEMENTS

Three kinds of data are illustrated here in order to show the extent of geographical and genealogical knowledge of the Iu

Mien and the degree to which their connections with other areas remain important to them.

1. Genealogy from Ban Lao Tsii Khuen (Phalae), Maechan, Thailand. The following patrilineal genealogy gives the spirit names of the ancestors, their titles (achieved in feasts of merit), and location of burial place. The genealogy indicates the movement of this lineage from Kwangtung (southeastern China) to Northeastern Thailand. The first name in each group is the spirit name of a male ancestor; the name(s) of wife (wives) follow. The first name gives the *fing* (clan) of the ancestor, held on the individual's behalf with respect to the spirit government. Thus ancestor No. 1 (the oldest) belongs to the Tang *fing*, and

TABLE 22
THE GENEALOGY OF TANG FU HIN

Gener- ation	Name (Clan, Spirit Name, Merit Title)	Location of Ancestor's Grave
1.	Tang Tseng Jet Loong	China: Kwangtung
	Pung Sii Jet Njaang	" "
2.	Tang Tsin Jet Loong	China: Kwangsi
	Tseu Sii Njej Njaang	" "
3.	Tang Tsoe Jet Loong	" "
	Tseu Sii Jet Njaang	" "
	Tang Sii Fam Njaang	" "
4.	Tang Liang Fej Loong	" "
	Tang Sii Jet Njaang	" "
5.	Tang Seng Jet Loong	" "
	Tang Sii Fej Njaang	" "
6.	Tang Hjaang Njej Loong	" "
	Tseu Sii Fam Njaang	China: Yunnan
7.	Tang Meng Fej Loong	" "
	Pung Si Njej Njaang	" "
8.	Tang Kiem Fej Loong	North Vietnam (?): Mung Soo
	Tang Sii Njej Njaang	North Vietnam (?): Mung Tin
	Lej Sii Njej Njaang	North Vietnam (?): Mung Tsung
9.	Tang Fa Liem	Laos: Mung Than
	Tseu Sii Tsie	Laos: Mung Lung
	Jang Sii Tsie	Laos: Mung Singh
10.	Tang Fa Tong	Laos: Nam Liang
	Tang Sii Tsie	Laos: Nam Khea
11.	Tang Fa Tsing	(Originally from Nong Tao, Muong Meung, Houei Sai, Laos; now living at Phalae, Thailand)
	Wife (still alive)	—
12.	Tang Fu Hin	(Living at Phalae, Thailand)

his wife belongs to the Pung. "Loong" indicates that he has made one of the higher and more expensive merit ceremonies, and for the same reason "Njaang" is added to his wife's name. Burial place is given after each name.

It is interesting to note that all the persons starting with Tang Fa Liem (No. 9) have only made the basic and cheapest merit ceremony. This is indicated by the word "Fa" for the men and the word "Sii" for their wives.

Because of the lack of maps, I have been unable to locate such place names as Mung Soo, Mung Tin, Nam Tsung, and Ming Than. My informants guess that they are in Vietnam.

2. *The Life Story of an Old Man.* X, who at seventy-three is the oldest male in Phalae, was born in Yunnan. When he was twelve years old, his father died, and one of his elder brothers became head of the household. One year later this brother also died, and their mother became head. She was then forty years old. Two years later his mother married again, and the new husband came to live in her house. She continued to be head.

X married for the first time at the age of twenty-five. He paid his wife's parents four and one-half taang* silver. He made the small marriage ceremony (the cheaper variant of the marriage ritual). He was then living in the village Huaj Palang, Mung Laa, Yunnan.

After his marriage he became household head. The following persons then lived in his house: (1) X himself; (2) his wife; (3) his mother; and (4) one son (now dead).

He became "small spirit doctor" when he still lived in Huaj Palang.

Six years after his first marriage he left Huaj Palang and moved to Nam Jong, Houei Sai, Laos. Five houses moved together. They reached Nam Jong after three days. They left Huaj Palang because the soil had become too exhausted for poppy cultivation. The elder brother of his wife led them. There was already one Yao house in Nam Jong when they arrived there.

He stayed in Nam Jong about ten years. He got no more children, and therefore he took one more wife. He paid seven and one-half taang silver for her. He gave four taang first and paid the rest during the following three years.

* Present value, one taang = 300 baht (Thai) = U.S. $15.00

Then the big headman, Kuej Tsou, called him to be headman in the village of Pha Bat, which had ten Yao houses. At the same time he became headman for seven Meo villages. In Pha Bat he also became "big spirit doctor."

He was headman in Pha Bat for six years. However, when his only son died, he did not want to stay there any longer, and he moved to the village of Mon Then Loo, Mung Paleo, in Kengtung, Burma. Thereafter he moved to the village Huaj Sang, Muong Meung, Houei Sai, Laos, where he stayed for four years. Then he moved back to Pha Bat and stayed there one year. His next move was to the village Huaj Maag, Maechan, Chiengrai, Thailand. After four years he moved to Phalae. This was fourteen years ago.

His first wife is still living with him in Phalae. The second wife left him and married a second time. With his second wife he had four children: (1) a son, who left with his mother; (2) a daughter, who married a man from Phalae (price: four taang silver, plus work for seven years); (3) a daughter, who married a Haw (Yunnanese) (earlier she had been married to a Yao, whom she left—X does not know where she is now); (4) a daughter who is staying with him.

Persons now living in the house include: (1) X himself; (2) his first wife, now age seventy-two; (3) a daughter from his second wife (who left him); and (4) the five-year-old son of this daughter (who has no father).

X has had very bad experiences buying children. When he still lived in Yunnan, he could not buy any because they were so difficult to get. Later on he bought, in all, six small children, who all died.

X's father was a smith, and his grandfather was big headman in Mung Saj, Yunnan, for an unspecified number of Yao, Meo, and Khmu? villages.

3. *Movements of a Forty-five-year-old Informant.* Y was born in Nam Kha village (now abandoned), Muong Meung, Houei Sai, Laos. He stayed there during the first eight years of his life. His father was big spirit doctor and high level headman over a number of Yao, Meo, and Lahu villages.

Y was eight years old when his father decided to move. There were then more than twenty houses in Nam Kha Village. Four

houses moved with the headman to Huaj Ho, Muong Meung
in Houei Sai, Laos (walking distance: half a day). (Y occasionally visits Huaj Ho, which now contains about fifteen houses.)
About fifteen houses went with a younger brother of the headman to Nong Tao (walking distance: one-half day to Nam Kha
and four hours to Huaj Ho).

When Y and his father arrived in Huaj Ho for the first time,
there were already over thirty houses in the village. Y's father
continued to be big headman as before. However, another man,
who lived there already, was small headman over this particular
village.

When Y was eleven, he moved to Huaj Sang, Muong Meung,
Houei Sai, Laos, a village of about ten houses now. This village
was founded by Y's father, who had found good soil not far
from Huaj Ho. He moved there with three households, all of
them relatives. Two years later there were about thirty houses
in the village. Y's father until he died continued to be headman
of the village and the big headman at the same time. At the
death of his father, Y, who was then twenty-four years old, took
over the functions of headman together with his eldest brother.
His mother, however, was leader of the household to which he
belonged.

When Y was thirty years old (about 1950), military operations
were carried out in the region, making living conditions very
difficult. Often Y and his family had to hide in the jungle.

Then together with a son of his father's younger brother and
another man, both from Nong Tao, he went to Thailand in order
to investigate possibilities of settling there. They found a suitable
place in Phalae (Ban Lao Tsii Khuen), Amphur Maechan. Thereafter Y's household from Huaj Sang and nine other households
from Nong Tao came to prepare the fields. Later on, houses
moved in from a number of other villages.

During his stay in Huaj Sang, Y visited the following Yao
villages for trading, as a spirit doctor, or "just for fun" (he also
visited a considerable number of villages belonging to other
ethnic groups): 1) Nam Kha and 2) Huaj Ho (which have already been mentioned); 3) Nam Hak, Mung Palaeu, Kengtung
(Burma)—walking distance from Huaj Sang, two days; 4) Siao
Nung Tao, Kentung, three-day walk; 5) Nam Tin, Mung Singh

(Laos), five-day walk; 6) Nam Oon, Mung Singh, four-day walk; 7) Chien San, Mung Singh, four-day walk; 8) Mung Noi village, Houei Sai (Laos), three-day walk; 9) Nam Wa, Houei Sai (Laos), three-day walk; 10) Phung Phaa, Houei Sai, one day's walk; 11) Nong Tao, Houei Sai, a half-day's walk; 12) Huaj Laj, Muong Meung, Houei Sai, a half-day's walk; 13) Bii Lae, Houei Sai, two-day walk; 14) Nam Kyng (in the hills), Houei Sai, two and one-half days' walk; 15) Nam Yong, Houei Sai, two and one-half days' walk; 16) Pha Ka Tung, Houei Sai, three-day walk.

During his stay in Phalae, he has visited the following: 17) Huaj Maag, Maechan (Thailand), walking distance, one day; 18) Mae Sarong, Maechan, two-hour walk; 19) Tung Baa Khaem, Maechan; 20) Noong Waen, Maechan; 21) Mung Wong, Amphur Mung Phon, Chiengrai (Thailand); 22) Nam Boo, Amphur Chiengrai; 23) Huaj Kang Paa, Maechan; 24) Ban Lao Suu Hjaang, Mae Sarong, Maechan; 25) Phadaeng, Chiengkham (Thailand).

GLOSSARY*

chuang ung thǎaj: the group that cooperates with respect to a single group of ancestor spirits

faᵖ bŭa: a person's spirit name

fing: clan (this word has no connection with *lēj fing*)

fiu tao mien: small headman, headman over one village

fiu tõo: to make merit

gjaa jəm kiu: the bridge of silver for the spirits, made of ritual paper money

gjaa tséᵖ: the highest grade of merit-making

hoo sii mien: mediator

hung gjáa: the king's government

jaang kéen: the world of men

jet peo mien hoo khii haj: "one house people that cooperates nicely," the household

jəm bung mien: hill people

jəm mung mien: valley people (*mung* is a Thai word, meaning city, nation, or people)

jəm keen: the world of spirits

jəm pɛɛng mien: valley people, as contrasted with mountain people

* Tone marks have the following values. ˇ: rising tone, ′: high tone, `: low tone, ˜: very low tone.

kwǎa táng: the lowest grade of merit-making

lāang: village, an aggregate of households

lēj: custom, or tradition

lēj fíng: customs of practical convenience, adaptation to external conditions, such as the authority of central governments

lēj njèj: laws of the universe, pertaining to matters of ritual

liing: power

lūng: a unit of measurement. Ten *lūng* = one *tεεng* = approximately ½ Kg. of Silver

meeng hǔng haj: success. This term is also associated with notions of good luck, favor from the spirits, etc.

mien: man

míen: spirit

sib míen mien: the ordinary ritual expert who takes care of the less important spirits, including ancestor spirits

mui mien: the leader of the marriage ceremony, the go-between

njaan: silver, or money

peo: house

peo tsíu: houseowner

phɔu tung: ordinary, non-ritual matters

Pien Húng: a creator-god who saved the ancestors of the Iu Mien during their "crossing of the sea"

Pien Húng fun fáᵖ: the descendants of Pien Húng, the Iu Mien

phiu jiu gjǎ koe: "crossing the sea," the origin myth of the twelve Iu Mien clans

saj zúng sɔu: ritual manuals, same as *tsɔu mien sɔu*

tɔu sáj: the middle grade of merit-making

tεεng: a unit of measure. See *lǔng*

tsaang laang haa laang: upper villages, lower villages, a politically organized group of villages

tsɔu míen sɔu: ritual manuals, same as *saj zúng sɔu*

tsien tshéᵖ: patrilineal relatives (descendants of the same known ancestor)

tsiep njej fíng: the twelve clans, referring to the total community of the Iu Mien

tsin: money

tsuang tsíu: the owner of the whole, the top chief

tsung míen: evil spirits

tum mien bǔa: a person's official name

tum saj kung: the great teacher, a high-level ritual expert who takes care of the spirit government

tum tao mien: big headman, or high-level headman

tum toong míen: the great group of spirits, central government of the spirit world

uən: the life spirit

ung thaj míen: ancestor spirits

djumaᵖ: the ritual headman of the village (Akha term)
nangɔɔ: the village contact man for outside political powers (Akha term, but probably not an Akha word)
nè tú thúu: to feed the spirits (Akha term)

REFERENCES CITED

BARTH, FREDRIK
    1964 Competition and symbiosis in North Baluchistan. Folk (Danske Etnografisk Tidsskrift) 6(1):15–22. Essays on human ecology, lectures delivered at the third meeting of Scandinavian Anthropologists, Copenhagen, May 9–11, 1963.

BENNINGTON-CORNELL ANTHROPOLOGICAL SURVEY OF HILL TRIBES IN THAILAND
    1964 A report on tribal peoples in Chiengrai Province north of the Mae Kok River. Bangkok, the Siam Society, Data Paper 1.

FREEDMAN, MAURICE
    1958 Lineage organization in Southeastern China. London, the University of London, The Athlone Press. London School of Economics, Monographs on Social Anthropology 18.

IZIKOWITZ, KARL GUSTAV
    1961 Lamet: hill peasants in French Indochina. Göteborg, Etnografiska Museet. Etnologiska Studier 17.

KANDRE, PETER
    1964 The Yao people of Thailand—notes on patterns in social interaction: leadership, decision-making in village communities, action-orientation. Unpublished field report for UNESCO, University of Göteborg, National Research Council of Thailand, and the Siam Society.

KANDRE, PETER, and LEJ TSAN KUEJ
    1965 Aspects of wealth accumulation, ancestor worship, and household stability among the Iu Mien (Yao). *In* Prince Dhani felicitation volume. Bangkok, The Siam Society.

LEBAR, FRANK M., GERALD C. HICKEY, and JOHN K. MUSGRAVE
    1964 Ethnic groups of mainland Southeast Asia. New Haven, Human Relations Area Files Press.

THAILAND, DEPARTMENT OF PUBLIC WELFARE
    1962 Report on the socio-economic survey of the hill tribes in Northern Thailand. Bangkok, Ministry of Interior, Department of Public Welfare.

YANG, C. K.
    1961 Religion in Chinese society. Berkeley, University of California Press.

YOUNG, GORDON
    1962 The hill tribes of Northern Thailand. Bangkok, the Siam Society, Monograph 1, 2d edn.

CHAPTER 17

The Lua? And Skaw Karen of Maehongson Province, Northwestern Thailand

PETER KUNSTADTER

SECTION I

THE SETTING

Although there are now regularly scheduled air stops in Maehongson and Maesariang, Maehongson Province is still one of the most isolated in Thailand. Until 1964 there was no all-weather road connecting this province with the rest of the country, and there is no railroad. Indeed, as is indicated by the fact that until the end of the Second World War the Indian rupee was the standard currency in the area, the Khun Yuam Valley probably had closer trade connections with Burma (especially the Salween Valley) than with the rest of Thailand. This situation has been changing in recent years, especially as the frontier with Burma has been closed, and as the teak trade on the Thai side has developed. A dry-season lumber road connecting Maesariang with the highway in the Maeping Valley was pushed through in the late 1950's, and an all-weather road has reached Maesariang and now is being extended rapidly in the direction of Maehongson.

Despite the shortage of modern transportation, the area has never been internally isolated—the valleys have always been routes of commerce, and, in spite of the rather rugged mountains, there has been a caravan route between Maesariang and the Maeping Valley for hundreds of years (see, for example, Hallett 1890). But it is only within the last few years that the region has been, even occasionally, in daily contact with the modern world and that cheap modern consumer goods and other benefits of modern civilization have become readily available.

[639]

HISTORY

The history of the region is of interest to us because it is considered to be important by at least the tribal people of the area. There is an amazing lack of sound historical information in the region, but what is important for influencing people's behavior and attitudes is what they *think* the history has been. People in the valley seem little interested in regional history. They have vague ideas that Northern Thailand was once ruled by a Prince of Chiengmai and that the area was subject to repeated raids and occupation by the Burmese. Some of them also know that the Lua? occupied the country even before the Thais. Many have heard of the legend of a magical contest between the Lua? King of Chiengmai, Khun Luang Wilanka, and the Mon Queen of Lamphun, Cham Tewi. According to this legend, which is also known to the Lua? still living in the mountains, the Lua? King wanted to marry Cham Tewi, and she set conditions which he could not fulfill—namely, that he throw a spear from the top of Doi Suthep, the mountain in back of Chiengmai, to the Queen's palace in Lamphun. After this, according to the legend, some of the Lua? fled the valley.

Descendants of the Prince of Chiengmai recall that the Lua? as well as other peoples of Northern Thailand in the area of Chiengmai used to pay tribute to the Prince. According to these recollections, the tribute was not onerous, amounting only to a few flowers or other specialized products. In return for tribute the Prince recognized the Lua? claim to the land. Some of the Chiengmai valley dwellers, who are apparently descendants of those Lua? who did not flee, remember that they were temple slaves of the Prince and now, because of their former slave status (they were called Kha Lua?, "slave Lua?"), may even refuse to admit that they were formerly Lua?. Such people now claim to be Northern Thai and for most purposes can pass as such. This change has taken place in the past couple of generations, since slavery was abolished during the reign of Chulalongkorn. There is no way of estimating the total number of Lua? who have become assimilated, in this or other ways, to Northern Thai culture and society, but it must be fairly large.

The Lua? in the mountains remember more of the details of

the early history. They claim, in fact, that they were the ones who originally built the town of Chiengmai and who built Wat Chedi Luang, the oldest temple in Chiengmai (the Chedi is now in ruins). In the old days, they say, they were Buddhists, but since they have moved to the mountains they have no priests and no one to teach them about Buddhism, so they worship the Lua? spirits of the mountains and jungles.

According to their recollection, the Lua? had the mountainous area of northwest Thailand pretty much to themselves for many years. About 150 years ago they lived in small scattered upland agricultural villages, but at about that time armed bands of raiders were in the area, and for mutual defense the small villages joined together into larger fortified settlements. Thus almost all present-day Lua? villages, at least the larger ones, were formed as federations, and the people still recall and recognize their separate village origins, which still have significance with respect to access to land resources. Only descendants of the village within whose territory fields are cut have free use-rights to cut upland fields there.

About 120 years ago Skaw Karens, coming from the west, began moving into the territory once held exclusively by the Lua?. At first they settled only on the mountain tops, in areas which the Lua? had abandoned when they were consolidating their villages. The Karens recognized the Lua? as lords of the land and paid them annual tribute of 10 percent of their rice crop. Each Karen village owed tribute to some particular Lua? village, within whose territory it was located. The Lua? recall that they were rich then and look back on this period as "the good old days" when they had many elephants, cattle, water buffaloes, and silk clothing.

The Lua? at this time were required to pay tribute to the Prince of Chiengmai or Lamphun. The old men of the tribe still remember stories of annual trips to make this payment, which, they say, was in the form of rice, roofing straw, and other products of the mountain region. They also relayed a portion of the tribute which the Karens had paid them, and in return the Prince recognized the Lua? claim to the land and their right to collect tribute from others, including even the Northern Thais, Shans, and Burmese who were beginning to settle in the Khun Yuam

[641]

Valley. The old men recall that the Prince could be persuaded to lower his demands for tribute in years when the harvest was poor.

As the Central Thai government extended control throughout the North in the early 1900's, the Prince of Chiengmai lost his right to collect tribute, as did the Lua?. The Prince lost most of his symbolic functions as a result of the Thai revolution of 1932.

As the Central Thai government took control, the Lua? became liable (as were the rest of the people in Thailand) for a rather heavy head tax. This was the beginning of a serious economic decline for the Lua? which has continued to the present day. Collection of the head tax stopped early in the 1930's. Taxes on land, animals, butchering, guns, and the brewing of liquor were substituted, and are collected with varying degrees of success. The government now apparently assumes that it owns all upland areas which are not occupied by house sites or subjected to irrigation. Apparently there is no formal recognition even of the hill people's use-rights to the upland areas.[1]

Over the past several generations the Karens have been increasing in number, building new villages, and taking over more and more of what used to be Lua? land. Usually they make token payments for the privilege of cultivating for the first year, thereafter assuming that they own the land.

TRIBAL POPULATION IN MAEHONGSON PROVINCE

As in all of Thailand, the census figures for tribal populations in Maehongson are inadequate. On the basis of available figures, Maehongson seems to have the largest counted proportion of tribal people: 27,000, or 40 percent, of those over five years of age are non-Thai-speaking, and presumably at least that percentage is tribal (a few of these 27,000 may be Burmese or Shans). There may be as many as 4,000 Lua? in Maehongson Province, of the total number of 9,000 given by Gordon Young (1962:85). All 1,300 of the Bwe (B?ghwe, Karenni, or Red Karens) Karens and all of the 600 Taungthu Karens reported by Young (*ibid.*)

[1] Clear title to house sites and irrigated fields may not be recognized either. For example, when the road was being built from Hot to Maesariang, irrigated fields of Karens were destroyed or damaged without compensation to their owners. Hill tribe people rarely register titles to their lands with the district office.

are in Maehongson. The remainder of the counted tribal population, about 22,000, are almost all Karens, most of whom are Skaw Karens, although there are also some Pwo Karens and some Lahu.

TYPES OF VILLAGES

Types of Lua? Villages. Within Maehongson Province there is considerable variability in tribal communities. At least three types of Lua? villages and one other type of settlement can be distinguished (see Table 23).

1. The most isolated of these types I will refer to as *traditional Lua? mountain villages.* Such villages range in size from twenty to one hundred or more houses. This type is exemplified by Ban Pa Pae, a village in which I resided for a total of over six months during 1964 and 1965. Pa Pae is about a day's walk away from the nearest market town, Maesariang. There are no markets or shops in this kind of village, but fairly regular patterns of trade occur for some commodities (e.g. fermented tea, kerosene, miscellaneous manufactured goods on special order) carried in by individual Lua?, or, more rarely, Karen entrepreneurs. The people are predominantly upland subsistence agriculturalists, though some young men may leave the village to seek wage work. They speak Lua? as their first language; most adults also speak Northern Thai and Karen. Dialect differentiation is so great among Lua? villages that people from more than one day's walk away may have to resort to Karen or Northern Thai in order to converse. There is little knowledge of Central Thai, and very few people are literate. There are few or no radios. The religion of these people is predominantly animist, although there has been some effort to missionize them, and most of them also consider themselves to be Buddhists, although they have few of the ordinary trappings of Buddhism (no temples, no priests, no knowledge of Buddhist scriptures; most houses have a shrine containing pictures of famous Buddhist priests, and some occupants have made images of the Lord Buddha). Although the headman of the village is officially recognized by the district office, the main contact by these people with representatives of the Thai government is with Border Patrol Policemen (there is a Border Patrol school in Pa Pae). Missionaries and anthropologists furnish contact with the outside world. Material culture consists primarily

[643]

TABLE 23
SOME CHARACTERISTICS OF LUAꞶ AND SKAW KAREN
COMMUNITIES AND SETTLEMENTS

Type	Isolation	Size	Relation to Thai Government	Language
1. Traditional LuaꞶ mountain village	Day's walk or more to market; no shops	100 to 300 people	Headman recognized; primary contact with BPP	LuaꞶ, N. Thai and Karen
2. Thai-ized LuaꞶ mountain village	Formerly on main caravan routes, now near highway; shops	Up to 1,000 or more	Recognized headman, public schools, contact with normal Thai officials	LuaꞶ, N. Thai, Karen
3. Thai-ized LuaꞶ valley village	Same as rural Thai; shops	Same size range as rural Thai	Same as rural Thai	N. Thai, little LuaꞶ
4. LuaꞶ migrants to valley towns	Same as other sections of town; shops	200 or more	Same as other sections of town; public schools	N. Thai emphasized, LuaꞶ, Karen
5. Mountain Karen village	One or more days' walk to market, no shops	Small, 10–20 houses, tend to send off colonies	Recognized headman for large village or group of small villages. Primary contact with BPP	Karen, very little and poor N. Thai
6. Rural valley Karen village	Variable, same as rural Thai	Larger, same size range as rural Thai	Same as rural Thai, but BPP provides some schools	Karen, some N. Thai, with strong accent
7. Town Karen	Same as town Thai	Large portion of Maesariang	Same as town Thai	Karen, N. Thai, C. Thai, English

(continued)

TABLE 23
(continued)

Type	Religion	Predominant Economy	Material Culture	Population Sources and Marriage Pattern
1. Traditional Lua? mountain village	Animism, nominal Buddhism	Upland subsistence agriculture	Traditional	Village endogamy, little recent in-migration
2. Thai-ized Lua? mountain village	Buddhism, animism	Upland subsistence agriculture, some wage work	Thai; little homemade clothing, tend to Thai-style house	Primarily endogamous, some Thai, Chinese moving in
3. Thai-ized Lua? valley village	Buddhism, some animism	Wet rice	Same as rural Thai	Primarily endogamous (?), some migration from Type 1
4. Lua? migrants to valley towns	Animism, Buddhism, Christianity	Wage labor, forest products, subsistence gardening	Mixed traditional and Thai, some weaving	Migration from many hill villages, and Lua? endogamy
5. Mountain Karen village	Animism, Christianity (Baptist, Catholic)	Upland subsistence agriculture, some elephant-drivers	Traditional "native" technology plus trade goods	Matrilocal marriage, often village exogamous
6. Rural valley Karen village	Animism, Buddhism, Christianity (Baptist, Catholic)	Wet rice for home consumption and sale, some wage labor, elephant-drivers	Some traditional technology retained, especially weaving	Matrilocal marriage, (?) village exogamous
7. Town Karen	Animism, Buddhism, Christianity (Baptist, Catholic)	Wet rice for consumption and sale, wage labor, crafts, shopkeeping	Like Thai, but weaving retained in traditional or modified styles	Locality pattern in marriage not strictly followed, migration in from rural and hill areas

of native technology: all of the women's clothing and much of the men's is homemade in traditional style, and almost all houses employ traditional style and materials. The population in the traditional villages is predominantly the result of endogamous marriages, with a few women brought in from other Lua? villages. In the past there was more in-migration of Karen and Khmu?. Pa Pae is described at greater length below.

2. The second type of village can be called the *Thai-ized Lua? mountain village*. This type includes such villages as Baw Luang and Kawng Loi. These villages, larger in size than most of the isolated mountain villages, may contain up to two hundred houses (a thousand or more people). They contain shops and limited markets. As a result of their location along caravan routes, they have been directly exposed to Thai or other lowland influences for hundreds of years. The Thai form of Buddhism has long been present; the head priest at Baw Luang claims the Buddhist temple there is over three hundred years old. Some of the priests are locally recruited. Along with Buddhism there is a strongly developed pattern of animism, similar to that found in isolated mountain villages. The first language spoken is Lua?, but everyone also speaks Northern Thai, and some speak Karen. Some of the people are literate, and there may be several radios in the village. The economy is primarily subsistence upland-rice agriculture, but there is also some wage work in the lumber business and in highway construction and repair. These villages, which were located on old caravan routes, are now on or near the highway, and daily bus transportation to Chiengmai and smaller towns is available. Contact with the government resembles that of rural Thai villages. (There is a public school in Baw Luang.) Technology in these villages is coming to resemble that of Thai towns. Houses are built more in Thai style, with tile roofs and the double-room pattern common in Northern Thailand. Men's clothing is purchased in stores (located in the villages). Little weaving is done; women wear purchased blouses, and if they have homemade skirts, they wear them in the Thai style (long wrapped skirts) instead of the short sewn version of traditional villages. The villages are predominantly endogamous, but some lowland Thais and Chinese have moved in.

3. The third type of village can be called the *Thai-ized Lua?*

valley type. These villages are to be found in the valleys, where, except for their histories and a few customs, they are today indistinguishable from the surrounding Thai communities. Such a village is Ban Hua Lin, Amphur (District) Sanpathong, Chiengmai Province. There are several other villages of this type to the north and south of Chiengmai, and several in the Khun Yuam Valley south of Maesariang. These villages often have shops in them, and villagers participate regularly in markets at nearby Thai market towns. The relationship of these villages to the Thai government is the same as that of any rural Thai village. The people are Buddhists; novices and priests are locally recruited, and there are temples in the villages. The language of the communities is Northern Thai—only a few of the older people know Lua?, and they may not admit to this knowledge. Degree of literacy is comparable to rural Thai villages. The predominant economy is wet-rice agriculture for sale and home consumption. Villages vary in degree of isolation, as do the rural Thai villages in the same area. Material culture is virtually indistinguishable from that of Northern Thai villages—only a few remnants of Lua? cultural patterns remain, such as burial in hollow log coffins instead of cremation in plank coffins. I have no information on sources of the population or marriage pattern except that in the case of Ban Hua Lin, connections have been maintained with one of the isolated mountain Lua? villages, Ban Myt Lawng. Families and individuals from Ban Myt Lawng move to Ban Hua Lin, where they first settle as laborers and eventually get land and houses of their own, becoming Thai-ized like other members of the community. I do not know if this pattern of immigration is repeated elsewhere.

4. A fourth type of settlement, not actually an independent community, is composed of migrants to the valley from isolated mountain villages. Two settlements of this type, Ban Phae? and Ban Ton Phrao, are located on the outskirts of Maesariang. Each of these settlements is forty or more houses in size. The settlements have small shops, but most marketing is done in the Maesariang market. The houses of the Lua? are not spatially segregated from the houses of Northern Thais or Karens who live in the same settlements. The relationship between these settlements and the Thai government is the same as for any similar

segment of a town. The children are enrolled in public schools, without distinction, except that some special attention has been given to them because of special financial problems or language problems (see Thailand: Introduction, section on Ministry of Education). The Luaʔ children are reported to be better than average students, and some have done outstandingly well in classes with Northern Thai and Karen children.

Most of the animistic customs of these people are lost when they move to the valley. Apparently the customs are not felt to be appropriate to the valley setting, and the extensive sacrificial feasts are considered too expensive. Some of the people become active Buddhists and may play important roles in the local temple organizations. The people are also subject to influence from missionaries, who have made a number of converts in one of the settlements (Ban Phaeʔ), but none in the other. The language of the migrants was Luaʔ, but they report that they make a conscious effort to speak Northern Thai in their homes, so that their children grow up speaking Northern Thai, with little or no knowledge of Luaʔ or Karen.

Most of the migrants have moved to the valley for economic reasons, such as insufficient food in the mountains, insufficient variety of food, or too difficult a life. In the valley the men take a variety of temporary wage-laboring jobs (working in other people's fields, working on roads, gardening, working for lumber companies, etc.). Those who have been living in the Maesariang area the longest may own their own irrigated land, or may be working for shares on someone else's land, but, aside from house plots and small gardens, the majority of them do not own land. Women do odd jobs and gather forest products (firewood, large leaves used in the market for wrapping) and are able to earn two or three baht (U.S. $.10–.15), or up to five baht per day in this fashion. Men can earn five to ten baht per day, about the same as other laborers in this part of Thailand. The gardens yield an important supplement to their diet. The migrants also raise chickens and pigs, but seem to have fewer of these than do their mountain relatives.

The source of these settlements is migration from many different Luaʔ mountain villages of type 1. The pattern of marriage, which in the mountains is village endogamous, becomes "tribal" endogamous in these settlements, virtually all marriages being between two Luaᴾ but with no apparent restriction to the village of origin. The residents of these settlements feel a sense of kinship with all Luaᴾ and may state that "all Luaᴾ are relatives." Visiting patterns with villages of origin are maintained. When people from the mountains go to Maesariang, they usually stay with their relatives or friends who have moved there from the same village, and the people who have settled in the valleys return occasionally to their original villages (some go once or twice a year; others go only for important ceremonies such as weddings).

The material culture of these migrants comes to resemble that of Northern Thais to some extent. Houses resemble in part those found in the mountains (roof style usually is maintained), but include the typically Northern Thai feature of putting the kitchen in a separate room. Men almost always dress in purchased clothing, in the style of Northern Thai peasants, but women frequently retain some of their traditional clothing styles and continue to do some weaving. Traditional customs are maintained in a less elaborate fashion—in marriage, for example, bride-price may be reduced, the ceremony is shortened from a week or more to one day, and the prolonged feasting is reduced to a single feast.

Types of Karen Villages. At least three types of Karen communities or settlements can be distinguished: isolated mountain villages, valley villages, and valley town settlements. The characteristics of these different types are fairly comparable to those outlined for the different kinds of Luaᴾ communities and settlements.

5. *Isolated mountain villages* of the Karen tend to be smaller than those of the Luaᴾ, ten to twenty houses being a common size. When they get larger than this, they tend to send off colonies to settle in nearby areas (a walk of ten minutes to half an hour or more). Village fission of this sort is explained by the people as being a result of arguments, or a desire to be closer to upland fields. Usually the daughter villages retain the name of the parent village and are distinguished from one another by reference to some well-known elder who lives in the village in question. Each new daughter village must have its own re-

ligious leader, but most often the daughter villages are still regarded as being under a single headman, usually the headman
of the parent village, who is officially recognized by the district
office. Villages of this type are scattered throughout the hills
of Amphur Maesariang. Some are quite close to the roads, while
others are one or more days' walk to transportation or to the
nearest market. None of these villages has shops. No accurate
count has been made of villages of this type. Headmen of groups
of these villages are recognized by the district office, but the
primary contact of these people with the Thai government is
through Border Patrol Policemen; occasional visits by anthropologists and missionaries bring contacts with the outside world.
Mountain Karens are generally monolingual, and those few who
speak Northern Thai do so with an accent so strong as to make
understanding very difficult. Dialect differentiation between villages apparently is not very great. The hill villages are primarily
animistic, although there has been missionary activity among them
by Baptists and Catholics for many years. A few children from
this type of village are attending public schools in Maesariang
and living at the Baptist Hostel. The Baptist church is well
enough established among Karens so that for many years some
of the evangelists themselves have been Karens. Some of the
mountain Karens consider themselves to be Buddhists and, like
the Lua?, have pictures of Buddhist priests in their homes. The
economy of these villages is predominantly upland subsistence
agriculture, with some irrigated agriculture and some elephant-
driving. Material culture is primarily of traditional native homemade type, supplemented by a few manufactured items (knives,
matches, kerosene, tin plates, pottery, etc.). The villages are
based on matrilocal matrilineal extended families, with males
often being recruited from other hill Karen communities.

6. *Rural valley Karen villages* are located in the larger valleys,
such as that of the Khun Yuam River. Their size is variable,
but tends to be larger than that of the mountain Karen villages.
Local headmen are recognized by the district office, but the usual
governmental services have not penetrated very far into the rural
areas among the Karens, and some responsibility for them (including providing some schools) has been taken by the Border
Police Patrol. Some of the children attend public school in

Maesariang and live at the Baptist Hostel. The language spoken in the homes is Karen, and some men speak Northern Thai, but with a strong accent. Valley Karen language is differentiated from hill Karen on the basis of vocabulary differences and some regular sound shifts (such differences appear even between hill and valley Skaw Karens). The predominant religion of these villages is animism, though there are some Christians as well. As among the Lua?, many of the villagers consider themselves Buddhist and have pictures of Buddhist priests in their houses. The economy of the valley Karen is based on wet-rice cultivation for home consumption and sale, supplemented by some wage labor and elephant-driving. Some traditional technology and material culture has been retained, but much has come to resemble rural Northern Thai. Weaving in traditional style is still done in every household. The marriage pattern is matrilocal, and kinship is reckoned matrilineally, but I do not know whether the villages tend to be exogamous or not.

7. *Valley town Karen settlements.* A large portion of the present population of the town of Maesariang is Karen. These people are no more isolated than other town dwellers; although they tend to live in neighborhoods with other Karens, there is no formal pattern of residential segregation. Their relationship to the Thai government is the same as that of other town dwellers. The children attend public schools. In the past some attended mission schools, and a few are literate in English as well as Karen and Thai. Some valley dwellers are wet-rice farmers, others are storekeepers, and still others are wage laborers or civil servants. There are few differences in material culture between town-dwelling Karens and town-dwelling Thais, except that many of the Karen women still weave in traditional style, or in modifications of traditional style, both for their own use and for sale. The pattern of matrilocal marriage is not followed consistently in the towns—marriages may be patrilocal or neolocal. The population of town-dwelling Karens is supplemented by migration from hill villages and rural areas.

This brief typology is enough to indicate that at least two variables are involved in determining the pathways followed by individuals or whole communities in "becoming Thai." A simple folk-urban continuum is not an adequate description. Degree of physical isolation is certainly one factor, and nature of the preexistent culture pattern seems to be another. The Lua? and Karen patterns seem to be significantly different in regard to the latter; rural valley Lua? villages seem to "become Thai" much more readily than rural valley Karen villages (cf. Hamilton 1963; 1965:1).

BAN PA PAE—A MOUNTAIN LUA? VILLAGE

Tribal Economy. The following remarks derive primarily from my field work with the Lua? of the traditional Lua? mountain village, Ban Pa Pae Amphur Maesariang, but are also applicable to other nearby Lua? and Karen mountain villages (for further details see Kunstadter 1965; 1966A). Ban Pa Pae is a village of about fifty houses and two hundred people. Unlike most Lua? villages, which are located on the tops of ridges, the houses of Pa Pae are clustered together on either side of a mountain stream.

Although they have some irrigated land, both the Lua? and Karen in the hills of Amphur Maesariang are primary swidden-rice cultivators. The cultivation of swiddens is done on a nine- or ten-year cycle, with an eight- or nine-year fallow period between each single year of cultivation. The Lua? population has been stable, having lived in settled villages for at least four or five generations, using the same field areas since the beginning of traditional memory—at least 150 years ago. This indicates that the system of farming is not as destructive to forest and soil resources as has been suggested by various authorities.

Wet-rice cultivation has been practiced in this area for only about forty years (the Lua? of Baw Luang have evidently had irrigation for much longer). At about this time some Karens tried unsuccessfully to imitate the irrigation techniques they had seen in the lowland valleys. Irrigation technology was successfully introduced, along with the appropriate rituals, by Northern Thais from Umeng (a village near Sanpathong, about twenty-five miles southwest of Chiengmai) who were employed for the purpose by some Lua? villagers. Knowledge of irrigation has now spread widely among both Lua? and Karen communities, but some Karens consider that the Lua? are more skillful, and employ them for the initial construction of dams and ditches. Irrigated fields now cover most of the available mountain-valley lands, and are being extended slowly up the hillsides each year. The Lua? have lost or sold much of their irrigated land to Karens as a result of inability to repay loans or mortgages.

No reliable figures exist to indicate annual income. Estimates by Lua? farmers in the village of Pa Pae for a two-year period indicate considerable annual and individual variation in yield. In a sample of fifteen households in the Lua? village of Pa Pae, the farmers estimated their own average production at about 85 tang (a tang is 40 liters) of unhusked rice per family, which loses about one-half its volume when husked. When converted to its cash value, this amounts to about 1,225 baht per year (U.S. $61.25), of which about 1,000 baht worth is consumed by the family itself, leaving a potential cash surplus of about 225 baht (U.S. $11.25).

The surplus rice is carried to Maesariang for sale, or sold or loaned to other Lua? or Karen villagers who have had poor rice yields. Cash income from rice is supplemented occasionally by sale of vegetables (mustard greens, chilis, onions, etc.), and live-stock (pigs and, rarely, buffaloes). The average total *cash* income per family is probably under 400 baht (U.S. $20.00).

Cash is spent on manufactured goods (matches, combs, kero-sene, plastic sheeting, iron tools, flashlights, and so forth).

Cash income of some families is supplemented by young men (bachelors) who go to work for a few months, or a year or more, in the mines near Chiengmai. The money they earn seems to be used most frequently as bride-price.

Despite the long-time familiarity with money, the economy is basically one of subsistence. People make most of their own houses out of materials they gather in the jungle, and feed them-selves with vegetables and rice from their gardens and fields and with their own chickens and pigs. They could be virtually independent of the market except for iron for tools (they can work the iron themselves) and salt.

Effects of economic development programs in tribal areas. The biggest governmental effort toward economic develop-ment in the region under discussion has been the building of an all-weather road connecting Amphur Hot with Maesariang, and eventually connecting Maesariang with the provincial seat of Maehongson. Construction of this road has been going on

[653]

for about five years, and had been completed by 1964 to the extent that it was possible to drive from Hot to Maesariang throughout most of the rainy season. The building of this road, and another one which was built parallel to it for about thirty kilometers by a lumber company, has had several effects on the tribal people living in the area. First, it has provided a temporary opportunity for wage labor for tribal people living in the construction area. Second, in one of the tribal villages, Kawng Loi (see Thai-ized mountain Lua? villages above), a construction camp was built, and the construction company also built a school and some demonstration gardens (apparently at the initiative of the chief of the construction crew, not as the result of any official governmental program). Third, the coming of the road through these villages has greatly increased villagers' opportunities for transportation, and also their access to manufactured goods. The same is true of Maesariang, where a whole series of new shops with a greatly increased variety of goods has grown up since fairly regular truck transportation became available. Thus new goods and new wants have been introduced to the local population. Fourth, although some of the tribal people along the roadway have been able to gain temporary employment, some of the traditional jobs (e.g. elephant-driving, caravaning) have been lost to them as transport has become mechanized. Fifth, what used to be fairly isolated country is now readily accessible, and some of the villagers alongside the roads say they are now unable to protect their livestock from pilferage. Thus roads may cause a lowered standard of living, through loss of traditional jobs and through actual robbery, at the same time as expectations are raised through temporary wage labor and the introduction of new varieties of consumer goods.

Economic effects of opium in non-opium-growing tribes. Opium is so important in determining the economic condition of such groups as the Meo and Yao (see papers by Geddes, Kandre, and Manndorff) that it is appropriate to discuss here the effects of opium in groups where it is not an important cash crop.

The chief opium producers in northwestern Thailand are apparently the Meo. As far as I know, the Lua? and Karen in this area only suffer from the effects of addiction, and do not benefit economically from extensive opium trade. In Amphur Maesariang

I have been told that Karens there grow opium primarily for their own consumption, or for local sale, not for trade to other parts of Thailand or for export. In Ban Pa Pae, the Luaꜰ village where I lived and worked, no opium is grown. There are two addicts in the village, who purchase their supply from Karens. Luaꜰ villages further to the north are reported to grow large amounts of opium, primarily for their own consumption, and Luaꜰ villages in the area west of Chiengmai are reported to have died out because so many of their residents became addicts. Addicts are feared because they are known to steal in order to get money to buy the drug.[2]

The addicts in Ban Pa Pae have given up cultivation of their rice fields and have sold or mortgaged their irrigated fields. They have been selling all their other property, and are now desperately poor. The other villagers are well aware of the effects of drug addiction. They take pity on the families of addicts: several Karen boys whose parents were addicts were employed by Luaꜰ villagers, and one young daughter of an addict was adopted by a Luaꜰ family.

There is no governmental program for rehabilitation of addicts; they are treated as criminals. One Karen addict was treated at the Baptist Mission in Maesariang, and the cure was apparently effective for at least six months. The effects of drug addiction among the opium-growing tribes are, no doubt, much more serious.

The absence of opium (or any other valuable product) as a cash crop has kept cash income at a low level as compared with the opium-growing tribes. This lack limits trade connections and general awareness of market and even political conditions in the outside world. This also means that these Luaꜰ and Skaw Karen are less likely (for better or worse) to come to the attention of government officials. As Manndorff has indicated in this volume, it was only as an afterthought that the Karens (by far the largest tribal group in Thailand) were added to the list of groups to be surveyed, and it was only within the past year

---

[2] Although the addicts in the village where I lived have not resorted to violence, the villagers are aware of an incident which took place several years ago, within a day's walk of the village. One Karen man was murdered, and another badly injured, when their home was entered by an addict in search of money and valuables.

(1964) that a Hill Tribes Division project was established in a Karen area.

Village organization. Present-day Lua? communities are confederations of older villages which came together over one hundred years ago for mutual defense. Each of these constituent villages retains its identity as a patrilineal descent group and has its own religious leader, known as a *lam,* who is the oldest man born into that group. Each group has slightly different patterns of religious observances which relate to spirits who protect the households or the community as a whole. These differences have been retained in spite of generations of intermarriage with other groups.

The constituent villages (*not* the present-day settlements as a whole) are the landowning units, and descendants of these groups retain their ancestral claims on upland agricultural fields. Each household in the present settlement is identified as belonging to one or another of the ancestral villages, and thereby has a traditional use-right claim on certain field areas. Membership in a constituent village is gained by being born into, or marrying into, a household which is already identified with one of the constituents. In the years since the villages were consolidated, much of the land (particularly that which lies far from the present village site) has been lost to Karens who moved into the area after the Lua? had clustered together in fortified settlements. This means that some of the constituent villages have lost most or all of their land, and members of these groups must beg the religious leaders of other groups for permission to cultivate in their areas. Use-rights to swidden fields are occasionally traded among members of the community, and sometimes are rented to Karens.

Most Lua? communities have a lineage known as *khun* (a Thai word meaning "lord") or *samang.* The senior man in this lineage is known as the big *samang;* he is the paramount religious leader for important village ceremonies. The big *samang* adjudicates violations of customary law and is regarded as the conservator of Lua? customs and traditions. He is identified with one or another of the constituent villages, and members of that group owe him allegiance. This means that they must pay him the leg of any large game animal they kill in the forest, and must give him one leg of every animal sacrificed on certain occasions. Some of the constituent villages were invited to join the consolidated settlement by the big *samang*—their descendants also pay animal legs to the present incumbent and receive the right of free access to upland field areas.

In spite of the differences between the constituent villages the whole settlement acts as a community on many occasions. Many of the agricultural activities are coordinated on a community-wide basis; many of the most important religious ceremonies require the participation of all households; and for administrative purposes the whole settlement is considered as a unit.

A village headman (*kae ban*) who is the civil leader of the community is recognized by the district office. He may or may not be the same person as the big *samang*. The headman has the right to draft villagers to act as policemen, and may hold law violators or suspected violators for the Provincial Police (this is very rarely done). He is responsible for collecting land taxes, which he transmits to the district office. He is also supposed to attend the monthly meetings of the village headmen at the district office, but actual attendance is only once or twice per year. He must provide hospitality for visiting officials, but collects the direct expenses (the cost of food and liquor) from the villagers. The district office pays the headman a monthly wage for these services. The headman is selected by the villagers, but the selection must be approved by the district office, which sometimes suggests acceptable candidates. The headman ordinarily serves for life, but he may retire if he feels he is no longer able to perform the duties of the office.

One or more assistant headmen (*salawat*) are also elected by the villagers, but they are not paid. In their selection of an assistant headman, and in discussing their choice for an eventual replacement for the present headman, the people of Pa Pae emphasize ability to speak and write Central Thai. They are quite aware of the need to conform to the requirements of Thai administrative bureaucracy. However, there is no indication that there is any lessening of the influence of traditional leaders in matters of religion or village custom.

The headman is responsible for enforcing Thai laws. This responsibility sometimes requires the headman to reconcile Thai laws with conflicting tribal traditions. Thus, apparently, one amusing custom has grown up around the Lua? wedding ceremony. The groom's family is required to kill a buffalo to feed the wedding guests. Thai law, however, requires that a tax be paid and a permit issued for slaughtering a buffalo. In order to avoid this, the wedding buffalo is led to a tree before dawn on the day of the feast. Most of the men of the village assist in putting a rope around the neck of the animal, and hanging the animal on a stout branch. After the buffalo is thoroughly dead, the headman is notified that "A buffalo has fallen out of a tree and killed itself," to which the headman replies, "Well, if that's the case, we might as well eat it." The whole thing is taken as a big joke.

Individuals are responsible for paying their license fees for brewing liquor, or for owning buffaloes or guns, directly to the district office. This they do with varying degrees of regularity. Some, but not all, of the villagers were required to go to Maesariang in February and March of 1964 to have their pictures taken and to pay a fee for an identification card. They had not received their cards by January 1965, and considered this to be just another form of taxation.

The villagers also have a form of taxation of their own. Each year, after the harvest, a meeting is held, and all the unpaid expenses of the village are added up. These include such things as the expense of official visitors who are fed at the headman's house, the expense of sending men to accompany the headman to district office meetings, the expense of sending someone out to secure sacrificial animals for village ceremonies, and the expense of sending men to fight forest fires which threaten the field areas of the village. Each man-day of work is evaluated at five baht. The total amount is divided by the number of households in the village, each house is then assessed its share, and the men who have worked are paid five baht for each day they worked.

There is no political organization of Lua? villages above the level of the village community.

Swidden agriculture follows a regular round: fields are cultivated for only one year before being fallowed for about nine. Households tend to return to the same field sites at the end of the fallow period, but the headman may reassign land in the event of obvious inequality. Ordinarily all households from the Luaᵖ community make their fields in one area in any one year. Decisions on location of the area to be cultivated and timing of the cutting, burning, and planting are made by community religious leaders. Individual choice of field sites within the selected area is confirmed by divination. The entire community cooperates in clearing firebreaks around the field area and in patrolling the margins when the fields are burned. If Karens are making fields in adjacent areas, they will join in clearing firebreaks, and coordinate their activities so their fields are burned on the same day. The Luaᵖ system of upland agriculture requires much more coordination of communal activities than does their irrigated farming (Kunstadter 1966B).

The village headman has the authority to fine people who cut their fields in the wrong places, or who start fires in the wrong place or at the wrong time. Certain virgin jungle areas are preserved in stream beds (where they help retard erosion), and an orderly pattern of field rotation is maintained. In the event of forest fires (which are deeply feared because they are known to reduce soil fertility in future years) village members must join in fighting the blaze, even though their own fields are not threatened.

Irrigated fields are individually owned; the title to use-rights no longer resides in the constituent village once the field has been cleared and levelled and the ditches and dams have been constructed. Irrigated fields can be bought, sold, rented, or mortgaged. The timing of activities in the irrigated fields depends on the completion of work in the upland fields. Cooperation in building dams and ditches is organized among a small group of friends or relatives, and labor is sometimes hired to work on these projects. Plowing and harrowing is usually done by the field owner himself, sometimes assisted by hired labor. Transplanting is done with the assistance of relatives and friends, and is organized in much the same way as planting the upland fields.

Although the Luaᵖ have individual ceremonies for healing and for honoring their relatives, by far the most common form of ceremony is communal. The major agricultural rites require cooperation from all households, as do weddings and funerals. Ancestral rites require joint action of whole sections of the village. Major rituals are led by *samangs, lams,* and their assistants, all working together.

The household, which is the primary unit of production, distribution, and consumption, tends to be limited to the nuclear or stem family. Older sons bring their wives to live in their father's house, but move out after a few years; the youngest son remains in his father's house after marriage and cares for his parents in their old age. In spite of the fission of households, the heavy agricultural tasks involve cooperation between large numbers of patrilineal and affinal relatives from all sections of the community. It is not considered pleasant to do any task alone, and even such marginal pursuits as fishing in the small mountain streams will usually draw a gang of twenty or more participants.

Karen villages are organized somewhat differently. Original inhabitants of a newly established village may come from one or more parent villages. Each village must have its own religious leader or *thipokawkosa,* and a new village cannot be started unless it has an appropriate person to act as one. The position of religious leader, according to my informants, is *patrilineally* inherited. This religious leader may or may not be recognized by the district office as the civil headman.

New villages are formed as a result of quarrels within the original villages. Such quarrels are most often related to division of property, especially land, and the main reason for people's moving out to new villages is often that there is too little land available around the old villages.

Unlike the Lua?, the Karen households tend to make their fields separately, wherever the land looks as if it will support a crop. Households rather than villages seem to be the landholding units. Decisions on the timing of agricultural operations are made by individuals (supported by various forms of divination), rather than by community leaders.

Duties and powers of the civil headman of a Karen village are the same as those in a Lua? village.

Lua?-Karen relations. Karens are ubiquitous visitors in Lua? villages; many Karens come to attend Lua? ceremonies and to partake in their feasts. The Lua? less frequently visit their Karen neighbors, although they occasionally go for special ceremonies, such as weddings, and sometimes go to trade, especially for sacrificial animals. The Luaꞏ consider Karen liquor to be inferior to their own, and though they are generally tolerant, they make fun of the Karen inability to speak Thai or Luaꞏ. They are also somewhat apprenhensive about Karen visitors, since many of the Karens are opium addicts.

In cases of severe or chronic illness, if Luaꞏ treatments fail, Karen doctors are frequently called in to treat Luaꞏ patients, and it is Karen specialists who tattoo Luaꞏ men and give them their sign of manhood. Some of the Luaꞏ, particularly those from the now landless constituent villages, resent the fact that the Karens have taken over much of what used to be Luaꞏ land. The Karens have done this either by squatting, or by paying "rent" for one year in upland areas, and then assuming perpetual use-rights. They have also made loans and foreclosed mortgages on irrigated fields. Karen sometimes borrow rice from the Luaꞏ, and a few Luaꞏ have acquired Karen fields, but most of the time the transactions go the other way.

Karen and Luaꞏ bachelors sometimes visit each other during the planting season, which gives them an opportunity to look at the other group's maidens. At present there is relatively little intermarriage (only one Karen husband and no Karen wives can be found in Pa Pae, and no Pa Pae individuals have married into Karen villages). But in the past Luaꞏ men occasionally brought Karen wives into the village. Several Karen boys come to live in Pa Pae every year to help in the irrigated fields; in return for this they are fed and clothed and given a payment in rice after the harvest. The Luaꞏ take pity on the Karens, whom they consider to be poorer than themselves, and are especially sorry for the children of opium addicts (one daughter of opium addicts has been adopted at Pa Pae).

It is hard to tell the relative wealth of the two groups, since they are both so near the subsistence level. The Luaꞏ have more ceremonies and eat more meat, but the Karens, over the years, have acquired a very substantial portion of the Luaꞏ land. Karen population in the hills is evidently increasing, while Luaꞏ population remains stable (partially because of emigration to the valleys).

Despite cultural differences and resentment over loss of land,

[661]

the Lua? and Karen feel that they are "relatives" because they have been living as neighbors in the mountains for many years. They recognize and perpetuate their cultural differences, but also feel a bond with each other, as mountain people, vis-à-vis the lowland Thai.

Relations with the Outside World—Border Patrol Activities. A Border Patrol Police School has existed at Ban Pa Pae for about five years, staffed by one or sometimes two policemen. Their activities have consisted of building the school and school furniture, for which they have gotten labor and supplies from the villagers, conducting classes, and building and periodically clearing a landing strip on a ridge above the village. Tools, and supplies (e.g. corrugated iron for roofing) have been provided by the BPP.

The school has been enthusiastically received by the parents and children of Ban Pa Pae, and almost all school-age children are enrolled in spite of the fact that enrollment is not compulsory. In fact the students get less schooling than they want. During more than six months of observation, school was actually in session only about six weeks. School was not held whenever there was any major ceremony or when there was an especially heavy work-load requiring the children (e.g. planting the upland and irrigated fields). School was also in recess for long periods while the teacher was in Maesariang awaiting delivery of material for the new school building or awaiting arrangements for bringing his family up to the village to live with him. The teacher who had been in the village for the longest period was very well liked, as was his wife. In addition to giving formal instruction to the children, he spent much time talking informally with the men of the village, trying to broaden their horizons with respect to the government of Thailand and, to a certain extent, the political situation in Southeast Asia. The villagers felt that merely by his presence (he made no attempt to arrest people) he discouraged bandits from coming to the village. The villagers are particularly afraid of opium addicts, who generally shun the village when the policeman is present.

The effect of his indoctrination can perhaps best be judged by the reaction of the villagers to an "invasion scare," at a time when the BPP man was not in the village. Early in the rainy season of 1964 some of the villagers had been to market in Maesariang and heard a rumor that a large number of men (1,100 or 11,000—the reports were not clear) were coming to invade Maesariang from Burma. It was said that these invaders might be Karens or that they might be Communists. The villagers were greatly agitated, but no consistent pattern or plan of action emerged. The reaction of one young married man is illustrative: "If anyone comes to this village, I'll shoot him." He was armed with a muzzle-loading match-lock. He told me that Communists are bad because "they take what you have away from you. If I have three or four pigs and three or four buffaloes they will take them away. That's not good." He then turned to me and asked, "What do Communists look like—are they big or small? What color are they—red or black?"[3]

The airstrip built at the direction of the BPP has been something of a fiasco. It has been cleared three times, each time after assurances that a plane would land. No plane has yet landed, nor has any big inspection by high officials taken place, although this has been promised (or threatened) several times. The village men were a bit discouraged after the third time they cleared the field (in January 1965) and said that it would be harder to persuade them to do work on it again in the future.

The Border Patrol have also furnished villagers with school clothing for the children, tools for the men (such as hoes, hammers, saws, an anvil), and vegetable seeds. A boar which was introduced in order to improve the breeding stock of the native pigs was carefully penned and fed for almost a year before it died—without issue. A school garden, which was started with great enthusiasm under the teacher's direction, was taken over by pigs and weeds when the teacher was absent from the village for over a month shortly after the garden was cleared and planted.

In the past year new BPP schools have been built in several nearby Karen and Lua? villages.

[3] The rumor later turned out to have sprung from the following incident. A Karen from Maesariang had reneged on his promise to provide supplies to some Karen refugees in Burma after taking money from them. The Burmese Karens threatened to raid Maesariang. The offending Thai Karen was arrested and transferred to a jail in Maehongson, apparently to decrease the danger of further incidents.

More important than the effect of the formal BPP programs has been the effect of the residence of one or more BPP men in the village. These men and their families have now become points of contact between the Lua? in the mountains and the Thai communities in the valleys. Even when the BPP men are not resident in the village, villagers who go to Maesariang stop to see them, get news and advice from them, and may stay with them overnight. The relationship which has developed between villagers and Border Policemen has been a good one and has provided a contact with the valley which previously did not exist. This is an example of the importance, in communities of this type, of loyalties based on personal relationships.

Missionary Programs. Apparently the earliest missionaries to work with the Lua? were the Presbyterians, who started missionizing just before World War II. They met with limited success in one village, La?up, but were forced to withdraw by the Japanese invasion. They made little effort after the war to return to this area. The New Tribes Mission started work with the Lua? in 1951, and in a meeting in the mid-1950's in which the "field" was divided, it was agreed to give the Lua? to the New Tribes Mission. They are an evangelistic group of Americans not associated with any organized church in the United States.

The New Tribes missionaries, of whom there are usually two or three among the Lua?, started by working with people who had moved down from the mountains to Maesariang and concentrated initially on learning the language and translating the Bible. The La?up dialect was selected as standard for making the phonetic transcription of the Lua? language because of the earlier missionary work which had been done at the La?up. It is too early to tell what effect this standardization of dialect will have on the Lua?, whose dialects are quite divergent.

The New Tribes Mission has no economic, medical, or educational program other than informal teaching of reading as one step in religious training. A fairly large number of Lua?, especially in the younger generations, became literate in this way in their own language, using a Romanized phonetic script. This literacy is not limited to Christian converts. Although there has been no development of a Lua? literature aside from portions of the Bible and some religious songs, the knowledge of writing has been used in non-religious ways. Young men have learned to write love letters to their girl friends, and patients (or their relatives) have received written prescriptions for animal sacrifices from Lua? curers in other villages.

So far there has been relatively little success in teaching the Lua? to use a Thai-alphabet phonetic transcription. The missionaries developed this script in 1963 in conformance with an effort to decrease the differences between Thais and tribal people. This effort met initially with some resentment from Thai officials, who claimed that it was designed to distort the Thai script. The officials eventually saw the ultimate value of the Thai phonetic script for increasing the integration of the tribes into the Thai nation by preparing tribal people for literacy in Thai.

Limited amounts of medicine are occasionally given or sold to the tribes-people, but the New Tribes missionaries also try faith healing. In their preaching they urge the Lua? to give up their beliefs in Lua? spirits and to put their faith in the Christian God. Sacrifices to the spirits are denounced as wasteful, and consumption of alcohol is decried. No substitution has been made for the communal feasting which is such an important part of the native socio-religious system. Singing is an important part of the weekly Christian services.

The New Tribes missionaries have had success in reestablishing Christianity in the village of La?up, where some converts had been made before the war. About twenty out of the hundred houses there are now at least nominally Christian. In Pa Pae two families had been converted (one for the second time), both because of chronic illnesses which had left them impoverished and unable to continue the Lua? method of treatment, which requires repeated sacrifices of animals. In the past, impoverished Lua? families have "become Karen" in order to avoid the expenses of Lua? religion. Such families moved to Karen villages, adopted Karen dress and speech, and raised their children as Karen. They still retained some ties of kinship and friendship with their old Lua? friends and relatives. Thus cultural conversion for financial reasons is an old pattern.

Roman Catholic missionaries have made two converts in La?up, again on medical grounds. According to informants, a young woman was in great pain from an acute illness when a Catholic priest was passing through the village. Her family was told that she would die unless she were operated on. The priest offered to take her to the hospital in Chiengmai if her entire family would convert to Catholicism, which they did. The Catholics ordinarily do not work with the Lua? and have not learned their language, nor do they have a Lua? Bible translation, so the services have to be conducted in Karen. The Catholics have no technical or educational program among these people.

Most non-Christian Lua? are deeply suspicious of missionaries and profoundly desire to maintain their traditional religion, which regulates their agriculture and social behavior: the time of cutting and burning the fields and planting are determined by religious leaders; religious leaders decide disputes concerning traditional customs; weddings and funerals (which are important communal events) are governed by religious custom. In other words, religion is integrated into all aspects of Lua? life in the mountain villages. Religious conversion (usually to Buddhism) seems much more appropiate to the Lua? in the valleys, where the whole pattern of life is quite different.

The Karens in Burma have been considered to be the mission field of the American Baptists for many years. The American Baptists also have established missions in Thailand which deal primarily with Karens. The Baptists have translated the Bible (over a hundred years ago), using a modification of the Burmese script, which they continue to use in Thailand.

The Baptists are probably the most liberal and enlightened missionaries in the area. They have established an agricultural experiment station in Chiengmai which deals largely with upland crops and livestock, and have attempted to introduce new crop methods among the Christian Karens. This has met with spotty success, not so much for technological reasons but because there are limited marketing opportunities for cash crops, transportation to markets is poor, and it has been difficult to persuade the Karens to cooperative effort in this sort of economic enterprise.

The Baptist education program has developed a boarding school or "hostel" arrangement for hill children. The children live at the hostel in Maesariang, located near a public school, which they attend. The parents contribute clothing and rice for the children. The children are supervised by houseparents who are educated Burmese Karen refugees.

A clinic has been established, and a hospital is being built in Maesariang, near the Baptist Mission. Practice is not limited to tribal patients, but they receive sympathetic treatment there, something which apparently they did not always get from the Thai doctor at the government clinic in Maesariang.

Missionaries, like the Border Policemen, form a point of contact between the Luaꜱ and Karen mountaineers and the valley dwellers. But the position of the missionaries in valley society is quite different from that of the policemen, since they are not a part of the dominant society or of the officialdom of that society. Occasionally the missionaries intervene on behalf of the hill tribesmen with government officials, for example in order to assure prompt and free treatment in the government clinic.

SECTION II: RECOMMENDATIONS

RECOMMENDATIONS FOR RESEARCH

In the past, little effort has been made to coordinate the various programs for hill tribes. Occasionally they overlap, compete, or conflict with one another. Hill tribes, just like everything else, have become enmeshed in a series of bureaucracies which are remote from the concerns of the isolated areas and which are often unresponsive to the needs under varying conditions which they are supposed to meet. It is encouraging that in Thailand enough recognition has been given to the needs for knowledge about hill tribes to assign an anthropologist to the Hill Tribes Division of the Public Welfare Department, to start a Tribal Research Centre, and to begin talking seriously about a census of hill tribes. The specific suggestions made by Dr. Geddes for research on hill tribes of the North, their social organization, economics, and agriculture, when completed can form the basis for rational decisions.

Many decisions will have to be made, and many policies decided. Among important issues which must be decided are those with regard to legal status, economic role in the nation, and language policy. These decisions should be based on research directed to these problems.

Research on Legal Status. Research should be done on the laws of Thailand to determine the implications of existing laws for tribal and minority populations. This research should cover at least the following topics:

(a) *Citizenship.* Are these people citizens? If not, what are the implications of their alien status, and if integration is desired, how can they obtain citizenship?

(b) *Land ownership.* Do they have rights to land? If not, how can their rights to land be secured?

(c) *Customary law.* What are the limits of legal systems based on tribal customs? What are potential conflicts between customary law systems and modern Thai law, for example with respect to family, inheritance, or religious practices? Since the areas in which these people live are usually remote from Thai courts, some thought should be given to ways of supporting customary legal systems as a means of preserving order in remote areas.

Research on Economy. Dr. Geddes (in this volume) makes a number of specific proposals for research on the economy of the hill tribes which are worthy of implementation. The first task must be an accurate mapping and census of the various groups, plus an outline of information on their economic patterns, to be followed by a detailed study of each major cultural group, including their patterns of social organization, upland agriculture, trade relations, and so forth.

In addition to Dr. Geddes' suggestion for studies of hill tribes in the hills, studies should be made of the patterns of assimilation of tribal peoples into lowland society. These patterns should be observed among the lowland Karen, Khmu?, and Lua?, all of whom, despite cultural, linguistic, and religious differences, have become more or less settled lowland peoples.

More attention in research should also be paid to the other large groups of potentially alienated minorities, such as the Thai Malay in the South, on whom only one monograph has been written (Fraser 1960; see also Thompson and Adloff 1955:158–165); the Cambodian and Kui in the East, who are inadequately known; and the various Thai sub-groups in the

North and Northeast, who are only beginning to be known (see Moerman's paper in this volume).

In regard to all of these studies of tribal and minority groups, attempts should be made to develop rapid techniques for determining the degree of cultural homogeneity or heterogeneity along lines relevant to economic and political development. It will be impossible ever to study intensively every variant of Lua?, Meo, or Karen, or Thai-Lue culture—each village is different. But not all of the differences are important for the purposes to which we have addressed ourselves.

Research on Language. Several major problems exist with regard to language. Dr. Geddes has addressed himself to some of these: the need to transcribe, analyze, and describe tribal languages, and to develop methods to teach them to those who will be working among the tribal peoples. Basic decisions must be made regarding the use of tribal or minority languages in schools, the earliest language of instruction, development of scripts and literatures in these languages, and the encouragement or discouragement of the perpetuation of these languages. Decisions on this point should be based on a review of the existing literature on the problems of bilingualism in other areas of the world (American Indians, Africa, India, etc.) (see Smalley 1964; UNESCO 1953). For the time being it seems evident that use of traditional languages for spoken communication (either by radio or in direct face-to-face relationships) is to be recommended.

RECOMMENDATIONS FOR ACTION

Coordination of Action. More and more agencies are becoming interested in the hill peoples. Many of these organizations have programs, but there is little evidence of coordination in planning or sharing of information. No overall policy is evident in these programs, many of which are aimed only at specific problems, and there are even contradictions between programs inherent in the ways in which they are carried out. Formal and informal mechanisms should be developed for coordination of planning and the sharing of information. The Tribal Research Centre is a step in this direction.

International Coordination. The scope of the problems involved, as evidenced by the papers in this volume, is not confined to Thailand alone, and efforts should be made to share knowledge and coordinate activities with other countries in Asia, through international scientific organizations, such as the Pacific Science Congress, or through existing international organizations such as ECAFE and SEATO.

Local Administration. If hill peoples are to be brought into participation in the life of Thailand, efforts must be made to increase their contacts at the *tambon* (commune) and *amphur* (district) levels of administration. This problem, of course, is not confined to tribal peoples, but is also applicable to rural people outside of the most readily accessible areas. *Amphur* officials will remain ignorant of conditions in the hills until they visit and see for themselves. Mechanisms of communication between tribal or rural minority groups and decision-makers must be developed or strengthened. The MDU (Mobile Development Units—see Huff's paper) and some of the BPP programs offer models for this task, but in part the problems of tribal administration have been problems of overcentralization which MDU and BPP programs do nothing to counteract.

Communication and Transportation. Contact between hills and lowlands, or between market and administrative centers and remote regions in difficult terrain can be increased by a program of trail-building, especially the building of all-weather foot bridges in regions subject to seasonal flooding. This should be done through the use of *paid* local labor, not *corvée* labor, and should be done during the slack season when labor is not required for agriculture. Such trails and bridges would make it much easier for people in remote regions to participate in lowland markets on more favorable terms (e.g. bringing rice to market during the rainy season when prices are high), as well as increasing speed of communication at all times of the year.

Border Patrol Police Programs. The Border Patrol Police programs have been only partially successful, primarily because projects are started, but not maintained with sufficient personnel or funds. These programs should be strengthened through further recruitment of staff and adequate financing.

(a) Schools which the BPP has established should be fully

staffed and should be kept open. Tribal people in the areas where schools have been built are anxious for education, have contributed to the construction of the schools, and should receive a return on their labor and expressed interest.

(b) Aircraft should be landed on airstrips built and maintained by tribal people, in order to indicate that the whole exercise is something more than a meaningless ritual or a new variety of *corvée* labor.

(c) Methods should be developed to enlist tribal people in the BPP. These people possess language skills and knowledge of the terrain which make them invaluable in attempting to secure the border areas. Training and informal contacts with lowland BPP members will improve the tribal people's knowledge about Thailand, and will increase knowledge among lowland BPP members about hill peoples. Units of the BPP in which tribal people serve should be fully integrated in order to achieve the benefits of this plan. This program should be based on voluntary enlistment, not conscription.

(d) BPP members should be adequately paid, through use of per diem or by other means, to insure that they will not have to impose on tribal people for free food or labor. Demands for free food and labor defeat the purpose of the BPP.

(e) Emphasis on economic development and education should be continued.

Police and Local Security. Police activities should be expanded in order to insure the physical security of the hill peoples and peoples in remote regions, many of whom fear robberies and raids.

Medical Care. One of the best ways of reaching the populations in remote areas is with medical care. Modern medical care seems to be universally desired, and is not seen as conflicting with native forms of treatment or native religion. Traveling medical units could be established on a more or less regular schedule, or more permanent installations could be made on main trails in hill regions. They should include specially trained local personnel as much as possible.

Population Control. The limited medical programs which have already reached the remote areas have had major effects on population growth rates. Family planning information should be made

[671]

available in remote areas, where population growth is liable to have almost immediate adverse effects because of the already marginal economic conditions. Although tribal people value children highly, they also express an interest in knowledge of family planning.

Building Loyalty. Attempts to build loyalty among the hill tribes should be undertaken by building loyalties to individuals. Some of the BPP programs are good examples of how this can be done. Individual loyalties, such as those won by BPP teachers, serve as points of contact between upland and lowland peoples, and are far more meaningful and effective than attempts to develop loyalties to abstract ideas or remote personages. These efforts should be coupled with development and strengthening of local self-government.

Legal Changes. National laws should be modified to accommodate the need to integrate tribal and minority peoples into the nation and to protect their legitimate interests, especially with regard to citizenship and landholding. Unrealistic or unenforceable laws, for example those concerning the cutting of upland fields, should be discarded in order to protect the traditional rights of making a living and to secure the territorial and often spiritual basis of the people.

Any program which is designed to promote the stabilization of upland peoples and to enhance their integration into the national society must take steps to preserve the basic resource of these people, their land. The integrity of land ownership is essential to the preservation of upland communities, and community structure must be preserved as the base from which effective development programs can be launched. This is not a plea for a "reservation system" such as that developed for American Indians. It is, however, a recognition that loss of land-base leads to social disorganization. As many years of experience with American Indians have taught us, social disorganization does not promote orderly social and economic development. Protecting the land-base does not mean that fences should be erected around the upland peoples and that they should be confined to upland areas. For many years upland people, as individuals, have migrated to valley communities, and this process will continue in the future to siphon off surplus hill population and to give opportunities for economic advancement. Rather than building reservations, it is to be hoped that measures will be taken to assure the upland communities of continued possession of their lands in the face of expansion of lowlanders into the upland areas.

A program designed to protect the land-base must take into account the very important differences between classes of land within a single group and between the different customs regarding ownership which are found among different groups. In discussing the Lua? and Karen in this paper, I have tried to indicate how different their customs are in these respects. Communal landholding is much more important among the Lua? than among the Karen. But both groups also recognize individual or family claims to land. Any general land law should be based on research into the various customs of landholding among the several upland groups.

Finally, we should note that hill tribesmen do not live in isolation, and that they are not unaffected by changes taking place in the lowland society. This means that some of the effects for tribal people of the development programs which are directed at rural Thailand in general should be recognized. Road-building may be an essential part of economic development, but modern roads do not, by themselves, promote better integration of tribal communities: roads may merely make it easier for lowland people to exploit the less sophisticated tribesmen. Mechanization of traditional occupations of tribal people, such as lumbering and caravaning, does not mean better jobs and higher wages for tribal people: it probably means their replacement by better trained and more highly skilled lowland people. The widespread distribution of cheap manufactured goods (clothing, packaging materials, etc.) does not always lead to an increase in the standard of living: it may mean that tribes-people are deprived of a market for their traditional products at the same time as they are introduced to new wants. More efficient bureaucratization, for example in the form of greater uniformity of regulations and greater dependence on written records, does not necessarily mean better administration of tribal areas: it may mean that the old basis of face-to-face contact between tribesmen and administrators is lost and flexibility to meet local customs and conditions is made more difficult. Unless such considerations are kept in mind, the

[673]

attempts at development may lead to increasing the gap between the tribes-people and the lowland majority.

REFERENCES CITED

FRASER, THOMAS M., JR.
  1960 Rusembilan: A Malay fishing village in Southern Thailand. Ithaca, Cornell University Press.
HALLETT, HOLT S.
  1890 A thousand miles on an elephant in the Shan States. Edinburgh and London, William Blackwood and Sons.
HAMILTON, JAMES W.
  1963 Effects of the Thai market on Karen life. Practical Anthropology 10(5):209–215.
  1965 Kinship, bazaar, market: the Karen development of a dual economy as an aspect of modernization. Unpublished paper presented at Asian Studies Association annual meeting, April 1965.
KUNSTADTER, PETER
  1965 The Lua? (Lawa) of Northern Thailand: aspects of social structure, agriculture, and religion. Princeton, N.J., Princeton University. Center of International Studies, Research Monograph 21.
  1966 Residential and social organization of the Lawa of Northern Thailand. Southwestern Journal of Anthropology 22(1):61–84.
  1966B Irrigation and social structure: narrow valleys and individual enterprise. Paper prepared for Eleventh Pacific Science Congress. Tokyo, mimeographed.
SMALLEY, WILLIAM A., et al.
  1964 Orthography studies: Articles on new writing systems. London, United Bible Societies.
THOMPSON, VIRGINIA and RICHARD ADLOFF
  1955 Minority problems in Southeast Asia. Stanford, Stanford University Press.
UNITED NATIONS (UNESCO)
  1953 The use of vernacular languages in education. Monographs on Fundamental Education 8. Paris, UNESCO.
YOUNG, GORDON
  1962 The hill tribes of Northern Thailand. Bangkok, the Siam Society, Monograph 1, 2d edn.

PART VIII: VIETNAM

THE ETHNIC Vietnamese, who form over 90 percent of the population both in North and South Vietnam, are a people who have adapted themselves to a lowland way of life. The culture of Vietnam shows many effects of contact with the Chinese, who occupied the country from 111 B.C. to A.D. 939 and again early in the 1400's.[1] The rural Vietnamese are generally intensive irrigated-rice cultivators. Following the period of Chinese domination they expanded southward from their Red River Delta homeland, along the narrow coastal strip of Indochina, staying in the lowlands where irrigation was possible. They destroyed the Cham kingdom which lay in their path, and by the mid-eighteenth century they took over most of the Khmer territory of the Mekong Delta (see Buttinger 1958: Map VIII).[2] The ethnic Vietnamese are still found in the two major delta regions of the Red and Mekong rivers, and along a narrow coastal strip connecting the two (see Service Géographique 1949). About two-thirds of the territory of Vietnam (the mountainous area) is occupied by minority or tribal peoples who, until recently, have been only marginally integrated with the lowland Vietnamese.

The present borders of Vietnam were defined by the French, who took over the territory after a series of wars between 1858 and 1883. The border which was established with Laos cuts across mountainous territory occupied primarily by tribal Tai, Meo, and Yao in the north, and various Mon-Khmer peoples (such as the Hre, Koho, and Bahnar) and Malayo-Polynesian-

[1] For history of Vietnam see Buttinger (1958) and Le Than Khoi (1955). Buttinger's book contains an extensive annotated bibliography. See Fall's two books (1963A, 1963B) for recent political and military history. See Jumper and Normand (1964) for a well-documented summary of contemporary problems in both North and South Vietnam, with a good bibliography. See Jumper (N.D.) and Auvade (1965) for further bibliographic references. See Hickey (1963) for a succinct analysis of Vietnamese society and some of the social differences between northern, central, and southern Vietnamese villages.

[2] The Khmers had at one time controlled the entire Mekong Delta, and were encapsulated or driven back into what is now Cambodia by the advancing Vietnamese. There is still a substantial Khmer minority in South Vietnam, and there are many Vietnamese in Cambodia around Phnom Penh, where they are an unassimilated minority, regarded as the forerunners of a Vietnamese invasion. The Cambodians have ample historical reasons to fear a continued Vietnamese movement to the west.

speaking people (such as the Jarai and Rhadé) in the south.[3] Although Tu Duc, the last independent Vietnamese emperor, attempted to expand his control over the southern highlands after 1863 (Buttinger 1961:103), this mountainous border was not controlled by the Vietnamese in the pre-colonial period, though they occasionally extracted tribute from some of the mountain people. The Vietnamese traditionally exploited the highlanders economically. Especially in the south, where highlanders did not develop an important cash crop, this exploitation increased after European technology had supplanted traditional mountaineer products such as elephants and medicinal plants. The mountaineers still required prestige goods and essential tools from the lowlands, but no longer had much of value to exchange. Trade was carried out by Vietnamese *cac-lai*, or traders, who were assigned specific trading territories by the Annamese government at Hué in return for collecting tribute from the mountaineers (Condominas 1951:78 ff.).

The French split Vietnam into three major administrative division—Tonkin, Annam, and Cochin China—but they also recognized the cultural and environmental differences between the lowland Vietnamese and the highland minorities. In the north, where the minorities were often organized in the form of petty principalities, the French tried a variety of techniques, apparently attempting to divide and rule (see McAlister's paper). In the south they established a different form of administration for the highlanders, eventually developing a form of direct rule in which customary tribal law was recognized (Hickey's paper). Relations between lowland Vietnamese and the highlanders were subject to fluctuations in French policy. The French alternately opened and closed the highlands to Vietnamese settlement, sometimes used Vietnamese, and sometimes French, and sometimes tribal administrative officers. Probably as a result of economic exploitation (the French used highlander *corvée* labor in southern highland plantations), there were tribal revolts, including

---

[3] For a general description of the ethnology of Indochina, including a selected bibliography of French sources, see Condominas (1953). For a description of the Vietnamese, Tho, and Black Tai of northern Vietnam see Hickey (1958). For a discussion of the Chinese minority, see Fall (1958). See LeBar *et al.* (1964) for brief summaries of the cultures of the various ethnic groups mentioned elsewhere in this introduction.

a revolt among the Jarai which was connected with a messianic movement, and which lasted until the late 1930's (Hickey 1957:9–10). But the French also won many friends among the mountain people when they acted as protectors from the Vietnamese.

McAlister discusses the ultimately unsuccessful French attempts to manipulate ethnic differences in order to prevent the Viet Minh from taking control over the northern highlanders during the French Indochina War. The French were more successful among the southern highlanders. Under the French the region of greatest concentration of southern highland peoples was known as the Pays Montagnard du Sud (or PMS, the southern mountaineer area), which was administratively separated from the rest of Annam. Relatively few roads were built here, and the area was not subject to as much economic development as were the lowlands. The French established the *cac-lai* trading system and some medical and educational services, and tribal leaders were sometimes allowed to govern at the district level and below. Though the policy was not consistent, Vietnamese settlement in the highlands was generally limited to a few of the larger towns such as Kontum and Pleiku.

In order to maintain control of the northern highlands, the French attempted to create a semi-autonomous Tai Federation (McAlister's paper). In the south the French detached five predominantly highland provinces from Annam and attempted direct administration there. This won favor with the highlanders, but frustrated the nationalistic ambitions of the Vietnamese— both the Viet Minh and the followers of the French candidate for emperor, Bao Dai. As a sop to Vietnamese nationalism the French made the five central highland provinces and the Tai Federation into crown territories under Bao Dai, after restoring him to the throne in 1946 (Condominas 1951:79; Joiner 1965:22). As a result the tribesmen were obliged to pay allegiance both to the French and to the Vietnamese.

McAlister tells us how the Tai Federation was taken over by the Viet Minh in spite of French efforts. The Viet Minh promised the Tai tribes as much or more independence than the French had granted. In 1955, only a year after the victory over the French at Dien Bien Phu, a Tai-Meo Autonomous Zone was

[679]

established, and the Viet Bac Autonomous Zone was established a year later. These zones included most of the area of the Tai Federation. The North Vietnamese went on to exploit pride in ethnic differences in their attempts to build national unity, and gave their minorities considerable autonomy at least in language and customs (see below).

By contrast, the South Vietnamese attempted to deal with their bewildering variety of tribal peoples by incorporating the high-land areas as an integral part of the nation. Highlanders were supposed to be considered citizens, and were made subject to the same laws and administrative structures as lowland ethnic Vietnamese. Tribal custom courts were abolished, and Vietnam-ese was supposed to be the language of instruction in all schools. The South Vietnamese struck at the heart of highland society with their land policy. Lowlanders, who were often refugees from the North or from Viet Cong-controlled areas, were resettled in the highlands, irrespective of previous claims of the highland-ers to the land. In some areas attempts were made to regroup the highlanders into centers which were supposed both to give them protection from the Viet Cong and to serve as centers for the Vietnamization of the highlanders. These centers resembled the strategic hamlets of the Mekong Delta (described by O'Don-nell; see also Osborne 1965). By 1963 as many as 209,025 high-landers were reported to have been resettled in strategic or tacti-cal hamlets (figure from Vietnam Press, w/e July 7, 1963, cited by Osborne 1965:39, who says the estimate is probably much too high). The highland regroupment plan evidently failed for reasons similar to those detailed by O'Donnell for the delta, plus the complicating factor of traditional antagonisms between low-land Vietnamese and the mountaineers. This policy with respect to the highlanders was evidently the expression of the personal philosophy of President Diem (Joiner 1965:26–27; see also But-tinger 1961).

The Communists have been quick to seize on the unsympathetic and unsuccessful attempts of the South Vietnamese Government to deal with problems of the mountain minorities (e.g. Burchett 1963: Ch. VI). The Program of the National Liberation Front (Viet Cong) specifically refers to the poor treatment which the minorities have received at the hands of the "U.S. Diem clique" and states its own policy:

To ensure the right to autonomy of the national minorities.

To set up, within the framework of the great family of the Vietnamese people, autonomous regions in areas inhabited by minority peoples.

To ensure equal right among different nationalities. All nationalities have the right to use and develop their own spoken and written languages and to preserve or change their customs and habits . . .

To help the minority peoples to catch up with the common level of the people by developing the economy and culture in the areas inhabited by them, by training skilled personnel from people of minority origin (Anon. 1963:29–30).

The similarity of this policy to the Constitntion of the Democratic Republic of Vietnam is obvious (see below, p. 684).

The Viet Cong have attempted to exploit the discontent of the South Vietnam tribesmen, but have not been completely successful. A Rhadé, Ybih (or Y Binh) Aleo, is the chairman of a committee of the National Liberation Front dealing with minorities. He is also a member of the NLF Central Committee and a vice-president of the NLF, and he leads a movement for the autonomy of the central highlands area (Joiner 1965:28; Burchett 1963: Ch. 5). This employment of a tribesman in positions of responsibility and leadership clearly parallels that used with great effectiveness by the Pathet Lao (see introduction to the Laos section of this book), and by the Viet Minh (McAlister's paper). The NLF program for autonomy of the highlands is directed not only against the U.S. and South Vietnamese presence, but also at improvement of the living conditions of the mountaineers. They claim to have improved the economic conditions of the mountaineers by introducing cattle-breeding, blacksmithing, and various handicrafts; and also claim to have introduced doctors and sanitation personnel, schools, and phonetic transcriptions for seventeen tribal languages (broadcast of South Vietnam Liberation Radio, December 21, 1965, of a report by Y Binh Aleo, President of the High Plateau Autonomy Movement Committee; see also Burchett 1965: 166 ff.).

The South Vietnam government's response to the situation has not been to attempt to match or beat the offers of the Viet Cong. The Americans (under CIA and Army Special Forces) have attempted to train and arm tribesmen in order to secure the highlands area, but this effort has met with resistance from the South Vietnamese government, which sees a strong armed mountaineer

population as a threat to national unity. The Americans have
ended up in the middle of a traditional antagonism: they wish
to arm the mountaineers so they can protect themselves against
the Viet Cong and restrict infiltration by the Viet Cong and
North Vietnamese into the highlands from Laos, but they find
themselves unable or unwilling to assist the mountaineers in their
desire for greater autonomy (see e.g. *New York Herald Tribune,*
October 10, 1965).

The mountaineers have occasionally taken matters into their
own hands and have rebelled three times in a little over a year
(September 1964, October 1965, December 1965). The available
journalistic reports are not sufficient to tell the complete story,
but the tribesmen have repeatedly asked for greater autonomy,
protection of their lands against lowland intrusion, better schooling and medical facilities, and greater representation in the central government. These demands are not surprising—they were
all evident as early as 1957 (Hickey 1957)—but they have been
repeatedly ignored by Saigon. What is surprising about these
revolts is the degree of organization which they evidently represent. The Rhadé, who were evidently the leaders of the rebellions,
traditionally were not organized above the level of the village
(LeBar *et al.* 1964:254, citing Condominas 1955:561 ff.). In spite
of the lack of traditional supra-communal organization, the revolt
in December 1965 took place simultaneously in five different
provinces, and the rebels managed to seize two provincial capitals before the revolt was quelled (*New York Times,* December
9, 10, 1965). It seems likely that this supra-communal organization was aided by two factors: the Rhadé were trained by the
French as administrators, and under the French "many of the
lower-echelon provincial positions and almost all of those at the
district level gradually came to be held by trained Rhadé"
(LeBar *et al.* 1964, citing Sabatier 1940:53–56). The second factor is probably the training and communication networks provided to the Rhadé and other tribesmen by U.S. forces. It is significant that FULRO (the Front for the Relief of the Oppressed
Races), a movement which claims to represent the united aspirations of the southern Vietnamese highlanders, and which is apparently based in Cambodia, also has a Rhadé leader, Y Bham
(see Oka 1965 for more information on Y Bham, the tribal revolts,

[682]

and FULRO).⁴ Though the leaders of the 1964 revolt were given amnesty, and promises were made to meet some of their demands (see Hickey's paper), apparently these promises were not kept. The South Vietnamese government's policy seems to be hardening—several of the 1965 rebellion leaders were executed (*New York Times*, December 28, 1965), and there is no evidence that any promises were made regarding reforms.⁵

North Vietnam has more minority peoples, and fewer different groups of minorities, than South Vietnam. These include various Tai-speaking groups such as the Tho, the Black, White, and Red Tai, the Muong, the Meo, and the Yao. In general, these groups

⁴ The program of FULRO was discussed at the Congress of Indochinese Peoples, which was convened by Prince Sihanouk early in March 1965. In a speech on March 13, at the conclusion of this congress, Y Bham Enoul outlined the historical background of the FULRO movement and its aspirations. He asserted that the "Austrienne race" (roughly equivalent to the people who are labeled "montagnards" of South Vietnam) came from the same origin as the Khmer people. He also said that strong and good politico-religious relations were maintained between the Austriennes and the Khmers throughout pre-colonial and most of colonial history. He traced the history by which the highlanders were annexed by the French to Annam, and refers to the conditions under which the French "arbitrarily, without consulting us, had, by decree No. 28, QT-DT dated April, 1952, reunited the PMS (Pays Montagnard du Sud, the country of the southern mountaineers) to the domaine of the Crown of Emperor Bao Dai." The mountaineers, he said, were not consulted about their own fate during the 1954 Geneva Conference. Y Bham concluded by saying that the Austrienne people have decided to unite and form their own front for their own liberation. (The full text of Y Bham's speech is reported in Réalités Cambodgiennes, 19 March 1965, pp. 9–10.)

Y Bham's argument concerning the identity of all of the "Austrienne race" is ethnographically (or at least linguistically) inaccurate, since there are two completely distinct language families represented among the highlanders. These are the Mon-Khmer languages (spoken by groups such as the Hrê, Koho, and Bahnar), whose languages are clearly related to the language of the Cambodians, and the Malayo-Polynesian languages (spoken by groups such as the Rhadé and Jarai) whose languages are unrelated to that of the Cambodians. Likewise, Y Bham's description of political and religious ties between the mountaineers and the Cambodians seems over-formalized. These arguments, however, formed the basis for Prince Sihanouk to maintain that Cambodia has an interest in preventing the genocide of the mountaineers by the South Vietnamese, just as he protested the treatment of the Cambodian minority in South Vietnam (in an interview at the conclusion of the Indochinese People's Conference, reported in Réalités Cambodgiennes, 19 March 1965, p. 8).

⁵ Preliminary reports indicate that the existing provinces will be maintained for the election of the constituent Assembly in September 1966—each province must have at least one seat. However, election districts are being constructed so as to assure minority representation—five seats have been set aside for mountaineer tribesmen, six for the ethnic Cambodian minority, and one for the Cham minority. Religious minorities, such as the Hoa Hao and Cao Dai, should also be able to elect representatives in the districts where they are concentrated (Apple 1966).

are closer to the cultural level of the lowland Vietnamese majority than most of the tribes of the South. In spite of the closer
cultural ties, however, the Vietnamese of the North have in the
past gotten along just as poorly with the mountain people as
have those in the South. Some of the minority peoples joined
in anti-Japanese actions during the Second World War, while
others remained aloof or accepted the rule of the Vichy French
and the Japanese military occupation forces. During the French
Indochina War, the hill and minority peoples both in the North
and the South were frequently loyal to the French. This was
particularly true of the Tai-speaking groups, concentrated in the
North, although the Tho were very quickly won to the Viet Minh
(see McAlister's paper).

The Viet Minh proclaimed the equality of tribal minorities
as early as 1945 (Jumper and Normand 1964:449). They continued their attempts to win the favor and support of minorities
after the Geneva settlement in 1954. Though the South Vietnamese Constitution is silent with respect to minority rights, the Constitution of the Democratic Republic of Vietnam makes specific
provisions for its minorities, for their rights to organize, and to
preserve their language and culture:

Chapter 1. Article 3.

The Democratic Republic of Vietnam is a single multinational state.

All the nationalities living on Vietnamese territory are equal in
rights and duties. The state has the duty to maintain and develop
the solidarity between the various nationalities. All acts of discrimination against, or oppression of, any nationality, all acts which undermine
the unity of the nationalities are strictly prohibited.

All nationalities have the right to preserve or reform their own
customs and habits, to use their spoken and written language, and
to develop their own national culture.

Autonomous zones may be established in areas where people of
the national minorities live in compact communities. Such autonomous
zones are inalienable parts of the Democratic Republic of Vietnam.

The state strives to help the national minorities to make rapid
progress and to keep pace with the general economic and cultural
advance (quoted in Fall 1963A:402).

The Constitution goes on, in Articles 92–96, to define the structure of People's Councils and Administrative Committees in the
autonomous zones. These provide for the establishment of these
structures along the same lines as in the ordinary districts and

provinces, except that in zones where there are several different minorities present, each is supposed to be represented in the People's Councils. A 1957 modification of the laws setting up administrative organs of the government recognized the differences in population density between upland (minority and tribal) and lowland (majority) areas. The sparsely settled mountainous areas, and even plains areas of the minority autonomous zones were allotted a per capita quota of deputies about three times as high as the quota for the lowlands areas (Ginsburgs 1963:195–197). Government services are supposed to be provided by cadres from the zone itself. The people in the autonomous zones can even organize their own self-defense forces, but these become an integral part of the Vietnamese People's Army under the central government as soon as they are organized. Likewise, although the autonomous zones are supposed to be able to control income and expenditures, they are required to deposit part of the revenue in the Central State Bank, and all aspects of the zone's development plan must be coordinated with the nation-wide plan (Fall 1963A:402; Ginsburgs 1962:211–230).

Two such zones were created: the Thai-Meo Autonomous Zone and the Viet-Bac Autonomous Zone, both located in the extreme north of the country, where the French had earlier attempted to establish a "Tai Federation."[6] Other attempts to create autonomous zones proved unsuccessful and were abandoned (Fall 1963A:150–151). All in all the policy of the North Vietnamese looks very similar to that of Communist China (see paper by Diao in this volume) and the Soviet Union (Armstrong 1965). Virtually identical policies are stated in the Program of the National Liberation Front of South Vietnam (quoted by Fall 1963A:422; cf. Ginsburgs 1962). As Hickey predicted in 1957, the propaganda value of the autonomous zones has evidently been quite great: similar statements turn up repeatedly in the demands of the mountaineer rebels in the 1964 and 1965 upris-

[6] See Honey (1962:10) for a description of some of the difficulties involved in maintaining control over the northern minorities; for more recent references see Joiner (1965:n. 13, citing Documentary Record of the Third National Congress of the Vietnam Lao Dong Party—North Vietnam, U.S. Joint Publications Research Service, Paper 7137, Washington, D.C., January 1961, pp. 375–384, and implementation of the Policy on Zonal Autonomy with Regard to the Various Nationalities in the Viet Bac Zone, U.S. Joint Publications Research Service, Paper 20739, Washington, D.C., August 1963). See also Jumper and Normand (1964:499–501) and Fall (1963A:148–152) for a discussion of North Vietnam's minority policies.

ings against their South Vietnamese commanders (e.g. Sochurek 1965; *New York Herald Tribune*, October 10, 1965; *New York Times*, December 19 and 20, 1965). Apparently the demand for tribal autonomy has been a continuing source of friction between the U.S. and South Vietnam governments (Anon. 1965A; 1965B; Mohr 1965).

The Democratic Republic of Vietnam (North Vietnam) has long recognized the significance of use of minority languages in building national solidarity, and, like the Chinese (Diao's paper), they have embarked on a program of linguistic research and reform and special schooling for tribesmen. The North Vietnam government has decreed that tribal or minority languages are to be used in areas where tribal or minority people predominate (Decree No. 206-CP, dated November 27, 1963, cited in Nguyen Kin Than 1964:32). Scripts have been created for Meo, Tay (Tho), and Nung, and standardized for Tai, using Tai Noir (Black Tai) as the standard dialect (Le Khac 1962:157). The pattern of operation seems identical with that reported for China (cf. Lin 1961; Ma 1962).

In spite of announcements that the minority language program has gone well, it has also been criticized for failures in basic research on minority dialects, in development of scientifically based scripts, in training of teachers, in translating texts and reference books, and in failure to use minority languages and scripts in official signs and notices in the minority areas. The announced policy now is to teach minority children first in their own languages before trying to teach them literacy in Vietnamese (Nguyen Kin Than 1964), and tribesmen are taken to a special school in Hanoi, where they are given political indoctrination and are taught how to be teachers in their own languages (Fall 1963A:152, and Tongas 1960:172, cited in Jumper and Normand 1964:501, n. 14).

In 1962 the tribal schools were reported to have 870 students, including members of the Khmer, E dê (Rhadé), Jarai, Bahnar, Sedang, and Cham groups, all of which have large populations in South Vietnam.[7] As early as 1957 the North Vietnamese were

---

[7] The fact that the South Vietnamese tribal students are attending North Vietnam schools is from Le Khac (1962:157). These students may have been recruited from among the 25,000 or so tribesmen reported to have gone north after the 1954 Geneva settlement (Joiner 1965:23–24). These included five or six thousand Rhadé (Hickey 1957:26).

making radio broadcasts to the central highlands of South Vietnam, using tribal languages (e.g. Rhadé and Jarai), and were infiltrating indoctrinated tribesmen and Vietnamese back into the area (Hickey 1957:26–27; Osborne 1965:49, citing broadcasts in Rhadé from Radio Hanoi of March 8, 1962, August 9, 1962, and November 15, 1962). No doubt these infiltrators have influenced the southern Vietnam highlanders to a certain extent, but the grievances of these highlanders predate the Vietnamese war, and the South Vietnam government has failed to deal with them effectively.

Joiner's well-reasoned conclusion is worth quoting at length on this point:

> The Central Vietnamese Highlands must soon be granted administrative autonomy. This is not an argument for secession of the large plateau region from the Vietnamese state. Rather it favors a reasonable political solution for an extremely dangerous situation. Administrative autonomy within the Republic of Vietnam would permit the highlands to remain politically an integral part of the nation. It would provide for needed administrative flexibility, permitting highlanders a much wider participation in their government, and allowing wider possibilities for solving unique highlands problems through implementation of programs geared specifically to tribal conditions. It would be the most effective technique for winning the cooperation of tribal leaders, by accepting local forms to the extent possible, and by giving tribal and village chiefs and headmen as well as village councils, elders, and even sorcerers a good deal of formal responsibility to serve as the operational government within their own territories. This delegation of authority to *de facto* tribal leaders would bring them within the framework of the administrative apparatus now operating throughout the highlands. They would be directly responsible to other highlanders who would assume higher administrative positions on both geographic and functional bases. (Joiner 1965:35–36)

To be sure, such a solution would involve a structural recognition of a basic division within Vietnam. But the recognition of this division might lead to a better integration, along the lines of developments in India (see Burling's paper), rather than the obviously unsuccessful attempt to ignore or abolish the differences between lowland and highland.

Vietnam is crosscut by a number of divisions which make the building of a modern nation extremely difficult. The political division between North and South—Communist and non-Communist—is only the most dramatic of these problems. The problems of integration of upland minorities, complicated as they are by ecological and economic differences, and reinforced by traditional ethnic antagonisms, indicate that the struggle now going on in Vietnam is much more than just two-sided. And, as O'Donnell indicates, the rural-urban split is a profound one, even apart from the conditions of warfare.[8] As Hickey has shown (1963:212, 213) the southern villages traditionally were even less closely tied to the central government than were those further north. The mandarin system was not established in the southern villages before the French arrived.

Unlike the Buddhist countries (Burma, Cambodia, Laos, and Thailand), Vietnam has no national religion which can serve as a symbolic or structural basis for national unity. The division between Catholics and Buddhists is well known. But it is not proper to think of Vietnam as a Buddhist country with a Catholic minority. In spite of the fact that many rural people consider themselves to be Buddhists, organized Buddhism is predominantly an urban phenomenon in Vietnam, and there is no unified national Buddhist hierarchy penetrating all rural areas, as there is, for example, in Thailand. Vietnamese Buddhism is split into a number of competing, politically organized sects. In addition there are other sects, such as the Cao Dai (Fall 1955, and Jumper 1959), which have been organized as politico-religious units, often in competition with the central government. The religion of many villagers is locally oriented and focused on ancestral shrines with highly specific locales and highly specific village kinship-based adherence (see for example Hickey 1964: Chs. 3, 8; and Landon 1947).

The people of Vietnam would have had a difficult time developing national unity even in the absence of a Communist-inspired war. In South Vietnam no adequate administrative infra-structure has been developed (Dorsey 1963 and Shaplen 1965), and

[8] For further documentation of the rural-urban dichotomy see Hickey's excellent study of the village of Khanh Hau (1964) and the introduction thereto by Mus (pp. xx ff.) See also Hendry's examination of the economy of the same village (1964), and Woodruff's administrative study (1960). For some of the consequences of the Vietnamese rural-urban gap in the U.S. aid programs see Hendry (1960; 1962) and Donnell (1966). Donnell also discusses the differences between Government of Vietnam and Viet Cong attempts to minimize or exploit this gap. For an analysis of the general problems of social cohesion and national unity in Vietnam see Mus (1952, esp. Ch. 24), and Fall (1962).

there is weakness at the top levels of government in spite of (or perhaps because of) years of attempts at support and manipulation first by the French, and later by the U.S. Certainly nothing in the South has developed to rival the organizational ability of the Communists of the North. The failure to develop effective bases of national solidarity, as starkly illustrated by the repeated tribal revolts, leads to the unhappy prediction that whatever may be gained by military means cannot, under present conditions, be consolidated politically once the fighting has stopped (cf. Fall 1965). The drama of warfare and concentration on military solutions has tended to obscure the lack of basic development of national unity in the political, economic, and social spheres.

REFERENCES CITED

ANON.
1955 Minorities under the Viet-Minh. Eastern World 9:17–18 (November).

1963 The voice of justice. Hanoi, Foreign Languages Publishing House.

1965A U.S. denies Saigon demanded recall of three officials. New York Times, September 15 (story datelined Saigon, South Vietnam, September 14).

1965B 500 Tribesmen affirm loyalty to Ky regime. New York Times, September 16, (story datelined Banmethuot, South Vietnam, September 15).

APPLE, R. W., JR.
1966 Buddhists and election: militants expected to win 40 to 50 seats in vote for Assembly Sept. 11. New York Times, 11 June (story datelined Saigon, 10 June).

ARMSTRONG, TERENCE E.
1965 Russian settlement in the north. Cambridge, University Press.

AUVADE, ROBERT
1965 Bibliographie critique des oeuvres parues sur l'Indochine Française: un siècle d'histoire et d'enseignement. Paris, G.-P. Maisonneuve & Larose.

BURCHETT, WILFRED G.
1963 The furtive war: The United States in Vietnam and Laos. New York, International Publishers.

1965 Vietnam: inside story of the guerrilla war. New York, International Publishers.

BUTTINGER, JOSEPH
1958 The smaller dragon: a political history of Vietnam. New York, Frederick A. Praeger.

[689]

1961 The ethnic minorities in the Republic of Vietnam. *In* Problems of freedom, Wesley R. Fishel, ed. New York, The Free Press of Glencoe, Inc.

CONDOMINAS, GEORGES
1951 Aspects of a minority problem in Indochina. Pacific Affairs 24:77–82 (March).
1953 L'Indochine. *In* Ethnologie de l'Union Française (Territoire Exterieur), Tome II: Asie, Océanie, Amerique, par André Leroi-Gourhan et Jean Poirier. Paris, Press Universitaire de France, pp. 514–678, bibliography pp. 997–1028.
1955 Introduction to "Chant épique de Kdam Yi," by F.-P. Antoine, Bulletin de l'Ecole Française d'Extrême Orient 47:549–615.

DONNELL, JOHN C.
1966 The war, the gap and the cadre. Asia 4:49–71

DORSEY, JOHN T. JR.
1963 The bureaucracy and political development in Vietnam. *In* Bureaucracy and political development, Joseph LaPalombra, ed. Princeton, N.J., Princeton University Press, pp. 318–359.

FALL, BERNARD B.
1955 The political-religious sects of Vietnam. Pacific Affairs 28:235–253 (September).
1958 Viet-Nam's Chinese problem. Far Eastern Survey 27(5):65–72 (May).
1962 Problèmes politiques des états poly-ethniques en Indochine. France-Asie 172:129–152 (March–April).
1963A The two Viet-Nams: a political and military analysis. London and Dunmow, Pall Mall Press.
1963B Street without joy: insurgency in Indochina, 1946–1963. London and Dunmow, Pall Mall Press, 3d revised edn.
1965 The second Indochina war. International Affairs 41(1):59–73 (January).

GINSBURGS, GEORGE
1962 Local government and administration in the Democratic Republic of Vietnam since 1954 (Part I). The China Quarterly 12:211–230.
1963 Local government and administration in the Democratic Republic of Vietnam since 1954 (Part II). The China Quarterly 14:195–211.
      These two articles are republished in a slightly different form, under the title "Local government and administration under the Viet-Minh, 1945–54." *In* North Vietnam today: profile of a Communist satellite, P. J. Honey, ed., New York, Frederick A. Praeger, pp. 135–165.

HENDRY, JAMES B.
1960 American aid in Vietnam: the view from a village. Pacific Affairs 33(4):387–391 (December).

1962 Economic development under conditions of guerrilla warfare: the case of Vietnam. Asian Survey 2(4):1–12 (June).

1964 The small world of Khanh Hau. Chicago, Aldine Publishing Co. Research Studies in Economic Development and Cultural Change, Bert F. Hoselitz, ed., University of Chicago.

HICKEY, GERALD CANNON

1957 Preliminary research report on the PMS. [Saigon] Michigan State University Vietnam Advisory Group, Field Administration Division.

1958 Social systems of northern Vietnam. Chicago, University of Chicago, Department of Anthropology, doctoral dissertation.

1963 Problems of social change in Vietnam. In Proceedings of the Ninth Pacific Science Congress of the Pacific Science Association, 1957. Vol. 3, Anthropology and Social Sciences, pp. 209–216. Bangkok, Secretariat, Ninth Pacific Science Congress.

1964 Village in Vietnam. New Haven and London, Yale University Press.

HONEY, P. J. (ed.)

1962 North Vietnam today: profile of a Communist satellite. New York, Frederick A. Praeger.

JOINER, CHARLES A.

1965 Administration and political warfare in the highlands. Vietnam Perspectives 1(2):19–37.

JUMPER, ROY

1957 Mandarin bureaucracy and politics in South Vietnam. Pacific Affairs 30:47–58 (March).

1959 Sects and communism in South Vietnam. Orbis 3:85–96 (Spring).

N.D. Bibliography on the political and administrative history of Vietnam: 1802–1962, selected and annotated. Michigan State University Vietnam Advisory Group, Agency for International Development, contract ICA c1126.

JUMPER, ROY, and MARJORIE WEINER NORMAND

1964 Vietnam. In Government and politics of Southeast Asia, George McTurnan Kahin, ed., pp. 373–524. Ithaca, Cornell University Press, 2d edn.

LANDON, KENNETH PERRY

1947 Southeast Asia, crossroads of religion. Chicago, University of Chicago Press.

LEBAR, FRANK M., GERALD C. HICKEY, and JOHN K. MUSGRAVE

1964 Ethnic groups of mainland Southeast Asia. New Haven, Human Relations Area Files Press.

LIN YUEH-HUA

1961 The minority peoples of Yunnan. China Reconstructs, December:26–29.

MA HSUEH-LIANG
    1962   New scripts for China's minorities. China Reconstructs, August:
            24–27.
MOHR, CHARLES
    1965   Saigon said to oust 3 aides of U.S. over tie to tribes. New
            York Times, September 13 (story datelined Saigon, South Viet-
            nam, September 12).
MUS, PAUL
    1952   Vietnam, sociologie d'une guerre. Paris, Ed. du Seuil.
NGUYEN KIN THAN
    1964   Problems in minority languages and writing. In Tap Chi Van
            Hoc [Literary Magazine], No. 12, pp. 64–72, Hanoi. Trans-
            lated by U.S. Joint Publications Research Service, Washington,
            D.C., JPRS:28, 472, Translations of Political and Sociological
            Information on North Vietnam, No. 137, pp. 31–40.
OKA, TAKASHI
    1965   Hill tribe leader in South Vietnam. Christian Science Monitor,
            December 27 (story datelined Saigon).
OSBORNE, MILTON E.
    1965   Strategic hamlets in South Viet-Nam: a survey and a compari-
            son. Ithaca, Cornell University, Department of Asian Studies,
            Southeast Asia Program Data Paper 55.
SABATIER, L.
    1940   Recueil des coutoumes Rhadées du Darlac. Hanoi, Imprimerie
            d'Extrême-Orient.
SERVICE GEOGRAPHIQUE DE L'INDOCHINE
    1949   Carte ethnolinguistique (care de l'Indochine au 2.000.000e).
            Dressé sous la direction de l'Ecole Française d'Extrême-Orient.
            Hanoi, Service Géographique National du Viêt-Nam.
SHAPLEN, ROBERT
    1965   The lost revolution. New York, Harper and Row.
SOCHUREK, H.
    1965   Americans in action in Viet Nam. National Geographic
            127(1):38–65 (January).
TONGAS, GERARD
    1960   J'ai vécu dans l'enfer communiste au Nord Viet-Nam et j'ai
            choisi la liberté. Paris, Nouvelles Editions Debresse.
WOODRUFF, L. W.
    1960   The study of a Vietnamese rural community—administrative
            activity. Saigon, Michigan State University Advisory Group.

Periodicals

NEW YORK HERALD TRIBUNE. New York.
NEW YORK TIMES. New York.
RÉALITÉS CAMBODGIENNES. Phnom Penh.

TABLE 24
POPULATION AND LINGUISTIC AFFILIATION OF ETHNIC GROUPS OF NORTH VIETNAM[a]

Group (Synonyms in Parentheses)	Est. Population in North Vietnam[b]	Location (in Order of Size of Population)	Language
Kinh (ethnic Vietnamese)	13,553,746	South Vietnam, North Vietnam	Viet-Muong: Vietnamese
Tho (Tay)	503,995	North Vietnam, Kwangsi	Tai: Central, several dialects[c]
Muong (Viet-Muong)	415,658	North Vietnam	Viet-Muong: Muong
Tai (Thai) (including White, Black, and Red Thai)	385,191[d]	North Vietnam, Laos, Thailand	Tai: Southwestern
Nùng[e]	313,998	Kwangsi, North Vietnam	Tai: Central
Meo (Miao)	219,514	Kweichow, Hunan, Szechwan, Kwangsi, Yunnan, North Vietnam, Laos, Thailand	Miao-Yao: Miao
Man (Yao)	186,071	Kwangsi, Kwangtung, Hainan, North Vietnam, Laos, Thailand	Miao-Yao: Yao
Hoa[f]	174,674	China, Southeast Asia	Chinese
San diu[g]	32,479	[not available]	[not available]
Cao lan[h]	22,543	[not available]	Tai (?), Miao-Yao (?)
Xa[i]	22,500	[not available]	Tibeto-Burman: Burmese-Lolo, Lolo group
Nhang	16,429	North Vietnam, Yunnan	Tai: Northern
San chi[g]	15,816	[not available]	[not available]
Lolo	6,898	Yunnan, Kweichow, Szechwan, Laos, North Vietnam	Tibeto-Burman: Burmese-Lolo, Lolo group
Van Kieu[g] (probably Brôu)[j]	5,486	[not available]	?Mon-Khmer: Katuic
U ni[g]	5,259	[not available]	[not available]
May[j,k]	(904)	North Vietnam	Mon-Khmer: ?Katuic

(continued)

[693]

TABLE 24
(continued)

Group (Synonyms in Parentheses)	Est. Population in North Vietnam[b]	Location (in Order of Size of Population)	Language
Laqua[k]	(200)	North Vietnam, Yunnan	Kadai:
Ruc (Rôc)[j,k]	(189)	North Vietnam	Mon-Khmer: ?Katuic
Kelao[k]	[not available]	Kweichow, Hunan, Yunnan, Kwangsi, North Vietnam	Kadai:
Lati[j]	(a small group)	North Vietnam, Yunnan	Kadai:
Nùng[g,k,l]	(a large group)	Southern China, North Vietnam, South Vietnam	Chinese: Nùng dialect
Sach[j,k]	[not available]	North Vietnam	Mon-Khmer: ?N. Laos
Total (1960 census)	15,916,955[m]		

[a] Sources: Population figures primarily from UNESCO (1964:315, Table 9) citing *Nhan Dan* (*The People*), November 2, 1960, North Vietnam, quoting 1960 census figures. Information on distribution from LeBar *et al.* (1964) and other sources as noted. Population figures in parentheses are from LeBar *et al.* (1964) and are not included in the 1960 census total. For information on methods of linguistic classification see notes accompanying the table of population and linguistic affiliation for Burma in the present volume.

[b] Groups whose populations are unknown are listed alphabetically.

[c] According to Gedney (1965), in North Vietnam, "the term Tho . . . is applied to many dialects of the Tai group, and there it is said to be a Vietnamese term. . . . Some of the dialects on the Kwangsi side of the border that I studied are [also] called Tho by their speakers." In some places the term Tho is considered to be derogatory, so the North Vietnamese have begun using the term "Tay" in official references to these people. Thomas (1965) adds that there is much confusion in classification between Tho and Nùng, some dialects of which are apparently mutually intelligible.

[d] The Tai population probably includes most or all of the following populations listed separately by LeBar *et al.* (1964): Lü (1,000+), Neua (?), Pa-y (533), Black Tai (344,191), Phutai (?), T'ou Lao (528), Trung-cha (180), Red Tai (?), White Tai (?).

[e] There is also a Chinese-speaking group known as Nùng (see *n.k* below).

[f] The Hoa are grouped by LeBar *et al.* (1964:72) with the Meo, but are considered by Skinner (1965) and Thomas (1965) to be ethnic Chinese. Skinner's estimate for 1965 population of ethnic Chinese in North Vietnam is 190,000.

(continued)

TABLE 24
(continued)

ᵍ This group is not listed by LeBar *et al.* (1964).

ʰ The Cao Lan are grouped by LeBar *et al.* (1964:88) with the Indochina Man (Yao), but they cite Arutiunov and Mukhlinov (1961), who consider the Cao Lan to be a separate Tai-speaking group. Population figure is from UNESCO (1964).

ⁱ The Xa are grouped with the Indochina Lolo, by LeBar *et al.* (1964:26), but they are listed as a separate group by UNESCO (1964).

ʲ Identification and linguistic classification from Thomas (1965).

ᵏ This group is not listed in UNESCO (1964).

ˡ Thomas (1965) states that there is a Chinese-speaking group known as Nùng in North Vietnam. A large number of refugees from this group have gone to South Vietnam.

ᵐ Census total includes 36,728 "other" tribal people.

REFERENCES CITED

ARUTIUNOV, S. A. and A. I. MUKHLINOV
    1961   Materialy po etno-lingvisticheskoĭ klassifikatsii narodov V'etnama [Materials for the ethnolinguistic classification of the peoples of Vietnam]. Sovetskaia Etnografiia 1:72–82.

GEDNEY, WILLIAM J.
    1965   Personal communication.

LEBAR, FRANK M., GERALD C. HICKEY, and JOHN K. MUSGRAVE
    1964   Ethnic groups of mainland Southeast Asia. New Haven, Human Relations Area Files Press.

OVERSEAS CHINESE YEARBOOK
    1964   Overseas Chinese yearbook. Taipei.

SKINNER, G. WILLIAM
    1965   Personal communication.

THOMAS, DAVID D.
    1965   Personal communication.

UNESCO
    1964   Demographic yearbook, 1963. New York, United Nations.

TABLE 25
POPULATION AND LINGUISTIC AFFILIATION OF ETHNIC
GROUPS OF SOUTH VIETNAM[a]

Group [Sub-groups (Synonyms in Parentheses)]	Estimated Population in South Vietnam[b]	Location (in Order of Size of Population)	Language
Vietnamese (Annamese, Kinh)	12,900,000[c]	South Vietnam, North Vietnam, Cambodia, Laos, Thailand, China	Viet-Muong: Vietnamese
Chinese	860,000[d]	China, Southeast Asia	Chinese
Cambodian (Khmer)	300,000 to 500,000[e]	Cambodia, South Vietnam, Thailand	Mon-Khmer: Khmeric
Jarai [(Djarais), Puan, Hodrung, Hrue]	150,000 to 160,000	South Vietnam, Cambodia	Malayo-Polynesian: Chamic, Plateau
Rhadé[f] [(Raday, Rdê, Edê, Radê[f]) Adbam, Bih, Blo, Kodrao, Krung, Mdhur, Rdê Kpă]	100,000 to 120,000	South Vietnam, Cambodia	Malayo-Polynesian: Chamic, Plateau
Hrê [(Davak, Davach), Rabah (Tava), Crêq (Kare), Hrê, Taliang]	100,000	South Vietnam	Mon-Khmer: Bahnaric, N. Bahnaric
Koho [Cil[g] (Chil, Kil[f]), Lat (Lach), Tring, Sre, Maa (Chau-Ma), Kalop, Laya, Pru, Riôn, Nop, Tala, Codon]	100,000	South Vietnam	Mon-Khmer: Bahnaric, S. Bahnaric
Bahnar [Tolo, Golar, Alaking, Jolong, Bahnar Bonom, Bahnar Rengao, Kontum, Krem]	75,000 to 80,000	South Vietnam	Mon-Khmer: Bahnaric, N. Bahnaric
Brôu [(Bru,[f] Baroo, Muong Leong, Leung, Kalo, Leu, Quang Tri Vân Kiêu)]	50,000	South Vietnam, Laos, North Vietnam	Mon-Khmer: Katuic
Cham [Cham, Cambodian Cham]	45,000 to 50,000+	South Vietnam, Cambodia	Malayo-Polynesian: Chamic, Coastal

(continued)

[696]

TABLE 25
(*continued*)

Group [Sub-groups (Synonyms in Parentheses)]	Estimated Population in South Vietnam[b]	Location (in Order of Size of Population)	Language
Nùng[h]	50,000[i]	Southern China, North Vietnam, South Vietnam	Chinese: Nung dialect
Sedang [(Hadang, Hotea, Hoteang, Rotea) possible sub-group: Sedang Todrah]	40,000 to 80,000	South Vietnam	Mon-Khmer: Bahnaric, N. Bahnaric
Katu [(Teu, Attouat, Kao, Khat, Thap, Nguôn Ta, Ta River Vân Kiêu, Phuong Katu)]	20,000 to 40,000	South Vietnam, Laos	Mon-Khmer: Katuic, very close to Phuong
Stieng [Bulach, Budip, Bulo]	30,000	Cambodia, South Vietnam	Mon-Khmer: Bahnaric, S. Bahnaric
Mnong, Central [(Pnong) Nong, Bu Rung, Bu Prang, Bu Nong Dih Bri, Bunor, Rohong, Preh, Cil[g] (Chil, Kil)]	20,000 to 40,000	South Vietnam	Mon-Khmer: Bahnaric, S. Bahnaric close to Koho[j]
Roglai, Northern [(Radlai, Raglai[f], Adlai)][l]	20,000 to 25,000	South Vietnam	Malayo-Polynesian: Chamic, Coastal
Cua [(Kor, Traw, Bong Miêu), mountain group (Kol, Dot, Yot), foothills group (Traw, Dong)]	20,000	South Vietnam	Mon-Khmer: Bahnaric, N. Bahnaric
Roglai, Southern [(Raglai[f])][l]	15,000 to 20,000	South Vietnam	Malayo-Polynesian: Chamic, Coastal, very close to N. Roglai
Chru [(Cado, Chrau, Churu[f])][l]	15,000	South Vietnam	Malayo-Polynesian: Chamic, Coastal, close to Cham

(*continued*)

TABLE 25
(continued)

Group [Sub-groups (Synonyms in Parentheses)]	Estimated Population in South Vietnam[b]	Location (in Order of Size of Population)	Language
Chrau [(Chrau Jro, Ro) Jro, Mro, Vôqtwaq, Vajiêng, Chalah, Vla, Prâng, etc.]	15,000	South Vietnam	Mon-Khmer: Bahnaric, S. Bahnaric
Pacoh [(Bô River Vân Kiêu), Pahi, ?Ta-ôih]	15,000	South Vietnam	Mon-Khmer: Katuic
Mnong Gar [(Gar, Mnong,[f] Pnom Gar)]	10,000 to 15,876	South Vietnam	Mon-Khmer: Bahnaric, S. Bahnaric[j]
Jeh [(Dié, Yeh) Jeh Perak, Jeh Brilar, Dràm, Langya]	10,000	Laos, South Vietnam	Mon-Khmer: Bahnaric, N. Bahnaric, close to Halang
Rengao	10,000 to 15,000	South Vietnam	Mon-Khmer: Bahnaric, N. Bahnaric, between Sedang and Bahnar
Tai [Black Tai, White Tai, Red Tai]	10,000 to 15,000[i]	North Vietnam, Laos, South Vietnam	Tai: Southwestern
Halăng [(Koyong)]	10,000	South Vietnam, Laos	Mon-Khmer: Bahnaric, N. Bahnaric, close to Jeh
Nùng [(Nong)]	10,000[i]	North Vietnam, Kwangsi, South Vietnam	Tai: Central
Hroy [(Báhnar Cham)]	6,000 to 10,000	South Vietnam	Malayo-Polynesian: ?Chamic, Coastal
Kwanh [(Mnong Kwanh, Kuen)]	5,000 to 10,000	South Vietnam	Mon-Khmer: Bahnaric, S. Bahnaric
Bih[l]	5,000 to 10,000	South Vietnam	Malayo-Polynesian: Chamic Plateau (dialect of Rhadé)
Bout[m]	5,000 to 10,000	South Vietnam	Mon-Khmer: Bahnaric, N. Bahnaric
Rai [(Seyu)]	5,000 to 10,000	South Vietnam	Malayo-Polynesian: Chamic, Coastal, close to Southern Roglai

(continued)

TABLE 25
(continued)

Group [Sub-groups (Synonyms in Parentheses)]	Estimated Population in South Vietnam[b]	Location (in Order of Size of Population)	Language
Rolom[n]	5,000 to 10,000	South Vietnam	Mon-Khmer: Bahnaric, S. Bahnaric
Ta-ôih [(Kantua, Tau-Oi[f])]	6,000	Laos, South Vietnam	Mon-Khmer: Katuic, close to Pacoh (may not be a distinct group)
Krung[m,o]	5,677	South Vietnam	Malayo-Polynesian: Chamic Plateau
Yao [(Iu Mien, Man)]	5,000[i]	Kwangsi, Kwangtung, Hainan, North Vietnam, Laos, Thailand, South Vietnam	Miao-Yao: Yao
Monom [(Bonom, Menam[f])]	5,000	South Vietnam, Laos	Mon-Khmer: Bahnaric, N. Bahnaric
Muong	5,000	North Vietnam, South Vietnam	Viet-Muong: Muong
Tho [(Tay)]	5,000[i]	North Vietnam, Southern China, South Vietnam	Tai: Central, several dialects
Các Giá Roglai[l]	2,000	South Vietnam	Malayo-Polynesian: Chamic, Coastal dialect differs from other Roglai
Striêng[p]	2,000?	South Vietnam, Laos	Mon-Khmer: Bahnaric, N. Bahnaric, possibly a Jeh dialect
Meo [(Miao)]	100[i]	Kweichow, Hunan, Szechwan, Kwangsi, Yunnan, North Vietnam, Laos, Thailand, South Vietnam	Miao-Yao: Miao
Brao [(Lave, Love) Krung]	[unavailable]	Laos, Thailand, Cambodia, South Vietnam[m]	Mon-Khmer: Bahnaric, N. Bahnaric
Cao [(probably a Katu group)]	[unavailable]	Laos, South Vietnam[m]	Mon-Khmer: Katuic

(continued)

TABLE 25
(continued)

Group [Sub-groups (Synonyms in Parentheses)]	Estimated Population in South Vietnam[b]	Location (in Order of Size of Population)	Language
Duan [(Duane,[f] same as Takua or Kayong?)]	[unavailable]	South Vietnam	Mon-Khmer: ?Bahnaric
Halang Doan[k]	[unavailable]	Laos, South Vietnam[m]	Mon-Khmer: Bahnaric, N. Bahnaric
Kayong [(Kagiuong, Ca Giòng, Katang)]	[unavailable]	South Vietnam	Mon-Khmer: Bahnaric, ?N. Bahnaric, close to Cua
Langya [(Lang Ya, ?Strieng)][q]	[unavailable]	Laos, South Vietnam[m]	Mon-Khmer: Bahnaric, N. Bahnaric
Loven	[unavailable]	Laos, South Vietnam[m]	Mon-Khmer: Bahnaric, N. Bahnaric
Ngeh	[unavailable]	Laos, South Vietnam[m]	Mon-Khmer: Katuic
Nhang [(Yay, Giai, Nyang, Giang)]	[a few]	North Vietnam, Yunnan, South Vietnam	Tai: Northern
Noang [(sub-group of Chru?)][l]	[unavailable]	South Vietnam[m]	Malayo-Polynesian: Chamic, Coastal very close to Chru
Noar	[unavailable]	Laos, South Vietnam[m]	Mon-Khmer: ?Bahnaric, N. Bahnaric
Phuong [(Huu River Vân Kiêu)]	[small group]	South Vietnam	Mon-Khmer: Katuic, close to Katu and Ta-ôih
Pru [classed by Thomas (1965B) as a Koho sub-group])	[unavailable]	South Vietnam[m]	Mon-Khmer: Bahnaric, S. Bahnaric
Sayan [(? a variant of Sedang)]	[unavailable]	South Vietnam[m]	Mon-Khmer: Bahnaric, ?N. Bahnaric
Sedang Todrah [(Didrah)]	[unavailable]	South Vietnam	Mon-Khmer: Bahnaric, ?N. Bahnaric, apparently distinct from Sedang language
Takua[r]	[a small group]	South Vietnam	Mon-Khmer: Bahnaric, N. Bahnaric?
Total South Vietnam (1960)	14,900,000	—	—

(continued)

[700]

TABLE 25
(continued)

[a] Source: Names of groups are those accepted as standard by Thomas (1965A), except as indicated. Following Thomas, the groupings are on a linguistic, not necessarily cultural basis. Underlined population figures are from Thomas (1965A). Those not underlined (unless otherwise specified) are from LeBar *et al.* (1964) and derive ultimately from a 1960 census reported in Tong-So Cac Sac Dan Thuong [the total highland population figures] by Nha Cong-Tac Xa-Hoi Mien Thuong [Bureau of Social Action for the Highland Area], Saigon, 1960.

Linguistic affiliation is from Thomas (1965A) for all those Mon-Khmer-speaking groups he has listed. Groups identified by LeBar *et al.*, but not by Thomas, are classified following LeBar *et al.*, according to their scheme, which is primarily *geographical*. These classifications are in parentheses. Tai-speaking groups are classified according to Li (1959, 1960). See notes accompanying the Burma population and linguistic affiliation table for further details on problems of classification.

Distribution of groups is from LeBar *et al.* (1964), Thomas (1965A), and other sources, as noted. Countries are listed in order of concentration of the group.

[b] Groups whose populations are unknown are listed alphabetically.

[c] Estimate for ethnic Vietnamese was calculated by subtracting minority and tribal populations from census total.

[d] Figure for Chinese is from Skinner (1965).

[e] Figure for Cambodian is from Buttinger (1961:120), apparently based on South Vietnamese government sources.

[f] Name used by LeBar *et al.* (1964).

[g] Thomas (1965B) states that these Koho sub-tribes have somewhat different cultures, and speak dialects of the same language with varying degrees of mutual intelligibility. LeBar *et al.* (1964) have considered them to be distinct, and give the following figures for population: Koho (10,000); Ma (30,000); Sre (30,000).

[h] Identification by Thomas (1965A, 1965B). Not mentioned by LeBar *et al.* (1964). The Chinese-speaking Nùng are renowned fighters.

Yao (Man, Iu Mien), Meo (Miao), Muong, Tai-speaking Nùng, Chinese-speaking Nùng, Black, White, and Red Thai, Tho, and Nhang have come from the North to South Vietnam as refugees (Thomas 1965A, 1965B; Kandre 1965).

[i] Thomas (1965B), quoting Georges Condominas, considers Gar to be a Mnong language, possibly mutually intelligible with some dialects of Mnong.

[k] Thomas (1965B) suggests combining Halang and Halang Doan, although LeBar *et al.* (1964:139) have listed them as separate.

[l] Bih, Chru (Churu), Noang, and Roglai (Raglai), all apparently Malayo-Polynesian speakers, are grouped together in the 1960 census figures, with a total population of 40,000.

[m] Identification by LeBar *et al.* (1964), not listed as separate group by Thomas (1965A), who says he has heard of no Brao, Loven, Cao, Ngeh, Pru, or Sayan languages in South Vietnam (1965B).

(continued)

TABLE 25
(continued)

ⁿ Identification and population estimate from Thomas (1965A), lumped with Mnong by LeBar *et al.* (1964:154).

º The Krung are classed as a sub-group of the Rhadé by Thomas (1965A).

ᵖ Identification and population estimate of Strieng are from Thomas (1965A, 1965B). They are not mentioned by LeBar *et al.* (1964).

ᑫ The Langya are classed as a sub-group of the Jeh by Thomas (1965A).

ʳ Identification by Thomas (1965A), not listed as a separate group by LeBar *et al.* (1964).

REFERENCES CITED

BUTTINGER, J.
1961 The ethnic minorities in the Republic of Vietnam. *In* Problems of freedom: South Vietnam since independence, W. R. Fischel, ed. New York, The Free Press of Glencoe, Inc., Ch. 6.

KANDRE, PETER
1965 Personal communication.

LEBAR, F. M., G. C. HICKEY, and J. K. MUSGRAVE
1964 Ethnic groups of mainland Southeast Asia. New Haven, Human Relations Area Files Press.

LI, FANG-KUEI
1959 Classification by vocabulary: Tai dialects. Anthropological Linguistics 1(2):15–21.
1960 A tentative classification of Tai dialects. *In* Culture in history: essays in honor of Paul Radin, Stanley Diamond, ed. New York, Columbia University Press, for Brandeis University.

SKINNER, G. WILLIAM
1965 Personal communication.

THOMAS, DAVID D.
1965A Vietnam minority languages (July 1965 revision). Saigon, Summer Institute of Linguistics.
1965B Personal communications.

CHAPTER 18

The Strategic Hamlet Program in Kien Hoa Province, South Vietnam: A Case Study of Counter-Insurgency

JOHN B. O'DONNELL

INTRODUCTION

This paper will consider some aspects of the counter-insurgency program conducted in the province of Kien Hoa in the Mekong Delta area of South Vietnam.* The physical, cultural, and historical setting and a brief description of the insurgents will be presented first, followed by a short analysis of the origins and aims of the Strategic Hamlet Program, discussion of the methods used and results obtained in Kien Hoa Province, and then some conclusions and recommendations which may be drawn from this experience.

Setting. Kien Hoa is one of the forty-five provinces of South Vietnam and is located fifty miles south of Saigon, where the Mekong River meets the South China Sea. On a map and from the air, the province looks like a giant green and brown paw—the elements of the paw composed of three large, long islands separated by the major channels of the Mekong. The edges of the islands are dense with coconut groves and swamp palms, the ends are large salt fields and mud flats covered with tangled mangrove and swampbrush, the interiors of the islands are made up of rice paddies crisscrossed by levees and canals. The total area of the province is 215,520 hectares (832 sq. mi.), with a population of approximately 550,000.

Although adjacent to the area where Khmer (the ancient Cambodian empire) influence has been greatest in South Vietnam, the people of Kien Hoa are almost entirely ethnic Vietnamese.

---

*John B. O'Donnell was the U.S. Operations Mission (AID) Provincial Representative in Kien Hoa from December 1962 to August 1964.

Because of the relative wealth of the province and the emphasis placed on education, they are better educated than their neighbors to the north and south.

Many of the great heroes of the Vietnamese past either came from or were associated with Ben Tre, which was the name of the province before it was changed to Kien Hoa by President Diem in 1957. Phan Thanh Glan, a leader in the early resistance against the French, *ca.* 1880, was born in Kien Hoa and, after attempting valiantly to deter the French from taking over Cochin China, committed suicide in protest against the French encroachment on Vietnamese sovereignty. Earlier, when Nguyen Anh, later proclaimed Emperor Gia Long, sought refuge in Kien Hoa after being driven from central Vietnam by the Tay-Son, he enlisted the support of General Truong Tan Buu, a native of Ben Tre, who became a key figure in Gia Long's long, difficult, but eventually successful, campaign to drive the Tay-Son from central Vietnam. The farmers and fishermen of Kien Hoa have perpetuated the legends of Phan Thanh Gian and Truong Tan Buu and are proud of being from the same area which produced these and many other national heroes.

Kien Hoa is an extremely rich province. The coconut groves of Kien Hoa provide over half of the fresh coconut and copra production for the entire country. The 1962 harvest of 196,000 metric tons of unprocessed rice ranked eleventh in the country, with an average yield of 1.8 tons per hectare, which ranked twentieth in the country. The other major income sources in Kien Hoa are fish, fruit, duck feathers, and tobacco.

Because of the superior education, rich tradition, and extreme pride of the people in Kien Hoa, which made them natural leaders in other revolutionary struggles, the agricultural wealth of the province, which provides money to support the guerrilla effort in Kien Hoa and other provinces as well, plus the difficult terrain at the edges and tips of the islands, which provides excellent concealment for training camps, hospitals, supply depots, munitions factories, rest and recreation areas, the Viet Cong have placed the "liberation" of Kien Hoa high on their priority list. In fact, captured documents have indicated that the Viet Cong attempted to make their effort in Kien Hoa their model for "liberation" programs throughout the Mekong Delta.

When the Geneva Accords were signed in 1954, Binh Dai, Ba Tri, and Thanh Phu at the tips of the three islands of Kien Hoa were designated regrouping areas for the Viet Minh who wished to go to North Vietnam. According to reports from people who lived in Kien Hoa at the time, many of the Viet Minh who were regrouped in Kien Hoa for transportation to the North did not leave, either deciding of their own free will to remain in the province, or, as with some, receiving orders to stay behind. A token amount of Viet Minh arms was turned in to the International Control Commission, and the rest were cached where they could be brought out again if and when the need arose. Many of those who did go north left behind members of their families—wives, children, parents, or brothers and sisters.

Following the exodus to the North, things settled down in Kien Hoa as the ex-Viet Minh went back to their rice fields and coconut groves to await the reunification of the two halves of Vietnam. However, the elections to reunify the country were never held. Some accuse Diem of refusing to hold the elections, others blame the Russians who were worried about the uprisings against the Communist agrarian reform program in the North. The truth probably lies somewhere in between, with both sides unwilling to take the chance of losing the election.

By late 1957, it became increasingly apparent that President Diem, having neutralized or virtually eliminated the threat from the Binh Xuyen, Cao Dai, and Hoa Hao, and having consolidated his power in Saigon and the other major population centers, was gradually extending his control to the countryside, employing many of the techniques of propaganda and political action used formerly by the Viet Minh. These developments alarmed the Hanoi regime and the former Viet Minh still living in the South, and it was evidently decided by the North Vietnamese government that the political, psychological, and military struggle which had brought the Viet Minh success against the French should be resumed. Accordingly, in early 1958 some of those who had gone north in 1954 began to reappear in their native villages in the South. Former Viet Minh who had remained behind in 1954 began to make the long trek north for indoctrination and training. Those who had returned from the North established themselves in the villages where government presence was limited or where the government had never completely succeeded in reestablishing its presence following the Viet Minh struggle.

The first step in resuming the struggle was to establish the security of what they designated their "base area." Small cells were set up in the remote villages, and intelligence and propaganda operations were begun. A dossier of the misdeeds of local officials and others loyal to the government was compiled, and a rumor campaign was mounted against these persons. When the proper climate of opposition to supporters of the My-Diem (U.S.-Diem) regime had been created, a campaign was started to win over, neutralize, drive away, or, if necessary, assassinate these officials, landowners, wealthy merchants, and other "My-Diem puppets."

As the pro-government presence was gradually eliminated, a shadow Viet Cong political apparatus was formed to replace it. As base areas were secured, intelligence agents and then propaganda and political-action specialists utilizing the intelligence gathered began to fan out into adjacent areas. The propaganda themes were simple—social justice, an end to corrupt and cruel government, land to the tiller, down with the Americans' puppet Diem, an independent prosperous Vietnam for the Vietnamese.[1]

Young men were taken into the ranks of the National Liberation Army. Men, women, and children were urged to contribute money and energy to the efforts of the National Liberation Front. Small raids, carefully planned and executed, were carried out against remote government outposts to capture weapons and ammunition for the National Liberation Army. Roads were mined and ambushes sprung to create an air of fear which would discourage the government troops and officials from visiting the rural areas except with strong military escort. Government attempts at suppression of the insurgency and retaliation against the Viet Cong tactics served only to add recruits to the growing National Liberation Army.

In addition to receiving reports of assassinations and attacks on outposts, President Diem learned of the deteriorating situation in other ways: farmers were dragging their feet on repayment of Government Agricultural Credit loans, land-service personnel

[1] See "Program of the National Liberation Front of South Vietnam," reprinted in Fall (1963: Appendix 4).

[706]

were having an increasingly difficult time collecting annual payments for land distributed under the land reform program of 1957, rural cooperatives were failing, landowners were unable to collect rent from tenant farmers, and troops were becoming increasingly hesitant to enter areas of the province where the guerrillas were operating.

Alarmed by these reports from Kien Hoa, President Diem in early 1960 appointed Lieutenant Colonel Pham Ngoc Thao to be Province Chief. Lieutenant Colonel Thao was a former regimental commander and later chief of counter-intelligence for the Viet Minh forces in Cochin China. Unlike most of his present fellow officers, he had not rallied to the French-sponsored Vietnamese government established in 1949, but had continued with the resistance forces until the end of armed hostilities in 1954. Upon arrival in Kien Hoa in 1960, Thao began to enlarge and improve the local military forces. He imported a large number of former Hoa Hao soldiers. The Hoa Hao are a militant religious sect who had set up their own, virtually autonomous, government in the lower Mekong Delta during the Viet Minh struggle. Following the war, they had been cleverly assimilated into the national political structure and, for all purposes, eliminated as a powerful political and military force.

The Hoa Hao brought into Kien Hoa were assigned specific areas of responsibility by Thao and through a combination of ruthless military tactics and a crude but effective campaign of psychological warfare and terrorism were able to drive the Viet Cong back from the edges of the main towns and villages. When Thao first arrived in Kien Hoa, his provincial headquarters was often fired upon from a small river by Viet Cong forces. After a few months the firing ceased completely, and the road which connected the provincial capital with Saigon was once again safe for traffic.[2] But the strong-arm tactics of Thao's Hoa Hao irregulars, although apparently initially effective, began to generate complaints from individuals loyal to the government over and above the constant complaints of Viet Cong sympathizers and

---

[2] O'Donnell's evaluation of Lieutenant Colonel Thao's effectiveness in this operation is confirmed independently by John McAlister (personal communication 1965, based on field trips in Kien Hoa Province, 1961). Thao had also been active in the development of the agroville program (Zasloff, N. D.). (Ed.)

became an increasing source of embarrassment for President Diem.

The President decided that Thao might be better used elsewhere and sent him off to Command and General Staff School at Fort Leavenworth, Kansas, and appointed in his place a young major, Tran Ngoc Chau, who was serving on the planning staff of the presidency. Chau was born and raised in Hue, the former capital of Annam. He was the son of an important mandarin who was an old friend of President Diem. Chau dropped out of school at the end of World War II and joined the nationalist forces who were preparing their campaign against the returning French. He was sent to Tonkin for training, where he had an opportunity to see and listen to Ho Chi Minh and Vo Nguyen Giap talk of the people's war and people's army. Chau was then assigned to the highlands of central Vietnam, where he rose in the ranks of the Viet Minh.

When the semi-independent Vietnamese government was set up by the French in 1949, he left the Viet Minh and returned to Hue. Subsequently he entered the Vietnamese Military Academy at Dalat and upon graduation was assigned to a Vietnamese battalion of the French Expeditionary Force and fought against the Viet Minh.

After the Indochina War, Chau continued in the army as a troop commander, inspector of Civil Guard and Self Defense Forces in the area immediately south of Saigon, and finally as a member of President Diem's planning staff, before being appointed Province Chief of Kien Hoa in May 1962.

With this introduction we can turn to a discussion of the Strategic Hemlet Program, its origin and aims, and the methods used and results obtained in Kien Hoa Province.

THE STRATEGIC HAMLET PROGRAM: ORIGINS[3]

The Strategic Hamlet Program of the government of President Ngo Dinh Diem was officially adopted on April 17, 1962, as the

[3] The Strategic Hamlet Program was preceded in Vietnam by a number of different resettlement and rural development programs. The Land Development Program has been outlined by Henderson (1961). In this program, which started in 1957, loyal Vietnamese peasants were to be resettled in areas such as the highlands around Pleiku and the Mekong Delta, which had served as bases for Viet Cong and other dissident groups. The aim of the program was to

vehicle for meeting the growing Viet Cong threat. Many individuals—Vietnamese, Americans, British, and French—have
claimed credit for its development. It is probably most accurate

---

develop or reclaim land which had been abandoned as a result of the war
or which had never been subjected to advanced agricultural techniques. Equally
important (or perhaps more important) was the idea that these resettlement
areas were to be of assistance in the political and military control of insecure
areas and were to serve as centers from which minority populations (e.g. the
montagnards) could be influenced.

The planning for the Land Development Program was based on earlier experience with resettlement programs for the 850,000 refugees who had come from the
North following the Geneva Conference in 1954. The program had to be abandoned in the delta region because the strength of the Viet Cong there made
it impossible to carry out the engineering tasks (ditching, damming, draining)
before the resettlement could actually take place. Resettlement in the highlands
encountered a number of technological and economic problems, and U.S. aid
was withdrawn from the project before it was implemented. Nonetheless, it
was pursued by the Vietnamese.

In 1959 a rural regroupment program was undertaken in which two kinds
of centers were to be set up: centers called *qui khu* for people believed to
be sympathetic, or potentially sympathetic, to the Viet Cong; and centers called
qui ap for families who were believed to be loyal to the South Vietnamese
government, but who were living in remote areas where they could not be
protected from the Viet Cong. The program was gradually abandoned when
it proved difficult or impossible to differentiate among the population according
to potential sympathy to the Viet Cong (even many government officials had
relatives in the North) and when the loyal families could not be convinced
that moving to the agglomeration centers was for their own good (see Zasloff,
N. D.: 6–8, for a brief review of the program).

The "Agroville Program" (Zasloff, N. D.:9–32; 1962–1963; Nguyen 1961),
which was begun later in 1959, was designed to concentrate rural population
for purposes of economic development and to prevent them from giving aid
to the Viet Cong. It did not, however, incorporate the self-defense features
of the strategic hamlets. It was hoped that the regrouped populations could
be linked up by a new strategic road system, that the program would stimulate
the development of more and more competent village administrators, that economic development would lead to better local finances for the villages, and
that a youth movement could be developed in the new setting to provide
future rural leadership.

As far as the peasants were concerned, the major disadvantages of the agroville
program were the forced abandonment of their homes, ancestral shrines, fruit
and shade trees, and familiar surroundings, forced indebtedness for new land
which they had not chosen, and unpaid *corvée* labor in the construction of
the new settlements. Since not all of the fields could be relocated, the peasants
were forced to walk several kilometers from the new settlements and could
not give their fields the continual attention they required. Local leaders in the
agroville projects were subject to great pressures from the Viet Cong, who
used peasant discontent with the program to great advantage. The agroville
program was gradually abandoned in 1961 and replaced by the Strategic Hamlet
Program. For further discussion of the Strategic Hamlets see Smith (1964),
and for a journalistic account of the background to the Strategic Hamlet Program
see Warner (1963). For a detailed comparison of the Strategic Hamlet Program
with similar programs in other countries see Osborne (1965). (Ed.)

to say that Councilor Ngo Dinh Nhu, brother and closest adviser to the President, was the prime mover in the development and execution of the program. The details of the program were worked out by a small group of Vietnamese officials (many of them former Viet Minh, including young Major Tran Ngoc Chau), assigned to the presidential planning staff. They included in the final program proposal the best elements of ideas presented from many sources—the British experience in Malaya with the "new villages," the experience of Vietnamese civilian and military officials who had already started security and political-social-economic programs in various parts of the country, the experience gained in the campaign against the Huks in the Philippines, the American frontier fort, the land development centers and agrovilles used by the Government of Vietnam (GVN) as resettlement centers for refugees from North Vietnam and colonization projects in undeveloped areas of the country, many of the elements of the strategy and tactics used by the Viet Minh in their campaign against the French, the counter-insurgency tactics developed by the French in Indochina and Algeria, and many other experiences and counter-insurgency theories.

Aims. The aim of the Strategic Hamlet Program, as stated by President Diem, was to create a "state of mind": the commitment of the peasants to the support of their government and resistance to the Viet Cong. It is essential that one remembers that the South Vietnamese government and the Viet Cong were in fact, *competing* in all fields for the loyalty and the support of the majority of the *people,* both believing that whichever side gained this loyalty and support would be the eventual winner in the complex struggle. The Viet Cong were attempting to force the government to withdraw from the rural areas to the large towns and cities where political subversion, economic strangulation, and increasing military pressure would result in a total collapse. This could be done only with the support of the rural population, to provide the manpower and money for the effort.

The government was attempting to reverse the process by forcing the Viet Cong back to their base areas, where they could be destroyed. Once again, the support of the rural population was essential. The Viet Cong believed that time was on their side; the GVN felt that their position of responsibility dictated a major accelerated effort.

To bring about commitments to the government, it was necessary to convince the peasant that he *should,* and *could,* successfully oppose the Viet Cong. Translated into more explicit terms, the Strategic Hamlet Program was intended to provide the average peasant and his family with the following things:

(a) a reasonable degree of safety;
(b) a reasonable livelihood;
(c) a reasonable amount of elementary justice;
(d) a reasonable chance for his children;
(e) a reasonable degree of status in his community;
(f) a reasonable degree of opportunity.

In addition to the major task outlined above, a second task and an overall objective were written into the program. The second task was to "teach through experience, the practices and processes, the requirements and rewards, of self-government." When both tasks had been accomplished, the final objective of "a stable, prosperous, self-governing nation offering adequate and equal opportunity and protection, under law, to all its loyal citizens, could be attained" (for more details on the aims of the Strategic Hamlet Program, see Bohannon 1963).

Methods Used. The tasks and objective, as stated, were (and are) basically sound and admirable goals for any government. The problem was to carry these goals from the point of talking about them to developing and executing programs which would bring about the desired results. As a result of the trips of Vice-President Lyndon Johnson and General Maxwell Taylor to Vietnam in 1961, the United States decided to increase its support to the government of Vietnam in its struggle against the Viet Cong insurgents. More U.S. military advisers were sent to Vietnam, and the military assistance program was increased.

Realizing that the political-economic-social-psychological aspects of the struggle were equally, or more, important than the military aspects, the Agency for International Development began to search for ways to intensify and accelerate non-military support. Accordingly, in early 1962 a special task force was set up in the U.S. Operations Mission (USOM)/Saigon to refocus ongoing aid programs and coordinate activities which contributed to the Strategic Hamlet National Plan with the Vietnamese government and U.S. military. In addition, a two-man team was sent to Saigon in May 1962 to survey the situation and prepare recommendations for increased AID support. Rufus Phillips, the leader of the team, had been an adviser to the Vietnamese army units involved in the reestablishment of GVN control in the Camau Peninsula and Interzone V (Binh Dinh and Quang Ngai provinces in central Vietnam) following the end of hostilities in 1954. He had later served as adviser to the Royal Lao Government during the establishment of the Action Civic program in that country. Bert Fraleigh, the other member of the team, had been with AID and its predecessor agencies since 1947, primarily in mainland China, Taiwan, and Laos, most recently serving as Operations Officer with USOM/Taiwan.

Phillips and Fraleigh, after several weeks of travel and discussion with GVN and U.S. officials in Vietnam, recommended that a special office for Rural Affairs (Counter-Insurgency) be established within the AID mission. This office would serve as the action unit for administering a decentralized program to support the GVN Strategic Hamlet Plan. The plan contemplated the assignment of a USOM representative to each of the provinces of Vietnam who would be responsible for administering a greatly increased non-military assistance program.

It was estimated that U.S. $10,000,000 in local currency would be required to get the program moving. This money would be used to help defray the costs incurred by rural families who would be required to move from the insecure areas into strategic hamlets, to support the recruiting, training, and deployment of government personnel who would work in the countryside, to support the training of local militia and hamlet officials, to cover a portion of the costs of self-help projects selected by hamlet residents, to support, as needed, psychological warfare and other complementary activities. It was also recommended that "Food for Peace" (Public Law 480, Title II) commodities and U.S. excess property items which would contribute to the counter-insurgency effort be imported.

AID/Washington accepted the recommendations, and Rufus

Phillips was selected to head the Office of Rural Affairs; Bert Fraleigh was transferred from Taiwan to be his deputy. The special purchase of U.S. $10,000,000 of local currency was authorized, and procurement of P.L. 480 and excess property requirements was started. Recruitment of provincial representatives was initiated by AID/Washington.

Phillips and Fraleigh started work with the GVN on developing more specific administrative procedures. As a first step, instructions were sent from Saigon to the province chiefs requesting the preparation of comprehensive provincial rehabilitation (strategic hamlet establishment) plans and detailed estimates of the funds, materials, and personnel required to carry out the plans.

When this writer arrived in Vietnam in October 1962, a few provincial rehabilitation plans had already been received in Saigon, and more were arriving daily. These plans were reviewed briefly by the Office of the Executive Secretary of the Interministerial Council, the Office of Rural Affairs of the U.S. Operations Mission, and the Strategic Hamlets Division of the U.S. Military Assistance Advisory Group (MAAG). A joint U.S./GVN team composed of the directors of these three organizations then made a field trip to the province concerned to work out any problems and to prepare a budget for USOM financial and material support and a calculation of MAP (Military Assistance Program) materials required which would be supplied through MAAG. These two documents were then presented to the U.S. Committee on Provincial Rehabilitation[4] and the GVN Interministerial Committee for Strategic Hamlets, where they were discussed and given official approval. The budgets were then cleared by the various GVN and U.S. officials concerned, and a check for a portion of the funds allocated (usually three months' operating costs) was drawn on the GVN treasury and delivered to the province chief by a representative from the Office of Rural Affairs.

The scope and depth of the provincial rehabilitation plans varied according to the imagination of the province chief concerned. In the case of Kien Hoa Province, Lieutenant Colonel

---

[4] This committee was also known as the "Trueheart Committee," a U.S. coordinating committee for provincial operations consisting of working-level representatives of all U.S. agencies in Vietnam, chaired by Mr. William Trueheart, the Deputy Chief of Mission.

Chau approached the preparation of his plan in a sensible way. Upon his arrival in Kien Hoa in May 1962, Chau immediately began an intensive study of the situation in the province. He visited every district and most of the accessible villages, talking to government officials, para-military commanders and their troops, businessmen, moneylenders, farmers, bus-drivers, captured Viet Cong, women, and children.

He read back in the history of Kien Hoa and its heroes, studied the flow of products and money between the towns and the countryside, reviewed the past production figures for copra, rice, tobacco, and fish, discussed the land reform program with landowners and tenant farmers, discussed the educational system with teachers, students, and parents, and analyzed the reports of enemy activities, both military and the complex political-psychological-economic combination.

During the six months from May to October, Chau studied the province from every angle. At the same time he strengthened his intelligence system to gather more information and also accomplished the very important task of instilling new hope and enthusiasm in everyone he contacted. In early November Chau presented his provincial rehabilitation plan to a joint GVN/U.S. committee in Saigon.

This writer was present at this meeting and was impressed by Chau's imagination and ability. His plan was well thought out, daring in some respects, and included details which conveyed his deep understanding of the strategy and tactics of the enemy and the measures that would have to be undertaken to cope with them. Chau's request for money, materials, and personnel was considered excessive by some members of the committee, so the whole group made a trip to Kien Hoa to discuss the matter further. They came away impressed by what he had already been able to do with the limited means at his disposal and subsequently authorized a major portion of his request.

The USOM support budget was prepared and approved and a USOM provincial representative (the writer) was appointed to assist and advise Chau in the implementation of his plan.

Under the terms of the piaster release agreement, a committee was established at the provincial level composed of the Chief of Province as Chairman, and the USOM Provincial Representative and the U.S. MAAG Sector Advisor as members. The latter officer was involved because each province was also considered a military sector, with the province chief as commander of local military forces and as civil administrator. All expenditures of provincial rehabilitation funds had to be discussed and approved by all three members of the Provincial Rehabilitation Committee. All questions were supposed to be resolved by the provincial committee with minimum reliance on the Vietnamese or American officials in Saigon.

The decentralization of responsibility *and* authority was one of the fundamental tenets of the Strategic Hamlet Program and a key element in its early success. The flexibility thus provided allowed the program to move ahead rapidly and to adjust fairly well to the constantly changing situation. The degree of independence and responsibility which the provincial committee assumed varied according to the confidence and aggressiveness of the province chief. Decentralization to this extent was a radical departure from past practice, and many Vietnamese at both provincial and central government levels found it difficult to adjust and did not use to the full advantage the responsibility and authority entrusted to them.

The struggle was at the grass roots level, and it was *sine qua non* of the Strategic Hamlet Program that the administration of the means to carry out the program be placed at the lowest practicable level. The risks inherent in decentralization of fiscal responsibility in a culture where the people often know and look the other way in cases of graft and corruption were to some extent compensated for by the presence of foreign observers in the person of the American members of the committee. There were cases of improper usage of funds which were uncovered by the American advisers and brought to the attention of the province chief and, in the case of Kien Hoa, many others which were uncovered by the province chief and passed on to the Americans. There were certainly cases of improper uses of funds which were not caught. It is difficult to generalize on, or even estimate, the degree of misuse of funds; but it is fair to state that this problem was of major concern to the American representatives in the field who attempted to assure proper use of funds and fiscal responsibility to the best of their ability.

It should be noted at this point that there were no known precedents for many aspects of the Strategic Hamlet Program, and new procedures of all sorts had to be established on an *ad hoc* basis. Fortunately, some of the personnel in the Office of Rural Affairs had had previous experience in Asia and assisted in the development of logistical and accounting procedures which were later combined and generalized for the whole country.

With the strategic hamlet support funds deposited in the provincial treasury and the military and civilian support items beginning to arrive in the province, the program began to move forward. The first step taken by the province chief was to initiate recruitment of personnel who would be responsible for guiding the rural population in the establishment of strategic hamlets.

Chau held a meeting of his district chiefs and instructed them to start recruiting candidates for the hamlet construction cadre positions. There were eight districts in Kien Hoa at that time; a ninth was created in early 1963. A quota was established for each district depending on the number and phasing of hamlet construction. While the district chiefs were recruiting men, the Chief of Province reorganized his provincial administration to deal better with the accelerated program.

The Special Assistant to the Province Chief for hamlet establishment (who ranked as a Deputy Province Chief along with the Deputy for Military Affairs and the Deputy for Administration) was a young major named Cao Minh Quan, who was born and raised in Kien Hoa and knew the province well. He was charged with the responsibility for setting up sites for training and developing programs of instruction for the hamlet construction cadre, village and hamlet officials and the hamlet militia. The central government had sent out sketchy instructions on training which were improved by the provincial staff; Chau contributed many ideas which were expanded by Quan.

Within a few weeks the construction and equipping of training sites was well underway and the recruits for the hamlet construction cadre had arrived in the provincial capital. The province chief dropped his other duties for two days and personally interviewed all the candidates. He then made the first of many decisions which were to add greatly to the effectiveness of his program but which eventually ran head-on into the opposition of the Saigon bureaucracy. Realizing that the success or failure of the program depended to a very great extent on the attitude or ability of the hamlet construction cadre, who would have direct contact with the villagers the government was trying so hard to influence, Chau decided that 900 piasters (U.S. $12.37) per month was not sufficient compensation for the work that he expected from these young men and women. He suggested that the provincial committee agree to the reduction of the number of personnel used in the program and to the use of the surplus funds thus created to pay those selected a higher salary. After consultation with the Assistant Director for Rural Affairs, this move was approved by the provincial committee. This is a good example of the flexibility built into the general program, which was an essential ingredient of its early success.

The persons selected then underwent an intensive training program conducted by the chief of the province, his special assistant for hamlet establishment, and various other provincial officials. The trainees were intelligent and appeared sincere in their desire to save their country. Chau's close personal attention to the recruitment and training was in good part responsible for their success in the field. Upon graduation from their training program, the candidates were organized into eleven-man teams. The team leaders were generally young men from the Provincial Office of the Ministry of Civic Action. This had been established about 1957 as the agency responsible for extending and strengthening government control in the countryside. The Civic Action men were usually capable individuals who had been fairly well trained in political/propaganda activities. Many of them had already had two or three years experience in Kien Hoa, working with the rural population. Most of the other team members had never worked for the government before.

The eleven-man teams were broken down into three sections, which were charged with different responsibilites. Three members of the team were responsible for gathering detailed information on all aspects of hamlet life, e.g. breakdown by population, by sex and age group, agricultural and livestock production, names and attitudes of families with members in the Viet Cong (we shall return to this later), agricultural credit loans granted

[717]

and repayment experience, existence and condition of schools, dispensaries, temples, churches, etc. These data were to prove invaluable for planning realistic social and economic improvement programs in the individual hamlets.

Three members of the team were responsible for organizing the hamlet residents into work groups and directing the construction of the hamlet defenses. The hamlet defenses usually consisted of a wide moat and a mud wall topped by a barbed wire fence which followed the perimeter of the population grouping.

This type of defense works was better suited to conditions found in the highland areas of central Vietnam, where the people tend to live in closely grouped clusters. In Kien Hoa, and for that matter in most of the Mekong Delta area, the people live in loose population groupings strung out along a road, canal, or river. The hamlet perimeters were in many cases four to five kilometers long, too long to be effectively guarded by the two squads of militia authorized for each hamlet.[5] The remaining four members of the team were responsible for explaining the philosophy and objectives of the strategic hamlet programs, organizing the hamlet residents into social and economic action groups according to sex and age, developing a hamlet charter, and arranging for the election of hamlet officials by secret ballot. These activities of the political/propaganda component of the team were the most important and, unfortunately, the least clearly defined and understood elements of the entire strategic hamlet process. In areas where the hamlet construction teams understood these elements and their importance and also possessed the personality traits which enabled them to convince the villagers of their integrity and sincerity and of the genuine concern of the government for their security and welfare, the people responded and started taking the first steps toward committing themselves to the government.[6] It was at this crucial point that the importance of careful selection, thorough training, adequate

[5] Unlike the older, compact, walled or hedged villages of northern and central Vietnam, the settlements in the delta are newer, more dispersed, and often strung out along water courses or roads (Hickey 1963:213). These delta villages are generally characterized by less cooperative action, for example in religious celebrations, than the villages further north. (Ed.)

[6] For an interesting discussion of the Communist approach to this problem, see "Population Control Techniques of Communist insurgents, a Sociological Analysis," Osanka (1964).

and continuing guidance, and constant attention to problems which affected the morale of the cadre became clearly evident. When the critical elements of understanding the program and establishing rapport were missing, the hamlet establishment phase often became a period of unpleasant, meaningless forced labor for the villagers. Although all of the physical steps might have been carried out, the hamlet was really nothing more than the population grouping now surrounded by a worthless mud wall, with a group of men who had been trained in military tactics and provided weapons, but had no desire to use them, a hamlet charter which was torn up by the Viet Cong agents who returned to the hamlet once the government cadre had left, and with "elected officials" who either fled the hamlet or agreed to cooperate with the Viet Cong.

A hamlet establishment team would generally stay in a hamlet from three to eight weeks, depending on the attitude of the population, degree of Viet Cong subversion, and other factors. When all the basic steps had been accomplished to the satisfaction of the cadre, the village officials, and district chief, a ceremony was held, usually presided over by the province chief or one of his deputies, to "inaugurate" the new "strategic" hamlet. The steps outlined above were the basic procedures for implementing the Strategic Hamlet Program. There were many other elements that will be discussed later in this paper. At this point, however, two important points should be made:

(1) The Strategic Hamlet Program was not intended to be a rigid program. As more experience was developed and the situation changed, old programs were refined or discarded, and new programs were initiated. The overall objective and the two tasks outlined earlier plus the basic procedural format remained the same, but the tactics used within this framework varied from area to area and from week to week. There are forty-five provinces in South Vietnam, and it has often been said that there are forty-five different wars going on. The Strategic Hamlet Program in each province, although applying the same basic procedural format, developed its individual character. This has been cited by some authorities as one of the basic weaknesses of the program. In the opinion of this writer it was the most realistic, if not the only, way to proceed. There were no standard prece-

dents for the program, and the tactics developed locally were often incorporated in the national plan as they were proven successful. There were many ways to bring about the commitment of the rural people. The tactics developed depended to a great extent upon the attitude, experience, ability, and initiative of the local leaders.

(2) The intangibles involved in changing a person's mind, which was the primary aim of the Strategic Hamlet Program, were often sidetracked or lost in the rush to *get things done*. Many officials, both Vietnamese and American, fell victim to a hypnotic preoccupation[7] with identifiable physical accomplishments, *numbers* of hamlets completed, *numbers* of "elections" held, *numbers* of militia "trained," and on and on. The urgency to move forward was great, the pressure from the enemy was always present, and very often the fundamental goal of the program was lost in numbers and the mechanics of everyday activities. It was extremely important to pause at frequent intervals to rethink the *reasons* for building hamlet defenses, the *reasons* for holding elections, the *reasons* for building schools and dispensaries, etc. Unfortunately, this was not done often enough, and the Strategic Hamlet Program in many areas, although apparently successfully completed, had not resulted in the commitment of people to the side of the government. This is not to say that physical accomplishments, speed, and urgency are not vital to the success of the program. They are all essential, but can become virtually meaningless, at times counter-productive, unless they are undertaken with the understanding continually re-thought and reinforced, that the fundamental goal is the attainment of an intangible—the creation of a state of mind, the commitment of men to a cause.

The conflict between physical and tangible accomplishments

---

[7] The insidiousness of numerical self-delusion can be illustrated by an encounter the writer had with one U.S. official in Saigon, who, when told that the Strategic Hamlet Program in the Mekong Delta was beginning to disintegrate, turned to a large chart behind him which showed *number* of hamlets completed, *number* of militia trained, *number* of rolls of barbed wire issued, etc., and in an outraged voice demanded an explanation, vigorously pointing out that it *couldn't* be disintegrating, that the figures indicated that it was moving ahead remarkably well, and that more figures were arriving daily! Unfortunately, this self-delusion had to be shattered by hard facts, and the emphasis on reporting was changed from quantitative to qualitative analysis.

and between quantity and quality, was the source of much discussion and friction. In Kien Hoa, Lieutenant Colonel Chau had worked out an ambitious timetable for hamlet completion. As the teams moved into areas which had been subjected to a long period of Viet Cong subversion and indoctrination, they found their task increasingly difficult. Accordingly, Chau modified his timetable and advised the teams to take more time in these hamlets. The slowdown of the program in Kien Hoa began to bring criticism from higher headquarters. Chau stood firm and refused to be pushed into a race with other provinces to see which one could report more numerical progress each month. During the same period this writer was also serving as USOM Provincial Representative in Long An Province, where the province chief was under even greater pressure to accelerate establishment of strategic hamlets. The province chief, Major Nguyen Viet Thanh, was a dedicated individual and responded to the pressure from Saigon by working day and night and urging his provincial and district staffs to move ahead faster. Standards were not observed as the teams moved rapidly from hamlet to hamlet. Masses of people were relocated, resulting in serious problems for the provincial government, and it soon became apparent that the program had been extended far beyond the capabilities of the province. The Viet Cong, who had been carefully plotting their response to the Strategic Hamlet Program, took advantage of this overextension and began an intensive military and psychological campaign against the government-"controlled" zones.

Included here is the General Narrative on progress from the Long An Provincial Representative's Report for June, July, 1963:

> The Provincial Rehabilitation program in Long An Province suffered some severe setbacks during the past two months. Viet Cong activity has picked up considerably—concentrating on attacking strategic hamlets, tearing down walls and fences, kidnaping young men, assassinating hamlet officials and in general destroying the morale and will to resist of the rural population. The hamlet militia have not performed well; the Viet Cong have entered completed strategic hamlets with trained and armed militia squads and have encountered no resistance. Why aren't the hamlet militia standing up to the Viet Cong? There appear to be a number of reasons—1) The militia do not seem to have confidence in their ability to resist the VC—rather than test their ability they are avoiding the enemy. 2) In many hamlets the

militia do patrol the defensive perimeter, lay ambushes and stand guard—but only until 2300 or 2400 at which time they all go to sleep, enabling the VC to penetrate with ease during the early morning hours. The situation may be corrected by the recruitment and training of additional militia who can then share the defensive assignments, allowing a rest period between patrols, guard duty, etc. (This problem has been discussed with the new province chief, Major Xinh, who plans to set up additional militia training centers which will double the present provincial training capacity.) 3) Long An Province is suffering from a critical shortage of troops—the limited number of troops are committed in great part to static defense (district towns, bridges, posts and security for hamlets under construction). Offensive operations against VC safe areas have been curtailed thus allowing the enemy a breathing spell to regroup and then strike at known government weak points. Because of the shortage of troops, few are available for reaction against VC attacks at night. The militia have come to realize that they will have to stand or fall alone, which has done nothing to improve their morale. The assignment of additional troops to Long An (at least one battalion) would do a great deal to improve the military situation and laterally the morale of the militia.

Another important factor in the present situation in Long An Province is the accelerated rate at which the establishment of strategic hamlets is being carried out. It appears that the massive relocation effort in March and April and May and the surge in hamlet construction during this period have overextended the provincial capabilities. There is a great need for consolidation activities in hamlets reported as completed. It has been strongly recommended to the new province chief that he recruit and train high calibre cadre to operate in small teams in completed hamlets to 1) examine hamlet defenses and defense plans; recommend improvements in current operating procedures; 2) examine hamlet development prospects and advise hamlet residents on self-help projects, NACO loans, collective development projects, etc.; 3) serve as personal representatives of the province chief to study the morale of hamlet residents and their attitudes toward the local and provincial administration—to report directly to the province chief an any cases of corruption or misconduct on the part of Government officials, to advise hamlet committee members on improvement of hamlet administration, etc. The province chief agreed with the need for this type of activity and is presently drawing up a plan for recruiting, training and deployment of such teams.

Early in July Major Nguyen Viet Thanh, province chief, was reassigned to Can Tho as IV Corps, G-3 [staff operations officer]. Major Nguyen Ngoc Xinh, former district chief of Sadec District in Vinh Long province was named as his replacement. Major Xinh does not possess the military abilities of Major Thanh, but is much more civic action oriented. He is very concerned with the people and intends to introduce programs which aim directly at winning their loyalty.

Essentially, the same sequence of events was repeated through most of the delta, resulting in the virtual collapse of many of the supposedly "completed" strategic hamlets during the summer and fall of 1963. Chau's approach was to be proven valid in later months when the Strategic Hamlet Program was disintegrating throughout the delta but the hamlets of Kien Hoa continued to resist bravely in the face of greatly increased Viet Cong military and psychological pressure.

Before moving on to some of the specific complementary programs developed and employed in Kien Hoa, we should take a moment to analyze what made Lieutenant Colonel Chau an effective counter-insurgent. First, he thoroughly understood and believed in the tasks and objective of the Strategic Hamlet Program. Second, he had the ability to translate his understanding of the strategy and tactics of the enemy and his ideas on how to meet them into action programs which could be carried out by others. Third, he possessed the initiative and self-confidence to use to full advantage the authority and flexibility allowed him under the decentralized concept of operations. Fourth, he had the courage and perseverance to move ahead despite the Viet Cong resistance and pressure and disagreements with the officials of his own government. Fifth, he had the administrative ability and insight to direct the complicated military-political-economic-social-psychological campaign against a ruthless, well-trained enemy. This paper is not intended to be an exposition of the virtues of Lieutenant Colonel Chau. However, any analysis of the program in Kien Hoa must take into consideration his unusual ability and his contribution to whatever success was achieved.

The complementary programs were many and varied. Because of time and security limitations, only a few of them will be discussed in detail. In meetings Lieutenant Colonel Chau would often say that his approach was very simple, composed of two basic elements: first, public relations; second, economic development.

In the "public relations" field, one program developed by

Lieutenant Colonel Chau was to prove extremely valuable in a number of ways. This was his version of a combined complaints-and-actions intelligence system. To carry out the program, the province chief instructed each hamlet deputy chief for security to set up an interview schedule which would include all members of all families of the village over a period of time. The interview, once the necessary rapport was established, would consist of three basic questions: (1) Do you have any complaints against anyone who works for the government, or for that matter, has anyone been giving you a bad time? (2) You know, the Strategic Hamlet Program is really intended to make things better for all of us—what do you think the government should do to make our lives better? (3) The Viet Cong don't bother us too much anymore—have you heard what they're up to? (What about Buu's brother who is with the Viet Cong— has Buu heard from him lately? How are things going for him? Do you think he might be interested in coming back to our hamlet and forget about carrying a rifle in the swamp? Now that the old village chief who used to give him such a hard time has been put in jail by the provincial officials, he really doesn't have much reason to stay away. Also, isn't he still pretty interested in Thanh's sister?)

Reports of these interviews were then sent to the provincial Complaints Bureau where they were condensed and passed on to the province chief daily. The people who were interviewed were also supposed to be informed that they could communicate directly with the province chief if they felt that the interview form might be too public a means to express their grievances.

Lieutenant Colonel Chau read these reports faithfully every day, taking action as required. If there was a report of corruption on the part of a village official or Self-Defense Corps (SDC) commander, he would order the next highest commander to make an investigation and report back to him with full details. If the charge was substantiated, appropriate disciplinary action was taken. Lieutenant Colonel Chau used members of his staff to make discreet investigations when he thought that the superiors of the accused might cover up for him.

The information on the Viet Cong activity, if tactical, was passed on to the district chief for follow-up. General information of strategic value, such as Viet Cong tax collection rate, current Viet Cong propaganda, potential defectors, was passed on to the Special Coordinator for Intelligence-Psychological War activities for inclusion in background documents or direct propaganda exploitation.

The information on the things the people thought the government should be doing in their hamlet or elsewhere were used as the basis for preparing *meaningful action* programs for economic and social development. The interview system was a continuing one. As the program developed, Lieutenant Colonel Chau noticed that some of the hamlet deputies were not sufficiently educated to do a decent job with the interviews, and that it was creating too much additional work for them. So he recruited several bright young people, trained them in the procedures, and sent them to village headquarters to do the same thing. It was much easier for them because they were able to read and write with facility and had no direct involvement with the grievances of the people. This was not a covert operation, and the people were encouraged to express themselves freely. The information gained from this activity contributed immeasurably to whatever success was achieved in the province.

It should be noted at this point that one decision that had been made during the formative stages of the Strategic Hamlet Program enabled the provincial committee to engage in activities which would otherwise have been impossible. When the budget categories were established for Strategic Hamlet Program support funds, it was realized that there would be many unforeseen expenses. Accordingly, 10 percent of the total provincial support budget was placed in a "miscellaneous" fund which could be used for projects not otherwise funded that were judged necessary by the provincial support committee. The Kien Hoa provincial committee made good use of the miscellaneous fund provided for many programs—probably the most significant among these were what Lieutenant Colonel Chau called his "public relations" programs.

In addition to providing limited support for the complaints and actions bureau, the provincial committee also authorized the publication of a bimonthly newspaper to acquaint the people of the province with the things the government was doing to improve the conditions in the province and also to report on the "actions" taken by the Viet Cong. Almost all of the news was local, and many pictures were included. The Viet Cong had been publishing a newspaper in the province for several years, distorting facts and pushing their own propaganda line. The government newspaper provided a much needed and effective device for getting the government story to the rural population. The provincial committee also authorized the formation and equipping of a provincial theatrical team composed of about thirty young men and women. The group was a great success, judging from the size and the response of the crowds they drew in villages throughout the province.

The GVN propaganda capabilities which had previously been judged adequate were, in fact, woefully inadequate when observed at a provincial level. Suggestions for improvements and lists of requirements began to come in from the provinces, and the GVN and U.S. staffs in Saigon began to respond. U.S. Information Service (USIS) jumped into the gap on many occasions, and USOM Communications Media Division started procurement of transistor radios, additional simple printing equipment (to augment the existing village newspaper kits), loudspeaker equipment, and other necessary hardware.

Lieutenant Colonel Chau was always looking for ways to improve his information programs, and so, when in early 1964 plans were worked out for importing several small (500-watt) radio transmitters for use in selected provinces, he became quite enthusiastic, remarking at one point that such a radio transmitter would be as valuable to the provincial rehabilitation program as one division of troops.

The provincial committee decided to embark on a joint campaign to get a radio station for Kien Hoa. Requests were prepared and submitted through Vietnamese government channels. Every visitor to Kien Hoa was asked to help get a radio transmitter. When provincial officials or U.S. provincial personnel went to Saigon, they repeated the request. The joint effort paid off, and the first of the new transmitters was installed in Kien Hoa in July 1964. This episode is included to illustrate another advantage of the presence of Americans in the decentralized system.

The request for the transmitter and many other provincial requests were given added emphasis by submission of an identical request through U.S. channels. American follow-up at all levels, up to and including direct conversation with President Diem and his successors, broke many bottlenecks and was one of the most important factors contributing to the effectiveness of the decentralized system.

In these and other propaganda programs (e.g. leaflets, posters, and direct personal contact with families with members in the Viet Cong to try to convince them that their sons or brothers or nephews should return to the government cause [see activities of hamlet team, above], helicopter- or aircraft-mounted loudspeaker broadcasts, etc.), Lieutenant Colonel Chau always emphasized the importance of basing the all-important local propaganda themes on local intelligence. In many cases the hardware for disseminating the message was available, but the individuals charged with the responsibility for preparing the message did not understand what they were doing and were more often than not poor writers. To coordinate these two important fields better, a special position was created on the provincial staff for a director of intelligence and psychological warfare activities.

Besides the "public relations" element of Lieutenant Colonel Chau's program, there were the very important "economic development" aspects which provided the basis for and follow-through on the public relations programs. There were far too many programs to go into them in any detail. Among them were the self-help program which was supported by release-agreement funds, Food for Peace (P.L. 480, Title II) supplies, excess property, and imported commodities such as cement, sheet roofing, reinforcing rods. In addition, programs were undertaken to improve the rural health program. For example, many of the village and hamlet health workers who had been trained in previous years had not been paid for quite some time. This problem was eventually solved through the efforts of the provincial committee, and the workers were brought in for back pay, training sessions, and pep talks.

In education, a hamlet school construction program was undertaken in 1963 with funds from the Asia Foundation and cement and roofing from Rural Affairs stocks. When this program was underway, a detailed survey of existing schools in the province was made by the IVS—International Voluntary Service (a forerunner of the Peace Corps)—volunteer assigned to the province, which served as the basis for a large-scale school improvement and construction program in 1964. The existing provincial vocational school was moved to a larger building, and additional tools were supplied from USOM/Rural Affairs excess property stocks. When this writer left the province, USOM/Education had shipped the steel frame for a huge new vocational school to be built on the outskirts of the provincial capital.

In agriculture, improved rice seed was distributed to about 15,000 farmers in 140 hamlets. The water problem, which was severe during the dry season, gave rise to a program for digging shallow concrete-lined wells and building concrete-block cisterns for catching rain water. (For a description of these and other projects, see USOM Activities Plan, Kien Hoa Province.)

The USOM Provincial Representative served very often as the catalyst for starting a new program, improving an existing program, or reviving a defunct program. The technical divisions of USOM provided invaluable guidance and assistance in these efforts.

When the Office of Rural Affairs was created, the technical divisions of USOM were not sure what role the new office would assume or what working relationships would be. As a result, there was some friction between Rural Affairs and technical division personnel at the beginning of the program. When it became apparent that the Provincial Representative could assist the technical divisions of USOM in spreading their programs throughout the country, something they had wanted to do years before but had been unable to do because of time and distance limitations, they pitched in and gave generously of their time and specialized talents to help the generalist at the provincial level.

These, then, were the basic elements of the Strategic Hamlet Program, which had been designed to achieve an intangible goal. Did the program achieve the hoped-for results? Had the *state of mind* been created? Had the people committed themselves to the government because they felt they *should* and *could successfully* resist the Viet Cong?

RESULTS OBTAINED

By mid-summer 1963, there were many indications that this "state of mind" was gradually being achieved in Kien Hoa. Included here is the "General Narrative on Progress" from the Provincial Representative for the months of June and July, 1963:

The Provincial Rehabilitation Program in Kien Hoa has reached a point during the past two months where encouraging indications of the progress of the program are reported daily. Hamlet militia and S.D.C. are working together to fight off Viet Cong attacks on strategic hamlets, increased intelligence from hamlet residents and defectors from the Viet Cong have resulted in inflicting damage against the Viet Cong, information on Viet Cong units have allowed provincial authorities to track and locate these units and launch successful operations against their bases, hamlet citizens are responding to ever-increasing security by building new homes, schools, hamlet offices, dispensaries, etc.

I have been able to make several field trips through the province and have been impressed by the progress which I have seen. Damaged roads are being repaired and new roads are being built; areas which were inaccessible except by helicopter six months ago can now be reached by jeep with relatively light escort.

In many hamlets, hamlet offices, information halls, dispensaries and schools have been built or are under construction. All of this construction has been accomplished by the hamlet citizens themselves through voluntary contributions and donated labor, with very little, if any, assistance from the government. (I am sure that the proddings of the village and district officials have played a major role in this burst of self-help; nonetheless, it is impressive to observe.)

The hamlet residents appear to be optimistic and anxious to improve their communities. Existing markets are busy and well-stocked; new market places are being built.

The Viet Cong still control or dominate large areas of the province, and the threat of Viet Cong attack is still ever-present, yet it appears that the Strategic Hamlet residents are gaining confidence in their ability to resist the V.C. The effective use of artillery and mortars at night in support of hamlet defenses, increasing numbers of militia to supplement the S.D.C. and Civil Guard (S.G.) troops in the area, provincial operations against Viet Cong safe areas—all of these factors are contributing to a growing willingness of the people to commit themselves to the Government and against the Viet Cong.

Relocation: All districts are relocating families as Strategic Hamlets are constructed. The relocation appears to be well-planned and ex-

[729]

ecuted. Food and money are provided to families when they are moved to their home sites.

Hamlet Militia: So far, the performance of the hamlet militia has been impressive. To date, 4541 militia have been trained. This is more than the number (20 per hamlet according to Provincial Release Agreement) authorized per hamlet. Col. Chau pursued a policy of training three men for each weapon and in some hamlets there are 30 or 40 trained militia with 10 or 15 weapons.

This policy has worked well—with more militia to share the responsibility of hamlet defense, there is less pressure on individual militia, who have an opportunity to rest between assignments. Also, the increased number of militia gives the hamlet residents a sense of security in numbers, a confidence in their ability to repel attack, and a willingness to stand up to attacking Viet Cong forces.

One hamlet I visited had thirty trained militia and ten weapons. When questioned on the value and effectiveness of the militia, the village chief responded, "We have one platoon now to fight against the Viet Cong—we would like one company." This same hamlet had been attacked one hour earlier by a V.C. group which had been driven off by the hamlet militia. In other hamlets, the hamlet militia are going out on night patrols and ambushes with the S.D.C. The large number of trained militia in this hamlet allows this type of activity which has proven beneficial to both the militia and the S.D.C.

Self-Help Projects: Self-help projects have been slow in getting underway. This is due in part to the fact that Col. Chau revised the orientation of the program in Kien Hoa and had to get the word to the people. Special five-day training courses were held in April and May to acquaint the hamlet chiefs with the new self-help concept, and applications are now beginning to flow in. Six projects have been approved and money was presented to the hamlets on 31 July. Forty applications are presently under study. Examples of proposed projects: 1) Hamlet purchases piglets which are distributed to individual farmers for raising—when pig is sold after one year, farmer keeps 60 percent of profit and hamlet receives 40 percent; 2) Hamlet uses 20,000 piastres provided by government plus 20,000 collected from hamlet residents to purchase copra from local residents, then arranges for transportation to market in province capital and keeps profit for improvement of hamlet facilities.

Health Programs: Province has difficulty retaining trained health workers. Although some 500 have been trained only 82 are working full time. Often these health workers are drafted by ARVN or recruited by CG or SDC. In other cases they receive no pay so are forced to find work which will provide them a livelihood. This problem is presently being studied by the province medicine chief and USOM representative to arrive at some practical solution.

Education Programs: Two buildings at Sun Dong Training Center have been renovated to provide two workshops for provincial vocational school. Work benches have been built and efforts are currently underway to obtain a generator, machine tools and more hand tools. The vocational school will concentrate on wood-working and forging and welding classes for the present. Dr. High, USOM Education, has assured us that Kien Hoa will be included in the 1964 Action Plan for Rural Trade Schools at which time the present work shops will be converted to dormitories for students from outlying districts. I intend to contact Vaughan Stapleton of IVS to find out whether we might be able to borrow an IVS vocational school advisor for two weeks or a month to help us finalize plans for the school.

Information Programs: Kien Hoa Today newspaper discontinued after issue 12 (June 15)—Province plans monthly magazine type publication with more photos and instructions to cadres and hamlet committees and militia.

Other:Youth Center: Plans now being developed by Reconstruction Chief for renovation of a large building in town to serve as Provincial Youth Center. Permission has been requested from Ministry of Interior for contact with Sacramento high schools to request assistance with equipping center. I am working on preparation of slide and tape presentation to send to Sacramento.

Coordination and Cooperation with Other Agencies (MAAG, etc.): Coordination with MAAG continues to be good, Sector Advisor and Intelligence Advisor keep USOM representative well posted on current military situation and Viet Cong activities.

Administrative: I plan to rent a house in Kien Hoa which will serve as an office and area to entertain Vietnamese officials.

Other Comments: On June 6, Lt. Col. Tran Ngoc Chau, province chief, was reassigned to Danang as mayor of that city. Major Le Huu Duc, deputy province chief for security, was designated Acting Province Chief. Major Duc is more militarily oriented than Col. Chau but assured me that he intended to follow closely the programs established by Col. Chau. Major Duc has been extremely cooperative and has demonstrated an understanding of the importance of civic action/people-oriented programs.

Other indicators of progress were captured Viet Cong documents which reported that the Strategic Hamlet Program was hurting them badly in many ways—young men were defecting to their native villages, intelligence agents were being arrested, tax collections were falling off, travel from base area to base area was becoming more difficult and more dangerous. On the other side, government tax collections and the National Agricultural Credit Organization loan repayments were increasing.

The program was apparently beginning to succeed, and not because a massive amount of financial and material aid had been provided to the province. The total value of the funds and USOM and MAP materials allocated to Kien Hoa during the six-months period from December 1962 to May 1963 was approximately one million dollars or the equivalent of two dollars per person. (At that, only approximately half the total allocation was used.) There is no doubt that the "hardware" helped a great deal, but more important, the people were beginning to *believe* in the sincerity and honesty of their own government and their own ability to resist the Viet Cong. In other provinces which had as much or more financial and material support and which had been initially less critical than Kien Hoa, the situation was much worse, e.g. Long An Province.

Although progress was being made throughout the province, the degree of progress in any given area depended to a great extent on the ability, honesty, and sincerity of the local officials, e.g. the district chief and, in even more direct contact with the rural population, the village chief and the commander of the local security forces and the catalyst hamlet establishment cadre. If these officials were responsive and fair, the program moved forward—even in the areas most heavily infested with Viet Cong political personnel, soldiers, and supporters.

An outstanding example of a successful leader of this type was Captain Huynh Anh Hoa who was the district chief in Binh Dai, at one time the worst district in the province. Captain Hoa was a native of Kien Hoa and had been involved in the struggle against the Japanese, French, and Viet Minh. He was a short, slightly chubby, happy-looking man, who showed several teeth missing when he smiled.

Riding with him in his battered jeep was an instructive experience in applied counter-insurgency techniques. Men, women, and children would wave as he drove by. He would stop occasionally to chat respectfully with an old man or woman, to speak seriously with a shabbily dressed hamlet militia man, or to fire a few questions at a passing bus-driver. As we drove away, the people he had talked with would be smiling and would wave until we were out of sight. Captain Hoa was a dedicated, capable, and brave man, but above all, he understood the people of Binh Dai, their needs and aspirations, and how to lead them.

One day in March 1964 when he was returning from a trip to resupply the men in a post that had been attacked the night before by a band of Viet Cong soldiers, the road erupted in back, under, and in front of the bus in which he and his men were riding. A murderous cross fire from the sides of the road poured into the bus. Hoa jumped out and began to rally his men for a counter-attack when he was dropped by a bullet through the forehead. By that time most of the soldiers were dead or badly wounded; the Viet Cong moved up to the bus and asked one of the wounded men to point out Hoa. They gave the dead body a kick, talked briefly among themselves, and then moved back into the coconut groves, their mission accomplished.

A new district chief was appointed immediately, but the program in Binh Dai began to sag. The new man was considered by the Americans in the province to be the best military planner on the provincial staff. He had also proved his courage and ability in several battles. When he arrived in Binh Dai, the Viet Cong followed up Hoa's murder with a vicious military campaign. They hit hamlet after hamlet, post after post, and the road was mined more and more frequently. The new district chief tried his very best, but he did not have Hoa's ability to motivate and lead people. Morale dropped, intelligence decreased, and defections from the Viet Cong decreased. When this writer left the province in August 1964, Binh Dai was still considered one of the more secure areas in the province, but things were definitely not going well.

There are others like Captain Hoa in Vietnam, but their number is decreasing with each passing month. A good district chief who does his job well becomes a marked man. He can anticipate death by a land mine, a sniper's bullet. He becomes a number one target for the Viet Cong, for he is their number one enemy. Other district chiefs who do not do their jobs or who use their positions as a means to line their own pockets survive, and they aid the insurgents' cause.

The real hope for defeating the Viet Cong rests with the Captain Hoas of Vietnam, not, with all due respect, with the military experts, nor with the road and dam builders, nor even with economic specialists. They are very important extensions of the program, but the Captain Hoas are the heart of the program. The military experts and others can become Hoas, not by simply going through the motions of wearing a constant vacuous smile, but by developing a deep appreciation of the needs and aspirations of their people. With this appreciation, a rapport can be established which will allow them to lead the Vietnamese people in a struggle for the attainment of those ideals which motivate the Chaus and Hoas of Vietnam as it did our own (U.S.) revolutionary leaders a little less than two hundred years ago.

The deterioration of the situation in Binh Dai was actually slower in coming than in the rest of the province, where a downward trend had started several months earlier. In June of 1963 Lieutenant Colonel Tran Ngoc Chau was summoned by President Diem and sent as mayor to Danang in central Vietnam, to quiet the Buddhists who had begun to agitate against the government. It was supposed to be a temporary assignment, and his military deputy was named acting province chief.

Major Duc was pleasant and well liked. He took over Chau's office and began to meet with the two U.S. members of the provincial rehabilitation committee. Chau had outlined those things he wanted done during his absence, and Major Duc began to carry them out. As time passed and Chau did not return, Duc became more and more unhappy with his difficult assignment and wanted to return to something he knew well—leading troops into battle. Decisions on new problems were needed, and he hesitated to make them. The program began to slow down. The repercussions from the suppression of the Buddhists in Saigon and central Vietnam were beginning to be felt in subtle ways. The civil servants at provincial level were disturbed by what was happening, their work was affected, and the program slowed down. Then came the November *coup d'état* which overthrew Diem. With the change in government things still did not improve. The central government was in complete confusion, and the generals were attempting to consolidate their power. The Viet Cong took advantage of the confusion and greatly benefited by intensifying the pressure. It became increasingly apparent that something would have to be done or all of the progress achieved during the first part of the year would be totally lost. Some programs staggered along, primarily because of the existence of a decision-making body at the provincial level (the provincial committee) with the authority and means to act.

The government called for submission of new "pacification" programs for establishment of "new life" hamlets. Some of the wrongs of the Diem program, such as forced relocation, forced labor, and forced contributions, were now outlawed. The programs submitted were, in most cases, technical improvements over the original plans. The Vietnamese and Americans had learned a great deal about the mechanics of the program during the past year. However, there was a disturbing emphasis on "control" of *territory* and "control" of *movement* and provision of more "hardware," which seemed to lose sight of the original concept of *influencing people* and bringing about a *commitment* to a *cause*.

Rumors of coups and counter-coups persisted, and morale began to falter—the Viet Cong continued to take advantage of the situation to intensify their activities. On January 30, 1964, the day General Khanh carried out his coup against the other generals, a reinforced Viet Cong company broke through the weakened defenses across the small river from the provincial capital at 6:30 in the evening and fired mortars and automatic weapons into the town and then withdrew. This was the first time that this had happened since the days of Lieutenant Colonel Thao (see p. 707). Exactly one week later, but this time at 6:00 in the evening, the Viet Cong attacked again, now with a heavier mortar barrage. Morale spiraled downward—officials moved their families to Saigon, wealthy businessmen and landowners moved into the provincial capital from the district towns which had also been hit by mortar attacks. Local security forces were defecting to the Viet Cong at an alarming rate.

And then in February 1964 a very unusual thing (for Vietnam) happened. Lieutenant Colonel Chau was reassigned to Kien Hoa. When he returned, he was shocked to find how badly the situation had deteriorated. He immediately took off on an inspection trip of every district—repeating the same evaluation study that he had made when he first assumed direction of the province. What he found was very discouraging. He determined that he would have to pull back many posts and withdraw from several strategic hamlets to regroup his force to reinforce those villages, hamlets, and posts which were still viable. He then put together another excellent program, which was an improvement over the original one because he had had time to evaluate his previous efforts during his absence from the province.

The downward spiral slowed, and then gradually the program began to move forward again, but this time it was much slower and more difficult. The central government was still in a state of complete confusion. Supplies were not moving out of Saigon. Many of Chau's best men had been killed. There was wrangling over the allocation of funds to the provinces. But despite all these obstacles things began to move. By August 1964 morale had picked up, intelligence was once again coming in, and the Viet Cong were again condemning publicly and complaining privately about the "American puppet" Chau.

The Vietnamese and Americans in the field have learned a little bit about insurgency—what causes it, how these causes are exploited by the Communists, how to combat it, and, hopefully, how to prevent it from developing in other countries.[8]

CONCLUSION

The Strategic Hamlet Program, as conceived by the central government and carried out in Kien Hoa Province, came close to meeting the requirements for defeating a Communist war of national liberation and achieving the political stabilization which would allow economic and social development to proceed in a well-ordered manner. However, there were several weaknesses which limited the effectiveness of the program. A few of the

[8] Additional information on the Strategic Hamlet Program is available from AID in Washington, including: "Notes on Strategic Hamlets," prepared by C. T. R. Bohannan, Office of Rural Affairs, USOM/Saigon, August 15, 1963; "U.S. Owned Local Currency Release Agreement between the Agency for International Development (AID), an Agency of the United States of America, and the Government of Viet-Nam, Kien Hoa Province Rehabilitation," Saigon, December 3, 1962; "Province Rehabilitation Plan: Kien Hoa Province," Saigon, March 6, 1964.

more important weaknesses and suggestions for improvement are listed below:

I. Weakness in the Program.

A. *The progress of the program depended too heavily on the attitude and ability of a few individuals.* If these were removed from the scene, the program did not move forward and often moved backward. This suggests three possible improvements:

(1) The entire program should have been spelled out much more precisely, in simple language, so that individuals at all levels would have come to understand and believe in the program. Once equipped with this understanding and belief, a constant flow of encouragement, reaffirmation of purpose, simple guide lines, and instructions should have been passed on to them to help them keep their eye on the objectives of the program.

(2) Continuing attention should have been paid to *careful selection,* thorough *indoctrination,* and *maintenance* of *morale* and *motivation* of all individuals involved in carrying out the program.

(3) The development of means by which the governed could prod the government into responsive action should have been encouraged. Further, this basic concept should have been translated into realistic action programs.

B. As more experience was gained, it became increasingly apparent that *there was too much emphasis on physical accomplishments.* Hamlet residents were provided with social and economic *facilities,* e.g. schools, health centers, newspapers, which are found in successful rural communities in other areas of the world, and then the people were expected to commit themselves to the government. *Too little emphasis was placed on solving those problems which were really bothering the rural population,* such as mistreatment by government officials, the lack of a simple system of justice, insufficient land, high land rentals, and high interest rate charged by money-lenders.

The Vietnamese government had attempted to meet some of these problems through laws and programs which limited land rentals, guaranteed the rights of tenancy for three to five years, provided agricultural credit at reasonable rates, etc. These programs, although quite good in theory, were not translated into realistic action programs. This failure can be traced to the poor caliber and low motivation of those charged with the responsibility for administrating the program at the province, district, village, and hamlet levels. Also, the mechanical procedures were too cumbersome to provide meaningful response to the needs of the people.

In areas where the basic problems of land, justice, and truly responsive government were handled well by the local officials, the people were willing to commit themselves to the government. In these areas hamlet residents demonstrated their confidence in the government by providing the social and economic facilities they needed through their own efforts with a minimum of outside assistance.

II. Suggested Improvements.

The shortcomings of the Vietnamese Strategic Hamlet Program might have been overcome by carefully applying the following broad concept of development which is based on our own (U.S.A.) successful experience.[9]

A. The preparation and continual proclamation of a statement of the aims and ideals of the government could provide something to which all citizens could rally and for whose preservation they would willingly risk their lives. We have such a statement in our Declaration of Independence and Constitution, strengthened and reaffirmed by the words of Patrick Henry, Thomas Jefferson, Abraham Lincoln, and others. The Vietnamese people have a good constitution (Fall 1963: Appendix 2) and a rich tradition of heroism and sacrifice for country which could serve as the basis for a declaration of aims and ideals. If properly presented and faithfully observed, this could become the rallying point for all the divergent interest groups, including many of the present Viet Cong supporters.[10]

B. The designers of the U.S. constitution and government were well aware of the necessity to create an atmosphere in which *struggle* (between haves and have-nots, management and unions, black and white, etc.) could take place with a minimum of vio-

---

[9] For an interesting discussion of this thought see "Ideology and Organization in Counterinsurgency," by Methvin (1964).

[10] The hard-core Communists could probably not be converted.

lence. Such an atmosphere allows and encourages citizens to present their aspirations and grievances with the knowledge that they can be satisfied under a system of law and without resort to violence. The Vietnamese government attempted to implement this concept when it included provisions for free elections of local officials, formation of social and economic action groups within the hamlets, and majority selection of self-help projects in the Strategic Hamlet Program. These measures were carried out fairly well in some areas, such as Kien Hoa Province, but much more emphasis should have been placed on translating this concept into practical, effective action programs.

The Viet Cong in Kien Hoa Province, and in South Vietnam in general, were far ahead of their opponents in understanding the political and psychological nature of the struggle and exploiting the grievances and aspirations of the peasants. The images they presented to the people were not those of a theoretical Marx, a dictatorial Stalin, or a power-hungry Mao, but more those of an inspiring Patrick Henry, a brave Robin Hood, or a just Abraham Lincoln. These statements of ideals and aims which they had prepared had great popular appeal among the rural population (see Fall 1963: Appendix 4).

Once they had seduced the people with inspiring slogans, they then maintained and strengthened their hold by continuous indoctrination, firm discipline, and the application of terror as needed.

Discussions with former Viet Cong leaders (Communist party members) revealed that they knew very well that they would have to seduce the people by presenting themselves as the champions of their aspirations and grievances. But once they gained complete control, they fully intended to turn South Vietnam into a Communist state.

This deception, carried out so well by the Viet Cong leaders, has resulted in the real commitment of a substantial percentage of the rural population. This belief and spirit cannot be defeated by military measures alone. The Viet Cong can be killed individually by bombs, machine guns, and artillery, but more will come forward to replace them as long as the people can be seduced or coerced to support the Viet Cong.

The people of Kien Hoa who had never lived under Commu-

[739]

nism were vulnerable targets for Viet Cong propaganda; those who had experienced Communist control, such as the resettled Catholic refugees from North Vietnam, resisted the Viet Cong fiercely. More emphasis should be placed on explaining the workings of, and conditions in, a Communist state such as North Vietnam, in terms that can be understood and believed by the peasants of Kien Hoa.

III. Effects of American Participation.

U.S. participation in the Strategic Hamlet Program was a major departure from conventional AID, MAAG, and USIS programs and should provide valuable lessons for future development programs.

The major features of the program were:

A. Decentralization of responsibility and authority.

B. Close coordination between U.S. government agencies and the Vietnamese government at central, regional (ARVN Corps—the country is divided into four corps areas), sub-regional (ARVN division—a tactical area composed of several provinces), provincial (ARVN sector comparable to U.S. state), and, in some cases, district (ARVN subsector—comparable to U.S. county) levels.[11]

C. American follow-up of downward and upward governmental communication which resulted in the breaking of many bottlenecks and the expediting of all aspects of the program.

D. The immediate and continuing availability of substantial amounts of money, P.L. 480 foodstuffs, and materials with sufficient U.S. participation in administration to:

(1) serve as a check on misuse of the support provided;
(2) provide a legitimate reason for offering advice on the use of the support provided.

The presence of Americans at the lower levels was an essential ingredient in any success the program achieved. Fighting a centuries-old tradition of tight central control, they gave confidence to local leaders and encouraged the central government to pro-

---

[11] This extension of coordinated U.S. activities to the lowest levels helped to assure that the policies and plans developed jointly in Saigon were translated into action programs at the grass roots level.

ceed with a decentralized program. The Americans, both military and civilian, played many roles in the provinces:

(1) They were observers and students—taking a graduate course in a people's war and in broader terms in political/economic/social development in general.

(2) They were friends and supporters—encouraging their Vietnamese allies.

(3) They were reporters—helping to shape U.S. understanding of the complex struggle.

(4) They were watchdogs (as much as a foreigner can be in an alien culture)—as much for the GVN as for the U.S.

(5) They were advisers, occasionally in guerrilla warfare and the political and psychological struggle, but more often in those things that Americans know best—hardware, procedures, bookkeeping, etc.

The Americans were all of these things and more and, as such, served as the *catalyst* which started and maintained the momentum of the program.[12]

A people's war and a people's army cannot be fought from the capital of the country alone. Responsibility *and* authority must be decentralized. Sufficient flexibility must be allowed at the lower levels of government to provide rapid and adequate response to local needs. Trust must be placed in carefully selected leaders. Mistakes will frequently be made, but the structure of government will be strengthened rather than weakened through this process.

RECOMMENDATIONS FOR RESEARCH

Mao Tse-tung has pointed out two obvious areas for research in the political/social/economic field: "Know your enemy. Know yourself."

Free world research in this field might be improved by approaching the problems in an underdeveloped area in the same way:

[12] When the majority of the U.S.-purchased local currency had been spent and had been replaced by GVN controlled currency, the practice of a three-man sign-off for expenditures was continued because the GVN officials knew that the U.S. personnel were honest, and were not convinced that their own men were. A side effect of the three-man sign-off was that the province chief felt that he could go ahead with the program because he had two people to share the blame or back him up if he got in hot water with the Saigon bureaucracy.

A. *Know your enemy:*

(1) Obtain all available anti-government propaganda and arrange to receive a continual flow of newly developed propaganda. Analyze the propaganda and identify those aspirations and grievances which the anti-government forces intend to exploit.

(2) Make a study of the political, psychological, and military tactics of the anti-government group to determine their strengths and vulnerabilities.

(3) Make an attempt to determine whether the anti-government groups are foreign-dominated. If they are not, determine the chances of the movement's succumbing to foreign domination and what policy or programs might be developed to prevent this take-over.

B. *Know yourself:*

(1) Undertake an in-depth study of the problems which the anti-government groups are exploiting in their attempt to win the support of the people. Prepare recommendations for corrective government action which may be required.

(2) Analyze the government civil service structure to determine methods for improving the caliber and motivation of governmental employees at all levels.

(3) Analyze the present status of upward communication to determine improved methods for allowing the people to express and satisfy their grievances without resort to violence.

RECOMMENDATIONS FOR ACTION

The Strategic Hamlet Program as applied in Kien Hoa Province suggests several action possibilities which might be applicable in other underdeveloped areas subject to Communist-inspired insurgency. A few of these action possibilities are listed below:

(1) Encourage thorough decentralization of responsibility, authority, and resources. American or other Free World advisers assigned at lower echelons of government could serve as catalysts in a decentralization process. The role of the Peace Corps in such an undertaking requires careful consideration.

(2) Identify, train, and motivate responsible local leadership, both government officials and non-governmental leaders. Training should include thorough yet simple explanation of the

interrelationship of government and the governed—showing contrast between western democracy and Communist exploitation of legitimate grievances.

(3) Encourage national leadership to work on improving attitudes and administrative procedures of governmental bureaucracy to provide truly responsive government. The complaints and action technique used by Province Chief Chau in Kien Hoa and earlier by President Magsaysay in the Philippines could be adapted to conditions in other countries. Rewarding of capable, honest civil servants and punishment of corrupt officials would greatly strengthen the national civil service.

(4) Stress immediate grass-roots programs as well as long-range national development. The avowed aim of the Communist world—China and Cuba in particular—is to use the technique of exploiting local grievances to create national wars of liberation which will bring to power groups which would be subservient to their plans for world domination. The U.S. and the Free World in general cannot afford to devote years to gradual national development while a clever, ambitious enemy is steadily subverting the rural and urban population.

REFERENCES CITED

BOHANNON, C. T. R.
  1963 Notes on strategic hamlets. USOM, Office of Rural Affairs, August 15. Saigon.
FALL, BERNARD B.
  1963 The two Viet Nams. New York, Frederick A. Praeger.
HICKEY, GERALD C.
  1963 Problems of social change in Vietnam. In Proceedings of the Ninth Pacific Science Congress of the Pacific Science Association, 1957. Vol. 3, Anthropology and Social Sciences, pp. 209–216. Bangkok, Sacretariat, Ninth Pacific Science Congress.
HENDERSON, WILLIAM
  1961 Opening of new lands and villages: The Republic of Vietnam's land development program. In Problems of freedom: South Vietnam since independence, Wesley R. Fishel, ed. New York, The Free Press of Glencoe, Inc., 123–138.
METHVIN, EUGENE
  1964 Ideology and organization in counterinsurgency. Orbis, Spring, Vol. 8.

NGUYEN KHAC NHAN
1961   Policy of key rural agrovilles. Asian Culture 3(3–4):29–49
        (July–December).
OSANKA, FRANKLIN MARK
1964   Population control techniques of Communist insurgents, a so-
        ciological analysis. Australian Army Journal, January, No. 17.
OSBORNE, MILTON E.
1965   Strategic Hamlets in South Vietnam: a survey and a compari-
        son. Ithaca, Cornell University, Southeast Asia Program, De-
        partment of Asian Studies, Data Paper 55.
SMITH, Major WILLIAM, JR.
1964   The Strategic Hamlet Program in Vietnam. Military Review
        44(5) (May).
UNITED STATES OPERATIONS MISSION
1962   U.S. owned local currency release agreement between the
        Agency for International Development (AID), an agency
        of the United States of America, and the government of Viet-
        Nam, Kien Hoa Province rehabilitation. USOM, December
        3. Saigon.
1963   Provincial representative's general narrative on progress, Kien
        Hoa Province. USOM, June and July. Saigon.
1964   Province rehabilitation plan: Kien Hoa Province. USOM,
        March 6. Saigon.
WARNER, DENIS
1963   The last Confucian. New York, Macmillan.
ZASLOFF, JOSEPH J.
N.D.   Rural resettlement in Vietnam: an agroville in development.
        Michigan State University Vietnam Advisory Group. Agency
        for International Development Contract ICA c1126.
1962–   Rural resettlement in South Vietnam: the agroville program.
1963   Pacific Affairs 35(4):327–340 (Winter).

CHAPTER 19

Some Aspects of Hill Tribe Life in Vietnam

GERALD C. HICKEY*

HISTORICAL AND CULTURAL BACKGROUND

Introduction. From an ethnolinguistic point of view, the Indo-chinese peninsula is one of the most complex areas of the world. Generally speaking, however, the ethnic groups that occupy the area can be placed in one of two categories: those that live in the lowlands (the plains, valleys, and deltas) and those that occupy the highlands. More than a geographical distinction, the highland-lowland dichotomy plays an important part in contemporary problems of the area. Historically, the location of a given ethnic group has had significance for its development, for the advances of civilization in the Indochinese peninsula have been restricted to the lowlands.

The primary sources of high culture in the Indochinese peninsula have been India and China. As it spread eastward, the great tradition of India molded the civilizations of the Thai, Lao, and Khmer (the predominant ethnic groups of present-day Thailand, Laos, and Cambodia) as well as of the Cham. (Although only an estimated 45,000 Cham survive today in central Vietnam, this once-populous group at one time dominated the kingdom of Champa, which declined as a result of wars with the Vietnamese that culminated in its defeat in 1471.) The great tradition of China is represented by the Vietnamese, who were sinicized during the thousand-year period of Chinese rule and who, since the tenth century, have carried this tradition southward in their expansion along the coastal plain to the delta of the Mekong River.

* Portions of this paper appear in a somewhat different form in The Major Ethnic Groups of the South Vietnamese Highlands RM-4041-ARPA, by G. C. Hickey, published by the RAND Corporation, April 1964, reproduced here by permission. Materials on the contemporary situation in Vietnam refer to mid-1965.

The highland groups of the Indochinese peninsula, on the other hand, have remained relatively aloof from these great currents of history. This is not to say that they have been completely isolated from outside contact or that their societies have remained unchanged. Many groups have long had contact with their civilized lowland neighbors, who in many instances are related linguistically. Sometimes the contact has been marked by conflict, and sometimes it has been largely symbiotic, resulting in the borrowing of culture traits. Also, since the mid-nineteenth century, a number of groups, particularly those in the southern Vietnamese highlands, have had contact with the French. Essentially, however, the highland people (*montagnard*) have not become part of any of the great traditions that have touched them; they have not been "civilized."

Linguistically, however, there is considerable variation among the hill tribes. The Rhadé and Jarai speak closely related languages that belong to the Malayo-Polynesian stock, which includes Cham; the Mnong, Stieng, Bahnar, and Sedang languages belong to the Mon-Khmer stock, which includes Cambodian. This does not imply formidable linguistic barriers, however, as groups speaking different languages (whether of the same stock or not) but located in contiguous areas are sufficiently familiar with one another's languages to communicate with relative ease.

A Brief Historical Sketch.[1] Between the ninth and the twelfth centuries, the highland area of southern Laos and Vietnam is mentioned several times in accounts of the intermittent struggles between the kingdom of Champa (whose capital city of Vijaya was on the coastal plain of what is now central Vietnam) and the Khmer empire (whose capital was at Angkor, near the Tonle Sap in present-day Cambodia). In those struggles the area was a buffer zone, which often passed from the control of one side to that of the other. In times of peace trade between the two kingdoms was carried on over a highland route. Occasionally, highlanders participated in events of the period; in 1149, for example, an army composed of Cham, Vietnamese, and members

---

[1] Except as noted, historical material on the highlanders comes from Bourotte (1955:1–133). This is the major historical source for the highlands of southern Vietnam.

of several highland groups fought an unsuccessful battle against an army of invading Khmer.

The year 1150 marked the beginning of a long period of Cham hegemony over most of the high plateau. This ended in 1471 with the defeat of the Cham by the Vietnamese, who then extended their authority to include some of the areas inland from the coastal plain. The greater part of the high plateau, however, remained ungoverned for several hundred years.

By the beginning of the seventeenth century Lao influence in the highlands as far south as the Boloven Plateau was increasing, and Khmer control extended over most of the Darlac Plateau. Accounts of this period mention the existence of the powerful Jarai sorcerer known as the Sadet of Fire, whom legend claims to be the guardian of the sacred Prah Khan saber of the ancient Khmer (see "The Sadets," below). In 1601 the King of Cambodia, the Sadet of Fire, and another Jarai sorcerer, the Sadet of Water, formed an alliance of friendship in which they pledged themselves to exchange gifts every three years. The exchanges continued until 1890, when Norodom became King of Cambodia, and have become the basis for a claim for "reunification" of the highlands with Cambodia (see below).

The seventeenth and eighteenth centuries were a period of considerable inter-group warfare in the highlands, and new contenders for control of the area appeared. The Vietnamese, in continuing their southward expansion, reached the delta of the Mekong River, and the Nguyen emperors followed the pattern of extending their control to highland areas adjacent to the coastal plain. The Siamese were expanding eastward and, after struggling with the Lao, assumed control over the Boloven Plateau. According to one eighteenth-century account, many of the inter-group wars were concentrated in the Darlac Plateau. There the Jarai were said to be raiding villages of neighboring groups, notably the Bahnar, and carrying off slaves which they sold to the Lao, and the Sedang also were reported as fighting with their neighbors.

The first Westerners reached the highlands in 1843, when Catholic missionaries of the Société de la Mission Etrangère de Paris traveled into the interior from the coastal town of Tourane (now Danang). In 1849 the first mission was established near present-day Kontum, and by 1851 there were four missionaries (three French and one Vietnamese) working in Bahnar villages. Because of the inter-group warfare of the period, the missionaries encountered great difficulties. The existence of the mission was temporarily threatened in 1862, when an epidemic struck down many of the Bahnar, whose sorcerers blamed the disease on the presence of the foreigners. The Sedang aggravated the situation by attacking Bahnar villages at that moment.

When the French occupied the delta of the Mekong River in 1859, agitation spread to the groups in the adjacent southern highlands. (Some sources contend that much of it was stirred up by the Vietnamese.) The Stieng in the vicinity of Thu Dau Mot revolted against the French, as did the Chrau in the area east of Baria (now called Phuoc Le). In the period that followed, the Siamese, French, English, and Germans were bidding for control of the Mekong River, and the southern Laotian and Vietnamese highlands assumed new importance. To secure their claim on the area, the French organized several exploratory missions, the first of which was the Gautier Mission of 1881. The aim of the exploration was to reach Hue in central Vietnam from the Mekong Delta by following the Donnai River, continuing northward, contacting the Stieng, Mnong, and Bahnar, and ultimately crossing the cordillera to Hue. The mission failed to achieve this end, however, when, upon reaching the confluence of the Donnai and the Da Houe rivers, the guides refused to continue northward. In his account of the expedition Gautier mentions a "king of the mois," Tong Hen, a man of seventy-five who trafficked in slaves and was recognized as a leader by some of the smaller groups.

During the second half of the nineteenth century the Nguyen emperors began sponsoring *don dien,* or military colonies, in the upland areas adjacent to the coastal plain, where members of the army were given land so that they might settle these new territories. In addition to forcing many highlanders to move further inland, the Vietnamese settlers exploited those with whom they came in contact. The *quan truong,* or leader of the settlers, often demanded rhinoceros horns or slaves of the local highlanders, and in 1883 several serious incidents prompted restraining action by the French administrators. (In one instance, a highland village headman was burned alive, and his wife slain, when he failed to supply the amount of *corvée* labor demanded by Vietnamese settlers.)[2]

The importance of the Darlac Plateau in the bid for control of the Mekong rose with reports in 1885 that the streams in the Sedang country contained gold and with persistent rumors of other mineral riches in the area. In 1888 the French administration organized an expedition to investigate the Sedang area and placed it under the leadership of Mayrena, a Belgian adventurer. On his arrival in the Sedang country, Mayrena made contact with Pim, a Sedang chief who had gained the support of many villages among the Sedang and Bahnar. Because of Mayrena's impressive appearance and his unusual physical feats, the Sedang leader concluded that he was a man of great *ae* ("mana" or "soul force"; see below, p. 758) and formed an alliance with him. Encouraged by the French missionaries, Mayrena attempted, through the leadership of Pim, to form a federation of ethnic groups in the area. The Jarai tried to resist Sedang hegemony, but without success, and, when several of the groups had bowed to Sedang leadership, Mayrena declared the area to be autonomous and named himself its ruler, "Marie I, King of the Sedang." He then sent notice of this new development to the French authorities and also asked their permission to transport minerals and other produce to the coastal towns for shipping. Should the French refuse, he added, he was willing to negotiate with the English, Germans, or Siamese. The affair was short-lived, however. When Mayrena went to Belgium in 1889, the French denied him permission to return to Indochina (Bourotte 1955; Dossier Mayrena).

In 1890–1891, a French exploratory expedition known as the Pavie Mission secured the rights of the French in Laos, expelling the Siamese from the highland areas they occupied east of the Mekong River. Accompanied by a band of Cambodians, Captain Cupet, a member of the Pavie Mission, traveled from Kratié in Cambodia to the highland towns of Ban Don and Kontum. The group encountered great difficulties, some of which had been provoked by a rumor among the Jarai that Cupet was responsible

---

[2] Vietnamese attempts to settle in the highlands and consequent problems for the hill tribes have continued up to the present day.

for suppressing the Cambodian king's gifts to the Sadet of Fire. Cupet, however, succeeded in impressing the Jarai (his compass was of particular interest to them), and they agreed to take him to the Sadet of Fire, who welcomed him cordially. Cupet noted in his account of the visit that the Sadet's followers seemed to pay him little deference. He also met the Sadet of Water and, although he had no gifts to offer the sorcerer, was able to form an alliance with him.

In 1900 there emerged another "king of the mois," Le Vo Tru. (Although the reports are not specific on this point, the name would indicate that he was either a Vietnamese or an acculturated highlander.) With a following of around nine hundred highlanders, Le Vo Tru raided the central coastal town of Song Cau, killing the French resident, his wife, and their guards. He and his band then assumed control of the area, until the Garde Indochinoise Provinciale arrived, captured the leader, and thus ended the venture.

During the first years of the twentieth century there was a marked increase in attacks on French military and missionaries throughout the highlands. In an attempt to restore order and gain the highlanders' support of the French, Odend'hal, a high French administrator, accompanied by a small unarmed band of Vietnamese (Odend'hal explicitly refused an armed escort), journeyed into the Jarai area. There he was welcomed by the Sadet of Fire, and the two men agreed to form an alliance. After they had shared a chicken, the Sadet prepared a special jar containing prescribed ingredients for a blood oath, and the Sadet drank from the jar. But Odend'hal refused, saying that he only drank water, apparently unaware of the import of such a refusal. The Sadet became angry and suspicious, and Odend'hal aggravated this by asking to be shown the sacred saber. Several days later a band of Jarai warriors slew the Frenchman and his assistants and burned their bodies.

In 1905 Darlac Province was shifted from Laos to Vietnam and a French Resident appointed. This increased French control and, according to Bourotte, diminished the power of the Sadets of Fire. Another "king of the mois" appeared during that year. He was Me Sao, of a poor Rhadé family that had known slavery. Me Sao and a small band of followers established themselves in the heights between M'drac and Ban Me Thuot and conducted raids on villages of the area to capture slaves whom they then sold. The mandarins of Phu Yen and Khanh Hoa were reported to have aided Me Sao in his activities and shared in the profits. As more and more villages fell under his control, Me Sao became bolder, until finally the Resident of Darlac dispatched troops to the area. Me Sao was turned over to the troops by his own followers, and he later died in prison.

The situation in Darlac Province improved considerably during the tenure of Sabatier, who was the Resident in the first quarter of the twentieth century. This energetic and intelligent administrator launched public works projects, improved the administrative services, and conducted systematic research on the ethnic groups of the province. Assisted by the able administrator Antomarchi, Sabatier founded a school system for highlanders as well as a medical service. The growing reputation of Darlac as an area of rich and fertile soil caused a land rush in 1925, and, within a period of a few months, over one hundred bids for land totaling 92,000 hectares were filed with the colonial administration in Saigon. Bidders were either individual planters or representatives of large French corporations interested in establishing extensive tea, coffee, or rubber estates in the area.[3]

To meet the demands of this new situation, the French administration undertook a study of the land question in the highlands, and in 1927 Sabatier issued two comprehensive reports, the first concerned largely with the land-tenure question and the second with recommendations for coping with the problems involved in developing the area.

The first report pointed out that, while some land was unclaimed, there were large areas carefully apportioned by individuals, families, clans, or villages. It emphasized also that land-tenure systems varied from one ethnic group to another. Specific information was given on the land system of the Rhadé, wherein, by the matrilineal rules of succession, rights to a given territory were vested in *po lan* (female proprietors), who held title for

[3] See "Documents de Colonisation Française en Territoreis Non Soumis à la Jurisdiction et à l'Administration Annamites," Ecole Française d'Extrème Orient, 1927 (manuscript in two parts). These are the reports prepared by Sabatier concerning the land-tenure situation in the southern highlands. They also contain recommendations for granting titles or leases to colonists.

their kin group. The limits of the territory were clearly defined, and the *po lan* was obliged by tradition to walk its boundaries periodically. She also was responsible for regulating swidden agriculture in the territory and prescribing punishments for offenses (including incest) committed within its limits (see Sabatier 1940).

The second report contained extensive recommendations for land settlement procedure. In essence, land unclaimed (*res nullius*) would be immediately available for colonization with the approval of the colonial administration, and title to the land could be granted. With land claimed by the highlanders, however, a colonist could only receive a *bail emphythéotique*, or ninety-nine year lease. In addition to the approval of the colonial administration, the bidder for a given piece of land would also need the approval of the highlander (or group of highlanders) claiming title to the land. For example, in parts of the Rhadé country it would be essential to have the accord of the *po lan* and headmen of villages within the territory concerned.

In addition, the report covered such topics as labor for the proposed estates. It strongly suggested keeping Vietnamese labor out of the highlands, pointing out that contact with the Vietnamese and Cham had always been deleterious for the highland people.

In addition to formulating the land policy in the highlands, the French extended to the entire area the administrative system established at the end of the nineteenth century for those portions then under their control. The largest administrative units were the provinces, and these were divided into districts, some of which were further divided into cantons. The villages were the smallest administrative units, and they retained their traditional leadership. Eventually, the whole highland area, designated as the Pays Montagnard du Sud (and usually referred to as the PMS), became a Crown Domaine (*Domaine de la Couronne*) directly under the control of the emperor.

Although the Rhadé cooperated substantially with the French administrators, other highland groups continued to resist their authority. In 1931 Gatille, chief of Snoul District, was killed by a group of Mnong while inspecting the construction of a new road designed to traverse the southern portion of the highlands.

Two years later Morere, the marshal of the local gendarmerie, was slain in the vicinity of Nui Bara. In 1934 and again in 1935 Camp Rolland, one of the most important military posts in the southern highland area, was attacked by a combined force of Mnong and Stieng.

Between 1935 and 1938 there was also considerable agitation among highland groups further north, in the Pleiku and Kontum areas. Among the Bahnar and Sedang there is belief in *ya*—the incarnations of powerful spirits in human form—and in 1935 a rumor spread that a *ya* had appeared in Phu Yen. It was said to be the child of a man named Ma Wih and a python, and was believed to be the incarnation of Set, bearded son of Kok Glaih, the Spirit of Thunder. Among the Bahnar, Sedang, and Jarai the news caused a great stir; it was interpreted as a sign that the promised "age of gold" had come. Pilgrims began flocking to the house of Ma Wih bearing offerings, for which Ma Wih gave them small bottles of "magic" water as a powerful talisman. The Sedang openly expressed their opposition to the French administration and attacked French outposts. The Jarai abandoned their fields, in the belief that in this new age they would be provided for without having to work. The administration finally stepped in and arrested Ma Wih. Before the tribunal Ma Wih argued that he had committed no crime; he simply had given water to the curiosity-seekers to satisfy them so that they would leave him alone. The trouble, he contended, was caused by the Spirit of the Forest. Ma Wih was released, and the agitation subsided.

The take-over by the Japanese on March 9, 1945, ushered in a new period of trouble for the highlanders and of loss of prestige for the French. Some highlanders aided the Japanese, while others fought them. When the French regained control at the end of 1945, the Viet Minh were operating in the Darlac Plateau and encouraging the highlanders to "fight the colonialist oppressors." In the years following, highlanders fought both on the side of the Viet Minh and on that of the French. With the Geneva Agreements of 1954 most of the southern highlands came under the control of the government of South Vietnam. A large number (the exact figure never was reported) of highlanders who had fought with the Viet Minh went to North Vietnam.

With the passing of the southern highlands to the Vietnamese, the PMS as an administrative unit was abolished, and the provincial administrations became directly responsible to the government in Saigon. Tribal hamlets were arbitrarily consolidated into villages for administrative purposes. Village chiefs were appointed by the district chiefs, subject to approval by the province chief.

Highland agents trained in North Vietnam manifestly began infiltrating the area in 1957, at a time when thousands of Vietnamese refugees from North Vietnam were being resettled in the highlands. By 1960 there were reported to be 51,695 Vietnamese settled on 21,186 hectares of land, most of it in the vicinity of Ban Me Thuot and Pleiku. The highlanders have also been subject to forced resettlement programs. By 1963 three large regroupment centers were functioning for the highlanders. Since 1960 the highlands have again become a buffer zone, this time in the struggle between the Viet Cong and the government of the Republic of South Vietnam (Birou (1963:1–12; Hickey 1956–1958).

Cultural Background: Economic Activities. Although there are many details of differences between the various highland groups, a number of similarities between them can be mentioned. Among the highlanders, the village is the most important economic unit. Whatever is needed by the people is produced in the village, and whatever is produced is consumed by village residents. All highland groups practice swidden agriculture (see below, pp. 765 ff.).[4] Upland or dry rice is the staple crop, but all the groups cultivate numerous secondary crops in the swidden after the harvest and in kitchen gardens within the village.[5]

They also raise chickens, pigs, buffaloes, and goats, and both hunting and fishing are activities essential to the sustenance of the group.

---

[4] Swidden agriculture often is referred to as "slash-and-burn" or "shifting" agriculture. In both French and Vietnamese literature it is called *ray*.

[5] More recently, some groups, notably the Rhadé and Sedang, have begun cultivating coffee plants in small estates, sometimes an individual effort, sometimes a group effort. See Dam Bo (Jacques Dournes) (1950:931–1208), the general source for most of the highland groups of South Vietnam. Feeling that the highland groups are too similar in their way of life to be separated, Dournes refers to them generically as "Pemsiens" (taken from the initials PMS, for Pays Montagnard du Sud).

Socio-Political Organizations. Politically, too, the village is the most important unit. Although the highland groups often are referred to as tribes, they have no tribal organization. Indeed, prior to the establishment of the French administration at the end of the nineteenth century, there was no political superstructure or recognized permanent leadership beyond the village. The present Vietnamese administrative system, similar in structure to the French, provides the only large-scale political organization in the highlands. Among the Bahnar, there are *toring,* or defined territories, collectively claimed by the villages within them, but these associations are designed to safeguard the villages' hunting, fishing, and farming rights, rather than to provide a political bond (Guilleminet 1949:383–384).

In the past there have been individual leaders who for a time gained political ascendancy over groups of villages, whole ethnic groups, and in some cases several groups, but the unions they achieved were short-lived. Notable among these leaders were some of the Sadets of Fire, powerful sorcerers who exercised considerable political influence among the Jarai and neighboring groups (see "A Brief Historical Sketch," above).

Normally, however, the highlanders' political activities are restricted to the village. The village political organizations of the various groups are quite similar, with political authority in the hands of the males. This authority is not diminished by the fact that the Rhadé, Jarai, and Mnong have matrilineal kinship systems, in which descent is in the female line, and the women own the houses, domestic animals, produce from farming, and gongs and jars (both prestige items) and also hold title to land (Hickey 1956–1958). Every village has a council of elder males, usually drawn from the household heads, and from among these elders the village headman is selected either by the council or by a consensus of adult villagers. Administration of the village, protection of the inhabitants, and organization of village rituals are the traditional responsibilities of the headman, assisted and counseled by the elders. After the arrival of the French the headman also provided liaison between the villagers and the district authorities.

Justice has traditionally been largely in the hands of the village headman and the council. Although family problems are supposed to be resolved by the head of the family, other conflicts, including violations of village customs, are dealt with by the village leaders. In the village-centered society of the highlands, customs and moral codes are deeply internalized. Villages have a strong collective spirit, and everyone in them shares in the same style of life and subscribes to the same set of values. Because the village society is small, breaches of custom do not go unnoticed, and the sanction of the community is brought to bear on offenders. With the exception of the Stieng, who hold the entire family responsible for the wrongs of one of its members, guilt usually is treated as an individual matter, and the guilty party must make his reparations to the community according to custom. The French organized tribunals for most of the larger ethnic groups, using codified native customs and appointing indigenous judges, but these tribunals were only for the problems that could not be resolved at the village level. The Vietnamese government abolished them and tried to replace native with Vietnamese law. This decision has since been reversed (see below, "Recent Government of Vietnam Legislation for Montagnard Tribunals").

The one outstanding variation on this pattern of village-centered justice is found among the Rhadé, where a certain jural authority rests with the *po lan,* or "proprietors of the land," senior females who hold title to clan land by right of inheritance (see pp. 751–52). As guardians of these strictly defined territories (any one of which may encompass several villages), the *po lan* grant permission to farm within the territory, and, in addition, perform rituals honoring the souls of the clan ancestors who reside in the territory. Should the territory be violated in any way, as by the occurrence of incest within it, it is the *po lan* who demands the penalty (Sabatier 1940).

In the past, inter-village warfare has been common among the highlanders. The French abolished it in areas where their control was well established, but it continues to occur among some groups. Other kinds of inter-village conflict, short of war, remain widespread. Institutions such as the aforementioned *toring* of the Bahnar, or clans among the Rhadé and Jarai which create inter-village kinship ties, serve to diminish wars and conflicts between villages. But among all the groups the favored means for avoiding conflict are the alliances. Through the father-son alliance or the "great *xep*" blood oath, for example, villages can prevent or end wars and other conflicts and can force bonds of cooperation. By the same token, of course, such alliances can be a means of gaining allies with whom to carry on a war more effectively. And families or clans can ally themselves so as to be able to carry out vendettas. One such instance occurred among the Mnong Gar as recently as 1949 (Condominas 1957).

There is some similarity in the social stratification of highland groups. Most villages have several wealthy families, who consti-tute a socio-political elite. Among some groups, such as the Rhadé and the Mnong, these families tend to intermarry, thereby perpetuating their elite roles. Sorcerers have high status in the highlands, and in some village societies they exercise political as well as religious influence. Although the French administration officially did away with slavery, there continue to be instances of it, particularly among the Stieng, Mnong, and Sedang.

Religion. The different highland groups share a great many religious beliefs and practices. All have origin myths concerning the beginning of their "race," by which they mean their own ethnic group. Usually the myth has an ethnocentric touch in that it presents the group's ancestors as the first humans to ap-pear on earth. (A number of the highland groups refer to them-selves as "the people.") The pantheon of spirits (called *yang* by all groups, regardless of language variations) is extremely large; there are spirits associated with the elements, with inani-mate objects, with the dead, and with animals and plants. Though some of the spirits are good, most are malevolent. The Rhadé have a hierarchy of deities, the highest of which is the Lord of Heaven (*Ae Die*); the Sedang believe in a pantheon of gods who die as men do.

All the highlanders live in the shadow of the spirits, which are believed to affect human destiny. Illness and misfortune are attributed to the spirits, and only the sorcerer can treat them. The usual method of propitiation is the ritual sacrifice of an animal. First, the victim will sacrifice a chicken, then, if that has no effect, a goat, and finally a buffalo. By such means of curing illness, more than one highlander has depleted his livestock.

The life of the highlander is accompanied by many diverse

rituals and governed by a myriad of taboos. The rice-planting cycle includes a system of rites designed to guarantee a good crop, and such things as house construction have their own series of fixed rituals. Families and clans abide by food taboos and obey interdictions against hunting certain animals or consuming certain plants. Villages sometimes are taboo to non-residents, as are houses on certain occasions. Another concept shared by all highlanders is *ae* ("mana" or "soul force"), which everyone is thought to have, but in varying degrees. Though the amount of *ae* that an individual has is intrinsic, it may be enhanced by the favor of the spirits. The degree of *ae* is manifested in a variety of ways. Unusual physical characteristics such as a powerful physique or a full beard, as well as such attributes as an extraordinary ability in hunting or in war, are regarded as signs of such *ae*. A person so endowed enjoys great prestige among the highlanders, and a manifestly large degree of *ae* is essential for anyone who aspires to be a leader.

There are sorcerers among all highland groups, and at least one is found in most villages. Because they are believed to be capable of contacting the spirits, their services are much in demand, and in some villages the sorcerers exercise as much influence in village affairs as the headman and council. Their ability to determine the source of witchcraft makes them personages to be feared. In 1949 the vendetta among the Mnong Gar alluded to earlier involved a sorcerer who had informed one family that it was being bewitched by another. Similar incidents in Jarai villages in 1957 prompted the district chief to collect all the sorcerers into one village so as to be able to control their activities.

The Sadets. Recent works by French ethnologists agree that there are at present a Sadet of Fire, a Sadet of Water, and a Sadet of the Wind. As already mentioned, early accounts about the highlands tell of a powerful Jarai sorcerer known as the Sadet of Fire. In the seventeenth century, this sorcerer and his confrere, the Sadet of Water (the two are never supposed to meet, for a meeting would bring great calamities), entered into an agreement with the King of Cambodia to exchange gifts every three years. Legend has it that, at some unspecified time long ago, a bond was established between the Sadet of Fire and the Khmer rulers. When a Cham king recovered a glimmering object from beneath the waters of a river, it turned out to be the Prah Khan, a sacred saber of Khmer royalty. While the Khmer came to possess the scabbard, for which King Jayavarman II (A.D. 802 to 854) is said to have constructed a magnificent reliquary, the Jarai obtained the saber itself, and it was entrusted to a sorcerer of Plei M'tao village, who became known as Master of the Saber or Sadet of Fire (Bourotte 1955).

According to Jarai tradition, the Sadet of Fire as keeper of the sacred saber derives his unusual powers from the host of spirits associated with the saber, which are believed to live in the Sadet. In addition to giving the Sadet unconquerable strength in battle, these spirits endow him with special power to dispel epidemics through ritual sacrifices. Students of highland ethnology vary somewhat in their accounts of the Sadets and in their views on the influence of these sorcerers on the Jarai and neighboring groups. Jouin (1951:73–84) contends that the last powerful Sadet of Fire was a Jarai named Y Thih, who lived in the village of Plei M'tao during the last half of the nineteenth century and that his successors are incorrectly referred to as "Masters of the Saber," whereas they should be called "Guardians of the House of the Saber" (Ae Buom) because they are not true Sadets. Other scholars maintain that Sadets such as the one responsible for the death of Odend'hal, and also the current Sadet, are true successors to the guardianship and consequently to the title (Ezzaoui 1940:169–174; Lafont 1963).

All ethnologists agree that it is traditional for kinsmen of the Sadet of Fire to slay him when he has grown old, but there are two versions of the method by which the new Sadet is chosen. According to one, the Sadet, prior to his death, throws his copper bracelet into the pool where the residents of Plei M'tao bathe, and whichever male emerges with the bracelet on his arm will be the new Sadet. Another version is that, after the death of the Sadet, young warriors of the Siu clan (from which the Sadet traditionally is selected) gather to sleep in the same communal house. While they are asleep, one of the elders demands, "Who will be Bok Redau?" and when one of the warriors answers in his sleep, "It is I," a cotton bracelet is placed on his wrist as a symbol of his new role (Bourotte 1955; Ezzaoui 1940).

[759]

The Sadet of Water, according to all accounts, functions more as a sorcerer than as a leader. He resides in the village of Plei M'tao Ea in Darlac Province, where he receives visitors who bring prescribed gifts, and he frequently travels about the area visiting villages to perform rituals that are intended to prevent or dispel epidemics due to droughts. Elderly Rhadé recall that on several occasions a Sadet of Water came to the town of Ban Me Thuot, remaining on the outskirts of the settlement as is the custom, and throughout the Jarai areas older villagers recall having seen him. Several recent sources report that there also is a Sadet of the Wind, who, although he plays no political role, has considerable mystical power (Condominas 1959; Lafont 1963).

Of the three, however, the Sadet of Fire appears to be the only one ever to have wielded political power. Although Captain Cupet on his 1890–1891 expedition recorded (as mentioned above) that the then Sadet's followers paid him little deference, various historical accounts credit other Sadets of Fire with considerable political influence on the Jarai and neighboring groups, and the Odend'hal affair in 1905 would indicate that the Sadet of Fire of that time was a leader to be reckoned with. Recent French ethnologists disagree on the role of the current Sadet of Fire. Father Dournes, a member of the Société de la Mission Etrangère de Paris who has spent a number of years among the Jarai in the Cheo Reo area, believes that the Sadet of Fire continues to have considerable influence; Lafont (1963) denies that the three Sadets enjoy the prominent roles today that they had at the time the French explorers visited the highlands.

THE PRESENT SITUATION OF THE VIETNAMESE HIGHLANDERS

Introduction. The situation among the highlanders is in a state of basic change now (May 1965). Since the rebellion in September 1964 the government has attempted to satisfy some of the desires of the highlanders in the hope of getting them to rally behind the government. First they held a conference at Pleiku in October, and the highlanders present represented most tribes, although as delegates some were simply civil servants from province and district offices, while some were real leaders—people who had been jailed after their uprising in 1958. Most of these were Rhadé, Jarai, and Bahnar. Missing was Y Bham, the Rhadé leader who spurred the 1958 revolt, was jailed, and had been released in February 1964. He was involved in the September rebellion, but either went voluntarily or was forced to go to Cambodia where he now appears to be a captive of a movement that calls itself The Front for the Protection of the Oppressed Races. This movement does not put out the Viet Cong line, but rather something that sounds like the Cambodians being excessively nationalistic (see below).

The leaders of the highland group (Rhadé, Jarai, and Bahnar for the most part) compiled the "aspirations" of all the groups represented and presented them to the Vietnamese authorities. These concerned giving the highlanders more (and stronger) representation in the central government, more role in the administration of their own areas, land titles (a very sore point with those whose land had been taken by the land development schemes initiated in 1957 when the Diem government began resettling northern refugees and central Vietnamese in the highlands—the government's attitude then was that the government owned all the land in the highlands), acceptance of more highlanders in secondary schools, universities, and the School of Administration. They also wanted their own army, direct American aid (i.e., not to go through Saigon), more schools, and medical facilities, and they wanted reinstituted their native tribunals, which had been suppressed by the Diem regime (see below). They also wanted their own languages taught in the primary schools along with Vietnamese.

The Vietnamese discussed these things with them, then General Khanh came to meet them. The Vietnamese would not agree to the army or direct American aid. There had been a rather vaguely organized Bureau for Montagnard Affairs organized in March 1964, and General Khanh announced that it would become a directorate and appointed Colonel Ya Ba as director. He agreed to most of the other things and began turning the wheels to get something done about it, but left office late in October. Mr. Huong was sincere, but was too beset and besieged by the Buddhists and students to do anything. There were rumblings of another revolt in the highlands, and the Vietnamese quickly appointed a number of highlanders to the Non-Commissioned Officers' School at Nhatrang and fifteen to the Officers' Training School at Thu Doc. The Ministry of Education announced a plan for expanded education in the highlands and a scheme whereby highlanders would get special consideration for their application to schools of higher education (the acceptance grade would be lowered 10 percent for them). In March 1965 a group of twenty-two highland leaders met with various ministers in Saigon. The tribunals were reinstated, the intention of granting land titles was made known, and a scheme for surveying land announced. So it can be seen that the situation is in a state of flux.

The Viet Cong and the Highlanders. Vis-à-vis the Viet Cong, there has been a marked change. Whereas in 1958 the Viet Cong propaganda was well done (things like hammering away at the mountaineers' fear that the Diem government was going to depose them of all land), in the past several years the Viet Cong have used terrorism, forced recruitment and labor in hill tribe villages, demand for rice and food, and direct attacks on resettled hill tribe villages resulting in considerable death and destruction. The highlanders now almost invariably describe themselves as "in-between." They do not want to support the Viet Cong (and are afraid of them), but they still are not lured by the government.

Hill Tribe Nationalism: Y Bham and the Front for the Protection of Oppressed Races. Y Bham, a leader of the Rhadé tribe from South Vietnam, has gone to Cambodia, where he is working for the formation of a United Front for the Protection of Oppressed Races (French abbreviation: FULRO) to be composed of the peoples of the South Vietnamese and Cambodian highlands. Though this movement has been widely reported in the public press, it is too early to judge the effectiveness of Y Bham's attempt to build a nationalist movement among the highlanders, who are now, as has been the case for centuries, caught in a struggle between their more powerful neighbors.

Legal Status of the Highlanders: History. Traditionally among the highlanders reconciliation of disputes and punishments for violations of customs were the affairs of family and village. Prior to the arrival of the French, the tribal laws were unwritten; they were expressed in terms of taboos and sanctions which all mem-

bers of the societies knew and respected. There was a well-defined moral order, with well-defined retributions and punishments for those who breached it.

The French administration allowed the traditional jural systems to continue, and some administrators began recording tribal
laws with a view to organizing native tribunals (hill tribe customs are codified in Gerber 1951; Guilleminet 1952; Lafont 1963;
Sabatier 1940). Tribunals were established in the province capitals of the high plateau. Hill tribe judges were appointed, and
the *coutumiers* (codified customs) served as a basis for adjudica-
tion. Cases brought to the tribunals were those which could not
be resolved on the village level. The procedures of these courts
were relatively simple. At Ban Me Thuot, for example, the judge,
an elderly respected man from Ban Don, would hold sessions
for the first five days of every month. The sessions were held
in a small room simply furnished, with a table behind which
the judge sat, and a few benches. The plaintiff and his party
sat on one side while the defendant and his group were on the
other. After each side had presented his case, witnesses were
heard, and the judge would refer to the pertinent law. The case
usually was resolved through discussion.

*Recent Government of Vietnam Legislation for Montagnard
Tribunals.* In response to the highlander request for the organization of "Customs Law Courts in the highlands and a Law Protection regime" (formally submitted at the Convention for Administrative and Military Affairs held in Saigon in March 1965), the
Government of Vietnam has promulgated a decree aimed at "reorganizing Montagnard Common Law Courts in the Central
Vietnam Highlands." The new courts are to deal with civil affairs,
"montagnard affairs," and penal offenses when both parties are
highlanders. Crimes and offenses committed by hill tribe service-
men, crimes against the nation, or those involving lowlanders
(ethnic Vietnamese) will be brought before the National Courts.

The law provides for courts at the village, district, and province levels. The Village Customs Law Court is presided over
by the Village Administrative Committee Chief, assisted by two
highlander assessors. Early in December each year, the chairmen
of village administrative committees and residents of the villages
prepare a list of twelve notables elected by the population. From

[763]

each list the district chief concurrently acting as Justice of the Peace will select two regular assessors and two deputy assessors for every village court. At least one weekly session is held if necessary. When a case is resolved, the decision is recorded and signed by the contesting parties, thus negating the right to appeal to another court. Right of appeal to a higher court is possible when the case remains unreconciled.

At the district level, the courts will be presided over by a President of the Court, who will be the district chief, and he will be assisted by two hill tribe assessors. There will also be a clerk-interpreter. The assessors will be selected from lists of hill tribe notables elected by the district residents. Sessions of the court will be held at least twice a month at district head-quarters. Cases within the jurisdiction of the district court include those appealed from the village courts, lawsuits on civil and commercial matters involving more than 500$VN and less than 1,500$VN, all kinds of minor offenses, "and cases considered traditionally as serious ones, such as offenses against religions and creeds, viz. desecration of graves, insults uttered during a ritual ceremony, disturbance of an oath-taking ceremony and offenses against deities."

A Montagnard Affairs Section of the court will be organized at the provincial level. This section will be under a Montagnard Presiding Judge, assisted by two hill tribe assessors, a national clerk who keeps the records, and an interpreter. The assessors, like those of the other courts, will be drawn from a list of elected notables. The Montagnard Affairs Section will sit once or twice a month, depending on demands. This court is competent to pass judgment on appeals from the montagnard district courts and actions which do not fall into the realm of the village or district courts.

This legislation restores the legal status of the native laws and tribunals which had been lost by the highlanders under the Diem regime as a part of the policy of total assimilation which resulted in an attempt to replace hill tribe social institutions with Vietnamese ones. This policy caused considerable resentment among the highlanders, who felt that their way of life was threatened, and this fear was seized upon by the Viet Cong in their propaganda. This was one of the bases of a strong appeal by the Viet

Cong, who could cite favorably the example of the autonomous zones in North Vietnam.

Although the new laws seem to be a step in the right direction, the overall effect may have been to structure hill tribe law in terms of the Vietnamese system. The highland villagers, like the Vietnamese villagers, will probably prefer to settle their own difficulties without recourse to outside authority.

AGRICULTURE AND LAND TENURE

The government of the Republic of Vietnam is currently preparing a program of distribution of land titles to the mountaineers. Other than problems associated with shifting of villages due to the war (none of the highlanders normally could be considered nomadic people—they may shift their fields but prefer to keep their villages in the same location), there are matters concerning highland agricultural techniques and land-tenure systems which I believe would be well to consider in formulating such a program.

Highland Agriculture. Swidden agriculture (also sometimes referred to as shifting or slash-and-burn agriculture) is traditional among the highlanders and continues to be practiced by most groups. Where there is available bottom land with water sources, the hill tribes usually practice paddy wet-rice agriculture, using techniques similar to those of the Vietnamese (and probably learned from them). Such fields can be seen along river banks throughout the highlands, in volcanic depressions such as those in the vicinity of Pleiku, and in level areas around Kontum town. In the area of Phu Bon there are also some extensive paddy fields belonging to the Jarai, and the Churu in the valley of Dran cultivate paddy using the Cham plow and water buffalo (they are supposed to have learned the techniques from the Cham centuries ago). Finally, in the Valley of the Winds inland from Quang Ngai, the Hrê have terraced paddy fields similar to the terraces of the Vietnamese along the coast.

Generally speaking, there are basic similarities in the swidden technique employed by mountaineers. Among most (if not all) groups it is a system of rotating agriculture wherein a plot is farmed for a given period—usually between one and three years—and then is left to lie fallow while the cultivators move to a series of other fields, returning to the overgrown plot in due time. The cycle seems to be fairly consistent with all groups. The fallowing period usually depends on the type of flora that predominates the area; if there is an abundance of fast-growing bamboo, for example, the fallow period probably will only be three or four years, while in areas where the growth is slower it may be eight to fifteen years.

To prepare the fields, first vegetation is cut, and usually all but the large trees are felled. After the brush and wood have dried sufficiently, fires are set and controlled as much as possible. The rubble is cleared, and the soil is raked. The men make holes with dibble sticks, and women follow, planting the seeds. During the growing period some weeding is done. Both men and women assist with the harvest, and the yield is stored in individual family granaries. Various secondary crops are planted in the swiddens, sometimes in alternating rows with the upland rice and sometimes after the harvest. Kitchen gardens and fruit groves usually are cultivated in the village near the house.

The Brôu, a group located in the vicinity of Ke Sanh, near the Lao border inland from Quang Tri, usually farm their fields one year (three years if there are large trees, which are thought to indicate good soil). When there is new mature vegetation on the field lying fallow—from five to eight years—the plot can be recultivated. One year is the normal planting for swiddens used by the Jeh, a group found near the Dak Pek area, northwest of Kontum. Their fallowing period is ten years.

In the vicinity of Phu Bon (Cheo Reo), the Jarai who practice swidden agriculture cultivate their fields for three years, and the Jarai to the east, in the Plei Mrong area, farm their swiddens for as long as five years, leaving the field for five to eight years before clearing and burning them again.

Selecting the site for a new swidden field usually involves inspecting the vegetation to determine whether the kinds of plants supported by good soil abound. This also may be accompanied by some type of divination; the Rhadé, for example, look for certain birds in the forest because they are an omen of fertility, while the Cheo Reo Jarai construct a shelter on the proposed site, and if the occupants dream of fish or deceased kin or acquaintances, it is a sign of fertile soil, while dreams of goats or dogs indicate the reverse.

It is often assumed that swidden agriculture is destructive. In his detailed study of swidden agriculture among the Hanunóo of Mindoro Island in the Philippines, Conklin (1957:154–155) warns against making negative judgments on this form of agriculture without realizing the variations that exist in it and without examining it objectively. Other anthropologists and agricultural economists such as Pendleton (for example, N.D.:33–52; 1962) have been doing research on the efficiency of using swidden agriculture in certain physical ecologies. In areas like the uplands of Thailand (similar in many respects to the highlands of South Vietnam) most farming is done on slopes, and the rains are torrential. Using the swidden method has the advantage of leaving the tree roots in the soil, which helps to retain the structure, and the dibble stick does minimal harm to the structure. If a plow were used in these circumstances, there would be grave danger of having the top soil wash away.

Land Tenure. When highlanders cultivate wet rice in paddys, ownership is well defined, as the limits of the land usually correspond to the extent of cultivation Among the Hrê, for example, everyone knows which family owns particular terraces, and these are passed from generation to generation.

The traditional land-tenure systems of groups practicing swidden agriculture vary somewhat between the different groups. The most complicated appears to be the *po lan* system of the Rhadé (described above, pp. 752 ff.). It is related to the matrilineal clan system wherein clan name, mobile goods, and land are passed down through the female line. The sub-clan has claim to a given territory, and title is vested in the *po lan* (literally "proprietor of the land"), usually an elderly female of the senior line. According to recent Rhadé sources, this system has been changing, particularly in the vicinity of Ban Me Thuot.

Among the Bahnar there is the *toring*, a territory in which several villages collectively control hunting, fishing, and farming rights. Outsiders, whether Bahnar or not, must have the approval of the villages' elders (*kra*) in order to enter and carry out any of the above activities.

Research thus far indicates that most of the other hill tribe

[767]

groups have village territories in which the residents farm. In some instances it is a very well-defined area; among the Jeh, for example, the *sal ja* is a village territory, and while outsiders are free to hunt or fish in the *sal ja,* they cannot dam a stream or farm without permission of the village leaders. With other groups the territory is less well defined; it simply is an area surrounding the village, where the residents farm, hunt, fish, and cut wood. It is in the order of things that villages respect one another's rights.

Among all hill tribes, each family cultivating a cycle of swiddens is recognized as owner of these fields. Villagers all know which fields lying fallow belong to fellow villagers, and their rights are respected. The rule seems to be that the first occupier of the soil has unwritten title to it.

Finally, there is an erroneous notion that the hill tribes claim all of the land in the highlands. The land-tenure systems noted above embrace only a portion of the area. The remainder is land *res nullius,* unclaimed by anyone.

REFERENCES CITED

BIROU, A. (O.P.)

    1963   Les sociétés coutumières face à leur developpment: les montagnards du Vietnam Sud. Epiphanie, January/February:1–12.

BOUROTTE, B.

    1955   Essai d'histoire des populations montagnardes du Sud-Indochinois jusqu'à 1945. Bulletin de la Société des Etudes Indochinoises 30:1–133.

CONDOMINAS, G.

    1957   Nous avons mangé la forêt. Paris, Mercure de France.

    1959   Chez les rois de l'eau et du feu. Marco Polo 24:47–60.

CONKLIN, H.

    1957   Hanunóo agriculture. Rome, Food and Agriculture Organization of the United Nations. F.A.O. Forestry Development Paper 12.

DAM BO (JACQUES DOURNES)

    1950   Les populations montagnardes du Sud Indochine. France-Asie, Numéro Spéciale, 5:931–1208.

DOSSIER MAYRENA

    N.D.   Dossier Mayrena. Ecole Française d'Extrême Orient, mimeographed.

EZZAOUI, J.
  1940   Une version de la légende des deux Sadets. Institut Indo-
         chinois pour l'Etude de l'Homme 3:169–174.

FALL, B. B.
  1963   The two Viet-Nams: a political and military analysis. New
         York, Frederick A. Praeger, Inc.

GERBER, T.
  1951   Coutumier Stieng. Bulletin de l'Ecole Française d'Extrême
         Orient 45:228–269.

GUILLEMINET, P.
  1949   La tribu Bahnar du Kontum. Paris, Imprimerie Nationale,
         Société Asiatique de Paris. Actes du XXIe Congrès des
         Orientalistes.

  1952   Coutumier de la tribu Bahnar des Sedang et des Jarai de
         la province de Kontum. Paris, E. de Boccard, Publications
         de l'Ecole Française d'Extrême Orient.

HICKEY, G. C.
  1956– Unpublished notes on the major ethnic groups in the southern
  1958   Vietnamese highlands collected during field trips between
         1956 and 1958.

JOUIN, B.
  1951   Histoire légendaire du Sadet du Feu. Bulletin de la Société
         des Etudes Indochinoises 26:73–84.

LAFONT, P.-B.
  1963   Toloi Djuat: coutumier de la tribu Jarai. Paris, Publications
         de l'Ecole Française d'Extrême Orient.

MAITRE, H.
  1912   Les jungles moi. Paris, Larose.

PENDLETON, R. L.
  N.D.   Some interrelations between agriculture and forestry, particu-
         larly in Thailand. Journal of the Thailand Research Society,
         Natural History Supplement 12:33–52.

  1962   Thailand. New York, Duell, Sloan and Pearce.

SABATIER, L.
  1940   Recueil des coutumes Rhadées du Darlac. Hanoi, Imprimerie
         d'Extrême Orient.

CHAPTER 20

Mountain Minorities and The Viet Minh:
A Key to The Indochina War[1]

JOHN T. McALISTER, JR.

DIEN BIEN PHU:

A PRISMATIC VIEW OF THE FIRST INDOCHINA WAR

During the first week of May 1954 newspaper headlines the world over told of French-led soldiers, about an infantry division in strength, who were surrounded in a mountain valley in northern Indochina. They were fighting for their lives against an adversary more than twice their size. The enemy commanded the encircling mountain heights, and from these positions they maintained a withering artillery fire which served to cover the advance of their battalions. Relief forces could not be marched

[1] The study of which this paper is a part is based largely on research conducted in the French Army Archives on the Indochina War at the *Service Historique de l'Armée* in the Chateau de Vincennes on the edge of Paris. I am most grateful to the Ministry of Defense of the Republic of France for having granted me permission to consult these archives. I am equally appreciative to the personnel of the *Service Historique de l'Armée*, who aided me in innumerable ways. I wish especially to mention the assistance of the Director, General Cossé-Brissac, the Chief of the Overseas Section, Lieutenant Colonel Jouin, and the head of the Indochina Archive, Major Michel Desirée, a courageous survivor of the Battle of Dien Bien Phu, with whom I worked most directly. According to the regulations governing my use of these archives, I am not permitted to make direct citation to the information I collected there. Similar conditions have been observed in the publication of two other works (Fall 1961; Tanham 1961) based on research at the *Service Historique de l'Armée*.

The research at the *Service Historique de l'Armée* was made possible by a grant from the Foreign Area Fellowship Program, a joint committee of the Social Science Research Council and the American Council of Learned Societies, which I acknowledge gratefully.

The preparation of this paper was supported in part by the Special Operations Research office, the American University, under Department of the Army Contract DA 49-092 ARO-7, through funds made available to the Center of International Studies, Princeton University. Neither the Foreign Area Fellowship Program, the Special Operations Research Office, the Department of the Army, nor the Center of International Studies is responsible in any way for the contents of this paper, nor for the views expressed herein.

VIETNAM: JOHN T. MCALISTER, JR.

overland because the battle site lay on the opposite side of a
wide stretch of enemy-controlled mountainous terrain, difficult
to traverse under the best of circumstances. Parachuted reinforcements, a possibility earlier, would now be dropped to an
almost certain death. If their transports were not knocked down,
their bodies would be riddled in the slow descent to the ground.
An air of desperation and helplessness became widespread. The
defenders of Dien Bien Phu seemed beyond redemption.[2]

For distant observers throughout the world, the battle being
waged in the beautiful and remote upland valley on the border
between Laos and Vietnam was symbolic. It was a microcosm
of the confrontation of the West with the Communist strategy
of expansion into the underdeveloped areas of the world. For
closer observers this global symbolism was overshadowed by the
specific issues which the combat posed. The French command
was attempting to halt the take-over of the mountain homeland
of the Tai[3] minority people in northwestern Vietnam. Prior to
Dien Bien Phu the French had been unable to stop the wide-
ranging operational maneuvers into unprotected sections of the
Tai highlands and adjacent areas of Laos by the military forces
of the Communist-led Vietnamese independence movement, the
Viet Minh. It was for this reason that the French hoped to maintain their influence in the Tai country by drawing the Viet Minh
into a fixed-position battle.

The issues represented by the Dien Bien Phu encounter also
had an underlying significance for the Viet Minh. The battle
was the culmination of their progress through the stages of military development prescribed by Mao Tse-tung in his writings
on the strategy of revolutionary warfare.[4] After a meager begin-

[2] The literature on the battle of Dien Bien Phu is large and growing. It
includes Catroux (1959), Devillers and Lacouture (1960), Ely (1964), Fall
(1961:Ch. 12; 1964; forthcoming), Grauwin (1954), Langlais (1963), Laniel
(1957), Navarre (1956), Tanham (1961:Ch. 4), Paillat (1964:Ch. 33), Pouget
(1964), Roy (1963;1965), Vo (1964).
[3] The word Tai is spelled thus throughout this paper in order to differentiate
the Tai language, tribes, highlands, and federation of Indochina from the Thai
people of Thailand (who are also speakers of a Tai language).
[4] Mao's important writings on revolution have been collected in Mao (1963).
This volume includes "Problems of Strategy in China's Revolutionary War" (December 1936), "Problems of Strategy in Guerrilla War against Japan" (May
1938), "On Protracted War" (May 1938), and "Problems of War and Strategy"
(November 6, 1938).

[772]

ning in December 1944, with a guerrilla band of only thirty-four men, the Viet Minh had, by the autumn of 1950, achieved a capacity for flexible big-scale encounters known as mobile warfare.[5] In less than three years of earnest combat, from 1947 to 1950, they had progressed from guerrilla warfare to the second stage of Mao's strategy, mobile warfare. They had demonstrated this capacity by decimating a French force of 10,000 men in a running battle along Vietnam's mountainous northeastern frontier in October of 1950. From this turning-point the Viet Minh waged three and one-half more years of mobile warfare in which they refused to accept a defined battle front. Such a war without fronts was also a war without territorial objectives. This was the case because the Viet Minh knew that control of territory was meaningless so long as French forces remained stronger and could reoccupy any lost ground. Because the Communists began with relatively weaker armed strength, they had to harass and wear down the French, build up their own forces, and keep on the move so that they could not be trapped and annihilated.

The Viet Minh's revolutionary war strategy was designed to force the French into a territorial defense. With their adversary's troops spread out and tied down, the Communists could concentrate a local force superior in numbers and firepower to wipe out the scattered and exposed French units. If a stronger French relief force approached to aid its beleaguered comrades, the Viet Minh would merely melt into the countryside, refusing combat. After seven years (1947–1954) of this harassment the French were anxious to get the Viet Minh to join in a fixed battle. Ironically, this desire played into the Communists' hands. The battle of Dien Bien Phu represented the Viet Minh's arrival at Mao's final stage of military development, that of fixed-position warfare.

After the lines of battle had been drawn at Dien Bien Phu in late 1953, the fate of those defending the isolated outpost in the highlands of northwestern Vietnam was hardly in doubt. The certainty of this outcome became apparent when elements of four Viet Minh divisions were concentrated around the Franco-Vietnamese positions. The French commander in Indochina, General Henri Navarre, believed that the Communists'

[5] The beginnings and growth of the Viet Minh armed force are documented in Anon. (1955A). Details on the December 1944 origins are found on p. 12.

strategic mobility and logistics were modest and that their force in the Tai highlands would be no larger than one division (Sheehan in Roy 1965:XVII). It was expected that this division would batter itself against the superior power the General had amassed at Dien Bien Phu. The tragedy of this miscalculation was that the French command was attempting to fight a fixed-position battle more than 180 air miles from its nearest base of support with only meager air transport capability, no real alternative means of surface reinforcement, no avenue for withdrawal, and without command of the surrounding heights. To the surprise of the French military leadership the Viet Minh had devised an ingenious logistic system which replenished the Communist-led force across the most rugged terrain in Indochina.

By the end of the first week in May 1954 France had suffered its worst defeat in nearly four centuries of colonial politics and warfare. A French-led force of seventeen battalions numbering more than 10,000 men surrendered to the Viet Minh after fifty-six days of bitter conflict. Although this loss represented only a small portion of the approximately 450,000 Frenchmen, Vietnamese, and men of other ethnic identities fighting against the Communists throughout Indochina, it finished almost seven years of French combat against revolutionary warfare.[6] Since the overwhelming majority of French-led forces remained intact, it seems clear that the battle of Dien Bien Phu was decisive for reasons other than military capacity. The Franco-Vietnamese forces still had the means but no longer had the will to continue.

The reasons for the decisiveness of the battle of Dien Bien Phu in ending the Indochina War are complex. Without a full exploration of this complexity, one sequence of explanation appears conspicuous. That France no longer wished to press the combat against the Viet Minh was primarily, if not exclusively, a political decision. But the domestic political pressures which caused such a decision were a response to the lack of French military and political success in Vietnam. The defeat at Dien Bien Phu was dramatic and overwhelming evidence of this unsuccessful pattern. Although the Viet Minh did not have a pre-

---

[6] Figures from Roy (1963:558–559). The total included approximately 300,000 Vietnamese, 54,000 French, 30,000 North Africans, 18,000 Africans, 20,000 Legionnaires, 15,000 Laotians, and 10,000 Cambodians.

dominant military or political position in northern Vietnam, much less the whole of Indochina, it was deemed wiser by the French to end the combat and get the best conditions obtainable by negotiations. A further investment of men and materiel appeared unwarranted since the Viet Minh had perfected a strategy which the French-led forces had been unable to master.

THE ETHNOGRAPHIC BACKGROUND TO THE INDOCHINA WAR

The success of Viet Minh strategy was due not only to their use of the concepts of Mao Tse-tung but also, and more importantly, the adaptation of their strategic thinking to the unique geographic and ethnic features of Vietnam. The development of a modest guerrilla force into a six-division army with mobile striking power was greatly facilitated by the character of Vietnam's geography, especially that of the northern portion of the country.[7] These advantages arose because Vietnam is not geographically unified with convenient natural avenues of communication. Isolated areas abound and offer refuge for guerrillas or ambush sites for mobile forces.

Overall, Vietnam is an hourglass-shaped country fragmented with mountain chains and held together by a thin coastal plain uniting two deltas at extreme ends of the territory. The dimensions of Vietnam's geography are its length of approximately 1,000 miles and its width of 300 miles at its widest and 45 miles at its narrowest point. More striking is the pattern of the country's population distribution. Roughly thirty million Vietnamese are crowded onto less than 20,000 of the country's 128,000 square miles of territory. They live on fertile deltas and coastal plains, while the remaining 100,000-plus square miles, mostly plateau and mountains, are sparsely populated (Condominas 1951:77).

This vast mountain area marks a sharp cultural dichotomy. It contains less than two million persons of various non-Vietnamese ethnic identities having a much lower level of cultural attainment than the lowlanders. While the Vietnamese who are crowded along nearly a thousand miles of narrow lowlands have a general ethnic and cultural homogeneity, the mountains are inhabited by a confusing ethnic mosaic of widely diverse peoples.

[7] The best general geography of the area is Great Britain (1943). Another geography is Canada (1953), and Dobby's book (1956:Ch. 20) is also useful.

Enough is known about the mountain minority peoples to make valid generalizations about their diversity, but information about them is so scarce that there is not even a precise number for the various ethnic groupings.

With the information available the non-urban ethnic minorities in Vietnam can be classified into three convenient categories. These general distinctions relate primarily to the location of the minority people, although this characteristic tends to reflect congruent patterns in social organization, relation to the land, and linguistic classification. By employing these criteria, it is possible to distinguish first, the minorities of the southern deltas who have inherited the decaying tradition of antique kingdoms; second, those primitive inhabitants of the plateau country of south central Vietnam; and finally, the occupants of the northern mountains whose ethnic and cultural ties span the adjacent frontiers with Laos and China. The first of these categories includes the lowland minorities, the Cambodians and Chams, whose history shows that they had the highest cultural development of the non-Vietnamese rural peoples. While they have not been totally assimilated, they do live interspersed among the lowland Vietnamese population, whom they resemble in basic characteristics such as wet-rice agriculture.

At the other end of the cultural spectrum are the approximately 800,000 inhabitants of the plateau area of south central Vietnam.[8] In contrast to the other minority peoples of the country as well as to the Vietnamese, these plateau inhabitants practice agriculture primarily for their own subsistence. Their lack of a highly valued cash crop has tended to reinforce the distinctiveness and cultural isolation of the plateau people from the lowland Vietnamese, especially with the decline of the latter's demand from the highlands for such items as elephants and medicinal plants. Another reflection of their distinctiveness as well as their culturally less advanced status among the peoples of Vietnam is that those on the plateau generally do not use irrigation and are forced to shift their cultivation to different plots periodically when the fertility of the soil is depleted. A further aspect of the distinctiveness of the plateau people is their lack of coherent

[8] The population figures for the south central plateau are a matter of dispute. The figure of 800,000 used here is from Condominas (1951).

social organizations beyond the level of the village, except for occasional coalitions formed under the auspices of charismatic leaders, usually on the basis of magic or religion (see Hickey's paper).

Rather than a homogeneity arising out of their cultural distinctiveness from the lowlanders, the people of the south central plateau have such a diversity among themselves as to constitute one of the most complex ethnic mosaics in the world. Some order can be introduced in the picture because most of the plateau people fall within two linguistic classifications. But the predominance of groups belonging to the Mon-Khmer and Malayo-Polynesian language families does not mean that a neat pattern of cultural congruity has emerged. Even though there may be a close similarity in language among the inhabitants of distant villages on the plateau, cultural similarities do not necessarily follow linguistic lines. The languages themselves are very diverse (see table of linguistic affiliation and population), and uniformity of language does not mean political coherence. Therefore, the wide disparity in population among the language sub-groups is not so meaningful as it might seem upon initial investigation. While population figures are always of questionable accuracy in Vietnam, it appears that four linguistic sub-groups, the Jarai, the Hrê, the Koho, and the Rhadé, compose more than half the population of the central plateau. The remainder of the people belong to a great array of linguistic sub-groups (see U.S. Army 1964:1–10; LeBar et al. 1964).

Since these groupings based on language classification represent neither cultural entities nor coherent social organizations, they do not represent institutions of potential usefulness for common action. It is the village (or hamlet) which remains the basic unit for human activity on the plateau, and this characteristic has carried with it consequences for the perpetuation of existing patterns of cultural diversity and backwardness. The confusion which any description of the wide cultural variations inevitably produces underscores the difficulties involved in promoting any more coherent social organization among the plateau peoples themselves or in developing any assimilation with the lowland Vietnamese.

The arc of mountains surrounding the Red River Delta in

northern Vietnam and forming a buffer with south China is the homeland of a third general category of non-Vietnamese minority people. Containing people culturally more advanced than those of the south central plateau, this northern upland territory includes peoples of four major language groups. Despite the number of different language families, the degree of dialect differentiation is not nearly so great in the north as in the south central plateau. For example, many of the Tai dialects are to some degree mutually intelligible. Principal among the northern upland minorities are the populous Tai and Viet-Muong who share the agricultural practice of cultivating rice under irrigation in the mountain valleys. The approximately 300,000 Viet-Muong appear to be relatively homogeneous, and are concentrated in the region to the west and the south of the Red River Delta. The approximately 800,000 speakers of Tai languages are more dispersed and culturally heterogeneous.[9]

The major Tai groups of Vietnam are the White and the Black Tai (named for the color of the upper garment their women wear), the Tho, the Tai-speaking Nung, and the Nyang (see LeBar et al. 1964 for summary descriptions of these groups). Not only are they scattered throughout the arc of mountains of northern Vietnam, but they also have close cultural ties to similarly labeled Tai groups in adjacent areas of Laos and China. Along the northeastern frontier of Vietnam the settlements of Tho, Nung, and Nyang have been made without respect to the international boundary. They extend into Kwangsi and Kwangtung provinces in south China. In the other direction across the northwestern frontier there are substantial groups of Black Tai in Phong Saly Province of northern Laos as well as further south around the Plaine des Jarres in the vicinity of the Laotian town of Xieng Khouang; Sam Neua Province in eastern Laos is inhabited by a group known as the Tai Neua, which is another subgroup of the Tai-speaking peoples who are found in the interior of southeast Asia from northeast Burma and Northern Thailand into south China (see map 15).

In sharp contrast to the people of the south central plateau

[9] The most appropriate estimate of the Tai-speaking population for the period under discussion is the figure of 830,000, given in Morechand (1952). Condominas (1953:642) estimated the Viet-Muong at approximately 250,000. This latter source contains an excellent bibliography on the ethnography of Indochina.

the Tai have traditionally had a sophisticated social and political organization beyond the village. The Tai village has had its identity and importance subordinated to a larger grouping generally known as the *muong,* which is traditionally a valley-bound principality. Especially in Black Tai society the highly stratified class structure has always functioned in terms of the *muong,* and within this framework the village has been relegated to a very minor position.[10] According to tradition all land in a *muong* belonged to the *Chau Muong,* the hereditary political and social leader who was almost always a member of one of the noble families which make up the Lo Cam class (Hickey 1958:140 ff.). As in the feudal system of the European Middle Ages the individual farmer, a commoner, had no title to the land he worked. The Tai farmer was not bound to the land in serfdom, but if he chose to depart, the land he worked reverted to the *muong* for redistribution. Besides controlling the land, the nobility (which is composed of the Lo Cam families) has successfully nurtured the belief that they have been divinely authorized to be the traditional leaders of the Black Tai. Throughout northern Vietnam and parts of northern Laos the Lo Cam have been recognized as the social and political elite. Moreover, they have buttressed this prestige by maintaining a monopoly over the wealth of the region. For these reasons the influence of the Lo Cam persisted despite sustained French efforts to break their hereditary prerogatives.

Although the Lo Cam have had a position of influence extending over a wide region, no political or social entity beyond the *muong* has emerged from Tai society. However, there is the belief among the Tai in the area northwest of the Red River Delta that the region was once organized into a political unit known as the Sip Song Chau Tai, meaning the federation of twelve Tai states. There never appears to have been such a centralized political organization. Instead, the Sip Song Chau Tai seems to have been more of a ritualistic entity within which the Deo family of Lai Chau were beginning to weld a centralized political structure at the time the French asserted themselves in the Tai highlands.

[10] The best single source of information on the Tai-speaking peoples of Vietnam is Hickey (1958). Information on the *muong* is found on pp. 194–195.

In general, it was the *muong* around which Black Tai politics and society was organized, and this pattern of autonomous upland-valley principalities has seemed to be prevalent among Tai-speaking minorities throughout northern Laos and Thailand. This decentralized configuration of power has been a consequence of the influential position of the *chau muong* as hereditary chiefs of these principalities. Unchecked internally in their authority, the autonomous *chau muong* have been barriers to the formation of any more coherent organization for common action in the Tai highlands of northwestern Vietnam. On the other hand, they have also been the obstacles to the external domination of the Tai country. Both the Vietnamese in earlier centuries and more recently the French were unable to break the ritual or temporal power of the *chau muong*, though the Chinese may have been able to do so in recent years in the Sip Song Pan Na of Yunnan (see Diao's paper), and the Siamese have done so in Northern Thailand.

The Tho are the largest minority in northern Vietnam. While they too have had a hereditary elite, their social and political structure is quite unlike that of the Black Tai. This is in part a result of the Tho having modified their culture in response to the Vietnamese efforts to assimilate them into the lowland tradition in the period following the sixteenth century. This policy of Vietnamization was carried out by mandarins sent into the Tho area northeast of the Red River Delta. Their mixed-blood descendants, known as the Tho-ti, became a hereditary aristocracy. Tho-ti were accorded the political prerogatives of a mandarinate, which among the Vietnamese was chosen on the basis of examinations and merit. Among the Tho, the Tho-ti functioned in a political system which conformed to the administrative structure utilized by the Vietnamese in the lowlands (Hickey 1958; 33 ff.).

Rather than leading to a hierarchical political or social structure among the Tho, this administrative system has merely allowed the Vietnamese to exert their influence over them more easily. The Tho-ti did not have autonomous bases of power except as a result of their social prestige. They acquired prestige by a hereditary monopoly over the alien Vietnamese culture and their ritualistic role in the religion of their people. Among the

Tho, unlike the Black Tai, the rice fields were privately owned, and the great majority of the Tho settlements consisted of dispersed homesteads formed into loose-knit agglomerations. Thus the powerful position of the *chau muong*, based on the feudal land system and the highly stratified society of the *muong*, has no analog with the Tho.

If there is a general pattern of upland social structure (to which the Tho are an exception because of their Vietnamese acculturation), it is the system of the Black Tai. In addition to its presence among the White Tai, a small group of Tai language speakers closely related to their Black Tai neighbors, this cultural pattern also seems to be characteristic of the populous Viet-Muong people, who are quite different in language but similar in agricultural practices to the Tai. Although less recent data is available on the Viet-Muong, it appears that they too have a strong tradition of a hereditary aristocracy which enjoys political prerogatives stemming from feudal control over the land as well as from ritualistic prestige (Condominas 1953:645).

The peoples sharing characteristics in social and political organization with the Black Tai are found, with few if any exceptions, to the west of the Red River. Thus among the inhabitants of upland valleys who practice irrigated-rice agriculture, there are peoples on either side of the Red River who have contrasting social systems. To the east there are the Tho, whose Vietnamized hereditary elite has made them subject to lowland control. Fiercely independent valley-bound principalities scattered throughout the highlands of the area to the west of the Red River and extending on into northern Laos have traditionally resisted lowland control.

Two smaller groups, the Meo and the Man (called Yao or Iu Mien elsewhere), complete the ethnic landscape in the mountains of northern Vietnam. Similar in cultural characteristics, these two peoples are juxtaposed as a minor ethnic theme against the major patterns in social and political organization of the more populous Tai, Tho, and Muong. In the juxtaposition many aspects of the situation of the mountain minorities in Vietnam and their relations to each other become clearer. One important distinction of the Meo and the Man is found in their habitat and agricultural practices. Unlike the Tai and Muong linguistic groups in northern

Vietnam the Man and the Meo do not inhabit the upland valleys and river bottoms, but live on the peaks and slopes above them. There they grow rice in dry-land shifting cultivation for their own subsistence. But in contrast to the dry-land cultivators of the south central plateau the Man and the Meo also have an important cash crop, the opium poppy (see Condominas 1953: 644–649).

The existence of a cash crop means that these mountaintop dwellers have been closely tied to the markets in the upland valleys where their opium is traded for goods produced in the lowlands or imported from abroad. The opium trade has traditionally involved a substantial number of intermediaries in the marketing of the crop. Instead of being a harmonious commercial relationship, the trade between the Man and Meo cultivators and the valley traders has often resulted in substantial tensions. These difficulties over prices and exchange have served to reinforce the independent spirit of the mountaineer cultivators and have strengthened their apprehensions toward most aliens. Another factor complicating these highland relationships is that the valley principalities, the *muong,* have frequently attempted to bring the Man and the Meo under their authority and to require tax or tribute from them. Thus the character of the relations between the valley rulers in the highlands and the opium-growing mountaineers has somewhat resembled that between the lowlanders and the highland valley *muong* themselves.

In their social and political organization the Man and the Meo are much more sophisticated than the dry-land cultivators of the central plateau. As might be expected, their society is also quite different from that of their northern neighbors, the highland valley-dwelling Tai and Viet-Muong. Although the extended families are much more important groups among the Man and the Meo than are the villages this has not been a barrier to political structures emerging beyond the village level. Thus relatively large Man and Meo social clusters have developed. But rarely, if at all, have they been on the institutionalized or rigidly structured basis of the *muong* of the Black Tai. Instead they have been formed around the capacities for mediation, or personal prestige of individual Man or Meo leaders, usually in localized situations (see Kandre's and Barney's papers). Broader groupings have been limited in part because settlements of these two peoples have generally been small and restricted to altitudes above 3,000 feet, where the opium poppy grows best. At these heights their settlements have been dispersed throughout southern China, northern Vietnam, Laos, and Thailand. Despite the absence of any larger unit of political centralization beyond the local clusters of influence, even on a ritualistic or mythological basis such as the Sip Song Chau Tai, there appears to have been considerable communication between these distant Man and Meo settlements.

It has been these broad networks of communication and social organization that have made the mountain minorities of northern Vietnam as a whole culturally distinct from those of the central plateau. As this survey of the ethnic landscape of the Vietnamese highlands indicates, the geographic location of these minorities offers a convenient means for categorizing groups having fundamental differences in culture. The classification based on location demonstrates that the separateness and minority position of the mountain peoples with respect to the lowland majority does not necessarily imply great difference in level of cultural development with respect to the Vietnamese. While such a disparity does exist with the people of the south central plateau it is obviously not the case with the valley-dwelling Tai of the north, who have a written language and supra-village political structures, as well as irrigated-rice agriculture.

Since these cultural variations are associated with distinct geographical areas, they allow for certain limited generalizations about the consequences of this diversity for relations with the Vietnamese. The low level of political organization of the south central plateau peoples has meant that they have not had the organizational capacity to resist lowland domination. Yet the cultural disparity which results from their lack of an organization for common action has also been a barrier to the Vietnamese in controlling the plateau people through a simple pattern of administrative control and acculturation as was the case with the Tho in the north. While these Tho are part of the same language family as the Black and White Tai, the Vietnamese were unable to break the autonomy of the Tai peoples to the west of the Red River. Although, after the Tho, these upland-valley Tai were probably the closest culturally to the lowlanders, it did not prove possible to overcome the independent spirit and power of the *chau muong* or to change the structured society on which his influence was based. The same fiercely autonomous attitude of the upland Tai has also been shared by the Man and the Meo who live on the slopes and peaks above their upland-valley principalities. The *chau muongs* have attempted to extend their authority over these mountaineer opium cultivators with the result that tensions similar to those between the Tai and the Vietnamese have frequently developed. These and various other kinds of tensions have emerged to affect Vietnamese relations with the mountain minorities as a consequence of the broad spectrum of cultural diversity among the peoples of Vietnam.

GEOGRAPHIC AND ETHNIC LIMITS TO VIETAMESE POLITICAL UNITY

In their wide diversity these geographic and cultural characteristics have limited the unity of Vietnam and its development as a nation. With these limits in mind it is hardly necessary to emphasize, from the perspective of contemporary events, the potentially disastrous consequences for the Vietnamese people of the disunity of their country.

The pattern of its historical development has also affected the unity of Vietnam. The history of the Vietnamese has been a story of their steady expansion southward from the delta of the Red River along the narrow coastal plain of what is now central Vietnam into the delta of the Mekong River.[11] This advance was not completed until the late eighteenth century and was achieved only through the military conquest of two kingdoms which stood in the path of the Vietnamese. One was Champa, a kingdom of Malayo-Polynesian people located in what is now central Vietnam. It finally succumbed to the Vietnamese in the late seventeenth century after almost nine hundred years of conflict and two centuries of retreat. South of Champa the Khmer (or Cambodian) Kingdom controlled the area around the present city

[11] The most authoritative source on the historical development of the Vietnamese is Le Thanh Khoi (1955). Masson (1960) is a useful short account. Buttinger (1958) is the standard English language history. The historiography of Vietnam is discussed in articles by Honey, Chesneaux, and Malleret, in Hall (1961:Ch. 9; 17; 23).

[784]

of Saigon and the delta to the southwest of it. During the course of the eighteenth century this fertile territory was conquered by the Vietnamese. But unlike Champa, which ceased to exist, Cambodia continued to prosper in the upper part of the Mekong Delta around its capital of Phnom Penh. The presence of approximately 45,000 Cham people in the vicinity of the coastal towns of Phan Thiet and Phan Rang and about 400,000 Khmer people in the Mekong Delta are vestiges of these once prominent kingdoms in what is now South Vietnam (see population table). Although living in strategic locations, the Chams and the Khmers have not created major problems for the unity of Vietnam since their conquest because of the smallness of their number and the lack of their political consciousness and activity.

This centuries-long southward expansion was not wholly beneficial for the Vietnamese. Disadvantages have arisen because this geographic advance went beyond their capacity to consolidate these gains through political centralization. Regionalism developed as the expansion strained the tenuous monarchical structure of politics. This trend was confirmed in a division of the country at approximately the eighteenth parallel, a condition which endured for almost two centuries from 1620 until 1802. Two claimants to central power in Vietnam fought each other from bases in the southern and northern regions of the country. In a pattern reminiscent of the present fragmentation of Vietnam the Portuguese and then the French aided the south, while the Dutch supported the north. The reunification of the country in 1802, by Emperor Gia Long of the southern faction, was attributable in large part to French aid in the form of ships and naval guns which gave the southerners superiority in mobility and firepower.

It was only sixty years later that France began its unsystematic and opportunistic efforts to acquire political control over territory in Vietnam and its two neighbors, Laos and Cambodia. In the brief period of unity there was no time to lay the foundations of a durable national state in Vietnam. Neither was there the political capacity for such an undertaking. It was this absence of political talent among Gia Long's successors, manifesting itself in provocations toward the French, that prompted the latter to seize territory as an informal compensation for their declining influence with their former clients.

In the uneven pattern of French occupation Vietnam was divided into three territories (Tonkin, Annam, and Cochin China), with different legal statuses and forms of administration. Through colonial policies of this kind France reinforced regional tendencies in Vietnamese politics, making them even sharper by creating new bases for division. It was for complex reasons growing out of these divisive colonial policies that roughly equal numbers of Vietnamese fought on both the Communist and French sides in the war between 1947 and 1954.[12] This colonial divisiveness also contributed to the settlement that partitioned the country after the Geneva conference of 1954 on almost exactly the same lines as in the early eighteenth century when France had begun her political adventures in Vietnam. This continuing fragmentation serves to underscore the historical lack of experience with the central institutions in Vietnam. It also puts into perspective the present conflict, which involves a contest to impose central control by the Communists and relatively unstructured attempts to resist this challenge by other Vietnamese. As the contemporary situation indicates, the unique geographical features and historical experience of Vietnam has meant that political centralization of even the lowlands has been an unresolved problem in Vietnam over the past three and a half centuries.

Besides these historical problems of political centralization, the Vietnamese southward expansion along the narrow coastal plain and into the Mekong Delta created another problem for the unification of Vietnam as a nation. Their expansion was confined to the coastal plain and deltas, so the plateau region of south central Vietnam as well as the mountains of the north were left untouched by Vietnamese settlements. As the foregoing survey has shown, these two highland areas contain peoples with very basic cultural differences, and their continued existence as unassimilated minorities within the territorial boundaries of Vietnam has posed problems of control for the Vietnamese.

Unlike the consequences of regionalism which developed as the Vietnamese became stretched out along the coastal plain

[12] Approximately 300,000 Vietnamese were fighting with the French by 1954, and they were opposed by 350,000–400,000 in the Viet Minh ranks (Roy 1963:558).

[786]

in their southward advance, the presence of the highland peoples did not cause an immediate challenge to political centralization. Because they were small in number, not usually expansive, and inferior in technical capacity and social organization, the mountain minorities only infrequently posed a threat to the security and well-being of the lowland Vietnamese. Such challenges were easily dealt with by networks of military posts common to the frontier areas of advancing civilizations from the American West in the nineteenth century to the northwest China campaigns against the Niens and other minorities. Continuous efforts were made to normalize relations with the mountain minorities by recognizing their autonomy in return for their accepting ritual investiture from the Vietnamese monarchy and rendering tribute to it as sovereign. With minor exceptions, this action tended to stabilize the mountainous interior frontier of the coastal-oriented lowland Vietnamese.

A major variation from this pattern of leaving undisturbed the cultural autonomy and political separateness of the mountain minorities occurred in the Vietnamese relations with the Tho. This group inhabits a territory that has been strategic throughout Vietnam's history. It lies across the major routes of communication from south China into Vietnam. This mountainous area has been a traditional invasion route for Chinese forces which repeatedly attempted to restore the domination that China exercised over Vietnam before 939. The Tho homeland, lying between the delta of the Red River and the China frontier in the northeast portion of northern Vietnam, is also close to the main concentration of the Vietnamese population. For this reason its mountains were a useful refuge for the Mac family, who retreated there after their unsuccessful attempt to usurp the throne of Vietnam in the late sixteenth century. From the region around the town of Cao Bang the Mac were able to continue their bid for political power by winning the support of the local Tho population and by receiving the aid of the court at Peking. For almost a century the Mac maintained their aspirations for legitimacy until the opposition Trinh family invaded their mountain redoubt and crushed them (Le Thanh Khoi 1955:250–251). After having overcome the Mac, they made efforts to deny the use of the Tho territory to future dissidents. These efforts included a concerted program of cultural assimilation carried out by Vietnamese mandarins. The result was the emergence of the Vietnamized elite, the Tho-ti. Through them acculturation took form in the adoption of a Vietnamese style in land regulations and religious practices, among many similar changes in Tho society. Because of the role their territory played in Vietnamese politics, the Tho were more influenced by Vietnamese culture than any other ethnic minority in Vietnam.

Because their location was more peripheral to the arena of Vietnamese politics, this type of beginning toward assimilation into Vietnamese culture did not occur with the other mountain minorities. Such isolation could not long remain the case once fresh moves were made toward political centralization in Vietnam. After the unification under Gia Long in 1802 much interest was shown in the territory of the two states developing in the lowlands of the Mekong River Basin: Cambodia and the three kingdoms of what later was to become Laos. If the competition for influence over these countries beyond Vietnam's interior frontier during the early nineteenth century had continued, it seems reasonable to assume that the cultural contact with the mountain minorities located between the Vietnamese coastal plain and the Mekong Valley would have started a trend toward assimilation. But these incipient developments came to an end with the imposition of French power. Instead of indigenous states finding a definition through local processes of politics, the French created out of their techniques of colonial engineering a territory known as Indochina.

French Indochina became an amalgam of colony and protectorates, joining together territories with extremely diverse and contrasting cultures, and with great disparities in their levels of social and political development. This political potpourri was a consequence of French ambitions in East Asia and Vietnamese ambitions along the Mekong. The princes in the Cambodian and Laotian areas accepted French protection willingly rather than have their role as pawns in a Siamese and Vietnamese rivalry for territorial influence continued. Perhaps as an outgrowth of their attitude of protecting the Cambodians and Laotians against Vietnamese encroachment, the French also sought to preserve the autonomy and the cultural distinctiveness of the mountain minorities. The most extreme example of this policy occurred in the central Vietnam plateau where the French prohibited the immigration of Vietnamese into certain areas (Condominas 1951:80).

At the same time they were guarding the autonomy of the upland peoples, the French were also attempting to establish direct rule among them. Inevitably, this effort involved circumscribing the established patterns of rule, and resulted in considerable tensions between those with traditional influence and those with positions created by the French. These tensions did not cause enduring problems among the upland Tai to the west of the Red River in northern Vietnam because their indigenous elite's influence was only slightly affected by French programs. This was not the case among the Tho, whose elite, as has been seen, did not have autonomous bases of influence. Not only did the position of the Tho-ti decline under French rule, but their misfortune also represented a check on Vietnamese cultural influence since this Vietnamized elite was the principal agent of assimilation among the Tho. As is indicated by this situation among the Tho, one of the important effects of the program of direct rule was to strengthen the barriers to assimilation with the lowlanders, which were being erected around all the minority people. Except in the case of the Tho, these barriers coincided with the interests of the minority peoples or at least with desires of their leaders.

The upland peoples responded to this protection of their autonomy by a loyalty toward the French which was demonstrated dramatically during wartime. One such sequence of events took place in March 1945, when the Japanese attempted to arrest all French military and administrative personnel in Indochina. Some elements of the French Colonial Army managed to escape into south China. This exodus included a detachment of Rhadé tribesmen, probably belonging to the *Bataillon de Tirailleurs Montagnards du Sud Annam,* who were led by Lieutenant Colonel LePage, the commander of the Fourth Batallion of the Sixteenth Colonial Infantry Regiment. Under extremely severe circumstances they made their way through more than eight hundred miles of jungle from the central plateau of Vietnam all the way to Yunnan Province.

[789]

During 1946, when these Colonial Army units returned from China, all of Vietnam seemed to be in revolt against the French. But the people of the Tai highlands welcomed these French troops as liberators, particularly because they put to flight Viet Minh cadres who were attempting to get a foothold there. A similar situation occurred the same year in the central Vietnam plateau where the returning European detachments of the French army were enthusiastically received. This attitude contrasted with the aggressive resistance shown in the lowlands of central Vietnam, which the French never reoccupied during the seven years of the Indochina War.

Such loyalties as these were the result of colonial policies which reinforced the cultural dichotomy between mountain and lowland peoples in Vietnam. They were a corollary to the divisive policies followed by the French among the Vietnamese, which had facilitated colonial rule over the three administratively distinct areas of the country. Through their colonial rule the French had given greater definition and structure to the centrifugal forces which had developed throughout Vietnam's history. As a result of the French apprehension toward institutions for cultural assimilation and political integration, a heterogeneous pattern of conflicting loyalties took form in Vietnam. Those highland as well as lowland groups loyal to the French did not have common interests or mutual trust. It remained for the seven years of war to bring out these latent antipathies and cast them in bold relief. During this prolonged conflict, the absence of coherent political support from their various client groups in Vietnam proved a severe limitation to the French. Faced with the sophisticated military-political strategy of the tightly structured Viet Minh, the political divisiveness which had once facilitated French rule now proved to be a great liability. It meant that France was forced to surrender to the Communists despite the fact that the bulk of its armed forces in Indochina remained intact.

THE NORTHERN INDOCHINA MOUNTAINS IN VIET MINH STRATEGY

When the Indochina War began in 1947, it was not surprising that the Viet Minh fled the lowland cities of northern Vietnam for the surrounding mountains. The French military force was concentrated in the cities such as Hanoi and Haiphong, but it was too small to have great effect in the extensive highlands, where it found mobility difficult and its enemies could easily hide. In this early period the Viet Minh forces were tightly organized and well adapted to the mountainous terrain, though much smaller than the French. Besides size there was also a great disparity in equipment and in the quality of training. Because of their inferior position, the immediate task of the Viet Minh was to preserve their own force while wearing down that of the French. At the same time they had to develop their capacities beyond the scale of guerrilla warfare if their aspirations for independence through military operations were to be fulfilled. Thus it was inevitable that the Viet Minh would adopt unconventional forms of warfare, for any conventional approach toward the French military contingents which stood between them and their political objectives would surely have failed.[13]

The Communists took advantage of the most conspicuous features of Vietnamese geography and society in order to maximize their meager military capacities. In exploiting the mountain-lowland dichotomy in northern Vietnam, the Viet Minh exposed the vulnerabilities of the larger and better-equipped French expeditionary corps. The telling advantage the French had enjoyed in the lowland cities was the capacity to concentrate superior troop strength and firepower in tactical situations. The dictates of unconventional warfare required that the Viet Minh deny this convenience to their enemy by dispersing their own forces in terrain where the concentration of superior forces against them was more difficult. Even in the lowlands, where the terrain favored the French, the Viet Minh successfully caused the French to extend their forces to perilously thin limits. The harassment of guerrillas hidden among a lowland peasantry whose loyalty the colonial regime could not command was similar in effect to the actions of the Viet Minh dispersed in the mountains. With their adversaries' forces spread out and tied down, the Viet Minh could then concentrate locally superior strength to wear down the French, a process which came to be known as *pourrissement,* or "rotting away."

[13] This condition is similar to that discussed by Janos (1963). Also useful in understanding this situation is Zawodny, ed. (1962), especially the article by Knorr (pp. 53–64).

While there was extensive combat in many regions of Indo-china, it was in the northern mountains of Vietnam, where they had fled initially, as well as in the adjacent areas of Laos that the Viet Minh were best able to implement their strategy. Their success also depended on the capacity of the Viet Minh simul-taneously to undercut French positions in the Red River Delta by a clandestine political organization which gave increasing safety to lowland guerrillas, as well as providing recruits for the mountain training areas. Yet in these enemy-controlled lowlands, as several dramatic instances of Communist defeat indicated, it was difficult if not impossible for the Viet Minh to develop beyond the scale of guerrilla harassment. Even with the French forces spread thin, the delta terrain allowed reinforcements to be concentrated quickly. But the simultaneous gnawing away at the defense positions and communications routes in the low-lands held down troops that were potential reinforcements for engagements in the mountains.

By contrast, the terrain in the upland regions facilitated the Viet Minh's achievement of local superiority in troops and fire-power because of the isolation of certain key areas from the centers of French strength. Having the enemy cut off from rein-forcements was not so much a factor of the distance from bases of the expeditionary corps as it was the geographic fragmentation of Vietnam, where upland valley areas are reached only by long narrow defiles. Defense posts set up in these mountain valleys by the French were perfect objectives for the Viet Minh guer-rillas since reinforcements, when they did come, could usually reach their besieged comrades only through easily ambushed corridors. Weapons taken from these overrun positions allowed the Communists to develop their capacities beyond the guerrilla level and to repeat their pattern of achieving tactical superiority in mountain isolation on an increasingly larger scale.

This exploitation of the mountain-lowland dichotomy in north-ern Vietnam for military success depended on an ability to create bases in the highlands and to maneuver from them without being tied down to a defense of territory.[14] In developing this capacity, the Viet Minh had capitalized upon a revolt launched among

[14] The history of Viet Minh techniques for creating political-military bases is discussed in detail by Lancaster (1961: Appendix II, pp. 418–428).

the Tho in 1940 around the town of Bac Son. At that time the entry of the Japanese occupation troops into Indochina diverted the attention of the French and presented the opportunity for an expression of pent-up frustrations. By providing an organizational structure for these smoldering passions, the Communists were able to establish a guerrilla base in the mountains of Vietnam during the Japanese occupation. Creating this guerrilla zone behind Japanese lines secured for the Viet Minh both legitimacy as a "resistance movement," and weapons from the Allies, who were then eager to tie down the Japanese by local harassment.[15]

As the Pacific war came to a close, these achievements yielded other important benefits. With the unexpected Japanese capitulation in August 1945, the existence of a disciplined and equipped armed force in close proximity to the cities of the Red River Delta was a vital asset to the Communists. It allowed them to get control over the capital of Hanoi and proclaim the independence of Vietnam. Despite this advantage, there followed almost a year of unsuccessful negotiations with the French. By the end of 1946 it had become apparent that if the Viet Minh wanted independent political power they would have to fight for it (see Modelski 1964). At this point the guerrilla base in the Tho homeland (known administratively to the Communists as the Viet Bac Zone) was once again invaluable, for it afforded a safe haven upon which the Viet Minh could fall back.

The Tho revolt of 1940 was understandable in view of their historical experience. This militant protest was sparked by the Japanese invasion that was directed along a traditional route leading from China across the Tho homeland. Taking advantage of an old pattern in which they were pawns between the invaders and the invaded, the Tho sought an outlet for their antagonism toward the French. Even though the Japanese appear to have supplied arms indirectly to the Tho and given qualified encouragement to them, the motivation for the uprising seems certain to have sprung from these mountain peoples themselves. Significantly, the 1940 revolt occurred in areas where the influence of the Tho-ti, though stymied by the French, was still strong.

---

[15] The Communists' role in the Bac Son uprising is documented in Central Committee (1960:66–69). The circumstances of the revolt in relation to the Japanese occupation are discussed in Marchand (1950:11).

Whether this factor means that the Bac Son rebellion was wholly attributable to the latent opposition of the Tho-ti is not clear. However, the Tho-ti seem to have been unable to provide the leadership for the rebellion by themselves, especially after the Japanese permitted the French to crush its main thrust. Yet the uprising was never completely stamped out. Because the Communist Party provided an organizational structure, the resistance was able to persist in the form of isolated pockets of terrorists.

The role of the Communist Party in the Bac Son revolt and in the organization of enduring guerrilla units among the Tho is illuminating in several respects. The tenuousness of the position of the Tho-ti as an elite within Tho society is suggested by their inability to provide the organizational structure for a continuation of the resistance. But the apparent widespread support among the Tho for the Communist-led guerrilla movement indicates that hostility toward the French was not restricted to their Vietnamized elite, which had been dispossessed by the colonial regime. Despite the organizational limitations of the Tho-ti, their Vietnamese cultural background enabled them to play a vital part in the formation of the guerrilla zone. Since they were the only Vietnamese-speaking elite of any mountain minority, they were in an unparalleled position to work with the Viet Minh to organize a highland guerrilla base within their traditionally defined territory. Moreover, because the Tho-ti had suffered at the hands of the colonial regimes, their interests tended to coincide with those of the Communists. This attitude was in sharp contrast to the elites of other mountain groups who looked upon the French as protectors from Vietnamese encroachment.

These and other special characteristics which set the Tho apart from their mountain neighbors presented the Viet Minh with a rare opportunity for getting a political foothold in Vietnam during the Japanese occupation. Yet this development contained an important element of chance. Although the Bac Son uprising was an expression of deep-rooted attitudes, it was the Japanese invasion through Tho territory that provided the vehicle for the protest. Whether the Viet Minh might have achieved similar political ties among the Tho without the spark of the Bac Son rebellion is an open question. However, the uniqueness of the

Tho among the highland minorities made them the most likely mountain ally of a Vietnamese political group. Without the combination of the Tho cultural distinctiveness and chance historical developments, it seems unlikely that the Viet Minh would have been able to establish such an effective guerrilla zone. This limitation would have had important consequences for the Indochina War.

If a mountain base area was as indispensable as it appears to have been to the Viet Minh in gaining control over Hanoi after the Japanese capitulation, and in affording a sanctuary for the protracted seven-year conflict, then the Communist relationship with the Tho was seminal. Attempts by the Communists to establish base areas in the Vietnamese lowlands had failed before the Japanese war.[16] In the aftermath of the Japanese capitulation the limited cadre of the Viet Minh had time to organize only the cities of northern Vietnam into a Communist political structure. Without the Viet Bac Zone prepared during the Japanese occupation, the Viet Minh might have been exposed to the military superiority of the French and annihilated before another suitable base could have been established. In addition to the security which it afforded, the Tho homeland occupies one of the most strategic locations in Indochina. It is close to the cities of the Red River Delta, but its advantage over other mountain redoubts was its contiguity with the Kwangsi-Kwangtung provinces of southern China, which made convenient a lively contraband trade in arms and ammunition. In their exploitation of the mountain-lowland dichotomy for military advantage, the Viet Minh could hardly have been more favorably situated than in the Tho territory.

The commitment of the Tho people to the Communists' military effort was also an impressive asset. While the White and Black Tai were welcoming the French Colonial Army on its return from Chinese exile in 1945–1946, Tho guerrilla units were

[16] The most spectacular attempt to create a lowland base occurred in 1930–1931 in the north central Vietnam provinces of Nghe An and Ha Tinh. It was crushed by the French, but it gave the Communists an opportunity for invaluable revolutionary experience. The story of this uprising is told by Tran Huy Lieu (1960). Another important attempt to create a lowland base occurred simultaneously with the Japanese intervention and the Bac Son revolt. This precipitous uprising was launched in the Mekong Delta in the autumn of 1940 and was quickly crushed by the French. See Mus (N.D.:12) for details of this revolt.

helping the Viet Minh to take over Hanoi. After the proclamation of independence in August 1945 the Minister of Defense in the first government organized by Ho Chi Minh was a Tho named Chu Van Tan. He became one of the three Tho generals in the Viet Minh armed forces and served as the commander of the Viet Bac base area for most of the war. The other Tho generals eventually commanded two of the six divisions mobilized during the Indochina War by the Viet Minh. These two divisions, the 312th and the 316th, were composed primarily of Tho numbering roughly 20,000 men in all. This was approximately 20 percent of the Viet Minh regulars as of 1954 and about 5 percent of the total estimated Tho population in the early 1950's. As these figures demonstrate, the Viet Minh were accelerating the social and political integration of the Tho with lowland culture through the process of revolutionary war. From modest guerrilla beginnings, a small Communist cadre became the catalytic agent in this integration. At the same time they helped to transform the most loosely structured of the northern mountain minorities into hierarchical political-military formations of great dedication and determination.

In terms of the utility of their territory and the commitment of their population, the contribution of the Tho to the military success of the Viet Minh was vital, if not absolutely decisive. While it is imprudent to anticipate the results of thorough historical evaluation, four turning-points in the military sphere of the Indochina War appear conspicuous as antecedents to Dien Bien Phu. All of them occurred in the northern Vietnam mountains or were intimately related to the lowland-mountain dichotomy. The first was the series of battles fought along the northwest border with China during the autumn of 1950. This engagement gave dramatic evidence that the Viet Minh had achieved mobile warfare capability.

Known as the battle for R.C. (Route Coloniale) 4, this encounter was fought along the sixty miles of roadway running southeastward from the town of Cao Bang to Lang Son. In this vicinity the road follows mountain defiles parallel to the China border at distances never more than thirty miles and usually about twelve miles from the frontier. French troops had occupied these frontier positions in 1947, when the bulk of the expeditionary corps had been hurled against the Communists' Viet Bac redoubt. Although this attack failed to eliminate the Viet Minh base area, it did permit the French to station forces between the guerrilla zone and the most convenient routes into southern China. However, this defensive posture did not prevent the Viet Minh from obtaining military supplies and training from China, particularly after the Chinese Communist victory in 1949 had brought their regular formations to the Vietnamese frontier. Thus, contrary to their expectations, this frontier guard duty had placed a substantial portion of the French army in an extremely exposed position—a situation they realized only belatedly.

Exploratory attacks by the Viet Minh in mid-September 1950, on border posts between the two garrison towns of Cao Bang and Lang Son forced the execution of the previously determined French policy of abandoning these frontier positions. In order to facilitate the withdrawal of the detachments at Cao Bang southeastward along R.C. 4, reinforcements were dispatched northwestward from Lang Son to link up with the retreating units. This maneuver by approximately 6,000 French-led troops was through mountainous terrain in which the Viet Minh had massed more than twenty batallions of infantry and artillery— much more than double the size of the expeditionary corps units. The annihilation of this frontier force was almost inevitable. Yet R.C. 4 was the only feasible escape route from these forward posts deep in Communist-controlled territory. Instead of blocking Chinese materiel from entering the guerrilla zone in the Tho homeland, the French frontier force had become encircled. The troops who surrounded them were the very ones who had received weapons and training from the Chinese despite the defensive presence of the French army.[17]

With virtually their entire 6,000-man contingent either killed, captured, or wounded, the French suffered in the battle for R.C. 4 their greatest defeat in colonial warfare since the Battle of Quebec. Naturally, the engagement was historically important for the Viet Minh too. It not only heralded their achievement of a mobile warfare capability, it also gave them unchallenged con-

---

[17] The most thorough account of the R.C. 4 battle is contained in Bodard (1965:395–603). Important information is also found in Fall (1961:27–28) and Marchand (1953:127–142).

trol over an area northeast of the Red River Delta extending all the way to the China border. Besides acquiring enough materiel to re-equip a full division from stocks the French hastily abandoned at Lang Son, this Viet Minh success enabled them to obtain supplies from China on a more regular basis. Such material advantages were extremely important to the Communists in building a regular force from their guerrilla foundations. Yet certain factors underlying the Viet Minh victory on R.C. 4 were of more lasting importance than its material rewards. The Communists had now demonstrated tactical and organizational achievements without which the additional quantities of materiel might have been meaningless.

The battle of R.C. 4 was the first operation in which the Viet Minh were capable of employing a division having both infantry and artillery units as a tactical unit. It was also the first engagement in which Tho fought in regular formations. The Tho comprised at least a third of the forces committed to the combat on R.C. 4. They were organized into two regiments, the 174th and the 209th—nuclei around which the 316th and the 312th Divisions were later formed—and they played important roles in the Viet Minh victory. In addition to reinforcing the predominantly Vietnamese 308th Division, these regiments distinguished themselves on several occasions, especially when the French columns left the roadbed of R.C. 4 and attempted to escape through the mountains. The 209th Regiment was credited with annihilating the French army troops in the vicinity of Dong Khe even though its own effectiveness was impaired by severe casualties. Further south around That Khe the 174th Regiment was responsible for neutralizing French reinforcements parachuted in to facilitate the retreat of the Cao Ban garrison.

While it might have been expected that the Tho who were fighting on their home territory would be well adapted to mountain combat, the Vietnamese were traditionally unused to activities—military or otherwise—in the highlands. Moreover, the Vietnamese personnel of the 308th Division were primarily volunteers from the lowland towns of Hanoi, Phuc Yen, and Vinh Yen. Their capacity for mountain operations had developed as a result of experience in progressively larger encounters beyond

the guerrilla scale as well as from three months of intensive training at the Yen Shan base in southern China's Yunnan Province.

Of course, this was not the first time that Vietnamese troops
had fought in the mountains. Guerrilla remnants of the tradi-
tionalist monarchy had made a last stand against French conquest in the late nineteenth century in almost the same location
as the Viet Bac Zone. Efforts to repel Chinese invasions over
previous centuries had also taken place there. But the events
of the Indochina War appear to represent the first time that
the Vietnamese consciously utilized their mountainous territory
in a strategy to win political and military power, and then
adapted large numbers of lowlanders to the task. While it is
true that Vietnamese had been engaged as workers in mines
throughout the mountains, and that Vietnamese shops had predominated in the mountain towns, these activities involved a
small number of persons. Therefore, that eventually 100,000 to
150,000 Vietnamese could achieve any corporate undertaking in
the highlands by adapting themselves to mountain living was
an important departure in their cultural history.

Equally as significant as the Vietnamese's newly developed
capacity to fight in the mountains was their ability to coordinate
their operations with a large number of Tho. The tightness of
their coordination in the R.C. 4 encounter indicated that the
Tho had been well integrated politically and militarily into the
Viet Minh structure. This too was a new departure. Previous
lowland experience with the Tho had only the purpose of creating a Vietnamized elite as an instrument of pacification and control. Now the Viet Minh were assimilating the Tho and offering
them the possibility for social mobility based on military and political talents. While the Tho-ti were probably in a favorable
position intially, opportunities for mobility were not restricted
to them. Through this social and political mobilization, the Tho
became such cohesive and effective fighters that they were able
to sustain wide geographic mobility. Not only did they participate in operations on the edge of the delta, but they were also
dispatched into the Tai highlands hundreds of miles to the west
of their homeland.

Besides this capacity to maneuver widely, there were other

advantages to the Viet Minh from their program of geographic adaptation and political mobilization for revolutionary war. One of these benefits was the ability of the Viet Minh adherents to acquire military effectiveness rapidly. Even though the Vietnamese and the Tho had received little or no military instruction during the colonial era, they learned the demanding skills of artillery and infantry tactics in the short space of less than three years. Moreover, they devised ways of employing these skills to wipe out French forces having more lengthy military experience. Because of their skillfulness in the fundamentals of military tactics, the Viet Minh were able to adopt the revolutionary war strategy of Mao Tse-tung with great success.

Yet Mao's stress on mobile warfare—his intermediate stage in the path to victory—seems to have meant combat by large armies on great plains such as that of northeast China where there was ample area to maneuver.[18] However, the difference in scale and location between these classic engagements in China and the battle of R.C. 4 did not mean that the combat in the Vietnamese highlands was a departure from mobile warfare. The Viet Minh had adapted Mao's theories to their own particular situation. This was perhaps most evident in mobile warfare where, as Mao says, "in order to draw the enemy into a fight unfavourable to him but favourable to us, often we should engage him when he is on the move and should look for conditions favourable to ourselves as the advantageousness of the terrain, the vulnerability of the enemy, the presence of inhabitants who can blockade information, and the fatigue and inadvertence on the part of the enemy" (Mao 1963:246). The Vietnamese Communists had at the battle of R.C. 4, the first major turning-point of the Indochina War, used terrain to compensate for their still small armed forces. They had shown themselves capable of rapid repositioning in their maneuvers against the French, using the mountains to their advantage rather than allowing them to be an obstacle. Across the path of the fleeing French army they had executed their quick pincer attacks with the precision of a basketball play.

Because of this brilliant success, achieved through the shrewd

---

[18] The story of the implementation of Mao's strategy in the Chinese revolutionary war is contained in Liu (1956:243–270).

use of mountainous terrain, the next turning-point in the Indochina War is a startling contrast. The Viet Minh seemed to abandon all the shrewdness they had previously displayed when they
boldly launched a series of frontal attacks on French positions
in the Red River Delta during the first six months of 1951. In
what may have been a desperate effort to gain a quick victory,
the Communists, in the first of these lowland attacks in January
1951, swept down from the mountains, penetrated to the edge
of the delta, and attempted to drive in the direction of Hanoi.
Having concentrated close to 30,000 troops in the vicinity of
Vinh Yen, about thirty miles northwest of Hanoi, the Viet Minh
forces made a convenient and attractive target. In their haste
the Communist leaders seem to have forgotten the asymmetry
of military advantages between the mountains and the lowlands.
With roadways crisscrossing the level delta expanse in the battle
area, river transport, and nearby airfield, the French had little
problem in assembling superior forces quickly. While ground
detachments fixed the Viet Minh location, French air and artillery bombardments rained tremendous quantities of shells and
bombs on the massed units of their enemy.[19]

The loss at Vinh Yen of 6,000 men (a fifth of the force they
had committed there) was the price for this Viet Minh gamble.
Although the Viet Minh seemed temporarily to regain their caution from the sobering effects of the Vinh Yen debacle, they
soon indulged themselves in another adventurous campaign.
After attempting unsuccessfully to lure French units into isolated
defiles among the foothills on the northern edge of the delta
during March and April 1951, the Viet Minh thrust through the
western flank of French delta positions in late May. Unlike their
plan in the combat at Vinh Yen, the strategy of the Viet Minh
was to coordinate their frontal attack on the Day River line along
the southwestern rim of the delta, with an attack inside the delta
itself. The infiltration behind French lines of two crack regiments
of the 320th Viet Minh Division was made possible by the creation of base areas in the populous delta through clandestine
political operations. Even this subtlety could not compensate for
their military inferiority, as the fragmented mountain terrain had

[19] Details of the battle of Vinh Yen, including a map, are found in Fall
(1961:30–35) and in Marchand (1953:143–150).

done earlier. Again, because of the ease with which they could concentrate superior forces in the delta, the French were able to prevent the Viet Minh from achieving mobile warfare in the lowlands.[20]

These stubborn frontal attacks on French delta positions had cost the Viet Minh dearly in personnel and materiel losses. Yet as their subsequent moves indicated, they had learned their bitter lessons during the first six months of 1951. In the third turning-point of the Indochina War, the Communists drew out of their successful and unsuccessful experiences a more effective exploitation of the mountain-lowland dichotomy. As a result of this new approach the Viet Minh were able to attain an equilibrium in strategic force with the French at the battle of Hoa Binh, which raged for four months between November 1951 and February 1952. This midpoint along the path to a Maoist revolutionary war victory was achieved through a flexible response to a French initiative that had attempted to break the Communists' hold on the mountains surrounding the delta. In the hope of disrupting the Viet Minh supply line leading from the central coastal plain to the Viet Bac Zone, the expeditionary corps had occupied the town of Hoa Binh. Located on the Black River only forty miles from Hanoi, this town was in the mountains well beyond the periphery of the delta, and far enough from lowland bases so that its occupation required a vulnerable extension of French forces (Fall 1961:41–55; Marchand 1953: Ch. 8).

In this offensive the French seem not to have been wholly attentive to the disadvantages of their decision. By seizing a point isolated by mountainous terrain and connected to the low-lands by a single road running through narrow defiles, they exposed themselves dangerously to the Viet Minh. As position warfare developed for the town of Hoa Binh and its adjacent airstrip, mobile warfare was launched by the Viet Minh against reinforcements on the routes leading from the delta. During this fighting the Viet Minh displayed the same tenacious qualities that had characterized their earlier combat. While whittling away at these offensive units along the Black River, the Viet Minh demonstrated a new dimension in flexibility. Regular units were once

[20] The Day River battle is covered in Fall (1961:38–41, Map p. 40) and in Marchand (1953:156–162).

again infiltrated into the Red River Delta, though not with the purpose of attacking fixed French positions. Their harassment served to expand the delta base areas, increase the pressure on the security forces there, and eventually force the redeployment of French units from the Hoa Binh salient (Marchand 1953:184).

The Viet Minh victory at the battle of Hoa Binh pointed to a new departure in Viet Minh strategy. Previously the Viet Minh had been conspicuously incapable of sustaining mobile or position warfare in the delta. Now they had shown themselves able to use what capabilities they possessed in the lowlands in conjunction with their main force in the highlands. This strategy held out the potential of undercutting the whole French position in northern Vietnam. Instead of frontal attacks on the delta, the Viet Minh would now gradually expand their bases in the lowlands. This would tie down increasingly large numbers of French troops to static security duty and prevent their use in mountain offensives. When remaining French positions in the highlands were attacked, a simultaneous initiative by Veit Minh forces in the delta would create an insoluble tactical dilemma. Caught in this strategic vise, the military resources of the French command could be slowly filed away.

Strengthened by the achievements of their new approach to revolutionary war startegy, the Viet Minh launched an offensive into the northwest highlands, the home of the White and the Black Tai, in the autumn of 1952. The Communists had never before been able to mount large-scale military operations in this region because of its distance from their principal base area and the hostility of the Tai toward them. Forming an operations area known as ZANO (*Zone Autonome Nord-Ouest*), the Tai highlands were the last significant northern Vietnam mountain area under French control. The area's importance stemmed not just from the Tai population whom the French had pledged to defend but also from its position as the gateway to Laos. If the French could not stop the Viet Minh from gaining control over ZANO, then all of northern Laos would be threatened.

As the Communist troops moved toward the Tai highlands, the French attempted to exploit their enemy's extended position. They drove into the rear of the Viet Minh's supply line in the vicinity of the upper Red River about midway between the Viet

Bac base area and ZANO. In this maneuver, termed *Operation Lorraine,* the French assembled the largest force they were ever to amass for a single operation in the Indochina War, 30,000 men. Shrewdly, the Viet Minh allowed the French to penetrate deeply into the rear of their lines. The deeper they went into the Communists' rear area, the more exposed the French units became. Tied to the roads because of their tanks and vehicles, the Expeditionary Force was a convenient target when it abandoned the hope of deterring the Viet Minh advance and began to withdraw (Fall 1961:72–100).

Unchecked, the Viet Minh now rolled into the Tai highlands. After skirmishes around the important French airfield-outpost at Na San, which could have been a battle like Dien Bien Phu, the Viet Minh broke off the engagement. As if by impulse they then sent their main units careening through the mountains into northern Laos.[21] Caught off guard, the French hastily dispatched reinforcements into Laos by air from the Red River Delta. The Viet Minh's mobility had now reached the point where they could throw the French greatly off balance and thereby gain tremendous strategic advantage. Their adaptation to mountain combat and their manipulation of the mountain-lowland dichotomy to compensate for material and numerical inferiority had yielded great benefits.

THE TAI HIGHLANDS IN THE MOUNTAIN POLITICS OF INDOCHINA

The French military operations area in the northwest known as ZANO had as its primary mission the protection of the Tai Federation. Originally this task was essentially a political function. It was to be achieved by supporting the President of the Tai Federation, Deo Van Long, by defending the capital located at Lai Chau near the China border, and by maintaining French influence among the Tai population and other minorities living within their territory. If these conditions were to be realized, it would be through the military strength of France. Yet this strength was becoming increasingly circumscribed by the Viet Minh's exploitation of the mountain-lowland dichotomy. The po-

---

[21] These Viet Minh thrusts into Laos are illustrated in Navarre (1956:Map p. 165).

sition of the Tai highlands became progressively more vulnerable with the immobilization of French power, and because of fundamental political shortcomings of the Tai Federation.

Sharp internal dissensions made the political unit a federation in name only. In reality it was used as an instrument by its president in an attempt to restore the prestige and authority his family had enjoyed before the French colonization of Indochina. So bitter were the antagonisms within the Tai population as a result of Deo Van Long's bid to restore familial power that they caused the virtual paralysis of common action by Tai not linked to him by kinship. Moreover, in particular instances the bitterness of some of his relatives outdid that of other upland Tai. Ironically, the task of maintaining the allegiance of the Tai (which was intended as a political mission) was sought by military means that were eventually undermined by political factors for which the French had no effective response.

The Tai Federation came into being on July 15, 1948, when the Provisional Statute was signed at Lai Chau. It is especially significant that the Federation was formally attached to the French Union in this grant of autonomy and had no legal relationship to Vietnam. This situation was altered in April 1950, after Vietnam had ostensibly become independent, when the Tai Federation was included in the domain of the Vietnamese Emperor, but its autonomy was not substantially diminished. This autonomous status depended not only upon the French protection from the Vietnamese—Communists or not—but also upon the character of their own politics, which made the Tai difficult to control by any outsiders. As a further complication to their politics various groups among the Tai had traditionally been eager and adept in using outsiders in attempts to establish hegemony over their rivals in the Tai highlands. Such a competition was in progress when the French penetrated during the 1880's into what later became Laos under the pretext of stopping Siamese pressure on the "kingdom" of Luang Prabang. (The Siamese had ostensibly gone to the aid of Luang Prabang, which was under attack from the Hô Chinese.)

The French wanted to confine the Siamese to a position west of the Mekong River by diplomatic and military pressure and in the process establish a protectorate over Luang Prabang. An important limitation to this approach was the turbulence emanating from the mountainous interior between the Mekong and the Red rivers. This political no-man's-land, unassimilated by any lowland principality and having little coherence of its own, had become an upland sanctuary for disparate marauding bands fleeing south from China following the T'ai p'ing Rebellion. In response to the anguished pleas of neighboring principalities, the Siamese had attempted to pacify this terrorized mountain area. But in the process the Siamese had antagonized the upland Tai of the Sip Song Chau Tai along the Black River. As a reprisal these Tai had attacked Luang Prabang in 1887 with six hundred mercenaries of the infamous Black Flags led by the eldest son of the *Chau Muong* of Lai Chau (Muong Lai), known by his Vietnamized name as Deo Van Tri. Even the principal figure of France's imperial expansion in Laos, Auguste Pavie, then in Luang Prabang, was forced to flee temporarily with the King. Although it had been unintended by the Tai, this incident convinced the French that they must secure their position at Luang Prabang by occupying the mountainous hinterland. Without this control of the interior they could hardly expect to checkmate the Siamese (Hall 1955:597).

During the spring of 1889 French military units operating from the Red River Valley reached the highlands of the Sip Song Chau Tai. After protracted engagements with Deo Van Tri's Black Flags, a settlement was achieved which called for the annexation of the Tai highlands to the French Empire (Hall 1955:598). With the reduction of this mountain turmoil the French were able to proceed with the consolidation of their position along the Mekong. But sixty years later, with the crumbling of the French position throughout Indochina, the Tai highlands were once again the linchpin between the Red River Delta and the Mekong Valley. The use of the Tai Federation as a natural avenue by the Viet Minh for a thrust into northern Laos, aimed at the symbolic royal seat at Luang Prabang, is more comprehensible in the light of these earlier events. The French concept of using the Tai Federation as a buffer to such a thrust is, however, much less understandable. Divisive tendencies among the Tai had aided the French in occupying the Sip Song Chau Tai, and during sixty years little was done to encourage cohesion, since this would have made the problem of colonial control more difficult. By 1954 this policy proved to be shortsighted.

Throughout the nineteenth century there had been fierce internecine struggles between the related ruling families of the *Muongs* of Lai Chau and Phong Tho. Known by their Vietnamized names as Deo, these rulers were actually members of the Lo Cam families who traditionally dominated the key posts of the *chau muong* in the Tai highlands. The Tai name of the leader of the Black Flag contingent was Cam Oum (instead of Deo Van Tri). His father, who was the *Chau Muong* of Muong Lai (Lai Chau), was Cam Sinh. By the time the French had reached the Sip Song Chau Tai, this father and son combination emerged as the most influential family group in the Black River area.

This advantage had been achieved over the Deo family of Phong Tho, who had predominated for most of the century. The Lai Chau rulers' achievement can be attributed to a series of judicious alliances with outsiders that had vaulted them ahead of their Phong Tho rivals. These profitable external compacts had included ones with the Viceroy of Yunnan, the chiefs of the various Black Flag pirate gangs, and even the Emperor of Vietnam. After the French occupation ended the possibilities of such outside alliances, the Lai Chau rulers nevertheless perpetuated their predominant position among the upland Tai. Despite the attempts of the French to break their influence, the Lai Chau faction preserved their prestige by carefully planned marriages, maintaining close contact with family branches at Pa Tan and Chieng Chan, and by keeping in touch with the rulers of Phong Saly and Luang Prabang in Laos.

The White Tai, among whom the Deo of Lai Chau and Phong Tho were predominant families, are a numerical minority in the northwest highlands, but they have historically enjoyed a commanding position of influence over the Black Tai. This seems to have been true no matter which family (Lai Chau or Phong Tho) was in ascendency. The maintenance of this advantage has required an extensive system of political operations and communications, since the Black Tai are found in scattered locations often at substantial distances from Lai Chau. Those familiar with these relationships have customarily talked of the "natural superiority" of the White Tai. They have been observed to be cold-

[807]

blooded and to have easily dominated the submissive Black Tai.

Whether this has been a result of deep-seated psychological factors or a consequence of White Tai skillfulness in playing off Black Tai jealousies, the dominance of the Deo of Lai Chau and their kin was clear when the French arrived. Moreover, in Pavie's 1889 treaty with Deo Van Tri, France confirmed this hegemony by recognizing their hereditary right over the Sip Song Chau Tai exclusive of Phong Tho. Specifically mentioned as being within their patrimony were the *muongs* of Lai Chau, Quinh Nhai, Phu Yen, Tuan Giao, and Dien Bien Phu. Yet this must have seemed like an empty gesture to the Deo of Lai Chau. Perhaps it was only intended as a salve to the damaged prestige of the defeated lords of the Sip Song Chau Tai.

Whatever this recognition meant at the time, it did not mean that the French were going to permit the Deo of Lai Chau to continue unchecked their influence over the Tai highlands. As will be recalled, the French launched a program to break the traditional patterns of power in the Tai highlands. This included the organization of the Sip Song Chau Tai into provinces along the lines of Vietnamese traditions in administration. Lowland influence was also apparent in the names of the new provinces, Lai Chau, Son La, and Phong Tho, which were taken from the Vietnamese appellations of the trading centers that became the capitals of these administrative units. Within each province the first subordinate echelon of administration was the district which contained several cantons known as Phu. The Phu were in fact the Muong—the traditional valley principalities of the upland Tai. The *chau muong*, which now became the office of the *Tri Phu* in the Vietnamized system, was made elective by the French. In spite of this maneuver members of the Lo Cam families tended to remain as *chau muong* (or *Tri Phu*) since their traditional prestige served to guarantee their election. Above this level, however, virtually all upland Tai, whether Lo Cam or not, were blocked from upward mobility in the administrative hierarchy. The district chiefs were in general Vietnamese, and above them was a French superstructure composed of both civilian and military officials. Commanders of military units stationed there tended also to exercise administrative authority since the location of the Tai highlands made them a part of the IV Military Region.

While this French colonial era did not destroy the basis for the influence of the Lo Cam families within their individual *muongs,* it obviously did eliminate the tenuous hierarchy of power that the Deo of Lai Chau had erected over the Sip Song Chau Tai. After fifty years of consolidating these instruments of colonial control, the Japanese occupation of Indochina in 1940 disrupted France's relationships among the upland Tai. Before the end of the occupation the Franco-Vietnamese superstructure in the Tai highlands was abandoned when its personnel fled to the safety of southern China. In the absence of these colonial restraints the underlying character of the diverse Tai factions was again expressed. Not unexpectedly the Deo family of Lai Chau showed itself strongly opposed to the reintervention of outsiders. This was but a natural corollary of their determination to regain the family's previous position of influence.

By contrast, the diffuse and compartmentalized family groups of the Black Tai around Son La were eager for external aid in order to prevent the reestablishment of the Lai Chau hegemony. To these apprehensive Black Tai it was the armed force and not the ideology of the Viet Minh that proved so appealing. Paradoxically, it was this flirtation by the Black Tai with the Viet Minh that enabled the Deo of Lai Chau to regain their preeminent position through French auspices. Alarmed by the threat of Communist influence in the strategic northwest highlands, the French, upon their reoccupation in 1945–1946, seemed willing to use the Lai Chau family's aspirations as a means of control rather than try to reestablish their pre-war superstructure.

The readiness of the French to entrust the Deo of Lai Chau with the leadership of their program for a Tai Federation was based on several contrasting factors. With most of the Vietnamese lowlands in open revolt against French rule it was no longer feasible to plan for a Vietnamese cadre in the upper echelons of administration in the highlands. Moreover, many of these Vietnamese officials had already fled to the Red River Delta to join the Viet Minh. Since any hope for continuity with the pre-war administrative structure was out of the question in the turbulent year of 1946, the French were casting about for alternatives. The Deo of Lai Chau were, in this situation, their natural allies.

During the hiatus of authority following the Japanese capitulation, the Deo had made strenuous efforts to curb the expansiveness of the Viet Minh in the Tai highlands. While the interests of the Deo and the French were similar in opposing the Vietnamese Communists, they were not congruent in all respects. As will by now be well understood, the White Tai enthusiasm against the Viet Minh stemmed from their desire to prevent the Black Tai from developing outside alliances. But the pressure by the Deo upon the Black Tai merely increased the alienation of the largest group of the Tai Federation. Eventually this vulnerability made the Federation a gateway rather than a barrier to the Viet Minh conquest of the northwest highlands.

AUTONOMY AND INTERNAL DISSENSION IN THE TAI FEDERATION: AN UNSTEADY BULWARK AGAINST THE VIET MINH

When the French colonial restraints were removed by the Japanese occupation, the Deo of Lai Chau could not immediately extend their authority over all of the Sip Song Chau Tai. As a consequence of French policies the Deo did not at that moment have even a firm grasp over all of Lai Chau Province. Obviously, their first objective was to consolidate their position within the White Tai area. This was accomplished by making members of their family the *chau muong* for all of the neighboring *muongs*, even to the extent of breaking the prestige of other Deo families. With this done their next step involved the annexation of distant *muongs* to Lai Chau Province. As a capstone of this maneuver, Deo Van Long was made chief of the province. Having this foundation of local power, he easily acceded to the presidency of the Tai Federation when it was created in provisional form in 1946. Despite French backing, however, Deo Van Long's move into the presidency did not give him complete control over the Tai Federation. In order to extend his influence over all the upland Tai, Deo Van Long had somehow to deal with the other two provinces in the Federation, Phong Tho and Son La.

Phong Tho was ruled by a rival Deo family of White Tai whose competitiveness did not go to the extent of seeking power through disruptive outside alliances. Deo Van An, the leader of the rival family, was persuaded not to be destructive to the Federation as a whole by his appointment as Chief of Phong Tho Province.

Although Deo Van An was a manageable political rival, his prerogatives as province chief were not adequate to hold his allegiance indefinitely. However, his varying demands as premiums for his loyalty were within the capacity of Deo Van Long to accommodate. Moreover, the location of Phong Tho Province meant that it was the first to encounter Viet Minh regulars when they began to direct their attention to the northwest highlands. This challenge made Phong Tho more dependent upon both the French and the Tai Federation for military assistance. While there were frequent disagreements on the amount and quality of military support, Deo Van An's White Tai nonetheless fought tenaciously for their home province against the invading Viet Minh.

Deo Van Long did not find Son La Province nor any of the Black Tai areas easily manageable. During the unsettled period at the end of the Japanese occupation there was a Viet Minh-sponsored uprising in Son La against both the Deo of Lai Chau and the French. Cam Van Zung, a Black Tai who led this protest, was in close alliance with the Viet Minh Interprovincial Committee, which had provided him with the weapons to initiate the rebellion. Naturally, the neutralization of this uprising was a key objective of Deo Van Long.

After this was achieved in early 1947, Bac Cam Qui, head of the Black Tai family of Thuan Chau, was installed as Chief of Son La Province. Cam Van Zung fled in defeat into the hinterland, seeking what safety and support the Viet Minh could afford. He and other Black Tai leaders were to be heard from again. Meanwhile, the Tai Federation's authority in Son La was based on Bac Cam Qui, whose loyalty stemmed from his personal hate toward the Viet Minh, who had killed his brother in 1946. Yet his reliability did not give Deo Van Long control over Son La Province. Indeed, it wasn't under the control of any group, but hotly contested by several. Unlike the situation in Lai Chau and even in Phong Tho there had been no pattern of centralization or emergence of a ruling family in Son La. Perhaps this was attributable to some Black Tai traditions in marriage, lineage designation, or other aspects of social structure. Maybe it was a consequence of the size of the Black Tai population, estimated at 100,000—a figure three times larger than the estimate for the White Tai. Possibly its cause was the scattered nature of their settlements. Whatever its origin there was a striking absence of political cohesion among the Black Tai—even on the potentially unifying theme of opposition to Lai Chau dominance.

Military force eventually became the primary method for coping with the dissension inside the Tai Federation caused by the antipathies to the Deo of Lai Chau. In the particular situation at Son La there seemed to be no political formula which could hold the allegiances of all the inhabitants of the province. As the uprising of 1945 had shown, the disaffection of the Black Tai was certain to be expressed militantly. The problem was complicated by the fact that political influence among the Black Tai was fragmented between five families. They included the Xa of Moc Chau in the southernmost portion of the province, the Hoang of Yen Chau, the Cam of Mai Son, the Cam of Muong La, and the Bac of Thuan Chau. Lacking a convenient response to the political expectations of these families, and apprehensive of their ties with the Viet Minh, Deo Van Long appointed Bac Cam Qui the Chief of Son La Province. Since the Bac family of Thuan Chau comprised almost a quarter of the population of Son La, it was probably decided that they would be the best clients among the Black Tai. Moreover, their *muong* was located in the north of Son La, making them the nearest group to Lai Chau.

Beyond size it seems that the Bac family had few purely political attributes of benefit to Deo Van Long. The appointment of Bac Cam Qui seems to have galvanized the opposition of the Cam and Xa families. The Viet Minh gave them guarantees which the Tai Federation, because of its hopes for political centralization, could not make. In allying with the Vietnamese Communists, the dissident Black Tai families did not have to give up their own local autonomy. The Viet Minh were careful to preserve the traditional social hierarchy of the Black Tai, especially after early attempts at land reform had taught them bitter lessons. This capacity to capitalize upon antagonisms within traditional structures of local influence emerged as one of the key hallmarks in Communist political operations in both the lowlands and the highlands. By providing the resources and direction to these local clusters, the Viet Minh was able to aggregate political power without having to organize completely new structures at the local level.

The case of the Black Tai, as well as that of the Tho, demonstrates that the ability of the Viet Minh to exploit these traditional antagonisms first paid off in the availability to the Communists of highly motivated fighters. Besides such a fighting spirit the dissident Cam and Xa families provided the Viet Minh with other advantages. One in particular derived from the fact that their traditional lands were concentrated in the southern portion of Son La Province. The natural defense of their homeland served to protect important Viet Minh communication routes into northern Laos, especially into Sam Neua Province adjoining Son La. In addition, the dissident families were able to assist the Viet Minh on the eastern bank of the Black River. There they formed a buffer between Lai Chau and the White Tai areas around Nghia Lo, Tu Le, and Than Uyen which were held in 1947 by Viet Minh of Tho origin.

Because of this armed dissidence by Black Tai families backed by the Viet Minh, the consolidation of the Tai Federation was blocked to the south and the east of Lai Chau. Lacking the political attitude or acumen to end the dissidence, Deo Van Long and his French advisers organized a Tai military force. By July 1947 there were two Tai battalions, each with 850 men including 150 French or Vietnamese cadres. Together with several companies of irregulars, this formed the Tai armed force. The First Battalion was considered the most effective of the two because it was composed of Black Tai from Dien Bien Phu and Thuan Chau. They showed themselves tougher and more courageous than the Second Tai Battalion, which was made up of White Tai from Lai Chau (Lhermite 1949:27).

During their formative period these units were employed in clearing the west bank of the Black River country. This task was completed by June of 1947, with the occupation by the First Tai Battalion of the river town of Suyut, located south of Moc Chau. This gave clear evidence of the dissension among the Black Tai. The dissident Black Tai families and the First Battalion were fighting against each other on behalf of outsiders because they could not unite to oppose or bargain with the Deo of Lai Chau. Despite the efforts of the First Battalion, the dissident famlies were not defeated but took to the bush. From mountain sanctuaries they continued their guerrilla harassment against the representatives of the Federation. It was not until the formation of the Third Tai Battalion in 1949 that this harassment was given a comprehensive response. Even this did not eliminate the guerrilla challenge but only held it to a limited scale.

As part of France's overall strategy in northern Vietnam a high priority was assigned to the occupation of the mountainous area lying between the Black and Red rivers. Although this area was separated from Lai Chau by the Black River Valley and two of the most rugged mountain clusters in all of mainland Southeast Asia, the Fan Si Pan (10,308 feet) and Pou Luong (9,793 feet), the population characteristics were the same as those west of the Black River. Because there were important concentrations of the upland Tai in this vicinity, Deo Van Long was anxious to extend his control over them. Fortunately for the Lai Chau family, his ambition coincided with the French military requirement for securing this important flank on their Red River Delta positions.

Once the region of the Tai Federation to the west of the Black River had been reasonably well consolidated in the summer of 1947, Deo Van Long and his French advisers turned their attention to the east. The operational plans they were developing specified two offensive thrusts. One in the north along the China border would be launched from Phong Tho with the objective of capturing the Red River port of Lao Kay and pacifying the upper valley area. The other called for a drive from the lower Black River town of Van Yen into the mountains to occupy the upland valley of Nghia Lo and then down the western slopes to take Yen Bay, an important Viet Minh logistics center on the Red River. Both of these offensives illustrated through the action they initiated many of the particular characteristics of the Tai highlands (Lhermite 1948:27–32).

Known as *Operation Benedictine*, the southern offensive was a fight for communications routes and upland valleys. The latter were a major source of rice so precious to the Viet Minh because the French strength denied them the delta harvest. These valleys would continue to be special objectives of the Communists throughout the Indochina War since rice was used to pay for their military supplies from China. Of course this meant that the upland Tai who grew the rice would be targets for the Viet Minh too. As a corollary there was the possibility that the Tai Federation could lose by insensitivity to local issues what they had gained through military operations. *Operation Benedictine,* however, assured them for more than three years a control over the mountain population west of the Red River.

This offensive and its northern counterpart were able to break the back of the Viet Minh resistance because their adversaries did not consist of regular troops. Although they were organized into regular formations up to the regimental level, these Viet Minh units consisted of unseasoned and untrained guerrillas. But they were not defeated by the French-led Tai. When their resistance proved ineffective, they fled to sanctuaries in the hinterland, leaving the towns and routes of communication in French hands. Until the Viet Minh victories along R.C. 4 in the autumn of 1950 shifted the balance of strategic forces in northern Vietnam, this military force was sufficient to keep the Tai highlands relatively calm and under French control. But as events led up to the invasion of the northeast by Communist regulars in the autumn of 1952, political issues made military control increasingly difficult.

The northern thrust to the Red River in 1947, called *Operation Geneviève,* illustrated some other characteristics about the northwest highlands. This offensive, led by the French-commanded White Tai of the Second Battalion, was launched through rugged mountain terrain which contained few passages. Key to their success was the capacity to encircle the main Viet Minh defensive position at the town of Coc Leu just across the Red River from Lao Kay. This enveloping advance of the Second Battalion was aided significantly by Meo partisans. After more than a month of patient effort these Meo were successful in getting into positions on the flanks and in the rear of the Viet Minh. Their pressure exerted simultaneously with the main attack served to divert the Viet Minh and make a victory easier to attain.

These maneuvers in *Operation Genviève* were excellent examples of the possibilities of employing partisans of the various mountain minorities to fight on ground familiar to them. By their agility, endurance, and knowledge of the terrain, the mountaineers possessed mobility and surprise in attack which was often decisive. As an extension of their armed force the mountain partisans gave a flexibility to French military operations which would have been difficult to attain otherwise. They served as guides, porters, and sources of information, and they were tenacious fighters, useful in mountain ambushes. Obviously, military qualities varied among the minorities as well as between groups within the same minority group. They played a major role in the war as long as the fighting in the northwest highlands continued its guerrilla pattern and combat was on a small scale.

Once regimental-strength contingents of both the French and the Viet Minh became engaged in the highlands, the role of the minority peoples declined quantitatively. Yet in many ways they became more valuable. With larger units fighting each other in the mountains, logistics and intelligence functions took on a new dimension. Mountain partisans frequently could provide the margin for victory through extended reconnaissance patrols or by finding little-known trails to improve mobility or reduce supply problems. Under larger-scale conflict, mountain minorities which were lost to the enemy as a result of political antagonisms could substantially reduce these advantages to one of the competing commands.

The performance in *Operation Genviève* did not mean that the French gained a clear-cut or permanent advantage from the highland minorities. Conflicting and easily changed loyalties complicated the task of recruiting dependable mountain partisans. Instead of becoming part of a socially mobilized military organization, these partisan groups tended to rely on their traditional social structure for combat organization. Their motivation to fight was stimulated by traditional attitudes and antipathies, including a combative spirit between neighboring people. These latent antipathies among the peoples living northwest of the Red River Delta were extremely intricate because of the complexity of the ethnic mosaic there. Since few institutions for peaceful resolution of differences among these groups has emerged, the area has experienced a long and bloody history of warfare.

By comparison the situation in the northeast was much more straightforward. The Tho were the predominant group numerically and inhabited the most strategic area in the region. With the exception of the Man (or Yao), the other smaller ethnic minorities lived in locations on the periphery of the Tho homeland. Because the Man had generally stabilized their relations with the Tho, the main source of tension in the mountain society of the northeast was with people coming from outside. The northwest highlands too had their concern with the outside, but as an added dimension it contained severe internal antipathies. These internal factors which made the northwest a politically and culturally diffuse social network also meant that it was a difficult area to defend. Outside pressure did not produce a unity against the intruder. Rather it was looked upon by some ethnic groups as an opportunity to gain an advantage over some internal adversary. Therefore, Deo Van Long's policy of minimizing the dissension within the Tai highlands by force was effective only so long as there was no strong military alternative. In this interim, before the Viet Minh regulars invaded the northwest highlands, the head of the Tai Federation made little effort to resolve some of the disunifying factors among his people. When the Viet Minh pressure was applied, these internal fissures began to show themselves.

A MINORITY WITHIN A MINORITY:
THE MEO AND THE POLITICS OF OPIUM

One of the most important political problems that Deo Van Long tried to manage by military force was his relations with the Meo. The inappropriateness and inadequacy of military measures of the Tai Federation in dealing with these people can be quickly grasped from information on their population and ecology. Within the Tai Federation there were almost 50 percent more Meo than there were White Tai. As will be recalled, the Meo generally live on mountain slopes above 3,000 feet, where they are dry-land cultivators. Since their habitation follows the terrain so closely, the Meo are usually found in clusters, but at widely scattered locations.

Probably because of their settlement pattern as well as their social structure, permanent political centralization has rarely occurred among the Meo. However, this has not meant that the

Meo have lacked regular communications with other members of their group at distant locations. In contrast to the image that might be suggested by information on their ecology, the Meo are a dynamic and sophisticated people. This characterization is partially validated by the facts that they have been migrating into Indochina since the early nineteenth century and that they are still on the move. This migration took Meo people into Laos in the mid-nineteenth century, and somewhat later they began to enter Thailand. Their history and kinship connections are well known even among the most far-ranging migrants. Common clan membership can serve as a bond between men from distant villages.

Although the settlements of the Meo have been scattered, they do follow a geographic pattern. This pattern reveals the direction of their migration, following a relatively well-defined course southward from China. On an ethnic map of Southeast Asia these Meo settlements appear like counterpoint to the main theme of Tai settlements. Their principal concentration outside of China is still to be found in the northern Indochina area. With few exceptions the Meo in Indochina are located between parallel lines running north-south from Muong Sing along the western edge of Sayaboury Province in Laos, as the western limit, and on the east from Ha Giang in Vietnam to the eastern edge of Sam Neua Province, Laos. Within this rectangle, 350 miles from east to west, and 400 miles from north to south, there is a distinctive ethnic pattern which, however, has little coherence of its own. Perhaps it has been the tension arising out of the struggle between the multiplicity of ethnic groups (including large populations of upland Tai, Hô Chinese, Man, Meo, and Khmu?) that has given this region special political definition.

Historically, this southward migration of the Meo has been a source of great unrest. It was turmoil in southern China that prompted the Meo exodus. In their determination to secure a new homeland, they clashed with the upland Tai and Man, laid waste much of the mountain area, and drove to the periphery of the delta before being checked by the Vietnamese (Hickey 1958:33–34). Despite the lingering antagonism their devastation had caused, the Meo were able to locate themselves in the northwest highlands of Vietnam. Their choice of high-altitude living sites not only meant a scattered settlement pattern, it also brought them into greater contact with the upland Tai than if they had been concentrated in one location, as were the Tho. Obviously, this increased the potential for friction since the valley-dwelling Tai wished to insure their security by controlling the Meo who lived on the heights above them.

In the early 1950's approximately 50,000 Meo lived in the northwest highlands. Another 30,000 were to be found east of the Red River in locations along the China border from Pa Kha to Cao Bang. As the war progressed, these Meo in the east became isolated at the rear of Viet Minh positions in the Tho homeland. Because of their traditional antagonism toward the Tho, the Meo *east* of the Red River fought tenaciously against the Viet Minh. The largest and most important of the eastern Meo clusters was in the vicinity of the Song Chay River northeast of the frontier town of Pa Kha. From this mountain redoubt Meo under the command of Chau Quan Lo persisted in harassing the Viet Minh.

In contrast to this situation east of the Red River, the Viet Minh in the northwest were not allied with the traditional enemies of the Meo but were fighting against them. This was an initial advantage to Viet Minh ambitions for receiving Meo support, but it had to be cultivated.

Unlike their eastern counterparts the Meo in the northwest did not inhabit peripheral locations but lived in areas within the heart of the Tai Federation. Their settlements were in five separate locations, the largest of which was in the mountains surrounding Dien Bien Phu. Here some 12,000 Meo were engaged in traditional agriculture. Due north, in the mountains between Lai Chau and Phong Tho, there were another 10,000 Meo. In the area between the Black and Red rivers there were two prominent Meo settlements. Each of them was grouped around the two towering peaks of the area, the Fan Si Pan, where there were about 10,000 Meo, and Pou Luong, having about 5,000 Meo inhabitants. Completing this pattern were approximately 10,000 Meo located on the mountain heights around Moc Chau and Phu Yen in the lower Black River Valley. The pattern thus formed becomes more distinct and comprehensible upon consulting an ethnolinguistic map. It is no exaggeration that the

Meo commanded the ramparts of the Tai Federation. Access to the northwest highlands from the east was virtually impossible except by traversing areas inhabited by the Meo. Key towns of the Federation were encircled by mountains containing Meo settlements. The Meo were a ready-made Trojan horse.

The antagonistic attitude of the Meo which the Viet Minh were to exploit was not merely a persistence of historical jealousies. By their continuing southward movement, their fierce independence, and their willingness to fight for autonomous settlements, the Meo perpetuated a spirit of distrust between themselves and the valley-dwelling Tai. Yet more fundamental than these antipathies was the friction that developed over the potential profit from the Meo's cash crop: opium. Because there were tremendous profits to be made in the marketing of the opium, the Tai and the other valley people, particularly Chinese and Vietnamese merchants, were eager to get the crop from the Meo. Unhappily for the northwest highlands, this did not lead to a harmonious commercial relationship between the producers and the merchants. It is not clear whether this was due to the absence of bargaining capacities among the Meo or an intractable conspiracy by the merchants. Nonetheless, the Meo felt that the merchants were taking advantage of them and depriving them of the fruits of their labor.

The antagonism over opium was related to that attributable to the Meo settlement patterns. Since the opium poppy grows best at altitudes of from 3,000 to 4,500 feet, the Meo settled in such locations even though their presence produced friction with the valley dwellers below. As can be easily seen from this precondition for cultivation, the production of opium had a sharp effect on the topographically stratified settlement pattern and complex ethnic mosaic of the mountains of northern Vietnam and northern Laos. So important a factor was this opium that it came to be one of the principal issues around which the politics of the Tai highlands was focused.

Under French colonial administration the cultivation of opium had been controlled on the basis of international agreements. This placed sharp limits on the Meo as well as on the Man and the Black Tai, who were also important cultivators of opium. The were allowed to grow the plant only on the conditions that they declare their product and sell it directly to the French public monopoly. In practice the mountain people never declared more than a third of their production. The remainder they sold as contraband in a trade that was established between the mountains of northern Vietnam and southern China.

The existence of such a trade was a great advantage once the Viet Minh got a foothold in the mountains during the Japanese occupation. It facilitated their getting weapons and ammunition in return for the opium crop of the highlands. Because other barter items were paltry when compared with the riches of opium, the Meo cultivators became special objects of military and political pressure. The mounting exigencies of the war meant that in addition to the traditional sources of friction over the marketing of the opium the Meo now became linked as never before to the issues of lowland politics. In this way they became involved in an unorthodox form of political integration.

The significance of this politics of opium can be seen by evaluating the magnitude of the crop. In the late 1940's and early 1950's the annual production of raw opium in northern Vietnam was estimated at seventy tons. Discounting the amount that was consumed by the Meo and other producers, it was estimated that in the year 1947 there were thirty-eight tons available for marketing. While there is no indication whether this was a typical amount, its value was put at approximately 400 million piasters or about sixteen million U.S. 1957 dollars.[22] This provides an interesting comparison with another major cash crop—the rice exported from all of Indochina, which jumped from 91,000 tons in 1947 to 233,000 in 1948 and in that year had a value of 452 million piasters.[23] Rice, unlike opium, was more completely controlled by the French and represented nearly 40 percent of the value of exports from Indochina. Potentially, then, the Viet Minh could have approached the income of the French from exports by gaining control over the opium of northern Vietnam.

The importance of this source of wealth to the Communist military machine is evident from the barter relationships that

[22] The estimate in U.S. dollars was calculated at a rate of 23.5 Indochinese piasters to 400 francs, to one U.S. dollar in the period prior to 1952. This exchange rate is documented in McCall (1961:93–94).

[23] Information on rice crop is from Haut-Commissariat de France en Indochine (1949:221–222).

developed during the year 1949 in the vicinity of Cao Bang. With six kilograms of opium it was possible to obtain through the contraband trade with southern China a light machine gun and 500 rounds of ammunition. An automatic rifle and 500 rounds of ammunition could be gotten for 4 kilograms of opium, and a rifle and 500 rounds of ammunition for 2.5 kilograms. On this basis the Viet Minh could have acquired 12,800 rifles and 6,400,000 rounds of ammunition if they had controlled all 38 tons of opium that was estimated as marketable in 1947.

This quantity of supplies would have been sufficient to equip an entire infantry division, an objective of utmost priority to the Viet Minh. Carrying the analogy further, it would have been possible to have equipped the six divisions of the Viet Minh regular army by 1952 through the barter of opium alone! While the Viet Minh never achieved this degree of barter, it is surprising that the annual labor of approximately 80,000 Meo and other mountain cultivators of opium could, even in theory, equip an infantry division. Yet such a relationship serves to underscore why the opium crop in general, and the Meo in particular, were of such concern to the participants in the Indochina War.

Although there is no information on the portion of the opium crop that the Viet Minh controlled, it is certain that they did not control it all, at least until their invasion of the Tai highlands in 1952. In fact the only real source of tax receipts for the Tai Federation was from the sale of opium. At its height in 1948, this amounted to 1.2 million piasters or about $52,000 in U.S. 1957 dollars. After 1951 this ceased to be a source of revenue for the Federation, a development which probably reflected the consequences of the Tai policies toward the Meo.

As a rough approximation it appears that there were between eight and nine tons of opium available annually for marketing in the Tai Federation. A little less than half of this amount, between three and four tons, was obtainable from the Meo who inhabited the heights around Dien Bien Phu, and another ton was usually available from the Meo of the Pou Luong mountain area near Nghia Lo. If these are accurate approximations, they indicate that about 20 percent of the marketable opium of northern Vietnam came from the territory of the Federation and that almost 10 percent of the total was produced around Dien Bien

Phu itself. While precise documentation is unavailable, it would appear from what information is accessible that the Dien Bien Phu area was the most concentrated producer of opium in Vietnam.

The antagonism between the Tai and Meo had come to a head in 1945 and was heightened with the formation of the Tai Federation. Prior to the Japanese occupation the Meo were responsible only to the French administration in the highlands. They were grouped together under the authority of Meo chiefs in the various provinces, but, as in the case of the Black Tai, it was hard to impose unity upon them. Efforts by the French in the 1930's to organize paramilitary units among the Meo and to name a Meo commander for all the units of Son La Province were a complete failure. The Meo treasured their autonomy even to the point of being uninterested in the unification of their own people. Supra-local political organization among the Meo in northern Vietnam has been on a purely *ad hoc* basis, and has not had the traditional legitimacy that the *muong* of the Tai has enjoyed.

There are two examples of Meo political centralization: the clusters around the leaders Chau Quan Lo in the Song Chay River Valley northeast of Lao Kay, and around Touby Lyfong in the mountains surrounding the Plaine des Jarres in north central Laos. These Meo units were at two geographic extremes of Indochina, and no prominent Meo leaders emerged in between. Social and political action among these Meo in between was probably on the basis of hamlet or local kin grouping. These smaller units appear to have been much more easily manipulated by the competitors in the Indochina War. Often this was not an advantage, since the Meo, like other mountain minorities, found it easy to switch sides. By comparison, the larger group (under Touby), probably because it is more resilient and has developed more specific interests, has been more consistent in its alignment. It also continues to play an exceedingly important role in Laotian politics, as it has over the past two decades (see Barney's paper). But these differences among the Meo, rather than explaining the basis for their behavior, merely raise more questions. Why such clusters of political organization as that of Touby's have appeared in some Meo areas and not in others is at present an unanswerable question, but its effects can be examined.

In 1945 the Meo became alarmed at what they saw to be a resurgence of White Tai hegemony in the northwest highlands. Those Meo in the vicinity of Dien Bien Phu reacted similarly to the Black Tai. They joined the Viet Minh rather than acquiesce to the curtailment of their autonomy. In return for pledges of full autonomy they rendered great service to the Viet Minh through their extensive knowledge of the mountains. Because of the social and political fragmentation of the Meo living in the Federation, the Tai were able to maintain at least some influence among them by arbitrary arrangements, but this waned as the Viet Minh pressure on the highlands increased.

From the beginning of their involvement in the northwest, the Viet Minh had been able to use the Meo without forcing them into any more rigorous organizational structure. Through a coordination of Meo activities in this loose arrangement, the Viet Minh benefited from the pressure exerted by the White Tai to absorb the Meo into a more centralized organization. In contrast to their operations in the Vietnamese lowlands, where they were establishing rigid superstructures for political mobilization, the Communists were able in the highlands to manipulate traditional structures without reorganizing them.

If persisting patterns of antagonism had not been present and the highlanders had been resilient and opposed to outsiders, the story of the Indochina War might well have been a different one. Since it has been customary to think of lowland-highland antipathies in Southeast Asia, this intra-highland pattern of antagonism is especially significant. Thus, by his precipitous action in trying to assert his authority over the Tai highlands, Deo Van Long had as early as 1945–1946 actually given the Viet Minh at least nominal control over the richest opium-growing area in the northwest and access to the heartland of the Federation.

DIEN BIEN PHU:

THE PRIZE OF THE TAI FEDERATION AND THE GATEWAY TO LAOS

Besides its opium production there were other reasons for Dien Bien Phu being the richest location in the Tai Federation. It is the largest upland valley in the northwest highlands and virtually the only place that wet rice can be cultivated on a scale approaching that of the Vietnamese lowlands. Consequently it had the highest rice yield of any *muong* under the control of Deo Van Long. In 1953 this production amounted to 4,000 tons, which was approximately 30 percent of the harvest available to the Federation in that year. Moreover, it was, with the exception of Hoa Binh, the largest population center northwest of the Red River Delta. Its 15,000 persons constituted 15 percent of the Black Tai people in Vietnam and about 5 percent of the total population of the Tai Federation.

Another aspect of Dien Bien Phu's importance was as a key avenue of communications from the northwest highlands into upper Laos. It was the closest point of significance in Vietnam to the Royal Laotian capital of Luang Prabang on the Mekong River. Via the Nam Ou Valley, the Lao royal capital was a straight shot to the southwest less than 150 miles away. Since the Mekong had been the direction of the Vietnamese expansion when the French had intervened, it seemed natural that it would again be a prime objective as France's power crumbled. Dien Bien Phu was not only the linchpin of the Tai Federation but also the gateway for Vietnamese expansionism to the west.

The importance of Dien Bien Phu to the northwest highlands was recognized by Deo Van Long. The impotence of the Tai Federation without Dien Bien Phu was in a sense an established historical fact. Deo Van Long probably looked upon the extensive upland valley as a part of his patrimony since the Pavie Treaty had specifically recognized the hereditary right of the Deo of Lai Chau over Dien Bien Phu as well as other highland locations. However, the French had not permitted the exercise of this right during their colonial administration. Under their auspices a Black Tai *chau muong* had governed Dien Bien Phu and had been responsible to the Vietnamese administrative superstructure in the highlands. Amid the confusion of 1945 a major change in this pattern occurred which had important implications for the Indochina War.

In the aftermath of the Japanese capitulation in 1945, Deo Van Long returned from voluntary exile to what had once been the Sip Song Chau Tai, the mountain kingdom of his ancestors. One of his first acts was to replace the *chau muong* of Dien

Bien Phu, Lo Van Hac, with his own son Deo Van Un. Lo Van Hac had served as *chau muong* of Dien Bien Phu from 1941 to 1945 and had won the respect of both the French and his own Black Tai people. Out of an awareness of this prestige Deo Van Long attempted to persuade Lo Van Hac to accept a minor administrative post. But the former *chau muong* fled Dien Bien Phu in anger and disgust, finding refuge among the Viet Minh. Deo Van Long kept the Black Tai leader's wife a prisoner in the hope that this would induce Hac to return, but it merely reinforced his determination against the White Tai. Within the Communist organization he found an outlet for his hostility, and rose to a position of authority.

French officials who knew Lo Van Hac from previous experience were convinced that only his hate of Deo Van Long, and not his regard for the Viet Minh, made him their adversary. In the years 1951–1952, they attempted to make contact with the Black Tai leader in order to induce him to defect from the Communists. This effort was blocked personally by Deo Van Long, who labeled the former *chau muong* a traitor to the Tai Federation. Yet little doubt of Lo Van Hac's importance and awareness of trends within the Viet Minh camp remained by the autumn of 1952. Upon the initial French evacuation of Dien Bien Phu, he returned to rescue his wife from her imprisonment. For almost a year thereafter, until November 20, 1953, Dien Bien Phu was in Communist hands. Undoubtedly Lo Van Hac played an important political and military role in the Communist preparations of this period. After the French reoccupied the valley in order to make their dramatic stand in the Tai highlands, the *chau muong* of the spot they had chosen as the symbol of their resistance in Indochina was firmly among the ranks of the Viet Minh.

Once the French decided to engage the Communists in position warfare in the Tai highlands, Dien Bien Phu was the obvious choice as the key battle area. Although Lai Chau was roughly equidistant by air from resupply bases at Hanoi, it did not lie astride any of the major invasion routes into upper Laos. Neither did the other important centers in the northwest highlands offer locations appropriate to the achievement of French objectives in defending northern Indochina. The French Commander in

Chief, General Navarre, made it clear that the creation of a "hedgehog" or a land-air base at Dien Bien Phu to support mobile operations was a compensatory action (Navarre 1956:218). It was intended to make up for the French incapacity in mobile warfare especially in the mountains of upper Laos and northern Vietnam. The existence of a fortified camp deep in enemy-controlled territory would, it was hoped, offer an attractive enough target to make the elusive Viet Minh stand and fight. In such an encounter it was expected that the French would be strong enough to wipe out the Viet Minh as they threw themselves against fixed positions.

By establishing a "hedgehog" base athwart the principal route into the upper Mekong Valley, General Navarre hoped to block the anticipated Viet Minh invasion of northern Laos. Had the Indochina War been a motorized conflict with dependency on roads, Navarre's purposes might have been achieved. But in the northwest highlands there were no "blocking positions" like those that had been so familiar to the French Commander as an armor officer in Europe (Catroux 1959:171–172). The Viet Minh traveled by foot across difficult mountain terrain, and depended on human chains of coolie porters for their supplies and on local mountaineers for their guides. Against this type of mobility the stronghold at Dien Bien Phu was ineffective and vulnerable. It could not block the Communist advance, but it could be blocked from sending out mobile strike forces. In early December 1953 two Viet Minh divisions pinned down the French garrison, while a third struck into Laos and down the Nam Ou Valley toward Luang Prabang. The uselessness of Dien Bien Phu in protecting northern Laos was now apparent. Its vulnerability to annihilation was becoming evident (Fall 1964).

The defense of Laos, as symbolized by protecting the seat of the old kingdom of Luang Prabang, was hardly a goal to inspire Deo Van Long. The subordination of the Tai Federation to such a task was a blow to the prestige of its president. Moreover, the choice of Dien Bien Phu, a Black Tai area, as the principal French base in the highlands was a severe reduction of the White Tai leader's influence. Reinforcing this "hedgehog" required the evacuation of Lai Chau and most other centers held by the French in the northwest. In this retreat and regrouping at Dien Bien Phu there was a certain bitter irony. The location dictated by geographic considerations to be the nodal point for their confrontation with the Viet Minh was the locality the French had allowed their Tai client to abuse politically. Rather than planning their operations so that military strategy was reinforced by political preparations, the situation was reversed. Ultimately, French-sanctioned political programs among the Tai proved to have great military liabilities.

With the abandonment of Lai Chau, Phong Tho, and the Black Tai areas of Son La Province, the French political influence in the northwest highlands was virtually ended. This was not a sudden event. The prestige of the French had declined as the Viet Minh threat mounted. Long before the withdrawal from these centers the three Tai province chiefs had been adamant in their demand that paramilitary units raised among their people not be used in other areas of the Federation. Under Viet Minh pressure the tenuous spirit of mutual assistance broke down completely. Bac Cam Qui of Son La and Deo Van An of Phong Tho would not permit the assignment of their militia units to Deo Van Long in Lai Chau. When they were dispatched by French command, the troops defected and returned to their homes. These were occasions for expression of pent-up antagonism against Deo Van Long as well as fear of the Viet Minh. Yet the same effect resulted when White Tai units were used outside of Lai Chau.

By regrouping their forces at Dien Bien Phu, the French lost most of the Tai paramilitary units they had helped organize. The partisan fighters were concerned about protecting their families and reluctant to leave their homes. For their part the three Tai leaders could not believe that the battle for Dien Bien Phu, even if a victory, could restore to them the influence they had known since 1945. Such cooperation as they gave to the French was passive and diffident. However, the loss of these leaders' militia units was not a substantial quantitative setback for the French. There were only about 1,100 in all, or roughly a battalion in strength. They had not been trained to fight together as a unit but were used in company strength of about 150 men each. In order to appease the French, Deo Van Long at least gave assurances that his troops would fight as guerrillas behind the oncoming Viet Minh. Despite his feelings of humiliation on leaving Lai Chau, the President of the Tai Federation followed the French to Dien Bien Phu, and after the battle was evacuated to France, where he continues to reside in retirement.

One major consequence of the French withdrawal to Dien Bien Phu was the loss of contact and communications with the peoples of the Tai highlands. They could no longer expect intelligence or other tactical assistance from the Tai whom they had abandoned to the Viet Minh. Neither could they hope for much cooperation from the Black Tai living in the valley of Dien Bien Phu or the Meo inhabiting the heights above. In a sense the loyalties of the people living within the French "hedgehog" were still commanded by their traditional leaders, who were absent but were attempting to exercise their authority from the ranks of the Viet Minh.

As a practical matter most of the Tai population in or out of Dien Bien Phu were weighing their chances against the possible outcomes of the looming battle. Their opting for the Viet Minh in large numbers was based on an important factor besides a belief in a Communist victory. By contrast with the tactical immobility of the French, the Viet Minh were maneuvering with great flexibility throughout the northwest highlands and into upper Laos. This mobility depended vitally on contact with the local population for supplementary food, intelligence and guides, and, most important of all, porters. The feat that General Navarre had believed logistically impossible—the massing of four Viet Minh divisions in the Tai highlands—was achieved only with the aid of an estimated 80,000 porters. The flexible tactics of the Viet Minh gave the mountain people an opportunity to participate which the French self-imposed immobility did not. Because the Communist mobility depended on this popular participation, their political action was geared to stimulate it.

With the French immobilized in the valley at Dien Bien Phu, the Viet Minh had the opportunity to establish their offensive positions unhurriedly. The battle did not begin in earnest until March 13, 1954, nearly four months after the French had reoccupied the spot. Because of French fixed-position defense, the engagement quickly established its character as an artillery duel. General Navarre had anticipated this development and expected to use his twenty-four 105-mm. howitzers and four 155-mm. howitzers to devastate the Viet Minh forces as they swooped down from the surrounding heights (Fall 1964). Any real possibility of effective Viet Minh artillery fire on French positions was discounted. The Communists would have to locate their weapons in view of French observers, who would then order counter-battery fire or an air attack to silence them. Anyway, Navarre believed that potential Viet Minh artillery positions would have to be behind hills, six to eight miles from the airfield and the center of the fortified camp. This was considered by the French commander to be well beyond the range of any possible enemy artillery (Navarre 1956:195–196). However, the Viet Minh actually held an almost continuous hill line with an average elevation in excess of 3,000 feet at a distance of only 5,500 yards from the center of the French camp. In front of this there was a secondary hill line with heights in excess of 1,500 feet that was only 2,500 yards from the main defensive positions, whose elevation was 1,000 feet. The results of the battle attest to the effectiveness of the Communist artillery from these ranges (Fall 1961:285).

The Viet Minh's artillery was the principal surprise in the battle of Dien Bien Phu. The French were hopelessly outnumbered by their enemy in heavy weapons. The Communists had twenty 105-mm. howitzers, twenty 75-mm. howitzers, an important but undetermined number of heavy mortars, sixteen 37-mm. antiaircraft guns, one hundred 50-caliber antiaircraft guns, and, during the battle, sixty-four new Russian 37-mm. antiaircraft guns are supposed to have arrived; in all they had more than two hundred heavy weapons (Navarre 1956:218). The French had to match this strength with their twenty-eight artillery pieces, for which they had insufficient ammunition. But quantity was far from being the sole or even the principal advantage to the Viet Minh. The effectiveness of the Communist artillery lay in positioning and in protection from counter-fire. General Navarre has described the procedures which achieved these advantages:

> The artillery had been dug in by single pieces. The guns had been brought forward dismantled, carried by men, to emplacements where they had direct observation of their targets. They were installed in shell-proof dugouts, and fired point blank from portholes or were

[830]

pulled out by their crews and pulled back in as soon as our counter-battery fire began. Each piece or group of pieces was covered by massed antiaircraft artillery put into position and camouflaged in the same manner as the guns. This way of using the artillery and AA guns was possible only with the "human anthill" at the disposal of the Viet Minh and was to make a shambles of all the estimates of our own artillerymen. (Navarre 1956:218–219, as translated by Fall 1961:289–290)

The three-thousand-foot ridge line along which the Viet Minh positioned their artillery was the home of the Meo of Dien Bien Phu. Precise information on the role of the Meo in establishing these gun implacements is lacking. However, evidence of wide-spread Meo participation with the Viet Minh in Son La and Lai Chau provinces is plentiful. For example, among the 3,200 coolies at work on supply routes for the Viet Minh in Son La Province during the summer of 1953, the Meo were the most enthusiastic. Moreover, their involvement with the Communists was not limited to labor brigades; Meo guerrilla units were active for the Viet Minh cause in the area between Son La and Dien Bien Phu in the period leading up to the battle. In view of this participation, and because of their alienation from both the French and the Tai Federation, it seems certain that the Meo also played an important part in the military preparations at Dien Bien Phu.

Seen from another point of view, the role of the Meo gains in perspective. If the French had been able to maintain the loyalty of the Meo of Dien Bien Phu in the same manner as the fidelity of the Meo northwest of Lao Kay, the military situa-tion might have been substantially different. Chau Quan Lo of the Song Chay River area with 2,000 Meo partisans, was able in 1953–1954 to tie down a significant body of Viet Minh troops through relentless guerrilla harassment behind Communist lines. A similar sort of response by the Meo of Dien Bien Phu, perhaps based on a sense of defending their homes against Vietnamese encroachment, would have been an invaluable asset to the French. Not only would this have denied to the Viet Minh assis-tance from the Meo in locating and camouflaging bunkers, but it also might have enabled the French to fight for the high ground and possibly destroy some of the enemy's artillery pieces.

Given all the other shortcomings in Navarre's planning, it seems unlikely that loyal Meo harassment could have turned the tide of battle in France's favor. Yet the decisiveness of the Communists' artillery fire suggests that the absence of Meo support might have altered the pattern of the battle.

As the battle evolved, withering artillery fire was turned on the French and their Tai allies. In the valley of Dien Bien Phu were three Tai battalions comprising one-quarter of the forces under French command when the battle began. The Anne-Marie outpost located northwest of the Dien Bien Phu airfield was held by the Third Tai Battalion. Much depended on them, since the camp had no means of re-supply except by air. When their position came under attack and was isolated from the main French base on March 18, 1954, the whole battalion defected with their weapons. The other two battalions were also unable to adjust to the necessities of fixed-position combat in open terrain. Under the pressure of the unceasing artillery barrages they too fled the field.

This confrontation of traditional mountain enemies was a significant theme in the battle of Dien Bien Phu. The engagement illustrated, as perhaps no other event in the history of the northwest highlands could have, the opposing interests of the peoples in the mountain area. Seen against the background of more than two centuries of conflict, the battle of Dien Bien Phu could be regarded as a fight for the Sip Song Chau Tai, in which the antagonists again enlisted external aid as they had in the past. Certainly this was an important factor in understanding the battle. Yet clearly there was much more to the encounter than this. Never before had so many of the ethnic groups of the Indochina area faced each other in combat as at Dien Bien Phu. Two out of the four divisions the Viet Minh had committed at Dien Bien Phu, the 312th and the 316th, were commanded by Tho generals and had a large percentage of Tho in their ranks. If the Tho had never before fought west of the Red River, far from their homeland, it was equally true that the Meo and the Black Tai had never had such potent allies.

It was characteristics such as these that distinguished the battle of Dien Bien Phu from the previous pattern of conflict in the Tai highlands. Unlike their lowland predecessors, the Viet

Minh were attempting to incorporate the minority people throughout the mountains of Indochina into the political system they were building. Exacting tribute or placing a puppet regime in power were to them anachronistic modes of operating. Their interests were best served by creating an organization for military participation which gave the minorities opportunities for mobility and status, but which sought to prevent intra-minority antipathies from being expressed. Since political integration in Southeast Asia is so often thought of as depending on economic and social prerequisites, it is instructive to note the Viet Minh's effectiveness in using military organization to achieve these purposes.

Moreover, the Viet Minh consolidated these political gains at the end of the Indochina War by the creation of the Tai-Meo Autonomous Zone—a Communist version of the Sip Song Chau Tai. The internal autonomy of the minorities of this zone was provided by a proportional representation on an Administrative Committee in which the Tai had ten seats, the Meo five, Viet-Muong two, Man one, Vietnamese two, while five were distributed to lesser minorities (Anon 1955B:17). Whether the Communists have attempted to break the traditional pattern of local political and social structure among the peoples of the Tai highlands is unknown. Since their great success militarily came from manipulating these traditional structures, it would seem risky for them to attempt policies in which the Vietnamese and the French before them had failed. Yet until they alter these structures to assimilate the minorities more closely to Vietnamese culture, there will continue to be the possibility of assertions of autonomy beyond Communist control.

In retrospect, it is clear Dien Bien Phu was not a victory for Communist orthodoxy but for Viet Minh shrewdness. It was not doctrine that outsmarted the French but a precise knowledge of the mountains and peoples of northern Vietnam. Yet in the newspaper headlines throughout the world the battle was pictured as a triumph for the brute strength of Communism made possible by the illicit and unstoppable aid of the Chinese. This was but another example of the difficulties of communicating subtleties of international events to newspaper audiences.

Perhaps more of the meaning of the battle could have been

conveyed by a traditional Laotian legend about Muong Theng, the original Tai name for Dien Bien Phu. It was in this upland valley at the dawn of creation that Praya Then, the King of the Sky, sent his son Khun Borom to earth. By the two wives he brought with him Khun Borom sired seven sons, and to each of them he assigned a specific territory. These seven Tai Kingdoms were: The Land of the Million Elephants (Lan Xang) or the Kingdom of Luang Prabang, the Land of Pouen or the Kingdom of Xieng Khouang in Laos, the Land of the Ho or the Sip Song Pan Na in Yunnan Province of southwest China, the Sip Song Chau Tai in Vietnam, the Land of the Youn or the Kingdom of Chiengmai in Northern Thailand, the Kingdom of Ayuthya in present-day central Thailand, and finally the Kingdom of Pegu in Lower Burma. According to this legend, Muong Theng (or Dien Bien Phu) was the center of dispersion of the Tai peoples throughout Southeast Asia and might as a consequence be considered the ethnic origin-point of the area (Coedes 1954:13–15).

This legend is of course a gross simplification. If it were true, it would help to resolve many of the mysteries in the complex ethnography of mainland Southeast Asia. Yet the legend is not completely mythological. It seems probable that at least the Laotians of the Mekong Valley and the Black Tai of the Plaine des Jarres around Xieng Khouang did originate at Dien Bien Phu or passed through there from some northern point of origin. However, what is inaccurate ethnographically may be suggestive and instructive politically. Because of its location Dien Bien Phu is the gateway to the lands of the Tai-speaking peoples in Southeast Asia, which stretch across the states of Burma, Thailand, and Laos, as well as southern China.

The victory at Dien Bien Phu was not, as preceding Viet Minh campaigns in Laos clearly showed, to fulfill only Viet Minh goals of incorporating all of the peoples within the colonially established boundaries of Vietnam into a nation-state. As subsequent events have confirmed, this triumph at Dien Bien Phu established the Vietnamese Communists as a power among the Tai-speaking peoples. It also identified them with traditional Vietnamese goals of driving to the Mekong and acquiring a hegemony over the peoples to the west. Since the Chinese themselves are not without designs over the strategically located Tai peoples, this victory would have brought Vietnamese and Chinese goals into conflict.

Future historians may well record that the cessation of the Indochina War was caused as much by Chinese concern over Vietnamese expansion as by French defeat. If succession to French sovereignty in all of Indochina is the fundamental goal of the Vietnamese Communists, as their extensive activities in Laos tend to indicate, then this cannot but threaten all of the mainland of Southeast Asia as well as China. Whatever the underlying designs of the Chinese and Vietnamese Communists, their interests in the unassimilated Tai-speaking minorities of the mountainous interior of Southeast Asia makes them one of the important focuses of political concern. Attention to their particular ethnic and geographic characteristics, rather than to abstract Communist theory, may offer the best insurance against their manipulation for Communist purposes.

MOUNTAIN MINORITIES AND THE VIETNAMESE COMMUNISTS: THE CONTINUING CONFLICT

The Communist victory at Dien Bien Phu in the spring of 1954 brought a halt to what is now called the First Indochina War. But it did not bring an end to the Viet Minh activities among the mountain minorities. This has continued with great intensity among the Tai-speaking mountain people of northern Laos and the fragmented groups of the two major language families living on the south central plateau. These operations in Laos have been a natural extension of the earlier invasions of the country in 1953–1954 by the Viet Minh's crack divisions. Following the Geneva Conference of 1954, however, it was risky for the Vietnamese Communists to launch such overt operations into upper Laos. In order to avoid potential international sanctions, the Viet Minh undertook political and paramilitary organizational activities among the minorities of northern Laos in an unobtrusive manner.

These preparations came to light in the summer of 1959, when the Laotian government charged that the Communist Vietnamese had invaded the two northern provinces of their country, Phong

Saly and Sam Neua.[24] Investigations by United Nations observers failed to prove any invasion by ethnic Vietnamese. Since Sam Neua and Phong Saly have congruent ethnic characteristics—in concentrations of White and Black Tai peoples—with the neighboring provinces of northern Vietnam, Lai Chau and Son La, it would not have been difficult to use non-Vietnamese troops from Vietnam.

Such a possibility underscores the ease with which Viet Minh influence could be extended into Laos by employing techniques that were so successful in the Tai highlands of Vietnam. A new Geneva agreement, that of 1962, was expected to bring a cessation to the Vietnamese-supported hostilities that erupted in 1959. Yet the best guarantee has appeared to be a traditional one. The fiercely independent Meo living on the heights around the Plaine des Jarres in central Laos have proven the most tenacious combatants against the Pathet Lao—the Laotian Communist movement. Like the Meo in Vietnam around Dien Bien Phu, the Meo of the Plaine des Jarres seem to have made their decision on non-ideological grounds. Those Meo of Laos who are fighting against the Communists do so not for ideological reasons, but because the Communists have tried to restrict their autonomy and deprive them of the benefits from their opium crop.[25]

Having obtained their success through the manipulation of traditional structures and antipathies, the Viet Minh have now, ironically, had these characteristics turned against them politically. The continuing conflict around the Plaine des Jarres provides fresh evidence of the persistence of the underlying political characteristics of the Tai highlands from the Red River in Vietnam to the Mekong in Laos. Now, just the reverse from Dien Bien

[24] Halpern and Fredman (1960) and Dommen (1965:119–125). Dommen (1965:124) states that the United Nations ". . . subcommittee took a plane to Sam Neua Province, where they interrogated a number of prisoners and refugees, several of whom were Black Thai."

[25] There are also Meo fighting with the Communists in Laos, led by Faydang, who continues to be an active participant in the Pathet Lao. See Fall (1965A). The theme of Fall's article is stated in his opening sentence: "In large measure the Laotian Communist movement appears to be based not on the ethnic Laotian lowlanders but on many of the minorities of Laos—Thai, Meo, and Malayo-Indonesian (i.e. Kha, Lao for slave) peoples." For additional information on Faydang and the pro-Communist Meo see Dommen (1965:72–76), the introduction to the Laos section of this book, and Barney's paper.

Phu, it is the anti-Communist Meo who control the hills and the strategic passes leading south and westward from the Plaine des Jarres. The Pathet Lao have taken the valley itself, but they have been unable to take the surrounding heights (Dommen 1965:242–250). The outcome remains in doubt, but the events do illustrate that the influence of the Viet Minh and their clients can be checked by political shrewdness in the ways of the mountain people or by unanticipated consequences of traditional alignments, as appears to be the case with the Meo of Laos. A long-term resolution of the problems of Laos or any of the states of Southeast Asia would probably require further assimilation of the mountain peoples to the lowland culture. Yet the Meo would probably resist any overt move toward forced culture change and loss of political autonomy just as tenaciously as they are now opposing the Communists.

The Viet Minh's interest in Laos has not been confined to the northern part of the country where the Tai highlands are. Because Laos shares a border more than two hundred miles long with Vietnam south of the seventeenth parallel, it has offered a more convenient avenue for infiltration than the narrow, forty-mile wide demilitarized zone that separates the two halves of the Vietnamese territory. Viet Minh positions in southeastern Laos support an infiltration route (the "Ho Chi Minh Trail") which leads into the south central plateau of Vietnam (Warner 1965). This plateau is the homeland of approximately 800,000 people speaking languages of the Mon-Khmer and Malayo-Polynesian families. During the Indochina War the Viet Minh did not have notable success in winning the loyalties of these minorities or employing them in military operations.[26] This contrast to the situation in northern Vietnam was attributable in part to the absence of centralized social or political institutions such as the Sip Son Chau Tai or even the *muong*. It was also due to the paternalistic attitude of the French administration, which gave a high priority to the protection of the *montagnards* from the lowland Vietnamese and the preservation of their customs and traditions.

Before the end of the Indochina War the only organizational

---

[26] This conclusion is drawn from Marchand (1952:169–176).

structures to exist beyond the local level in the southern high-lands were French-sponsored paramilitary units. They were di-vided into units speaking the same minority language, and usu-ally commanded by a French cadre. Demonstrations of loyalty to the French by these units were frequent, and there is little to suggest that they ever defected to the Viet Minh. This does not mean that the Communist Vietnamese were not effective in exploiting the highlands of south central Vietnam for military advantage. The tragic story of the annihilation of the French regimental combat team, *Groupement Mobile*, on R.C. 19 at An Khe in June 1954, attests to their effectiveness.[27] But their adapta-tion of guerrilla and mobile warfare to the southern highlands was almost exclusively with Vietnamese, not tribal troops. By the end of the war in 1954 the Viet Minh had a full division, the 305th, in their Interzone V (south central Vietnam) and a total of 25,000–30,000 regular troops. Thus the situation in this area was just the reverse of that in northern Vietnam. The Viet Minh controlled the Vietnamese lowlands, and the French controlled most of the highlands where the minority peoples lived. With the implementation of the Geneva agreement, the Viet Minh evacuated this area south of the seventeenth parallel and brought most of its regular troops to the north.

The relative absence of intra-minority antagonisms in the south central plateau and the French protection of these minorities from the lowlanders had given the Viet Minh few political oppor-tunities to exploit. But these opportunities increased with the advent of the Republic of Vietnam. Out of a concern over the potential for infiltration into the southern highlands the govern-ment of Ngo Dinh Diem sought protection by moving approxi-mately 100,000 ethnic Vietnamese into the area. By placing these Vietnamese in strategic locations, President Diem expected to increase the security of the highlands against Viet Minh exploita-tion. At the same time about 25,000 mountain people were re-grouped at six sites as an added precaution (Gittinger 1959:27). Rather than enhancing the security of the region, these programs antagonized the mountain minorities to an extent that had not

---

[27] The facts of this most important operation on the south central plateau during the Indochina War are related by Fall (1961:Ch. 9).

previously existed. At the same time the Viet Minh launched a program of propaganda and indoctrination of the plateau people that included radio broadcasts in their languages and the training of cadres among the various minorities. Through these techniques the Vietnamese Communists hoped to capitalize upon the discontent of the southern highlanders and establish the political bases for guerrilla and mobile warfare operations (Buttinger 1961:109; Hickey 1957:26–27).

Despite the shortcomings of the policies of the Republic of Vietnam, the Communists' political experience has not been so successful in the southern highlands as it was in earlier years in northern Vietnam. Instead, another political trend has emerged. This has been the gradual development of a movement for autonomy of the highlands. It has been both anti-Communist and anti-Republic of Vietnam. The trend gained momentum through programs to train the mountain minorities as paramilitary and "special forces" in the fight against the Communists. This gave the highlanders an opportunity for military training, organizational experience, and combat equipment more widespread than anything previously known. By the autumn of 1965 approximately 18,000 men had been organized into formations known as civilian irregular defense units (Keatley 1965). With these assets the southern highlanders had a vehicle for the expression of their discontent. Their smoldering antipathies erupted on September 19, 1964, when 3,000 heavily armed mountaineers revolted in five United States Army Special Forces Camps, killing twenty-nine Vietnamese, capturing a hundred more and seizing twenty Americans as hostages. The conciliatory efforts of the Americans and the responsiveness of the Vietnamese succeeded in quelling the revolt and restoring order (Sochurek 1965:38).

The leaders of the uprising proclaimed their movement the *Forces Unifiées de Lutte pour la Race Opprimée* (that is, united forces for the struggle for the oppressed races, or FULRO), which has its own flag and a set of political aims that are addressed to the Americans and the Republic of Vietnam (Fall 1965:70). Most of the members of the movement seem to be from one minority group, the Rhadé, which is generally considered the most culturally advanced of the southern highland peoples. As part of the reconciliation in September 1964, they were given certain specific promises by the representatives of the Republic of Vietnam. These included a variety of political reforms which would ameliorate the condition of the highlanders and resolve many areas of friction between them and the Vietnamese. The Republic of Vietnam has not been quick to honor these promises, and the uprising of 1964 was threatened in September and repeated in December 1965 (Sheehan 1965A; 1965B). There is concern that FULRO will be driven into the Communist camp. Since a centralized organization among the highlanders has emerged in FULRO, it would now be more convenient for the Communists to deal with the southern minorities according to their established pattern of operations. By holding out promises of an autonomous zone similar to that of the Tai-Meo area in the northwest, the Communists might capitalize on the goals of the southern highlanders and turn them actively against the Republic of Vietnam and the allied forces assisting them.[28]

Since the ethnic composition of Indochina is one of the most complex in the world, it is to be expected that the political and social problems arising from this characteristic will also be complicated and protracted. However complex, these problems have not proven to be insoluble. They have been amenable to those who have shown themselves most knowledgeable concerning the particular characteristics and goals of the various mountain peoples and capable of responding to them. In all but a few instances this type of understanding has been by the Vietnamese Communists.

REFERENCES CITED

ANON.
  1955A Ten years of fighting and building of the Vietnamese People's Army. Hanoi, The Foreign Language Publishing House.
  1955B Minorities under the Viet Minh. Eastern World, November.
BODARD, LUCIEN
  1965 La guerre d'Indochine: l'humiliation. Paris, Gallimard.

[28] The details of the National Liberation Front program for the minority peoples and an extensive review of current military-political problems of the south central plateau are found in Joiner (1965).

BUTTINGER, JOSEPH
    1958   The smaller dragon: a political history of Viet Nam. New York, Frederick A. Praeger.
    1961   Ethnic minorities in Vietnam. *In* Problems of freedom: South Vietnam since Independence, Wesley R. Fishel, ed. New York, The Free Press of Glencoe, Inc.

CANADA, DEPARTMENT OF MINES AND TECHNICAL SURVEYS
    1953   Indo-China: a geographical appreciation. Ottawa.

CATROUX, General
    1959   Deux actes du drame Indochinois: Hanoi, juin, 1940; Dien Bien Phu, mars-mai, 1954. Paris, Libraire Plon.

CENTRAL COMMITTEE OF PROPAGANDA OF THE VIET NAM LAO DONG PARTY AND THE COMMITTEE FOR THE STUDY OF THE PARTY'S HISTORY
    1960   Thirty years of struggle of the Party, Book I. Hanoi, Foreign Languages Publishing House.

COEDES, GEORGES
    1954   A propos du site de Dien Bien Phu. Tropiques: revue des troupes coloniales 370:13–15 (fevrier).

CONDOMINAS, GEORGES
    1951   Aspects of a minority problem in Indochina. Pacific Affairs 24:77–82 (March).
    1953   L'Indochine. *In* Ethnologie de l'Union Française (territoires extérieurs), tome second: Asie, Océanie, Amérique, par André Leroi-Gourhan and Jean Poirier. Paris, Presses Universitaires de France, pp. 514–678.

DEVILLERS, PHILLIPPE, and JEAN LACOUTURE
    1960   La fin d'une guerre: Indochine 1954. Paris, Editions du Seuil.

DOBBY, E. H. G.
    1956   Southeast Asia. London, University of London Press.

DOMMEN, ARTHUR J.
    1965   Conflict in Laos: the politics of neutralization. New York, Frederick A. Praeger.

ELY, General d'Armee PAUL
    1964   Memoires: l'Indochine dans la Tourmente. Paris, Plon.

FALL, BERNARD B.
    1961   Street without joy: Indochina at war, 1946–1954. Harrisburg, Pa., The Stackpole Co.
    1964   Dien Bien Phu: a battle to remember. New York Times Magazine, May 3.
    1965A   The Pathet Lao: a "liberation" party. *In* The communist revolution in Asia: tactics, goals, and achievements, Robert A. Scalapino, ed. Englewood Cliffs, N.J., Prentice-Hall, Inc.
    1965B   The second Indochina war. International Affairs 4 (1) (January).

forthcoming   Ordeal of Dien Bien Phu. Philadelphia and New York, Lippincott.

GITTINGER, J. PRICE
1959   Terminal report of J. Price Gittinger, United States Operations Mission to Viet Nam. Saigon.

GRAUWIN, Medecin-Commandant
1954   J'étais médecin à Dien Bien Phu. Paris, Editions France-Empire.

GREAT BRITAIN, NAVAL STAFF, NAVAL INTELLIGENCE DIVISION
1943   Indo-China, Geographical Handbook Series, B. R. 510.

HALL, D. G. E.
1955   A history of Southeast Asia. New York, St Martin's Press.

HALL, D. G. E. (ed.)
1961   Historians of South-East Asia. London, Oxford University Press.

HALPERN, A. M., and H. B. FREDMAN
1960   Communist strategy in Laos. Santa Monica, California, The RAND Corporation (RM-2561).

HAUT-COMMISSARIAT DE FRANCE EN INDOCHINE, AFFAIRES ECONOMIQUES
1949   Annuaire statistique de l'Indochine, douzième volume, 1947–1948. Saigon.

HICKEY, GERALD CANNON
1957   Preliminary research report on the High Plateau. Saigon. Michigan State University, Vietnam Advisory Group, mimeographed.
1958   Social systems of northern Vietnam. Chicago, University of Chicago, Department of Anthropology, doctoral dissertation.

JANOS, ANDREW
1963   Unconditional warfare: framework and analysis. World Politics 15 (4):636–646 (July).

JOINER, CHARLES A.
1965   Administration and political warfare in the highlands. Vietnam Perspectives 1(2):19–37 (November).

KEATLEY, ROBERT
1965   South Vietnam tribes threaten a rebellion against Saigon control. Wall Street Journal, September 1, p. 1.

KNORR, KLAUS
1962   Unconventional warfare: strategy and tactics of internal strife. The Annals of the American Academy of Political and Social Science 341:53–64 (May).

LANCASTER, DONALD
1961   The emancipation of French Indochina. London, Oxford University Press.

LANGLAIS, Colonel PIERRE
1963   Dien Bien Phu. Paris, Editions France-Empire.

LANIEL, JOSEPH
1957 Le drame Indochinois de Dien Bien Phu au pari de Genève. Paris, Librairie Plon.

LE THANH KHOI
1955 Le Viet Nam: histoire et civilisation. Paris, Les Editions de Minuit.

LEBAR, FRANK M., GERALD C. HICKEY, and JOHN K. MUSGRAVE
1964 Ethnic Groups of Mainland Southeast Asia. New Haven. Human Relations Area Files Press.

LHERMITE, Lieutenant Colonel
1948 Les opérations Benedictine et Genviève. Tropiques: revue des troupes coloniales, 300 (juin).

LIU, F. F.
1956 A military history of modern China, 1924–1949. Princeton, N.J., Princeton University Press.

McCALL, DAVY HENDERSON
1961 The effects of independence on the economy of Viet Nam. Cambridge, Mass., Harvard University, Department of Economics, doctoral dissertation.

MAO TSE-TUNG
1963 Selected military writings of Mao Tse-tung. Peking, Foreign Languages Press.

MARCHAND, Colonel JEAN
1950 L'Indochine pendant la guerre mondiale. Section de documentation militaire de l'Union Française (janvier).
1952 Dans la jungle 'moi.' Paris, J. Peyronnet et Cie.
1953 Le drame Indochinois. Paris, J. Peyronnet et Cie.

MASSON, ANDRE
1960 Histoire du Viet Nam. Paris, Presses Universitaires de France.

MODELSKI, GEORGE
1964 The Viet Minh complex. *In* Communism and revolution: the strategic uses of political violence, Cyril E. Black and Thomas P. Thornton, eds. Princeton, N.J., Princeton University Press, pp. 186–194.

MORECHAND, G.
1952 Notes demographiques sur un canton Meo blanc du pays Tai. Bulletin de la Société des Etudes Indochinoises 27:354–361.

MUS, PAUL
N.D. Problèmes de l'Indochine contemporaine; le formation des partis annamites. Paris, College Libre des Sciences Sociales et Economiques, P.M. 1.

NAVARRE, HENRI
1956 Agonie de l'Indochine (1953–1954). Paris, Librairie Plon, nouvelle edition.

PAILLAT, CLAUDE
1964 Dossier secret de l'Indochine. Paris, Presses de la Cité.
POUGET, JULES
1964 Nous étion à Dien Bien Phu. Paris, Presses de la Cité.
ROY, JULES
1963 La bataille de Dien Bien Phu. Paris, René Julliard.
1965 The battle of Den Bien Phu. New York and Evanston, Harper and Row.
SHEEHAN, NEIL
1965A Tribesmen mutiny in Vietnam camps. The New York Times, December 19, p. 1.
1965B Tribal revolt stirs Vietnam highlands but fails. The New York Times, December 20, p. 2.
SOCHUREK, HOWARD
1965 American Special Forces in action in Viet Nam. The National Geographic 127 (1):38–65 (January).
TANHAM, GEORGE K.
1961 Communist revolutionary warfare: the Vietminh in Indochina. New York, Frederick A. Praeger.
TRAN HUY LIEU
1960 Les Soviets du Nghe-Tinh (de 1930–1931) au Viet Nam. Hanoi, Editions en Langues Etrangères.
U.S. ARMY, SPECIAL WARFARE SCHOOL
1964 Montagnard tribal groups of the Republic of South Viet-Nam. Fort Bragg, North Carolina, U.S. Army, Special Warfare School.
VO NGUYEN GIAP
1964 Dien Bien Phu. Hanoi, Foreign Languages Publishing House. Revised and enlarged edn. (also in Vietnamese and French editions).
WARNER, DENIS
1965 A cautionary report on Laos. The Reporter, December 2:35–38.
ZAWODNY, J. K. (ed.)
1962 Unconventional warfare. The Annals of the American Academy of Political and Social Science 341 (May).

PART IX. THE ROLE OF

PRIVATE FOUNDATIONS

The Asia Foundation's Programming for Tribal and Minority Peoples in Southeast Asia

HARRY H. PIERSON

INTRODUCTION

Guide Lines of Foundation Activities. The programs under-taken by the Asia Foundation with respect to tribal and minority peoples in Southeast Asia are carried out in accordance with guide lines of two kinds:

First, the Foundation's Articles of Incorporation, which reflect three purposes, two of which are pertinent to the subject of the paper:

(1) To support individuals, voluntary groups, and private, quasi-governmental and governmental institutions whose aims are the modernization and development of their own societies;

(2) To encourage cooperation among Asian, American, and international organizations that are working toward these same goals.

Second, country guide lines which are developed from the needs of the country concerned as viewed by the Foundation's resident representative within the limits imposed by (1) the Foundation's general purposes (above), (2) the Foundation's capabilities as an American organization working in Asia, and (3) the available funding.

In broad terms, those guide lines which are germane to projects relating to tribal and minority peoples reflect expressed national needs in regard to the integration of minorities, the achievement of development goals within a changing but reason-ably stable and peaceful social environment, the development of human resources, the development of research and study of social problems (especially by nationals of the countries them-

[847]

selves), and the role of minority peoples in the total social and economic development process. These objectives are, of course, to a consideable degree interlinked and mutually supporting.

Basic Operating Principles. Operating principles, which are fundamental to the Foundation's approach in the various countries of Southeast Asia, determine the individuals, groups, institutions, or government agencies which will be assisted and the types of programs undertaken. The most important of these principles are:

1. Asian initiative and support are essential to any constructive measures of lasting benefit. Therefore, most of the Foundation's assistance is in the form of grants to projects designed and administered by Asians themselves. The Foundation is firmly of the belief that such projects are most likely to be pertinent to local needs, to induce local support, and to become enduring assets in the countries concerned.

2. Resident representatives are essential to sound program development. A safeguard is thus provided against the unintentional imposition of preconceived American solutions that may be inapplicable or inappropriate to the Asian problem under consideration. Furthermore, the Foundation is enabled to extend assistance in whatever form may best encourage and supplement local effort, and therefore increase the probability of success of the project.

3. Since its limited resources do not permit the Foundation to undertake projects requiring large-scale financing, assistance is predominantly in the small grant field for projects which show promise of leading to greater and more sustained activity under local or other sponsorship.

In the light of the above guide lines and operating principles, it is not surprising that the Foundation has occasionally been asked to assist local projects having to do with tribal and minority peoples. For instance, a basic need to which the Foundation has responded in many Asian countries (and not only in relation to tribal and minority peoples) is for research to develop data with which adequate development program planning can be undertaken by Asian governments. It has been found that although the Southeast Asian countries by and large have been the subject of research and study by outsiders, they have seldom been the subject of research by their own people. This phenomenon has deep roots, of course, and there is no intention here to deprecate the tremendous contributions made to our knowledge of Asian countries by outside researchers.

Since World War II, however, many Asians have been trained in research methods and have returned to their own countries, where they have identified important areas of research. Thus local people are rapidly moving from positions of bystanders and informants to become active participants and planners. Under these conditions, research is becoming a part of the planning habits of government and private institutions and agencies, and its results are being fed back promptly into the system.

With particular reference to programs for tribal and minority peoples, the Foundation has on occasion been able to respond to requests for assistance in research which grew out of local concern for the integration of such peoples into national affairs. This concern underlay the Hill Tribes Research Project initiated in Thailand in 1961 by the Department of Public Welfare with a grant from the Foundation. This was the initial phase of a program which is reported on in this book by Dr. Hans Manndorff. Positively, the Thai government desired to find ways to incorporate the hill tribes more closely into the body politic without destroying their culture. Negatively, the threat of Communist subversion and the consequent threat to the integrity of Northern and Northwestern Thailand were also factors to be taken into consideration, although these factors seem to have become explicit only some time after the movement to find ways of integrating the hill tribes into the Thai nation began.

The origins of the Hill Tribes Research Project illustrate how a number of independent streams of thought and organizational interests can sometimes coincide at a point in time and result in the creation of a new activity possessing considerable potential for further development. In early 1959 the Public Welfare Department was already involved in a pilot resettlement program. Mr. E. J. Tavanlar, a Filipino specialist on land settlement was attached to the Department under arrangements with the Food and Agriculture Organization (FAO) in order to act as an adviser on the resettlement project. Both Mr. Tavanlar and the Director General of the Public Welfare Department were aware of the need for research prior to undertaking any major resettlement efforts. The Social Affairs Division of ECAFE (Economic Cooperation in Asia and the Far East) was interested in research because of its concern with the narcotics problem. The Southeast Asia Treaty Organization (SEATO) had become interested and had made a direct grant to the Siam Society to help collect tribal artifacts. The Director of the Border Patrol Police, already active in educational and social service programs for the tribal groups at that time, was also interested in research as a necessary prelude to improved work. This atmosphere led to a series of discussions in 1959 among personnel of the Department of Public Welfare with members of the Asia Foundation and the Social Affairs Division of ECAFE in 1959 looking toward the creation of a research project (see Manndorff's discussion, in this volume, of the Socio-Economic Survey of Hill Tribes).

By contrast, experiences in Burma and Laos have also taught the Foundation that it is not always so easy to discern a consensus within some Asian governments about possible ways of assisting in the solution of tribal minority problems. For this reason, it is a matter of policy that the possibility of working on tribal and minority problems be thoroughly discussed with the appropriate agencies of a central government, and a real effort exerted to be certain that the programming envisaged meets with the approval of every interested local center of power. Thus, during the late 1950's in Burma, both the central civilian government and the senior leaders of the Burmese army were very much concerned about the possibility of subversion of tribal groups by Chinese Communists, the Americans, Shan nationalists based in Thailand, etc. This unanimity of attitude, however, did not encourage foreign aid programs addressed to the problems of minority groups. With the formation of the Frontier Administration in 1960–1961, the Burmese army (as the primary agency in the work of defining the new frontier with China) took a much greater interest in social and educational work among the tribal groups. Though this heightened interest brought some measure of improvement in the treatment of tribal groups, it did not affect the long-standing inhibitions placed upon foreign aid agencies to do anything about promoting appropriate research and social improvement measures among the tribal people.

[850]

The Burmese army created internal programs for dealing with some of the problems of the tribal minorities; the national policies of Burma never encouraged foreign programming addressed to such groups.

The foregoing remarks only serve to point up, of course, the reasons for the Foundation's insistence on responding to local initiative and allowing projects to be carried out in the manner and through means considered by their local sponsors to be most appropriate for the circumstances. It might be noted here that this approach permits the Foundation to be represented by program administrators who are not necessarily highly trained specialists in particular aspects of the local culture, mores, etc.

The practical application of the Foundation's guide lines and operating principles is illustrated in the following section, which deals with programming for tribal and minority peoples in Burma, Laos, Malaysia, Thailand, and Vietnam.

FOUNDATION PROGRAMMING FOR HILL TRIBE AND
MINORITY PROJECTS IN SOUTHEAST ASIA

Burma[1]. Because of the policies of the government of Burma during the period from 1952 through 1959 with regard to assisting the educational, economic, and social development of the individual states of the Union of Burma, the Asia Foundation never sought direct and active programming with hill tribes or state governments in that country. The Union Government at Rangoon did permit program exploration by the Foundation in the states; but, for the most part, such explorations were to be confined to programs of central government agencies operating in the states.

A notable example of this kind of programming was the 1958–1961 project, with the National Registrar of Co-operatives[2]

[1] The section on Burma was prepared by Mr. James J. Dalton, Director, Review and Development Department, and former Asia Foundation Representative in Burma.

[2] Prior to March 2, 1962, when the present Revolutionary Council Government of Burma seized control of the government, the cooperative movement in Burma was a state-supported venture designed to ". . . reform the social system by means of a new economic system which would not favour private enterprise. . ." (Dr. Mya Maung, in an unpublished research paper on agricultural cooperation in Burma, June 1962, p. 28). The cooperative movement included Primary So-

covering costs of experimental training classes for leaders of cooperative societies in various state centers. The classes were organized and managed by the National Registrar of Co-operative
Societies (NRCS) with headquarters in Rangoon. The classes
were attended by an average of forty-five individuals, and students included the presidents, secretaries, committee members,
and members of local "co-op" societies in each area. The instruc-
tors were qualified personnel employed by the NRCS. Courses
taught included: Co-operative Principles, Accounting, and Administration. Among noteworthy features contributing to the experimental character of the classes, the following are
representative:

(1) The classes were residential, and there was always uncer-
tainty as to how many officers of local co-op societies could attend extended courses.

(2) The interval of training was varied, for purposes of experimentation, to range between one week and four months in order
to learn about the optimum time that could be given to certain
courses of training.

(3) The locations for the training were varied according to
plan. Problems of transport, style, and size of the surrounding
co-op societies, language of instruction, etc., all were factors in
determining location.

Classes were held in Tiddim, Falam, and Paletwa, Chin Hills;
Myitkyina and Bhamo, Kachin State; Sandoway and Kinmaw,
Arakan; Kyaukme, Taunggyi, Kengtung, Loilem, and Lashio,
Shan State; and Pa-an, Karen State. Due to the termination
of Asia Foundation assistance to Burma in December 1962, a
planned, full-scale evaluation of the experimental work was never
completed. However, preliminary observations at that time indicated that such field-training efforts might be uneconomic and
diffuse when compared to the creation and management of a
centrally located cooperative education training center. Plans for

---

cieties, Township or District Wholesale Societies, and National Wholesale Cooperative Societies. The sectors of the economy in which these societies were
to operate included agricultural produce, fisheries, cottage industries, production,
internal marketing, and foreign export. The major stress on the development
of the societies by the government during the period from 1947 to 1962 was
in internal marketing or consumer cooperatives, and in agricultural "co-ops,"
or Agricultural Procos (Producers' Multipurpose Co-operatives).

the creation of the latter training entity have not been implemented since the current Revolutionary Council Government of Burma came to power in 1962.

Another example of programming with central government agencies operating in the states is the project of the Armed Forces Rehabilitation Board in both the Shan and Kachin states. This Board's multi-faceted program is a deliberate attempt by the Burmese army to develop a 100,000-acre farming tract in the Shan State and another 10,000-acre tract in the Kachin State. It is also designed to meet certain sociologically-oriented needs within the army cadres. These needs concern, in part, the fact that a portion of the regular army is now nearing retirement age after twenty years of service. Facilities are already being developed within the army for retraining men in vocational trades for return to civilian life. Arrangements have also been made to provide employment opportunities to such trained men in government-owned enterprises. Since this had not been done to any large extent in the past, in matters concerning return to the land by retired army personnel, the present project was developed for such a purpose. Men opting for such a form of pre-retirement training activity are assigned to the Board's farm project three years prior to retirement. They thus get essential training and form a technically qualified labor corps capable of handling mechanized farming equipment. They are given individual houses and small garden plots; but the major areas farmed remain the property of the Board, and any profits derived are divided on the basis of scales for skills, hours of work invested, etc.

Aside from these various goals, the effort also represents an attempt by the army to extend its influence into non-Burman areas of Burma (those areas not inhabited primarily by ethnic Burmans) through the introduction of productive, socialist-oriented farm settlements in the Shan and Kachin uplands. The aim, particularly in the case of the Shan State, is to show the people of that state how the so-called feudal systems of authority, tradition, land use, etc., to which they cling are not suited to modern (Socialist and Burman) ways of doing things.

The area involved for the Shan project is 100,000 acres which formerly belonged to several feudal chieftains (sawbwas) in the Loilem area. The population in the area is small, and the villages tend to cluster on the higher hills. The areas developed by the Board as extensive farming lands are in the broad low valleys. Limited water supply, as well as a small, impoverished population, has always retarded the agricultural development of the region. By introducing mechanized farming on a large scale and installing deep-well mechanical pumping, the army Board's project has injected a much higher level of technology and farm investment than ever witnessed before in the area. None of the local farmers can imitate it without the kind of help now being extended to them by the Board in peripheral training projects, because they lack the capital and know-how. The principal crops in the project are upland wheat, corn, barley, and rye. Since Burma has to import a large amount of wheat per year the main emphasis in this large project is on the production of high-yield, healthy, drought-resistant varieties of wheat.

The Asia Foundation's role in this effort was merely that of supplying some experimental seed grains for test. At one time, also, the Foundation arranged to supply an Israeli grain production expert as an adviser; but the development of direct contractual relationships between the governments of Israel and Burma for supplying a number of Israeli technical advisers to this project superseded such an arrangement. To date, the activities of the Board still flourish, and in recent years efforts have been addressed to supplying some technical advice, seeds, fertilizers, etc., to surrounding small farmers such as those of the Pa O tribal groups in the Central Shan region.

In 1959 and 1960 the attitude of the central government toward the state governments began to change with regard to economic and other forms of assistance. It was finally recognized that an expanded effort would have to be made to foster the growth of several states, and increased allocations of central government funds as well as foreign aid were directed toward this problem. Thus, starting in 1959, the Asia Foundation—maintaining constant consultation with the central government—began to explore various possibilities with state governments. This led to the following representative projects:

1. A tax survey of the Shan State by a team of economists from the University of Rangoon. The purpose was to provide the state and central governments with factual data about the

deficiencies of the existing land, sales, vehicle, and other tax systems, in order to lay the basis for more efficient tax assessment and collection practices.

2. A system of agricultural training awards, administered by the Kachin State government, for young Kachin students graduating from the Kachin School of Agriculture in Myitkyina.

3. A system of supplying agricultural equipment to resident middle schools in the outlying areas of the Kachin State. The equipment was used by the students, under the direction of competent agricultural technicians employed by the Kachin State, for training purposes and to augment the income of the middle schools.

4. Assistance to a social service organization of Buddhist clergy interested in establishing the beginnings of a social service system in the Kachin, Shan, and Kayah states. The organization, known as the Social Service Sangha, worked with state governments and the central government in creating small health-care clinics, orphanages, and schools for handicapped children.

Since the assumption of power by the Revolutionary Council Government of Burma in March 1962, the Social Service Sangha has not been very active in the constituent states of Burma. Instead it continues to work in central Burma, where among the Buddhist monasteries and orphanages associated with this organization, over a thousand orphans and handicapped children are given lodging and some forms of vocational training by interested lay Buddhists.

In no case did the foundation ever carry out direct programs with tribal groups, even though in some instances the central government did not appear to oppose such work. Examples are the Pa O in central Shan State and the Lisu in Kachin and Shan states. The reason, in these and other cases, was that the Foundation saw the importance of an organized program supported and guided by the central government. At that time, and until the creation of the Frontier Administration in 1960–1961, no well-planned and organized central government program existed for the hill tribe peoples. With the creation of the Frontier Administration, the Burma army assumed a large measure of responsibility for such work, and thereafter security problems tended to override development considerations, with the result that no further efforts were made by the Foundation to develop programs in the states. In 1962 American foundations in Burma (including the Asia Foundation) were asked by the government of Burma to terminate their operations.

Looking back on programming in the tribal minorities areas in Burma, it is clear that the Foundation did not consciously undertake to study the processes of modernization as they occur among tribal peoples and the effect these processes have on tribal society. For this reason, its assistance went to what could be considered peripheral projects (in tribal or ethnic minority programming) such as formal education and technical schooling. Such projects were important because they underscored the Foundation's desire to help the central government foster national integration and an increased measure of economic and social development in the constituent states of Burma. On the other hand the effectiveness of such projects is questionable because of inability to mount essential preliminary research. A program on agricultural scholarships, for instance, was not related to the realities of swidden agriculture: what problems are both solved and created by training someone from the tribal groups or a citizen of a constituent state to run a tractor? It is understood that the government of Burma now gives increased priority to research into the customs of tribal peoples before attempting to develop economic and social programs in the hill areas.

Two research projects representative of this interest are those undertaken recently by the Rangoon Institute of Economics (formerly the University of Rangoon Economics Department) and the Anthropology Department of the Rangoon Arts and Science University. In the latter case the research concerns some of the Padaung people in the Kayah State and involves language study. The ultimate purpose is to develop means by which several selected Burmese army officers and civilians may be instructed in the language, so that they may better perform a number of agricultural training and community development functions among the Padaung people. In the former instance, the research concerns the land-use practices of the Pa O people in the central Shan State and how those practices have been affected by the various forms of taxation and administrative control by the Shan State and central government.

Laos. Foundation programming among tribal groups in Laos has been of a very limited nature. Some projects which were undertaken on behalf of the Meo tribal people were largely concerned with the welfare and well-being of persons who had been displaced from their homes to the Vientiane area by Pathet Lao military action.

One project was of special interest, however, because it helped to elucidate a governmental policy with regard to the hill tribes. This project had to do with the printing of a Meo primer so that the Meo children could become literate in their own language in addition to the Lao language. Despite close coordination between the Foundation and interested government officials, this undertaking incurred the opposition of Prince Souvanna Phouma and reflected his policy of equating Lao acculturation with Lao nationhood. Generally speaking, among the government officials in Laos, the attitude is that there is no tribal problem, even though there are more tribal peoples than there are Lao. Some friends of Laos consider this official disregard of the cultural differences and special needs of the tribal groups as one of the important reasons for the disaffection of many tribal peoples in the country. On the other hand, this policy does make it at least theoretically possible for tribal people to become sufficiently assimilated to be eligible for appointments to government positions, because *if* the tribals obtain and accept Laotian education, they acquire the same qualifications for government service as the Laotians themselves. Research on the pros and cons of this problem would be most welcome.

Malaysia. Because of the multi-ethnic communal nature of the Malaysian population, the Foundation's programming in Malaysia was an attempt to respond to the strong drive of the central government for national unity. Prior to the establishment of Malaysia, projects in the Federation of Malaya and Singapore took account of the importance of inter-communal cooperation and harmony. Because they dealt with Malay and Chinese (majority) populations, such projects are probably not within the purview of this book, except for ones which provided radio sets for the aboriginal settlements through the Protector of Aborigines, in order to help give the aborigines a greater sense of participation in the life of the Malayan nation and access to broader educational opportunities. Another assisted the Borneo Literature Bureau in Sarawak to develop publications designed to help increase literacy and build a democratic citizenry. These publications include writings in the indigenous languages of Iban and Kadazan. The Borneo Literature Bureau, the publishing agency, also publishes in English, Chinese, and Malay.

Since Malaysia Day and the establishment of a Foundation office in Jesselton, Sabah (North Borneo), programming with respect to Bornean tribal groups has increased. The general purpose of such work has, however, remained the same. A corollary of this work is the identification and development of modern leadership among the tribal groups.

Projects undertaken in the foregoing connection include scholarships for Dayaks, Kayans, and other indigenous peoples to enable them to finish high school; for the training of native peoples in Sabah in business methods; assistance in the contrastive analysis of the Kadazan (or Dusun) language with English to help improve English teaching; the provision of tutor-teachers to help qualify fifty native junior members of the Sabah state civil service for senior jobs or university entrance; and furnishing a linguist-educator to supervise the introduction of new English teaching methods in the primary schools of Sarawak, which enroll pupils of diverse language backgrounds.

Thailand. In Thailand the Foundation has carried out more systematic and comprehensive programming with respect to tribal and minority peoples than in any other country of Southeast Asia. Over the past ten years ministerial policies have begun to develop, and the approaches to the problems of the hill tribes and minority peoples have varied according to the ministry's view of its mission and the degree of enlightenment of high officials.

For instance, the Border Patrol Police—a branch of the Ministry of Interior—have as their principal mission the maintenance of law and order in the border areas. The exact origins of an interest, on the part of the Border Patrol Police, in providing educational training and other social services to tribal groups is unknown to us. That this kind of work has been in existence for some years is attested by the following excerpt from a draft article written in February 1960 by an American ethnologist working in Thailand:

> The Thai Border Patrol Police (BPP) now constitute a conscious instrument of gradual assimilation. This organization, apparently out of sheer propinquity to the ethnic minorities living in remote border areas and the necessity of dealing with them, has taken it upon itself, or had thrust upon it, cultural responsibilities which are not normally within the domain of the simple guardians of law and order. The BPP has established throughout much of the hill area, where ethnic minorities are most numerous, a series of schools in which the instructors are policemen. The primary objective of instruction in these schools is to bring a knowledge of the Thai language to the children of groups for whom that language is not the native form of speech. . . .

Health and sanitation measures are also taught. However, these activities are clearly secondary to the major duties of the BPP, which are in intelligence-gathering, police work, and similar fields. Consequently, the instruction of hill tribe children has to be suspended when police duties intervene.

More or less concurrent with the foregoing developments, the Department of Public Welfare—also a branch of the Ministry of Interior—began a program to resettle some of the hill tribes in the Northeast in permanent villages. This activity apparently grew out of a slowly developing awareness on the part of several high government officials that the hill tribes presented actual and potential problems for the government with respect to foreign subversion. They were also concerned about the (reported) deleterious effects on the watersheds of deforestation caused by swidden agriculture and the raising and/or transportation of opium. Crudely stated, the response seems to have been a decision to try out a resettlement program which would bring the hill tribe peoples into controlled areas, where they could be watched and at the same time encouraged to take up more permanent and legitimate agricultural pursuits. However, the Department of Public Welfare was led by an enlightened person and staffed by a growing number of persons who were trained in research and appreciated the importance of research-based action. Close acquaintance of the Department's personnel with

personnel of the Asia Foundation led to the discovery of an interest in hill tribes research and the beginning of conversations
in 1960 which resulted in the Foundation's extending financial
assistance to the Department to enable it to carry out a program
of field research before the resettlement program was
implemented on a large scale.

So far as the Foundation knows, the Hill Tribes Research
Project represented the first time a Thai government agency had
made a research survey before making a plan for socio-economic
development. The importance of this step need not be labored.
The details of this project and related grants by the Foundation
are pursued further in the separate paper by Dr. Hans Manndorff, who has been intimately involved with hill tribes problems
in Thailand for a number of years.

In making these grants, the Foundation has attempted to meet
national needs for social integration of minority peoples, the development of research and study of social problems, and socio-
economic development, and indirectly the development of
trained leadership through the team research system which was
adopted. However, it cannot yet be said that the program has
been successful, as it is not clear that there is any real commitment on the part of the Thai government to see the hill tribes
problem as a national one requiring basically *civil* administration.
Until recently, responsibility for the area has been left, more
by default than by intention, to the Border Patrol Police, perhaps
because of the belief that only a small number of persons, relatively speaking, were involved and the feeling that the budget
was too limited to cover such a large geographical area. One
of the advantages of the research project was, therefore, that
it would provide an opportunity for work with the tribal peoples
in a way that would nicely complement the police and military
sphere of concern.

It has been possible to see some progress. The Department
of Public Welfare has become deeply involved and has established a special division to work on hill tribes problems. Significantly, the Ministry of Education has also become involved recently and has set up a special unit to deal with education in
the tribal villages, and the Asia Foundation has financed some
of this work. The missing element is a sense of any fundamental

commitment by the Thai government *as a whole* to the prompt and effective integration of the tribal peoples into the nation.

The Foundation believes that its assistance has been an important factor in encouraging the civilian elements of government to become interested in putting large funds into hill tribes programming. The cooperation of several United Nations agencies, SEATO, and the Siam Society of Thailand has already been enlisted, and personnel has begun to arrive to undertake advisory tasks in specialized areas for which the Thais do not yet have the necessary trained people.

Another salutary result of the programming carried out to date is the change from the original attitude of solving hill tribes problems by resettlement to one which recognizes that civil government action and services must take place *in situ*—in other words, services must be taken to the tribes rather than bringing the tribes to the services.

The Department of Public Welfare projects involving the research program, the provision of an adviser (Dr. Manndorff), the training of mobile extension teams, and the printing of the report of the socio-economic survey in English, comprise the Foundation's major response to the needs of Thailand in this particular area. The Foundation is now reducing its hill tribes projects because many other agencies and organizations with larger funds at their disposal are entering the field.

In addition to the above program, the Foundation has, over the past few years, supported a number of small projects for research, publishing, and collection of artifacts of tribal peoples, assistance to schools enrolling hill tribes pupils and to the pupils themselves, and on one occasion has encouraged college students to do elementary social research among the hill tribes. In that instance a grant of April 1964 provided a month's per diem for eight members of the Voluntary Student Group for Hill Tribe Development, of the Faculty of Arts, Chulalongkorn University, who spent one month of their vacation period studying the social, cultural, and economic environment of hill tribe people and in carrying out research on local tribal languages.

Finally, it should be mentioned that the Foundation has responded to requests for assistance in respect to the Malay-speaking Muslim population of southern Thailand, which has had national integration as its goal. A number of relatively small projects, undertaken for the most part in answer to requests from the Thai government's Ministry of Education or regional and provincial education officers, but also from the Thai Library Association and the Education Society of Thailand, have been assisted in providing incentives to schoolchildren and adults to learn the Central Thai dialect, enabling specialists in language-teaching to introduce improved methods of teaching Thai to children, and providing reading materials in the Malay language for small village and mosque libraries. It is hoped that these efforts will help break the vicious circle of inability to speak and read Thai language and lack of education in general, which has kept the Thai Muslims in three of the four southern provinces of the country from entering government service and national life. A project has recently been started to teach the Malay language to Thai officers, whose first language is Thai, and who are posted in areas inhabited mainly by Thai-Malays.

Vietnam. Over the past five years, intermittent grants have been made by the Foundation to support Vietnamese efforts to create a greater national consciousness among the hill tribe (*montagnard*) peoples of South Vietnam. The Foundation does not view these grants as forming an integrated program. Rather, for the most part, they have supported a series of Vietnamese efforts during the period 1960–1963 to improve educational facilities for certain tribal peoples. For example, the Koho tribe has received aid for a primary school building and school books as well as agricultural training courses through private organizations such as the Association of Parents of Students of the High Plateau Area at Chrong Tambor, the Mission Evangélique at Dalat, and the International Voluntary Service. Rhadé tribal villagers in Banmethuot Province have received training in agricultural techniques, and the Jarai and Bahnar mountain tribes have been provided with special educational courses for young people through the Mission Etrangère at Cheo Reo, Kontum Province. School buildings for children of undesignated tribes, as well as agricultural demonstration courses for resettlement villages, have been provided through hill tribe centers and the International Voluntary Service.

Work has also been done with the Buddhists, who are a minority in Vietnam. Most of the projects are small and have provided books, equipment, teaching aids, and travel. The most substantial assistance has gone to the Institute for the Execution of the Dharma, for various purposes connected with their social work program. The idea has been to help identify and support leadership capable of constructive social action, and to encourage constructive community action.

CONCLUSIONS

Among the conclusions which might be drawn from the foregoing exposition are the following:

A. In the countries of Southeast Asia, government awareness of the actual and potential problems which arise from domestic efforts to integrate minority people into the national body politic, and from external efforts to use the dissatisfactions of minority peoples for subversive purposes is, relatively speaking, just beginning to crystallize.

B. Government attitudes toward research by outside scholars on all aspects of hill tribe life are quite closely correlated with the position of the nation in respect to alignment or non-alignment with the major contending international forces.

C. External organizations wishing to foster research or programs in respect to hill tribes and minority groups would be well advised to make sure that projects for those purposes are understood and accepted by the central government of the country concerned.

D. External organizations interested in assisting programs which involve hill tribes and minority groups should make every effort to use their funds to encourage local government agencies to base their planning on thorough research into socio-cultural factors of such groups.

E. Commitment by central government authorities to sound programs managed by the non-disciplinary or non-security agencies of the government should precede the financing of projects, or should be a major goal of projects assisted by external organizations.

F. Hill tribes programming is closely related to work in stimulating the improvement of social science research and teaching in indigenous institutions of higher learning.

G. The Asia Foundation's programming in respect to hill tribe and minority peoples in Southeast Asia is, by and large, not far enough advanced at this time to permit useful evaluation of its effects. Furthermore, there is a great need for more research by local scholars, backstopped by foreign scholars; this in turn emphasizes the need for more training of local people in the theory and techniques of social science research.

PART X. APPENDIX

TABLE 26
POPULATION AND LINGUISTIC AFFILIATION OF ETHNIC GROUPS OF CAMBODIA[a]

Group (Synonyms in Parentheses)	Estimated Population in Cambodia[b]	Location (in Order of Size of Population)	Language
Khmer (Cambodian	3,500,000	Cambodia, South Vietnam, Thailand	Mon-Khmer: Khmeric
Chinese	435,000[c]	China, Southeast Asia	Chinese
Vietnamese	400,000[d]	South Vietnam, North Vietnam, Cambodia	Viet-Muong: Vietnamese
Stieng	30,000+[e]	Cambodia, South Vietnam	Mon-Khmer: Bahnaric, S. Bahnaric
French	6,000[d]	—	Indo-European: French
Brao	3,000+	Laos, Thailand, Cambodia	Mon-Khmer: Bahnaric, N. Bahnaric
Saoch	172	Cambodia	Mon-Khmer: ?Khmeric
Cham	[unavailable]	South Vietnam, Cambodia	Malayo-Polynesian: Chamic
Chong	[unavailable]	Cambodia, Thailand	Mon-Khmer: Khmeric
Jarai	[unavailable]	South Vietnam, Cambodia	Malayo-Polynesian: Chamic
Kui	[unavailable]	Thailand, Cambodia	Mon-Khmer: Khmeric
Pear	[unavailable]	Cambodia	Mon-Khmer: Khmeric
Rhadé, (Radê)	[unavailable]	South Vietnam, Cambodia	Malayo-Polynesian: Indochina Plateau
Thai (Siamese)	[unavailable]	Thailand	Tai: Southwestern
Cambodia Total (1962 census)[f]	5,740,115		

[a] Source: Information on distribution and population from LeBar *et al.* (1964), except where noted. Linguistic classification primarily from Thomas (1965A, 1965B). See notes accompanying Burma population figures for further details on methods of linguistic classification. Estimate for Khmer population is for 1959.

[b] Groups whose population is unknown are listed alphabetically.

[c] Estimate of Chinese population is from Skinner (1965); at a press conference in Phnom Penh in March 1965 Prince Norodom Sihanouk gave an estimate of 300,000 Chinese in Cambodia.

[d] Figures released at a press conference of Prince Norodom Sihanouk in Phnom Penh, March 1965.

[e] Figure for Stieng is derived from data cited in LeBar *et al.* (1964:157).

[f] Figure for total Cambodian population from Réalités Cambodgiennes, 19 March 1965, Supplement A.

REFERENCES CITED

LeBar, Frank M., Gerald C. Hickey, and John K. Musgrave
    1964   Ethnic groups of mainland Southeast Asia. New Haven, Human Relations Area Files Press.
Skinner, G. William
    1965   Personal communication.
Thomas, David D.
    1965A   Vietnam minority languages (July 1965 revision). Saigon, Summer Institute of Linguistics.
    1965B   Personal communications.

Periodicals

Réalités Cambodgiennes, Phnom Penh.

INDEX

Index

The letter "m" preceding a number refers to the map of that number.

Armed Forces Rehabilitation Board of Burma, 853
Armstrong, T., 8n, 685
ARPA (Advanced Research Projects Agency), 745n
Arsa Meksawan, 475
Arutiunov, S. A., and A. I. Mukhlinov, 695n
Asia Foundation, 392, 533, 543, 549; aims of, 847f; in Burma, 851–56; in Laos, 857; in Malaysia, 857f; operating principles, 848; programs, evaluation of, 863f; relations with Asian governments, 850n; research, 848f, 854f; in Sabah, 858; in Thailand, 383f, 849, 858–62; in Vietnam, 727f, 861ff. *See also* action programs, private foundations in
Assam, 11, 45, 75, 135, 215–29; population in, 205; position of minorities in, 36; tribesmen in, 224
Assamese, in Burma, 117
assimilation, 38, 42, 51, 59; hypotheses concerning, 46f; "passing," 17; in Thailand, 391, 394, 554f. *See also* Burmanization; integration of minorities; Vietnamization
Attopeu Province, Laos, 297
Australian government: aid to Thailand, 543, 554f
Auvade, R., 677n
AVS (American Volunteer Service), 55

Ba Mali, in Sarawak, 331
Bac Cam Qui, Black Tai leader, 811f
Bac family of Black Tai, 812
Bahnar, in Vietnam, 677, 683n, 686, 747, 761; land tenure system of, 767; missionaries among, 748; political structure of, 755
Bailey, F. G., 36
Bajau, in Sabah, 354
Balembangan Island, Sabah, 355
Balipara Frontier Tract, Assam, 217
Ban Akas, Thailand, 464
Ban Don Luang, Thailand, 464
Ban Fa Huan, Thailand, 429
Ban Houei Sai, Laos, 233
Ban Hua Lin, Thailand, 647
Ban Kut Rua Kham, Thailand, 461n, 464
Ban Lao, Thailand, 464
Ban–Mai, Thailand, 518–22
Ban Myt Lawng, Thailand, 647
Ban Na Khu, Thailand, 461n

Ban Nong On, Thailand, 430n
Ban Oj, Thailand, 406
Ban Pa Pae, Thailand, 479n, 643, 652f
Ban Phae?, Thailand, 647
Ban Phalae, Thailand, 583
Ban Phon Thum, Thailand, 461n
Ban Ping, Thailand, 401n, 402–24
Ban Ton Phrao, Thailand, 647
Ban Yan (Wan-Yang), Thailand, 494–518
Bang Chan, Thailand, 419
Bangkok, Thailand, 235
Bao Dai, Emperor of Vietnam, 679, 683n
Baptists: in Burma, 97. *See also* American Baptists; Karen; missionaries
Barth, F., 627
Battle of Day River, 802n
Battle of Insein, 98
Battle of Vinh Yen, 801n
Baw Luang, Thailand, 646
Bawlahké, Kayah State, Burma, 77, 99f
Belaga, Sarawak, 329
Benedict, P., 85
Bengali minority, in Assam, 225
Bennington-Cornell Anthropological Survey, 13, 573, 620f
Berelson, B., and G. A. Steiner, 470
Bernatzik, H., 271n, 278, 288
Bhamo District, Burma, 75, 120, 135, 141
Bhu Lom Low *nikhom*, Thailand, 532
Bible Societies of Southeast Asia, in Thailand, 390
bilingualism, 22, 133, 135, 669; in India, 220; in Malaysia, 338; in Thailand, 513, 518. *See also* specific languages, countries, peoples; multilingualism
Binh Xuyen sect, in South Vietnam, 705
Birou, A., 754
Bisaya, in Sarawak, 321
Black Flags of the Tribal Tai: in Thailand, 234n
Black Tai: and French administration, 825f; internal dissension among, 814; lack of political cohesion, 812; in Laos, 236–38; Lo and Cam families, 236, 237, 779, 812; in North Vietnam, 678n, 683, 649n; relations with Viet Minh, 809f, 811–13; in Southeast Asia, 11; in Vietnam, 778, 807–10, 820f
Black, White, and Red Tai (Thai), 296. *See also* upland Thai, in Laos

Kirghiz, Korean, Laku, Li, Lisu, Meo (Miao), Mongolian, Nasi, Puyi Pu-i), Sibo, Thai, Tibetan, Tung, Uighur, Yi (*see also* Lolo), 180. *See also* separate headings under languages

China (People's Republic of), minorities in: agricultural development of, 190f; attitudes toward, 179; autonomous areas, 171, 186, m4; autonomous governments of, 173, 174f, 181–84; cadres, 175f, 197; and class 177; collectivization of, 189; cooperatives among, 187n; discrimination against, 177f, 198; distribution of, 170; education of, 176; elections among, 173f; government policies on, 28, 169–201; and industrialization, 191; kinship and marriage among, 195f; land reform, 186–91; language, policy, 32, 179–81; publications, 180; research on; 180f, 193; scripts, 179ff, 193n; literacy of, 193f; modernization of, 186–91; nationalism among, 200f; "nationality," definition of, 169n; non-Han, 492; political control of, 178; population, 149, 169–201; and public health, 194; radio broadcasts to, 181; reforms and social structure, 196n; religions of, 194–96; Tai-speaking, 185–197; taxation of, 192f; tribal feudalism among, 187f

China Inland Mission, *see* Overseas Missionary Fellowship

China, Nationalist (Nationalist China, Republic of Taiwan): 198, 492f, 510; minority policies in, 174n. *See also* Nationalist Chinese

Chinese: becoming Thai, 492; bandits in Burma, Laos, and Thailand, 493f; economic role in Southeast Asia, 36

Chinese Church of Indonesia, in Thailand, 392n

Chinese Communists, 150; in Sarawak, 319–20; organization, in Sarawak, 320

Chinese empire, 30, 117

Chinese influence: in Sabah, 354; in Vietnam, 787. *See also* influence of civilizations: Chinese

Chinese interests in Tai peoples, 834f

Chinese jars, trade among Murut of Sabah, 358

Chinese Moslems (in China *see* Hui),

in Thailand, *see* Haw; Yunnanese Chinese

Chinese overseas minority: 12, 35; in Burma, 114, 492; in Cambodia, 24n; in Laos, 239, 272, 492; in Malaysia, 264f, 307, 309f; in Sabah, 354, 355; in Sarawak, 311n, 318–20, 329, 344, 346, 349; in Singapore, 309; in Thailand (*see also* Haw; Yunnanese Chinese), 369, 373, 375, 390, 392n, 401, 487–524, 526n, 573; in Vietnam, 492, 678n

Chinese traders: 117f, 489f; in Borneo, 359; in Laos, 261, 281, 284n

Ching-po, 149, 170, 185f, 196n. *See also* Jinghpaw or Kachin

Chomsky, N., 106

Christian Brethren Mission, in Thailand, 390

Christian Mission, in Sarawak, 350

Christianity: among Yao, 585n, 595, 630; and political identity, 120; in Assam, 215; in Borneo, 324, 330; in Burma, 96; in India, 205, 220; in Laos, 242, 288, 289, 290, 292; in Malaysia, 330, 338f; in Sarawak, 321; in Thailand, 388–91, 498. *See also* missionaries

Chu-Ko Liang (K'ung Beng), 490n, 491n

Chu Van Tan, Gen., 796

Chuang, in China, 23n, 169, 183, 185n, 517n. *See also* China: languages

Chulalongkorn, King of Thailand, 389, 640

Chulalongkorn University, Thailand, 533, 548f, 861

Chung-chia, in China, 185n, 517n

Church of Christ in Japan, in Thailand, 392n

Church of Christ in Thailand, 391, 392n

Church of South India, in Thailand, 392n

CIA (U.S. Central Intelligence Agency), 55, 56, 640n, 681f, m3, m4

Civilian Irregular Defense units, South Vietnam, 56, 839

Clarke, Sir C., 336, 347

"closed, corporate community," definition of, 39

Cochin China, 678

Coedes, G., 834

cognitive models, 105

Colombo Plan, 301, 345, 544

colonial administration, 206, 241
colonialism, 18, 37–39; in Borneo, 341;
in Burma, 77, 120; in India, 206,
219f; and land tenure, 20; in Laos,
234, 241, 243, 246, 278f, 295; in
Malaysia, 307f; in Sarawak, 343f
Colson, E., 59
Communist activities: in Laos, 233; in
Malaysia, 310f; in Thailand, 388, 441,
473f, 500
Communist Party of India, 225
Community Development (CD) in
Thailand: 420, 448n, 465–67, 491
Condominas, G., 52, 678, 678n, 679,
682, 701n, 757, 775, 776n, 778n,
781f, 789
"Confrontation," Indonesia and
Malaysia, 57, 310, 339f; in Borneo,
322, 329, 332; economic effects of,
in Kalimantan and Sabah, 359;
effect on tribal economy, 333;
geography of, 318; in Sabah, 355f,
362–64; in Sarawak, 318, 322, 334
Confucianism, in Thailand, 373
Congress of Indochinese Peoples,
Phnom Penh, 24n, 683n
Congress Party, in Assam, 224, 225
Conklin, H. C., 102, 564, 767
cooperative movement in Burma, 851nf
corvée labor, 18, 241; and action
programs, 670; in Sarawak, 351; in
Thailand, 671; in Vietnam, 678
Cosse-Brissac, Gen., 771n
counter-insurgency, in Thailand, 425f
cultivation, see agriculture
cultural boundaries, 10, 31–35; and
caste, 216. See also demographic
boundaries
cultural background: in Laos, 261–63
cultural conversion, 34f. See also
assimilation, integration
cultural development: of population
groups, 16f
cultural identity, see cultural
boundaries
cultural discontinuities, 109
cultural group, 40
cultural-social change, 105, 139
culture: definition of, 40n; change, in
Sarawak, 326f; ideal vs. real, 106;
symbolic aspects in, 139. See also
assimilation, integration
Cupet, Capt., 749f, 760
Curtis, L. J., 405
customary law: among Lua? of
Thailand, 657f; in Burma, 28n; in

India, 218; in Sabah, 359f; in
Sarawak, 345–47; in Thailand, 377f,
378n; in Vietnam, 28n, 678

Da Houe River, Vietnam, 748
Daghor, in China, 175
Dalai Lama, 183
Dalton, J. J., 851n
Dam Bo (Jacques Dournes), 764n
Dambrö language, 399n
Darlac Plateau, Vietnam, 747; and
control of Mekong River, 749;
Khmer control of, 747; lowland and
French settlement in, 751. See also
Vietnam highlands
Darlac Province, South Vietnam, 55
Dayaks, in Sabah, 354, 858. See also
Land Dayaks (Dusun), Sea Dayaks
(Iban)
De Young, J. E., 61
Democratic Republic of Vietnam
(DRV), 684. See also North
Vietnam
demographic boundaries, 32. See also
boundaries
Dent, A., 355
Deo family of Tai, 779
Deo Van An, chief of Phong Tho, 810f
Deo Van Long, president of Tai
Federation, 804f, 810, 825, 825f
Deo Van Tri (Cam Oum), chief of
Black Flags of the Tribal Tai, 806,
807–808
Desiree, Maj. M., 771n
Deutsch, K. W., 38, 39, 40n, 41, 42,
46, 47, 52
Devillers, P., and Lacouture, J., 772n
Diem, Ngo Dinh, 55f, 681, 705, 706f,
708, 734, 761, 764, 838
Dien Bien Phu, 679, 771; artillery battle
of, 829–32; bibliography, 772n;
economic importance of, 824f; ethnic
antagonisms in, 832; ethnic
composition in, 825ff; French
military strategy in, 827; geographic
importance of, 825; significance to
Tai, 834; strategic importance of,
826f
Dobby, E. H. G., 775n
Doe Van Un, Prince of Dien Bien Phu,
826
Doi Chiengdao nikhom, Thailand, 532
Doi Musser nikhom, Thailand, 532
Dommen, A. J., 234n, 240n, 243, 836n,
837
Donnai River, Vietnam, 748

Oppressed Races), 25, 53f, 66, 682f, 761f, 839f
Funan, 525
Furnivall, J. S., 140

Gandhi, Indira, 206n
Garo, in India, 227
Garo Hills, Assam, 206, 217
Gautier Mission of 1881, Vietnam, 748
Geba, of Burma, 111. *See also* languages
Geddes, W., 549
Gedney, W., 85, 88n, 258n, 400n, 694n
Gekhu, of Burma, 112. *See also* languages
Geneva Agreements of 1954, 244, 705, 753
Geneva Agreements of 1962, 233, 235, 247, 295, 836
Geneva convention of 1954, 235, 295, 683n, 709fn, 786, 835
Genghis Khan, 180n
geography, 8, 9, 10
Gerber, T., 763
German Romanticist thought, and social science theories, 103
Ghurkas, in Sarawak, 327
Gia Long, emperor, 704, 787, 788
Ginsburgs, G., 685
Gittinger, J. P., 838
Goffman, I., 107
Government Alliance Party (Malaysia), 337
Governor, powers of, in Assam, 218
Graham, D. C., 271n, 287
Graham, W. A., 405
Grauwin, Med.-Com., 772n
"Great Hanism," in China, 199
"great tradition" religions, 21
"Greater Thai" ethnolinguistic classification, 431
Grierson, G. A., 84n
guerrillas, Chinese: in Burma, 493; in Republic of Taiwan, 493
Guilleminet, P., 755, 763
Gullick, J. M., 307
gumchying gumsa, 138, 139
gumlao, 43, 138
gumrawng gumsa, 139
gumsa, 43, 135, 138f

Hainan Island, 85
Haka-Chin, in Burma, 108. *See also* languages
Hallett, H., 489f, 526n, 639

Hall, D. G. E., 748n, 806
Halpern, A. M., and Fredman, H. B., 836n
Halpern, J. M., 21, 236, 239, 239n, 242, 244, 257nf, 261, 271n
Hamilton, J. W., 115, 652
Han Chinese: in China, 5, 150, 185
Hani (Ha-ni): in China, 170, 172, 183, 185
Hanunóo of Mindoro Island, 767
Harrisson, T., 343
Harris, M., 144
Harvey, G. E., 118
Haw, 32, 487–524; contact with British Information Service, 510; definitions of name, 488, 490f; dialect, 490; ecological position of, 487; economy of, 487; history of, 489f; international implications of, 487f; loyalties of, 523n; migrations of, 488; and opium, 35; origin of, 488f; and political unrest, 818; population, 487–92; refugees, 488–92; refugees in Burma, 488; refugees in China, 488; refugees in Laos, 233, 805; refugees in Thailand, 234n, 376, 404, 487n, 526n, 546, 555; role in culture change, 529; role in Thailand, 526f. *See also* Hui, Yunnanese Chinese
Hawaii, 86
headhunting, 45n; among Nagas, 206; in Borneo, 339, 356f; in Burma, 118; in Sarawak, 346f
Heine-Geldern, R., 19
Henderson, W., 7n, 60n, 708n
Hendry, J. B., 688n
Hickey, G. C., 237, 453n, 677n, 678n, 679, 682, 685, 687, 688n, 718n, 754, 779, 780, 818, 839
"High Plateau Autonomy Movement Committee" (NLF), 25
"hill peasants," 18
Hill Tribe Development and Welfare Program, Thailand, 267, 564, 376
hill tribes in Thailand: characteristics, 527; economy, 668; education, 382; effects of economic change, 673; effects of road-building, 673; employment restrictions, 548; land ownership, 642; languages, 669; legal status, 668, 672f; protection of land base, 672f; research on (*see also* Tribal Research Centre, Thailand), 549, 553–81, 667–69; strategic significance of, 56
Hinduism, 115; in Assam, 215; in

238, 350, 369, 586. *See also*
agriculture
Islam, 21, 32; in Borneo, 324, 330, 342;
in Malaya, 341; in Malaysia, 307,
309, 338f, 341f; in Sarawak, 319,
321; in Thailand, 428, 491. *See also*
Muslim; Hui in Thailand
Iu Mien, *see* Yao
Iwata, K., 238
Izikowitz, K. G., 18, 237, 238, 262,
584n, 623f

Jacob, P. E., and J. V. Toscano, 41
Janos, A., 791n
Japanese: in Borneo, 339; in Burma,
143; in India, 221; in Indochina, 684,
789; in Laos, 240, 274n, 278, 281,
289; in Malaysia, 310; in Sarawak,
348; in Thailand, 664; role in
Indochina War, 793
Jarai, in Vietnam, 54, 356, 683n, 686;
agriculture of, 766; history of, 747;
kinship system of, 755; political
structure of, 9n, 755f; relations with
French, 749f; slave trade,
Vietnam-Laos, 747; sorcerers,
758–60; in Vietnam revolts, 761. *See
also* sadets
Java, 7, 39, 319; peasants in, 39
Javanese: in Borneo, 329
Jayavarman II, King of Khmer, 759
Jeh (in Vietnam): agriculture of, 766;
land tenure of, 768
Jesuits: in Thailand, 388
Jinghpaw: in India, *see* Singhpo; in
China, *see* Ching-po
Johnson, L. B., 711
Joiner, C. A., 24n, 55, 679, 680, 685n,
686n, 687, 840n
Joint U.S. Military Advisory Group
(JUSMAG), in Thailand, 434
Jones, L. W., 315n
Jouin, B., 759, 771n
Judd, L., 369, 390, 392n
Jumper, R., 688
Jumper, R., and Normand, M. W., 55,
677n, 684, 685n, 686

"Kachin": as label, 102
Kachin: becoming Burman, 51, 141,
143; becoming Shan, 17, 34, 44; and
British, 143; in Burma, 14, 44, 46,
50, 75–77, 93–146; and Chinese,
135f; ecology of, 140; and Japanese,
143; and Shan cultural influence,

135–38, 140–42; and Sino-Burmese
border, 144; and World War II, 143
Kachin political system, 138. *See also
gumsa* and *gumlao*
Kachin social system, 43f, 112, 140
Kachin State, Burma, 7n, 24f, 38,
43, 132
"Kachin tribes," definition, 89n
Kachin tribes: in Burma, 30, 79, 134;
in China, 149, 196n
Kadazan (Dusun), in Sabah, 354
Kaladan River, in Burma, 97
Kalasin Province, Thailand, 452,
461n, 467
Kalimantan (Indonesian Borneo), 7, 12,
328, 340f
Kam, *see* Tung
Kanchanaburi Province, Thailand, 369
Kandre, P., 584n, 603n, 701n
Kandre, P., and Lej Tsan Kuej, 590n
Kansu Province, China, 173
Kantarawadi, Kayah State, Burma, 99
Kapuas River, Kalimantan, 328
Karen: agriculture, in Thailand, 565;
becoming Thai, 651f; in Burma, 75,
76, 94–124; community structure,
660; economic relations with Lua?,
36; entrepreneurs, in Thailand,
643–49; as ethnic category, 111;
intermarriage among, 661; languages,
22nf, 89n, 666; literacy, 376;
National Defense Organization
(KNDO), in Burma, 26, 93, 99;
National Union, in Burma, 26;
nationalists, in Thailand, 387;
political structures of, 9n; population,
in Thailand, 642f; rebellion, in
Burma, 26, 46; rebels, in border
areas, 8n; refugees, in Burma, 663n;
refugees, in Thailand, 13, 30, 44, 51,
114, 360, 374, 380, 389–92, 480,
528, 529, 534, 546, 547, 549f, 563,
576n, 668; tribes, in Burma, 30. *See
also* Pwo Karen; Skaw Karen
Karen State, Burma, 24f, 38
Karenni, in Burma, *see* Kayah
Karen-ni (Red Karen) State, Burma, 99
Kato, relations with Yao, 616f
Kaufman, H. K., 7n, 61
Kawa (Wa): in China, 170, 183,
185, 186
Kawilorot, Prince of Chiengmai, 389
Kawng Loi, Thailand, 646
"Kayah": in Burma, 38, 44, 50, 71, 77f,
78n, 94–124; as ethnic label, 111;
Kayah State, Burma, 38, 44, 94ff,

99f, 109; synonyms for, 75, 99; in Thailand, 111

Kayan: in Borneo, 318, 319, 331, 342; in Sabah, 858; in Sarawak, 321, 337, 346

Kayan-Kenyah: in Sarawak, 347

Kazakh, in China, 170, 183

Keatley, R., 839

Keen, F.G.B., 544

Kelabit: in Borneo, 318, 319, 322f, 331, 342, 356; in Sabah, 340; in Sarawak, 321, 327, 337, 346, 356

Kelao, in China, 156. *See also* Ch'ilao

Keningau, Sabah, 361

Kennedy, R., 315n

Kenyah: in Boreno, 318, 319, 331; in Sarawak, 321, 337, 344, 346

Keyes, C. F., 432, 433, 438n, 441n, 442n, 648

"Kha," 528; definition of, 236n; in Laos, 13, 24, 234, 246, 258n, 261; in Thailand, 433, 464

"Kha," meaning in Lao language, 241

Khammouane Province, Laos, 244, 297

Khamu (Khmu?), 528; becoming Yao, 594; relations with Yao, 616. *See also* Khmu

Khanh, Gen., 56, 761, 735

Khanh Hau, Vietnam, 688n

Khasi: in India, 220, 225, 227

Khet Phatanakane, 301. *See also* village clusters in Laos

Khmer: and FULRO, 54; history in Indochina, 677n; history in Vietnam, 677, 703, 746

Khmer kingdom, 10n, 11, 784f

Khmer minority: in Vietnam, 8n, 54, 787

Khmer Serei movement, 8n

Khmer-speaking peoples, 10

Khmu? in Laos: 238, 241, 269, 296, 389; agriculture, 272; culture change among, 238f; economy of, 242, 248f; political structure of, 242

Khmu? in Thailand: 374, 390, 392n, 643, 668; minorities, and political unrest, 818. *See also* Khamu

khon doi, 528

Khon Kaen, Thailand, 441

khon muang (Yuan), in Thailand, 406, 528

khon pa, 528

Khone Falls, Mekong River, 235

Khong Khai, Laos, 273

Khun Luang Wilanka, king of Chiengmai, 640

Khun Yuam Valley, Thailand, 374, 639

Khun Yuam Valley: connections with Burma, 639

Khwae Noi River, western Thailand, 44

Khyn, in Thailand, 406

Kien Hoa Province, South Vietnam, 703, 706–44; economy of, 704; geography of, 703; history of, 704f; Viet Cong in, 704

Kimanis, Sabah, 355

King of Burma, 30

king, as symbol of national unity, in Laos, 240n

king of Siam, 30

king of Thailand, 382, 513

Kingshill, K., 405

kinship, 115

kinship systems, 114f

kinship ties, 13

KMT (Kuomintang), *see* Nationalist Chinese

Knorr, K., 791n

Koho, in Vietnam, 677, 638n, 701n, 862

Kong Le, 240n, 275nf

Korean Presbyterian Church, in Thailand, 392n

Koreans, in China, 170, 183

Kratie Province, Cambodia, 24n

Kuala Lumpur, Malaysia, 336

Kuchinerai District, Thailand, 467

Kuching, Sabah, 355

Kuching, Sarawak, 355

K'uei Pi, 184n

Kui, in Thailand, 373, 380n, 668

Kun-ming (Kunming), China, 191, 499, 510

Kunstadter, P., 33, 34, 125, 243, 479n, 480, 576n, 652

Kuomintang (KMT), *see* Nationalist Chinese

Kutsung, in China, 159. *See also* Woni or Hani tribe

Kwangsi Province, China, 149, 517n, 778

Kwangtung Province, China, 778

Kweichou Province, China, 118

Kyaw Thet, 127, 129, 132, 145

Kyébogyi, Kayah State, Burma, 77, 99

Labuan Island, Sabah, 355

Ladejinsky, W., 7n, 55

Lafont, P.-B., 759, 760, 763

Lahahan Kayan, in Sarawak, 347

Lahu: becoming Yao, 594; guerrillas in Burma, 518; lack of literacy among,

621; in Laos, 269, 296, 634; migration
of, 11; political structures of, 9n;
relations with Yao, 616f; in Thailand,
374, 390, 506, 518, 527f, 533f, 549f,
620, 643
laissez-faire policies and political
development, 58
Lakua, in China, 170, 183, 185
Lamet: becoming Yao, 594; compared
with Yao, 623f; economy of, 623f; in
Laos, 238, 248, 389; in Thailand, 623;
world view of, 624
Lampang, Thailand, 479n
Lamphun, Thailand, Mon Queen of,
640
Lamphun, Prince of, 30, 52
Lamphun Province, Thailand, 491
Lan Chang, Laos, king of, 431
Lan Xang, Laos, 234
Lancaster, D., 792n
Land Dayak: in Borneo, 318; in
Kalimantan, 329; in Sarawak, 321,
329, 331, 344, 346, 349
land law, in Thailand, 377
land ownership, in Thailand, 376, 540f,
642n
Landon, K. P., 688
Langlais, Col. P., 772n

LANGUAGES (general): as basis for
minority groupings, 132; in Burma,
census of, 79; classification of, 78–89;
classification, in China, 23n;
classification in Thailand, 374n; and
cultural homogeneity, 133; dialect
boundaries, 78; dialect differences,
86; and education, Southeast Asia,
16; glotto-chronology of, 86; historical
relationships, 78f; mutual
intelligibility of, 86; official policies
on, 22f; policies: in Burma, 128; and
education, 669; in Laos, 243f, 266f,
292f, 857; in Malaysia, 308f, 858; in
Thailand, 375, 382; reform, in North
Vietnam, 686; romanization of scripts,
in China, 180f; use in national integration, 23

LANGUAGES: Akha, 374n, m15;
Arakanese, 116; Atzi, 116, 132;
Austroasiatic, 114, 116; Bahnar, 746;
Bahnaric, 85; Bih, 86; Black Tai,
m15; Black Tai, script for, 237; Bodo
group, 212; Bré, 109, 111; Burman,
116, 119; Cambodian (Khmer), 746;
Central Karen, of Burma, 111;
Central Naga, 212; Central Thai, 23n,
382; Cham, 86, 746; Chin, 116;

Chinese, 23n, 85, 119, m15;
Chinese-related, 79; Chuang, m15;
Chuang-Tung, 86; Dravidian, 89n;
Eastern Naga, 212n; Gauri, 116;
Geba, 109; Gehku, 109; Haka, 108;
Hani, m15; Haw (Hô, Yunnanese
Chinese), m15; Hré, in Vietnam, 777;
Iban, 858; Jarai, 86, 746; Jari in
Vietnam, 777; Jinghpaw (Ching-po),
76, 116, 119, 132f; Kachin, 78,
116, 132f; Kadai, 85, m15; Kadazan,
858; Kam-Sui, 85f; Karen, 109, 116,
374n, 651; Katuic, 86, Kayah, 78,
109, 111; Kelao, 86; Khasi, 85;
Khmeric, 85; Khmu', m15; Khün,
m15; Koho, in Vietnam, 777; Korean,
180; Kuki-Chin group, 212n; Lahu,
374n, m15; Lamet, m15; Lao, 238,
m15; Lao Thai, 78; Laqua, m15;
Lashi, 116, 132; Lati, m15; Li of
China, 180; Lisu, 374n; Lolo, m15;
Lue, m15; Malacca, 85; Malay in
Thailand, 307, 321, 862;
Malayo-Polynesian, 677, 683n, 777;
Manchurian, 180; Manumanaw
(Münü), 109, 111; Maru, 132;
Miao-Yao, 84, 374n, 375, m15; Miao
(Meo), m15, 85; Mikir, 212n;
Minchia (Pa-i), m15; Mongolian,
180; Mon-Khmer, 290f, 296, 677,
683n, 777, m15; Mnong, 746; Mon,
85; Munda, 85; Muong, m15;
Northeast Thailand, 22nf, 431;
Northeastern Thai, 22nf, 78; Nung
(Tai-speaking), m15; Nung-Rawang,
116; Nyang (Nhang), m15; Pa-y,
m15; Padaung, 109; Palaung, 85;
Pali, 625; Phuthai, m15; Red Tai,
m15; Rhadé, 86, 746; Rhadé, in
Vietnam, 777; Saek, m15; in Sarawak,
321; Sedang, 746; Shan-Tai, 132;
Singhpo (Jinghpaw, Ching-po),
212n; Sino-Tibetan, 79, 374n, m15;
Skaw Karen, m15; Standard Burmese,
116; Stieng, 746; T'in, m15; Tai,
84–86, 683f, 778, m15; Tai and
Kam-Sui-Mak, 85; Tai, in China,
185n; Tai Dai, 132; Tai Dau, 132;
Tai Leh in China, 193n; Tai Leng,
132; Tai Lung, 132; Tai Na, in China,
193n; Tai Neua, m15; Tai Nui, 132;
Taungyo, 116; Tavoyan, 116;
Tenasserim dialect, 89n; Tho (Tay),
m15; Tibetan, 180; Tibeto-Burman,
79, 374n; Tibeto-Burman,
Burmese-Lolo, m15; Viet Muong,
m15; Vietnamese, m15; Wa, m15;

369, 374, 390, 528, 563, 639–40
acculturation, 649; administrative connection with Thai government, 49, 657–60; agriculture, 652–53, 658f (see also swidden agriculture, dry-rice cultivation, irrigated agriculture, wet-rice cultivation); ancient Buddhism among, 641, 643–49, 666; and BPP (Border Patrol Police), 662–64 (see also Border Patrol Police); animism among, 641, 643–49; attitude toward central government, 47n, 48; attitudes toward Communism, 663; attitudes toward missionaries, 666

becoming Karen, 34; becoming Thai, 48, 640, 380n, 651f; and BPP (Border Patrol Police), 662–64 (see also Border Patrol Police); bilingualism, 643–49

cash crops (see also agricultural change, irrigated agriculture), 648, 653; in Chiengmai, 31; Christianity among, 664–67; communication among, 643–49; community structure of, 656–60; contacts with Chinese, 646; contacts with Thai, 646; control of village resources, 659

economic relations with Karen, 36, 641, 661; economy of, 643–49, 652f; education of, 662f; effects of literacy on, 664f

household structure, 660
influence of Thai civilization on, 652f; intermarriage, 643–49; irrigated agriculture (see also agriculture), 652, 659; isolation of, 644f

land ownership (see also hill tribes, land ownership, legal status of tribes), 642, 651, 656; language (Mon-Khmer group), 47, 643–49, 664f; leadership among, 656f; legal status, 375; lineages, 656–60; literacy among, 643–49; in lowlands, 668

markets, 646; material culture of, 643–49; and medical care, 661; migration to lowlands, 647–48; missionaries among, 643–49, 664–67; multilingualism, 22nf
"nationalism," 649
opium addiction, 654f
payment of tribute, 640, 642; population in Thailand, 642
relations to central government, 644f, 646; relations with Karen, 641, 647f, 660–62; relations with Northern Thai, 647f; relations with other groups, 641; relations with Prince of Chiengmai,

641; religion, 479, 480, 644f, 659f, 665 (see also animism, Buddhism, Christianity); response to "Communist" threat, 662f; romanized script for language, 664
schools for, 646; settlement patterns of, 641, 644f; as slaves (Kha Lua?), 640; standard of living, 661; swidden agriculture, 658
and taxation, 642, 657f; Thai influence among, 646; trade, 643–49; traditional history, 640; types of villages, 643–49
use of missionary script, 377; use of Thai script, 665
village administration, 657–60
wage work by, 648, 653
Luang Prabang, Laos, 234, 239, 269, 297
Luang Prabang, Laos, princes of, 234f, 240
Luce, G. H., 108
Lue, see Thai-Lue
Lushai Hills, Assam, 217
Lushai of Assam, see Mizo
Lux, T. E., 438n, 444n, 460n

Ma, in South Vietnam, 701n
Ma Chuan-kuo, Gen., 522nf
Ma Hsueh-liang, 23n, 161n, 180n, 193n, 686
Ma Wih, Vietnam highlands religious leader, 753
MAAG (U.S. Military Assistance Advisory Group), in South Vietnam, 713, 731
Mac family of Vietnamese, 787
Macartney, C. A., 126
Madagascar, 86
Madoc, G. C., 310n
Mae Cham District, Thailand, 577
Mae Sod District, Thailand, 546
Maechan nikhom, Thailand, 532, 583
Maehongson Province, Thailand, 109, 374, 383, 479n, 547, 639–74
Maenam River Valley and delta, 10
Maenom (P'anlung), Thailand, 505
Maeping Valley, Thailand, 639
Maesariang, Thailand, 383, 639, 647
Magsaysay, president of Philippines, 743n
majority-minority: in Borneo, 330f
malaria, 301; in China, 194; in Thailand, 384f, 438, 510. See also public health under country headings

Melanau, in Sarawak, 349
Melanesia, 86
Mendelson, E. M., 96, 114
Meng-Huo (Beng Haw), 490n

Meo (Miao), 36; agriculture, 568f;
becoming Yao, 594; bilingualism,
621; competition for land, 568f;
economy, 577; elite, 274f; history,
274n, 278f, 286; income, 577;
migration of, 11, 271, 577, 818;
minorities, and political unrest, 818;
and opium, 35, 568, 577; political
organization of, 9n, 278–82, 823f;
population distribution, 271;
relations with Haw, 577; relations
with Karen, 577; relations with Yao,
616f; use of tribal labor, 568; in
China, 149, 169, 185, 186, 238; in
Kwangsi Province, China, 298;
in Kweichow Province, China,
298; in China, representation of, 183;
in Yunnan Province, China, 298

Meo, in Laos: 9, 235, 238, 241, 244,
248f, 269, 274, 296, 298, 405, 621,
634; administration, 280;
administration in Xieng Khouang
Province, 273; agriculture, 283–85;
and Buddhism, 292; and Christianity,
288, 292; anti-Communism among,
836f; authority structure of, 276;
citizenship, 282; culture change,
289–93; clans, 275f; Communists,
409; division of labor, 285; economy,
282–85, 289f, 298f; education, 290f,
857; folklore, 286–89; history, 271f,
274f; in Laos civil war, 279; in
Xieng Khouang Province, 272;
inheritance, 286; intermarriage, 291;
"invasion" of Thailand, 402f; kinship,
275–78; land ownership, 285; radio
broadcasts to, 269f; newspaper for,
292n; livestock, 284f; loyalties, 292;
marriage, 277f; material culture, 285f;
military organization, 245, 275f, 281;
nationalism of, 282; political change,
290; political organization, 281f;
polygyny, 278f; refugees, 275, 293,
303; relations with Lao, 273f;
religion, 285–89; residence pattern,
276f; role of in Laos, 36f; separate
state for, 25n; settlement of disputes,
280; social structure, 248n, 275f;
opium in Laos, strategic importance
of, 836 (see also under opium);
village composition, 277ff

Meo, in Thailand: 9, 298, 369, 374,
390, 479n, 516, 523, 527f, 533f, 546,
549f, 555, 576f, 654; agriculture,
565–67; ecology, 565–69; language
of, 516; legal status, 375; radio
broadcasts, 386; migration, 567–69;
missionary activity among, 390;
on Thailand border, 8n

Meo, in Vietnam: 249, 287, 298, 677,
683, 694n, 781–84; conflict with
Tai and Yao, 818; ecology, 817f;
economy, 782; motives for joining
Viet Minh, 824; and opium, 817–24;
population, 819; relations with
lowlanders, 782; relations with Tho
and Viet Minh, 819; role in Battle of
Dien Bien Phu, 831–35; social
organization of, 782f; and the Tai
Federation, 817, 819f; in war against
Viet Minh, 815f
Meo-French paramilitary units in
Indochina War, 823
Mesoamerica, 39
messianic movements: among Jarai in
Vietnam, 679; among Jarai and
Sedang in Vietnam, 753; among
Khmu? in Laos, 242; among Meo in
Laos, 242
Methvin, E. H., 433n, 437n, 738n
Miao, see Meo
Micronesia, 86
migration, 6, 9, 11, 33, 34, 525–30
Mikir Hills, Assam, 217
Military Advisory Command, South
Vietnam, 56
military caretaker regime of 1958–1961,
Burma, 94
military training in Vietnam Highlands,
839
military, role in development programs,
482. See also, MDU, Thailand
millenary cults, 110. See also messianic
movements

Minorities and Tribes: and action
programs, 56; adaptation to central
governments, 10; attributes of, 4n,
15–17, 42; autonomous areas for
(see also Assam, China, India, North
Vietnam), 149; as buffers, 108, 118;
cultural change among, 9; definition
of (see also ethnic labels, cultural
boundaries), 134, 369; derogatory
terms for (see also "kha"), 9, 108,
490, 528; discrimination against, 9;
and ecological distinctions, 113, 136;

economic distinctions of, 113f;
government policies on, 23–29, 171;
integration of (*see also* assimilation),
143, 145; international implications
of, 8n, 45, 53, 65f; language
distinctions among, 115f; and
majorities, 134; markets and trade,
110, 117f, 135; migrations of, 12; and
missionaries, 130; and nationalism,
129; political development of, 116f,
119; pluralism of, 145; relations with
central governments, 29–54; religious
distinctions among, 114f; resistance
to change, 32; and secession, 171;
self-identification of, 76; social
science theories concerning, 101f;
social structural distinctions among,
114f; sophistication of, 9; as source of
instability, 126f; standard of living,
9; symbolic interaction of, 138;
symbols of distinctness, 110. *See also*
tribes.
  in Assam: 216f, 224–25; population,
216f
  in Burma: British policy on, 129;
international implications of, 29;
government policies on, 98f, 145;
national representation, 50; political
rights of, 95
  in Cambodia: 53; international
implications of, 24n
  in China: on borderlands, 149; in
Chinese revolution, 150; "divide and
rule," 127; government policies on, 25,
149–51; rebellions of, 199–201; and
self-determination, 197
  in India: administration of, 217;
attitudes toward majority, 219;
attributes of, 215; autonomous areas
for, 220–23; conflict with majority, 219;
cultural integration of, 228; economic
development, 227f; economic
integration, 228; economic relations
with majority, 205; government of, 217;
government policies on, 213n;
international implications of
(India-Pakistan), 221; international
implications of (India-China), 221;
relations with majority, 205;
representation of, 206, 216f, 222, 225;
symbolic distinctions, 219f
  in Indonesian-Malaysian
"Confrontation," 66
  in Kalimantan, 348
  in Laos: assimilation, 242, 247; and
Laos civil war, 246, 262–66; derogatory
term for, 241; education, 300;

language policy, 300; medical care,
300f; modernization of, 246; relations
with majority, 239, 241, 248, 261, 302;
representation, 241, 243–46, 608, 616f
  in Malaysia: administration of, 308;
British colonial policies on, 309
  in New World, 144
  in Sabah: 62; language policies on
365; legal status of, 360
  in Sarawak: administration of,
345–47; attitudes toward, 336, 342;
conflict resolution, 346; land laws
concerning, 348f; legal relations with
majority, 344f; and natural resources,
350f; population, 331; representation
of, 336, 347, 348n; self-rule, 346f;
taxation, 351f
  in Thailand: attitudes toward central
government, 401–24; communication
with central government, 393f, 401–24;
economic relations with Thai, 393;
education, 376f, 382; government
policies on, 539–43, 554–56; language
policies on, 376f, 385f, 479, 502, 513;
language research on, 573; legal status
of, 375–77, 529, 540; loyalties, 416;
nationalism of, 387f; ownership of
resources (*see also* land ownership; land
laws), 376n, 392f; population, 369–78,
relations with other minorities, 528;
representation of, 50f, 380, 430, 539,
607; symbolic importance of food, 442
  in Vietnam: 53; and national unity,
786–90. *See also* Vietnam highlanders
  in North Vietnam: autonomy of, 151,
249; government policies on, 25
  in South Vietnam: international
implications of, 53; and National
Liberation Front (NLF), 25;
representation of, 683n
minority group: definition, 131–35
minority problems, social science
approaches to, 125–31
minority relations (intra-minority
relations): and cultural exclusivity,
104; effects of colonialism on, 127;
historical background of, 127f;
religion and, 96; and social
philosophy, 102
Mishimi Hills District, Assam, 217
Mission Etrangère, in South Vietnam,
862
Mission Evangelique, in South
Vietnam, 862
missionaries: in Borneo, 356; in Burma,
96f, 389; conflicts among, 391; in
Laos, 291–92; and literacy, 46f; and

modernization, 46f, 141; relations
with minorities and central
governments, 667; role in annexation
of Chiengmai, Thailand, 389; in
Thailand, 388–92
Mizo, in Nagaland, 206
Mizo Hills District, Assam, 206,
217, 219
Mizo National Front, in India, 223
Mizo National Front, in Nagaland, 206n
Mnong (Viet-Muong), in Vietnam,
757, 778; elite, 757; kinship system
of 755; relations with French, 752f;
slavery among, 757; sorcerers
among, 758
Mnong Gar, 757
Mobile Development Unit Program,
Thailand, *see* MDU
mobile extension scheme, Thailand,
536f, 546, 548
Mobile Information Teams, Thailand,
433f
mobilization, 39, 42; and social
disorganization, 53; of unmobilized
peasants, 39. *See also* action
programs
Modelski, G., 793
modernization, 3–66; attitudes of
minorities toward, 58; desire for
among tribes, 26; effects on
rural-urban gap, 673; effects on
tribal economy, 52; in India, 226–28;
and MDU model villages program,
Thailand, 458–70; role of political
agencies in, 49. *See also* action
programs
Moerman, M., 32, 112, 406, 420, 421,
423, 430, 432f, 440, 442, 444
Mohr, C., 53, 686
moi, see minorities, derogatory terms
for
Mon, in Burma, 50, 75, 94, 114, 116,
130; migrations of, 12; in Thailand,
373, 390, 640
Mon-Khmer languages, *see* languages
Mon-Khmer languages, Northern Laos
group, m15
Mon-Khmer languages, Palaungic
group, m15
Mon-speaking peoples, 10
Mon National Defense Organization, in
Burma, 26, 93
Mon in Burma, nationalism among, 116
Mon refugees, in Thailand, 373
Mondulkiri Province, Cambodia, 24
Mongolians, in China, 170, 172;

attitudes toward Chinese, 178; in
government of Inner Mongolia, 174;
representation of, 183
montagnards of South Vietnam, 55, 66,
745–69. *See also* minorities in
Vietnam; Vietnam highlanders
Moorman, F. R., 544, 568
Morechand, G., 271n, 287, 778n
Moseley, G., 150
Mosel, J. N., 435n
Moslem, *see* Muslim
Mount Kinabalu, Sabah, 353, 363
Mrabri, in Thailand, 374
multilingualism, 22fn. *See also*
bilingualism
muong (Tai principality), 779–84
Muong, in North Vietnam, 683
Murchie, G., 448n
Murphy, C. J. V., 233
Murut, in Borneo, 331
Murut, in Sabah, 340, 353, 354, 356;
agriculture, 357f; economy, 356,
358, 359; loyalties, 363; material
culture, 356, 358; military actions,
363; relations with British, 363;
subtribes, 356
Murut, in Sarawak, 321, 333, 337, 347
Muslim, 21f; council of Thailand, 480;
minority in Thailand, 372n, 401,
480f, 491f, 497f, 861f; in Malaysia,
330
Mussuh, *see* Lahu
Mus, P., 688n, 795n
Mya Maung, Dr., 851n

Nadel, S. F., 107
Naga Hills, Assam, 217
Nagas, 205, 206n, 220–23
nai amphur, importance of in
Thailand, 475–78
Nakhon Panom Province, Thailand,
432, 454, 457n, 461n, 464
Nam Khyng, Laos, 583
Nam Tha Province, Laos, 296f
Nan, Thailand, 369, 409, 547;
Thailand, Prince of, 405, 408
Narai, King of Ayuthaya, 388
Nash, M., 77n, 114
Nasi, in China, 170
"nation," concept of, 103; definition
of, 40
nation-building, 3–66, 119; among
Thai-Lue in Thailand, 419; and
Buddhism, 469; in Burma, 24f; and
the colonial legacy, 129;

national unity, 21, 50; and national
unity in Malaysia, 330
religions: in Laos, 240; in Southeast
Asia, general, 21f. *See also* under
names of individual religions and
sects
religious syncretism, 22
research: on hill agriculture, in
Thailand, 544–46; on hill tribes,
Thailand, 549, 553–81; on
modernization of tribes, in Burma,
856; needs, Thailand, 535; relation
to government, 472; on tribal
languages, Sabah, 858; on tribes, in
Laos, 259
research programs, Thailand, *see*
Department of Public Welfare,
Tribal Research Centre
reservation system, United States, 59.
See also American Indians, Indian
Reorganization Act
resettlement, 7n, 12, 60; in Burma, 7n,
144; in Cambodia, 7n, 24n; in
China, 7n; in Indonesia, 7n; in Laos,
7n; in Malayan Emergency, 264f; and
modernization, 264–66; of refugees
in Laos, 264–66; in Sabah, 361f; in
Sarawak, 320n; in Shan and Kachin
States, Burma, 853f; in South
Vietnam highlands, 838f; in
Thailand (*see also nikhom*), 7n, 467,
535, 544–46, 859f; in Vietnam, 7n,
708nf
revitalization movement, among Meo
in Laos, 292. *See also* messianic
movements
"revolution from above," in Thailand,
483
Rhadé, and FULRO, 682f; customary
law, 756; elite, 757; "king of the
mois," 750f; kinship system, 755; land
ownership (*see also po lan*), 751f,
767; in North Vietnam, 686n;
political structures of, 9n; relations
with French, 752f; role in Vietnam
highlands, 682, 839f; in South
Vietnam, 54, 55, 683; in South
Vietnam, agriculture of, 766; in
South Vietnam, cash crops of, 764n;
in Vietnam, 678, 681, 686; in
Vietnam tribal rebellions, 761; in
World War II, 789f
rightists, in Laos, 244
Roi-et Province, Thailand, 431
role complementation, 108
roles, 106f

Roman Catholics, in Burma, 97
Roux, H. and Tran Van Chu, 271n
Roy, J., 772n, 773, 786n
Royal Lao Government, 8n, 273;
minorities policy of, 245
Ruey Yih-fu, 238
Rupen, R. A., 174n, 180n, 184n, 195n
rural Chinese ("Haw"), in Northern
Thailand, *see* Yunnanese Chinese
rural minority, *see* minorities
rural-urban gap, 17, 27; in Thailand,
423, 425, 432n; in Vietnam, 688
Rusk, Dean, 443
Russian Communists, 197
Russians, in Kalimantan, 350

Sabah (British North Borneo), 12,
307, 317f, 340; administration of,
340; administration of minorities in,
360; agricultural change, 361f;
Americans in, 355; education in, 361;
ethnic distributions in, 340;
European influence in, 354;
geography of, 353; history, 354f;
land law in, 361f; medical care in,
361; military operations in, 353;
natural resources, 358; population of,
353f; research on tribal languages,
858; religions in, 330; taxation,
361–62; transportation in, 353; hill
tribes in, *see* hill tribes; minorities
Sabah Border Scouts, 356, 359, 363
Sabatier, L., 682, 751nf, 756, 763
sacred kingdoms, 19. *See also*
Buddhist monarchy
Sadets (Jarai sorcerers), 747, 750, 755,
758–60; current role of, 760;
functions of, 759; relations with
Cambodia, 747, 758f; succession of,
759. *See also* Jarai
Sahlins, M. D., 18n
Sai Kham, Chao, 273ff
Saifudin, 183
Saigon, South Vietnam, 291, 353
Sak-Kadu, in Burma, 108
Sakai, in Sarawak, 342
Sakonnakhorn Province, Thailand, 432,
445, 461n, 462, 464
Salween River, 528
Sam Neua Province, Laos, 244, 245n,
258n, 269, 296, 297, 780
Sam Thong Refugee Center, Laos, 273,
299f
Sama Duwa of the Kachin, in Burma, 95
Sangha, *see* Shan Buddhist organization
in Burma

Sip Song Chao Tai (Twelve Tai Principalities), Northwest Vietnam, 236f, 243, 779, 783, 807, 833

Sip Song Pan Na, Yunnan Province, China, 237, 780 (see also Hsi-Shuang Pan-Na)

Sithdone Province, Laos, 244n

Sithone Komadam, 246

Skaw (Sgaw) Karen, in Burma, 110–15

Skaw (Sgaw) Karen, in Thailand: 113, 390, 639–74; acculturation of, 651f; animism among, 650; and Buddhism, 650; Christianity among, 650; district differentiation among, 650; economy, 644f; education, 650; history, 641; intermarriage, 644f; isolation of, 650; language, 644; local administration, 650; material culture of, 644f, 650–51 migration, 641, 651f; multilingualism, 650–61; opium addiction, 654f; relations with central government, 651; religions, 644f, 650, 651; settlement patterns, 641, 644f; village organization, 649–52

Skinner, G. W., 89n, 258n, 373, 375, 399n, 694n, 701n, 867n

Slimming, J., 310n

Smalley, W. A., 23n, 238, 242, 258n, 272, 373, 377, 380n, 383, 390, 399n, 669

Smith, D. E., 77n

Smith, Maj. W., Jr., 709n

Smith, R. M., 7n

So, in Thailand, 433, 464

Soai, in Thailand, 373

Sochurek, H., 55, 56, 686, 839

social stratification, 205

social systems, theory of, 93–124

"Socialist Education Movement," in China, 192

Societe de la Mission Etrangère de Paris, 760, 862

"a society," concept of, 101

socio-cultural integration, 40

Son La uprising, 811

sorcerers, see Sadets

Souphanavong, Prince, 303

South Korea, 250

South Vietnam, 57, 235; administrative divisions of, m13; Communist appeals to, 739f; Constituent Assembly of, 683n; Constitution of, 684, 738; control of minorities in, 709n; decentralization of administration, 742f; decline of administration, 706f; delta villages in, 718n; elections in,

705; government of, 8n; government relations with hill tribes, 53; National Liberation Front (NLF) in, 8n, 24n; language policies in, 680; minority legal status, 684; minorities policies, 680–83, 687, 763–65, 840; recommendations for research, 741f; refugees in, 709n; resettlement programs in, 680

South Vietnamese, relations with minorities, 680–83

Southeast Asia Treaty Organization, see SEATO

Southwest Union University, China, 499

Souvanna Phouma, Prince, 245, 302, 857

Spanish Americans, 41

Special Division of the Chins, Burma, 38

special forces, see U. S. Army Special Forces

specialized organizations, 49

Sre, in South Vietnam, 701n

Srivijaya, 525

Stacey, T., 310n

State Religion Act, Burma, 96–98, 120

Stern, T., 44, 52, 110, 115, 369, 373f, 378, 380n, 384n

Steward, J., 40

Stieng, in Vietnam, slavery among, 757

Stung Treng Province, Cambodia, 24n

strategic hamlets: American role in, 740; decentralized administration, 740; defense of, 718f; deterioration of, 734; education programs in, 731; intelligence systems in, 724–27; local newspapers in, 725f; local radio in, 726; medical care in, 730; role of militia in, 731; training personnel in, 717–19; U.S. aid to, 740f. See also action programs in Vietnam

strategic hamlet program: 57, 59, 703, 706–44; aims, 71f; costs, 732; decentralized administration in, 715, 740; education program, 727; evaluation of, 720f, 736–41; origins, 707–28; methods, 711–28; propaganda program, 727; public health measures, 727; results, 721–41; Viet Cong reaction to, 719, 721, 733, 739f

subsistence agriculture, 20, 35, 139. See also agriculture

Sulu, in Sabah, 354

Sun Yat-sen, 198

Sutherland, H., 233

sorcerers in (*see also* Jarai sorcerers), 758–60; South Vietnamese administration of, 754; South Vietnamese legislation on, 763–65; taboos in, 758; tribal revolts against French, 748–53; Viet Cong action in, 762; Viet Minh in, 753f; Vietnamese control of, 747f

Vietnam highlanders: 241, 745–769; aspirations of, 761; characteristics of, 776; land tenure among, 767f; legal status of, 762f; nationalism among, 762; in North Vietnam, 753

Vietnam hill tribes, *see* Vietnam highlanders

Vietnam minorities, role in French Indochina War, 771–884; geographical classification, 783

Vietnamese: expansion of, 6, 677n, 784–90; in Cambodia, 8n, 24, 54, 677n; in China (Ching), 159; in Laos, 237, 272; of North Vietnam, 678n; in Thailand, 430n; relations with Vietnam highlanders, 678; in South Vietnam, 56; southward expansion of, 11

Vietnamization of Tho, 780ff, 788. *See also* Tho in Vietnam

Vijaya, 746

village cooperation, in Thailand, 444–47

village headmen, role in Thailand action programs, 422–24

Vo Nguyen Giap, 708, 772n

Wa (Kawa) in Burma: 45, 75, 118; and Chinese, 149

Wa State, Burma, 19

Wachirawut, King of Thailand, 435

Wagley, C., 144

Wallace, A. F. C., 292

Walterhouse, H. F., 443

Wanat Bhruksasri, 575

Warner, D., 273, 709n, 837

Wars of national liberation, 743n

Weiner, M., 43

Wells, K. E., 389, 390f

westernization, 97

Westwood, T., 310n

wet-rice cultivation, 76; in Thailand, 14. *See also* agriculture, irrigated agriculture

White Tai (Tai Blanc), in Vietnam, 683, 694n, 778; relations with Black Tai, 807–11; relations with Viet Minh, 811f. *See also* Tai

Whyte, W. F., and Williams, L. K., 471

Wiens, H., 187n

"wild Wa," in Burma, *see* Wa

Wilhelm, H., 161n

Williams-Hunt, P. D. R., 60n

Wilson, D. A., 27, 39, 430

"winning hearts and minds," 56. *See also* action programs

Wolf, E., 18n, 39, 40

Woodman, D., 129, 142

Woodruff, L. W., 688n

World Bank Advisory Group, Thailand, 433n

World Health Organization (WHO), in Sarawak, 334, 346; in Thailand, 384

World War II, 18, 75, 126, 141–43, 216, 221, 235, 240, 249, 278, 281, 292n, 375, 392n, 492f, 664, 708, 753, 789f; in Indochina, 684; in Malaysia, 310

Worldwide Evangelization Crusade, in Thailand, 390

writing systems, *see* languages

Wulff, R., 386

Xa, in North Vietnam, 695n

Xa family of Black Tai, 812

Xieng Khouang, Laos, 272, 778; prince of, and Meo, 246; princes of, 234f, 273

Province: 233, 295; administration of, 273; civil war in, 272f; ethnic distribution in, 271f; governor of, 235, 242; transportation in, 272f; relations with Annam, 273; relations with rest of Laos, 273

Y Bham Enoul, Rhadé leader, 682, 683n, 761f

Y Binh Aleo, 681

Y Thih, Jarai sadet, 759

ya, spirits of Bahnar and Sedang, 753

Ya Ba, Col., 761

Yang, C. K., 622

YAO (In Mien, Man): 5n; adaptation to administrative change, 622; adaptation to central governments, 586f; adaptation to economic change, 609; adoption, 36, 585n, 594, 634; afterlife, 614n; ancestor worship, 590nf; and Chinese, 149; attitude toward central governments, 48; attitudes toward lowlanders, 621; attitudes toward other hill tribes, 621; bilingualism, 625;

Other books published for
The Center of International Studies
Woodrow Wilson School of Public and
International Affairs

Gabriel A. Almond, *The Appeals of Communism*
Gabriel A. Almond and James S. Coleman, editors, *The Politics of the Developing Areas*
Gabriel A. Almond and Sidney Verba, *The Civic Culture: Political Attitudes and Democracy in Five Nations*
Richard J. Barnet and Richard A. Falk, *Security in Disarmament*
Cyril E. Black and Thomas P. Thornton, editors, *Communism and Revolution: The Strategic Uses of Political Violence*
Robert J. C. Butow, *Tojo and the Coming of the War*
Miriam Camps, *Britain and the European Community, 1955–1963*
Bernard C. Cohen, *The Political Process and Foreign Policy: The Making of the Japanese Peace Settlement*
Bernard C. Cohen, *The Press and Foreign Policy*
Charles De Visscher, *Theory and Reality in Public International Law*, translated by P. E. Corbett
Frederick S. Dunn, *Peace-making and the Settlement with Japan*
Harry Eckstein, *Division and Cohesion in Democracy: a Study of Norway*
Richard F. Hamilton, *Affluence and the French Worker in the Fourth Republic*
Herman Kahn, *On Thermonuclear War*
W. W. Kaufmann, editor, *Military Policy and National Security*
Klaus Knorr, *On the Uses of Military Power in the Nuclear Age*
Klaus Knorr, *The War Potential of Nations*
Klaus Knorr, editor, *NATO and American Security*
Klaus Knorr and Sidney Verba, editors, *The International System: Theoretical Essays*
Peter Kunstadter, editor, *Southeast Asian Tribes, Minorities, and Nations*
Sidney J. Ploss, *Conflict and Decision-making in Soviet Russia*
Lucian W. Pye, *Guerrilla Communism in Malaya*
James N. Rosenau, editor, *International Aspects of Civil Strife*
James N. Rosenau, *National Leadership and Foreign Policy: A Case Study in the Mobilization of Public Support*
Rolf Sannwald and Jacques Stohler, *Economic Integration: Theoretical Assumptions and Consequences of European Unification*. Translated by Herman F. Karreman
Richard L. Sklar, *Nigerian Political Parties: Power in an Emergent African Nation*
Glenn H. Snyder, *Deterrence and Defense*
Harold and Margaret Sprout, *The Ecological Perspective on Human Affairs, With Special Reference to International Politics*
Thomas P. Thornton, *The Third World in Soviet Perspective: Studies by Soviet Writers on the Developing Areas*
Sidney Verba, *Small Groups and Political Behavior: A Study of Leadership*
Karl von Vorys, *Political Development in Pakistan*
Myron Weiner, *Party Politics in India*
E. Victor Wolfenstein, *The Revolutionary Personality: Lenin, Trotsky, Ghandi*
Oran R. Young, *The Intermediaries: Third Parties in International Crises*

Map Section

Map 3. CHINA—*Administrative Divisions. Redrawn from China: Provisional Atlas of Communist Administrative Units (CIA/RR GR 59-20). Washington, D.C., U.S. Department of Commerce, Office of Technical Service, 1959, and modified with more recent information.*

Map 4. CHINA—*Minority Autonomous Administrative Divisions of the Southwest. Redrawn from China: Provisional Atlas of Communist Administrative Units (CIA/RR GR 59-20). Washington, D.C., U.S. Department of Commerce, Office of Technical Service, 1959, and modified with more recent information.*

Map 9. THAILAND—*Administrative Divisions. Redrawn from map of Thailand prepared by Thai-American Audiovisual Service, July, 1962.*

Map 13. SOUTH VIETNAM—*Administrative Divisions. Redrawn from Population Density Map of South Vietnam, Scale 1:500,000, U.S. Army Corps of Engineers, Army Map Service, Edition 1-AMS, 6-64.*

Map 15. NORTHERN INDOCHINA—*Distribution of Languages.* Sources:

LeBar, Frank M. *et al.* Ethnolinguistic groups of Mainland Southeast Asia, map accompanying Ethnic Groups of Mainland Southeast Asia, New Haven, Conn., Human Relations Area Files Press, 1964.

Service Géographique de l'Indochine, Carte Ethnolinguistique prepared under the direction of l'Ecole Française d'Extrême Orient, 1949 edition.

Young, Gordon. The hill tribes of Northern Thailand. Bangkok, Siam Society, second edition.

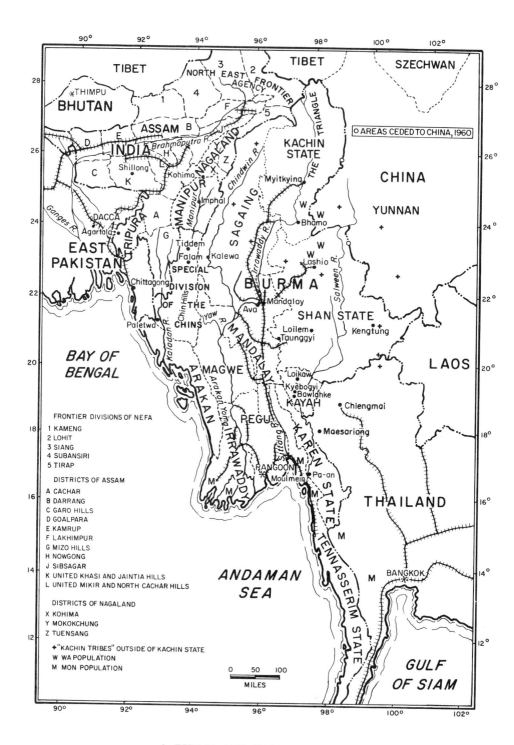

1. BURMA AND EASTERN INDIA

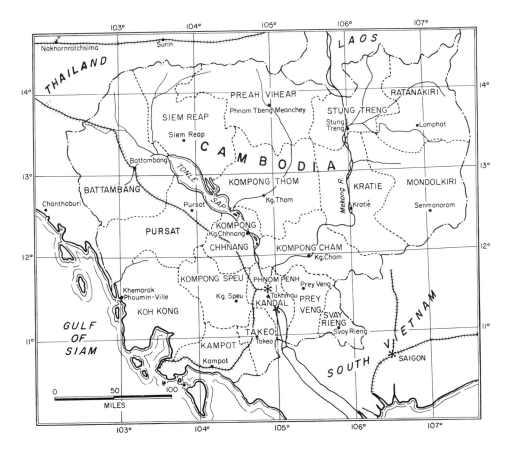

2. CAMBODIA

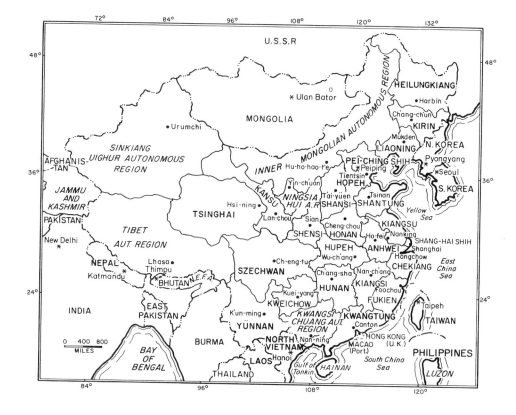

3. CHINA—ADMINISTRATIVE DIVISIONS

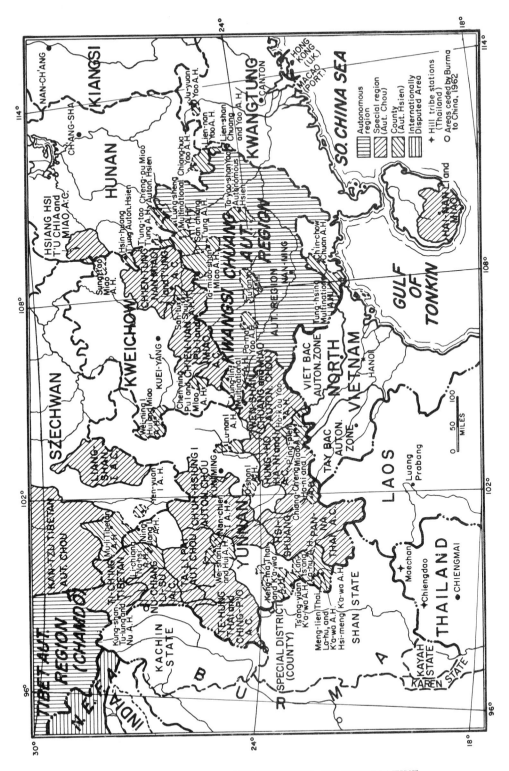

4. CHINA—MINORITY AUTONOMOUS ADMINISTRATIVE
DIVISIONS OF THE SOUTHWEST

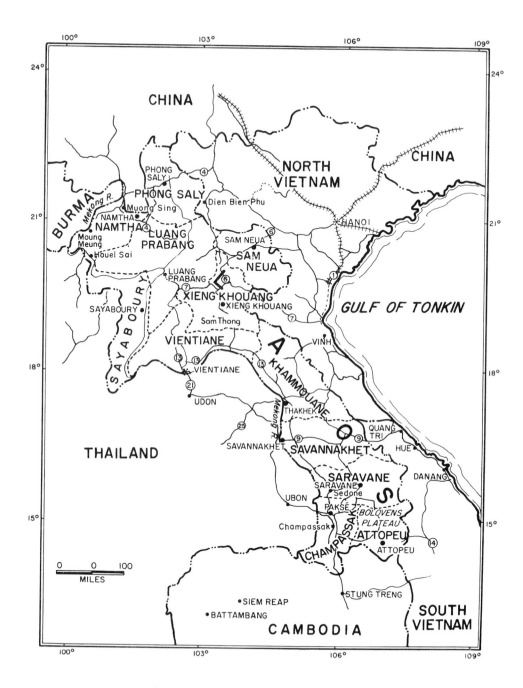

5. LAOS—ADMINISTRATIVE DIVISIONS

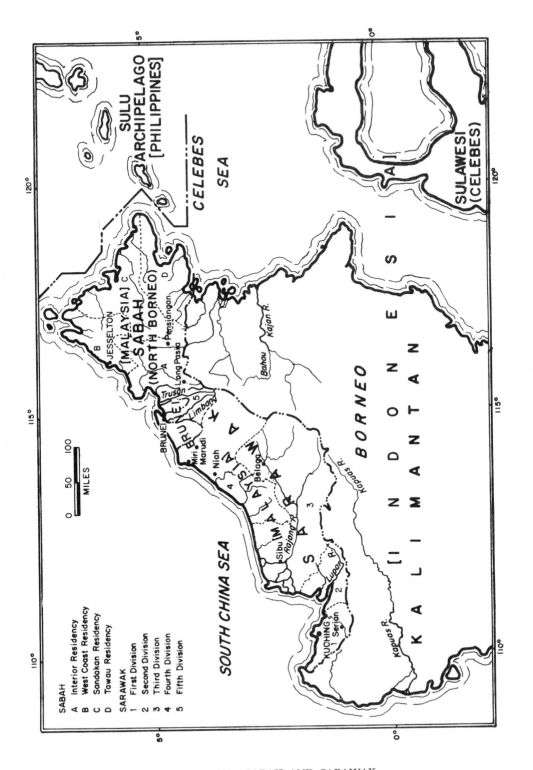

SABAH
A   Interior Residency
B   West Coast Residency
C   Sandakan Residency
D   Tawau Residency

SARAWAK
1   First Division
2   Second Division
3   Third Division
4   Fourth Division
5   Fifth Division

SULU
ARCHIPELAGO
[PHILIPPINES]

CELEBES
SEA

SULAWESI
(CELEBES)

[MALAYSIA]
SABAH
(NORTH BORNEO)

JESSELTON

Pensiangan

Long Pasia

Trusan

Bahau

Kajan R.

BRUNEI

Limbang

Miri

Marudi

Niah

Belaga

Sibu

Rajang R.

Kanowit R.

Lupar R.

KUCHING

Serian

Kapuas R.

Kapuas R.

SOUTH CHINA SEA

BORNEO

[INDONESIA]

KALIMANTAN

MILES

0   50   100

6. MALAYSIA—SABAH AND SARAWAK

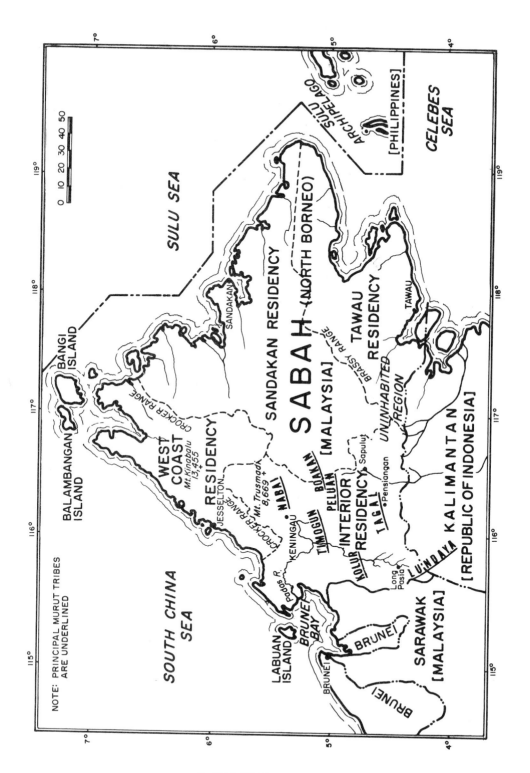

SABAH (NORTH BORNEO) [MALAYSIA]

SULU SEA

CELEBES SEA

SULU ARCHIPELAGO

[PHILIPPINES]

SANDAKAN RESIDENCY

SANDAKAN

BRASSY RANGE

TAWAU RESIDENCY

TAWAU

UNINHABITED REGION

BANGI ISLAND

CROCKER RANGE

WEST COAST RESIDENCY

Mt.Kinabalu 13,455 +

JESSELTON

CROCKER RANGE

Mt. Trusmadi 8,669 +

NABAI

BUAYAN

PELUAN

Sapulut

INTERIOR RESIDENCY

Pensiangan

TAGAL

BALAMBANGAN ISLAND

SOUTH CHINA SEA

TIMOGUN

KENINGAU

KOLUR

Padas R.

Long Pasia

LUNDAYA

KALIMANTAN [REPUBLIC OF INDONESIA]

LABUAN ISLAND

BRUNEI BAY

BRUNEI

BRUNEI

SARAWAK [MALAYSIA]

BRUNEI

NOTE: PRINCIPAL MURUT TRIBES ARE UNDERLINED

0 10 20 30 40 50

7° 6° 5° 4°

119° 118° 117° 116° 115°

7. MALAYSIA—SABAH

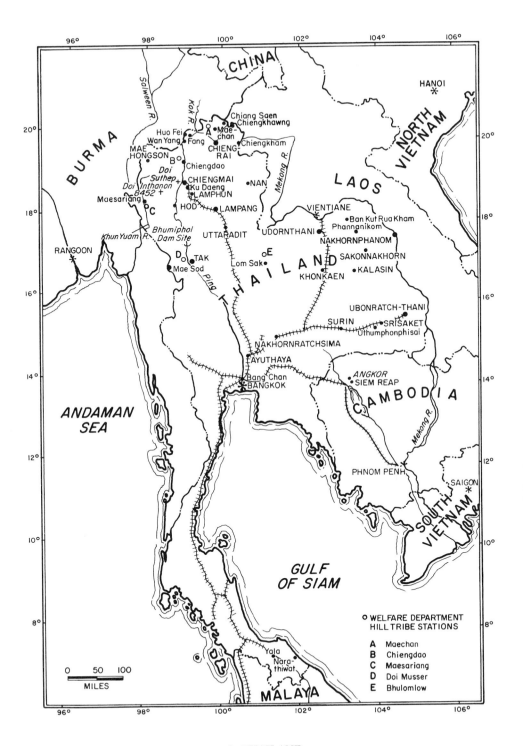

96°   98°   100°   102°   104°   106°

CHINA

HANOI

Salween R.

BURMA

Kok R.

Chiang Saen
Chiengkhawng
Mae-chan
A
Huo Fei
Wan Yang Fang
CHIENG-
RAI
Chiengkham

MAE
HONGSON
B
Chiengdao
Doi
Suthep CHIENGMAI
Doi Inthanon Ku Daeng
8452 LAMPHUN
Maesariang
C
HOD

NAN

Mekong R.

LAOS

NORTH
VIETNAM

VIENTIANE

Ban Kut Rua Kham
Phannanikom

Bhumiphol
Dam Site UTTARADIT

UDORNTHANI

NAKHORNPHANOM

RANGOON

Khun Yuam R.

LAMPANG

D TAK
Mae Sod

Lom Sak

oE

SAKONNAKHORN

KHONKAEN

KALASIN

THAILAND

Ping

UBONRATCH-THANI

SURIN SRISAKET
Uthumphonphisai

NAKHORNRATCHSIMA

AYUTHAYA

ANDAMAN
SEA

Bang Chan
BANGKOK

ANGKOR
SIEM REAP

CAMBODIA

Mekong R.

PHNOM PENH

SAIGON

SOUTH
VIETNAM

GULF
OF SIAM

○ WELFARE DEPARTMENT
HILL TRIBE STATIONS

A Maechan
B Chiengdao
C Maesariang
D Doi Musser
E Bhulomlow

0 50 100
MILES

Yala
Nara-
thiwat

MALAYA

8. THAILAND

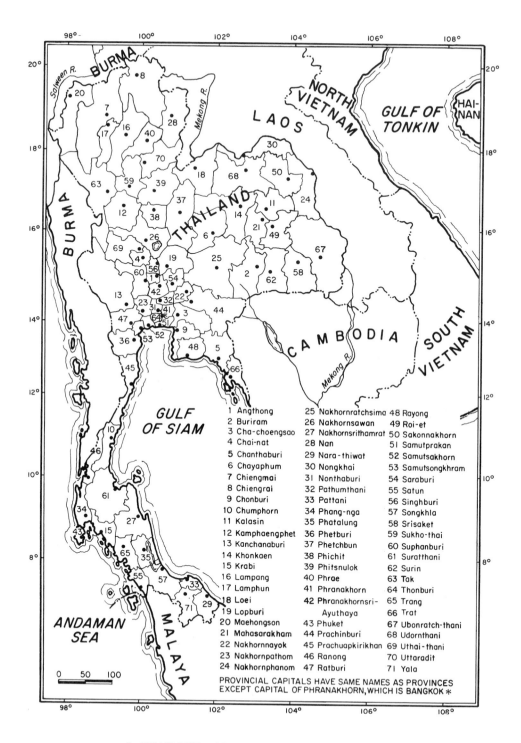

1 Angthong	25 Nakhornratchsima	48 Rayong
2 Buriram	26 Nakhornsawan	49 Roi-et
3 Cha-choengsao	27 Nakhornsrithamrat	50 Sakonnakhorn
4 Chai-nat	28 Nan	51 Samutprakan
5 Chanthaburi	29 Nara-thiwat	52 Samutsakhorn
6 Chayaphum	30 Nongkhai	53 Samutsongkhram
7 Chiengmai	31 Nonthaburi	54 Saraburi
8 Chiengrai	32 Pathumthani	55 Satun
9 Chonburi	33 Pattani	56 Singhburi
10 Chumphorn	34 Phang-nga	57 Songkhla
11 Kalasin	35 Phatalung	58 Srisaket
12 Kamphaengphet	36 Phetburi	59 Sukho-thai
13 Kanchanaburi	37 Phetchbun	60 Suphanburi
14 Khonkaen	38 Phichit	61 Suratthani
15 Krabi	39 Phitsnulok	62 Surin
16 Lampang	40 Phrae	63 Tak
17 Lamphun	41 Phranakhorn	64 Thonburi
18 Loei	42 Phranakhornsri-	65 Trang
19 Lopburi	Ayuthaya	66 Trat
20 Maehongson	43 Phuket	67 Ubonratch-thani
21 Mahasarakham	44 Prachinburi	68 Udornthani
22 Nakhornnayok	45 Prachuapkirikhan	69 Uthai-thani
23 Nakhornpathom	46 Ranong	70 Uttaradit
24 Nakhornphanom	47 Ratburi	71 Yala

PROVINCIAL CAPITALS HAVE SAME NAMES AS PROVINCES
EXCEPT CAPITAL OF PHRANAKHORN, WHICH IS BANGKOK *

9. THAILAND—ADMINISTRATIVE DIVISIONS

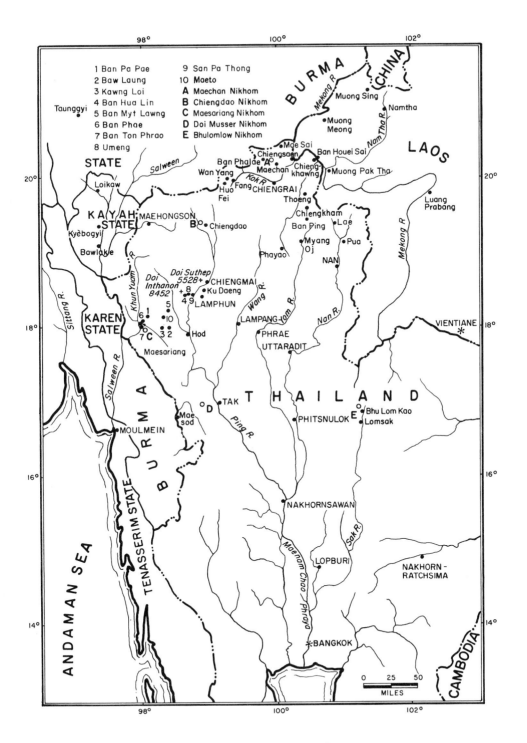

1 Ban Pa Pae
2 Baw Laung
3 Kawng Loi
4 Ban Hua Lin
5 Ban Myt Lawng
6 Ban Phae
7 Ban Ton Phrao
8 Umeng
9 San Pa Thong
10 Maeto
A Maechan Nikhom
B Chiengdao Nikhom
C Maesariang Nikhom
D Doi Musser Nikhom
E Bhulomlow Nikhom

BURMA
CHINA
Mekong R
Muong Sing
Namtha
Muong Meong
Nam Tha R.
LAOS
Taunggyi
STATE
Salween
Mae Sai
Chiengsaan
Ban Houei Sai
Ban Phalae
Maechan
Chieng-khawng
Muong Pak Tha
Wan Yang
Koh R.
Fang
CHIENGRAI
Thoeng
Luang Prabang
Huo Fei
Chiengkham
Ban Ping
Lae
Mekong R.
Loikaw
KAYAH STATE
MAEHONGSON
Chiengdao
Myang Oi
Pua
Kyèbogyi
Phayao
NAN
Bawlake
Doi Suthep 5528+
Doi Inthanon 8452
CHIENGMAI
+ 8
Ku Daeng
Wang R.
Nan R.
VIENTIANE
KAREN STATE
LAMPHUN
Khun Yuam
5
6
10
4 9
LAMPANG
Yom R.
Sittang R.
7 C
3 2
Hod
PHRAE
UTTARADIT
Maesariang
THAILAND
Salween R.
Mae sod
D
TAK
Ping R.
PHITSNULOK
E
Bhu Lom Kao
Lomsak
BURMA
MOULMEIN
TENASSERIM STATE
NAKHORNSAWAN
ANDAMAN SEA
Maenam Chao Phraya
Sak R.
LOPBURI
NAKHORN-RATCHSIMA
BANGKOK
CAMBODIA
0   25   50
MILES

10. THAILAND—DETAIL

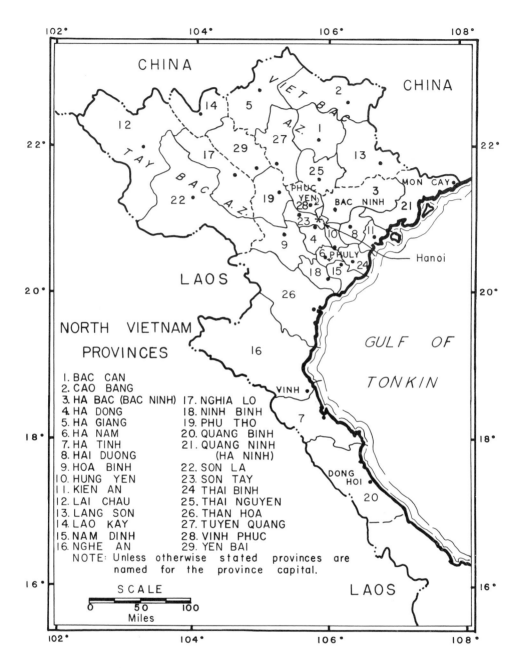

CHINA

CHINA

VIET BAC A.Z.

TAY BAC A.Z.

LAOS

NORTH VIETNAM
PROVINCES

1. BAC CAN
2. CAO BANG
3. HA BAC (BAC NINH) 17. NGHIA LO
4. HA DONG   18. NINH BINH
5. HA GIANG   19. PHU THO
6. HA NAM   20. QUANG BINH
7. HA TINH   21. QUANG NINH
8. HAI DUONG   (HA NINH)
9. HOA BINH   22. SON LA
10. HUNG YEN   23. SON TAY
11. KIEN AN   24. THAI BINH
12. LAI CHAU   25. THAI NGUYEN
13. LANG SON   26. THAN HOA
14. LAO KAY   27. TUYEN QUANG
15. NAM DINH   28. VINH PHUC
16. NGHE AN   29. YEN BAI
    NOTE: Unless otherwise stated provinces are
          named for the province capital.

SCALE

0   50   100
      Miles

PHUC YEN 28
BAC NINH
PHULY
Hanoi

GULF OF

TONKIN

VINH

DONG HOI

LAOS

11. NORTH VIETNAM—ADMINISTRATIVE DIVISIONS

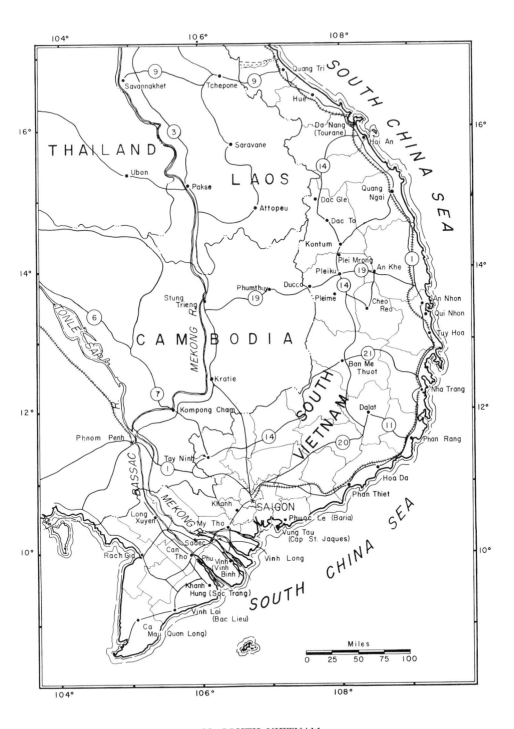

104°   106°   108°

⑨ Savannakhet   Tchepone   ⑨   Quang Tri   SOUTH CHINA SEA

Hué

16°   THAILAND   ③   Saravane   LAOS   Da Nang (Tourane)   16°

Hoi An

⑭

Ubon

Pakse   Dac Gle   Quang Ngai

Attopeu   Dac To

Kontum

14°   Plei Mrong   ①   14°

Pleiku ⑲   An Khe

Phumthuy   Ducco ⑭

⑲   Pleime   Cheo Reo

Stung Trieng   An Nhon

⑥   Qui Nhon

TONLE SAP   Tuy Hoa

CAMBODIA   ㉑   Ban Me Thuot

MEKONG R.   SOUTH   Nha Trang

Kratie   VIETNAM   Dalat   12°

12°   ⑦   ⑪

Kompong Cham   ⑳   Phan Rang

Phnom Penh   ⑭

Tay Ninh   Hoa Da

①   Phan Thiet

BASSAC   Khanh   SAIGON

Long Xuyen   MEKONG   My Tho   Phuoc Le (Baria)   SOUTH CHINA SEA

10°   Sadec   Vung Tau (Cap St. Jaques)   10°

Rach Gia   Can Tho   Phu Vinh (Vinh Binh)   Vinh Long

Khanh Hung (Soc Trang)

Vinh Loi (Bac Lieu)

Ca Mau (Quan Long)

Miles

0   25   50   75   100

104°   106°   108°

12. SOUTH VIETNAM

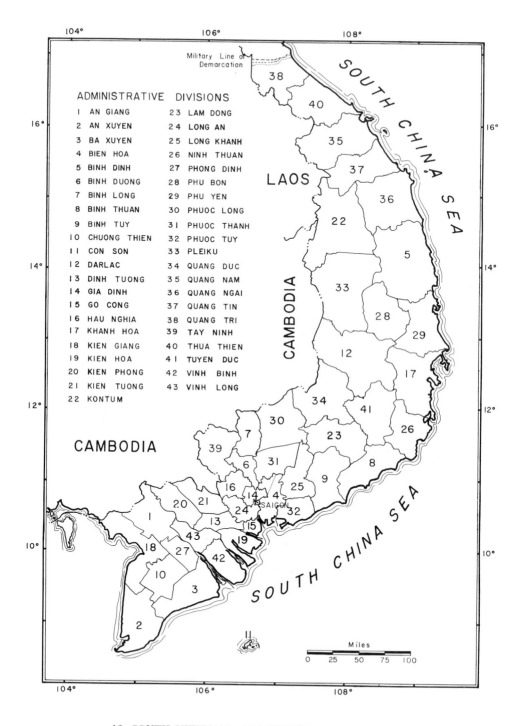

ADMINISTRATIVE DIVISIONS

1	AN GIANG	23	LAM DONG
2	AN XUYEN	24	LONG AN
3	BA XUYEN	25	LONG KHANH
4	BIEN HOA	26	NINH THUAN
5	BINH DINH	27	PHONG DINH
6	BINH DUONG	28	PHU BON
7	BINH LONG	29	PHU YEN
8	BINH THUAN	30	PHUOC LONG
9	BINH TUY	31	PHUOC THANH
10	CHUONG THIEN	32	PHUOC TUY
11	CON SON	33	PLEIKU
12	DARLAC	34	QUANG DUC
13	DINH TUONG	35	QUANG NAM
14	GIA DINH	36	QUANG NGAI
15	GO CONG	37	QUANG TIN
16	HAU NGHIA	38	QUANG TRI
17	KHANH HOA	39	TAY NINH
18	KIEN GIANG	40	THUA THIEN
19	KIEN HOA	41	TUYEN DUC
20	KIEN PHONG	42	VINH BINH
21	KIEN TUONG	43	VINH LONG
22	KONTUM		

13. SOUTH VIETNAM—ADMINISTRATIVE DIVISIONS

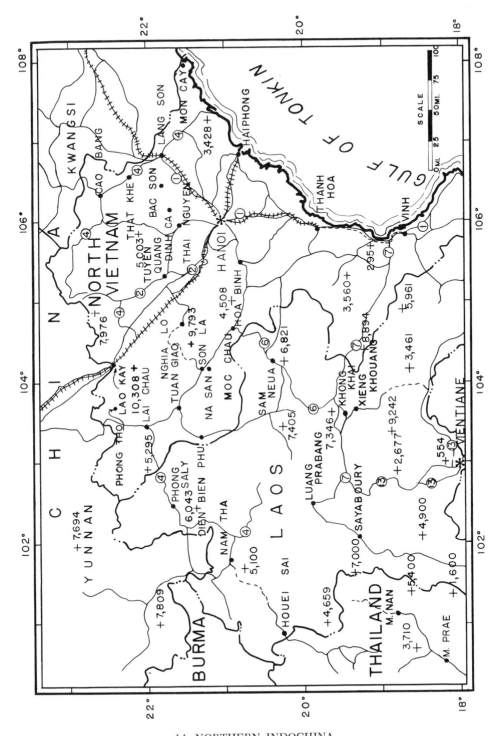

14. NORTHERN INDOCHINA

VIET-MUONG
  1. Vietnamese
  2. Muong
MIAO-YAO
  3. Miao (Meo)
  4. Yao (Man)
MON-KHMER
  N. Laos Group
  5. Khmu'?
  6. Lamet
  7. T in
  Palaungic Group
  8. Wa
TAI
  Southwestern Group
  A. Black Tai
  B. Khün
  C. Lao
  D. Lue
  E. Pa-y
  F. Phuthai
  G. Red Tai
  H. Tai Neua
  I. Yuan (Khon Myang)
  J. White Tai
  Central Group
  K. Nung
  L. Tho (Tay)
  Northern Group
  M. Chuang
  N. Nyang (Nhang)
  O. Saek
SINO-TIBETAN
  Chinese
  Q. Chinese (several
     dialects)
  R. Haw (Ho, Yunnanese
     Chinese)
  Tibeto-Burman Burmese-
     Lolo
  S. Akha
  T. Lahu
  U. Lolo
  V. -Hani
  W. -Woni
  X. Minchia (Pai)
  Karen
  Y. Skaw Karen
KADAI
  a. Laqua
  b. Lati

15. NORTHERN INDOCHINA—DISTRIBUTION OF LANGUAGES